Clinton Library
35444001952646
971.2 CON
Conway, John Frederick
The rise of the new West

JUL 29 2014

THE
RISE *of the*
NEW WEST

D1738603

THE
RISE
of the
NEW WEST
THE HISTORY OF A REGION IN CONFEDERATION

JOHN F. CONWAY

JAMES LORIMER & COMPANY LTD., PUBLISHERS
TORONTO

Thompson-Nicola Regional District
Library System
300 - 465 VICTORIA STREET

Copyright © 1983, 1994, 2006, 2014 by John F. Conway

All rights reserved. No part of this book may be reproduced or transmitted in any form or by any means, electronic or mechanical, including photocopying, or by any information storage or retrieval system, without permission in writing from the publisher.

James Lorimer & Company Ltd., Publishers acknowledges the support of the Ontario Arts Council. We acknowledge the financial support of the Government of Canada through the Canada Book Fund for our publishing activities. We acknowledge the support of the Canada Council for the Arts which last year invested $24.3 million in writing and publishing throughout Canada. We acknowledge the Government of Ontario through the Ontario Media Development Corporation's Ontario Book Initiative.

Cover design: Meredith Bangay
Cover image: iStock photography

....

Library and Archives Canada Cataloguing in Publication

Conway, John Frederick
[West]
        The rise of the new West : the history of a region in Confederation / John F. Conway. -- Fourth edition.

Revision of: The West : the history of a region in Confederation / J.F. Conway. -- 3rd ed. -- Toronto : J. Lorimer, c2006.
Includes bibliographical references and index.
Issued in print and electronic formats.
ISBN 978-1-4594-0624-7 (pbk.).--ISBN 978-1-4594-0626-1 (epub)

        1. Canada, Western--History. 2. Federal-provincial relations--Canada, Western--History. 3. Canada, Western--Politics and government. 4. Canada, Western--Economic conditions. I. Title. II. Title: West.

FC3206.C66 2014   971.2   C2013-907873-8
C2013-907874-6

....

James Lorimer & Company Ltd., Publishers
317 Adelaide Street West, Suite 1002
Toronto, ON, Canada
M5V 1P9
www.lorimer.ca

Printed and bound in Canada.

3 5444 00195264 6

Cross over the continent to the shores of the Pacific, and you are in British Columbia, land of golden promise, I speak not now of the vast Indian Territories that lie between — greater in extent than the whole soil of Russia — and that will ere long, I trust, be opened up to civilization under the auspices of the British American Confederation. [Cheers]

Well, sir, the bold scheme in your hands is nothing less than to gather all these contries into one . . . [Cheers]

Hon. George Brown, during
the Confederation Debates
in the Province of Canada's
Assembly, February 8, 1865

CONTENTS

PREFACE *to the* 2014 EDITION

The West's place in the Canadian political firmament has changed dramatically. Key structural and political continuities must be acknowledged: a fundamental reliance on natural resource production and processing, largely for export; grievances about the West's place in the political and economic structure of Confederation; and the pandering to regional politics in battling Ottawa and Central Canada by successful premiers. Most Westerners continue to believe the West's priorities get short shrift in Ottawa and in the nation's corporate boardrooms, and the West's political clout in national decision making is less than deserved.

This long cherished view was challenged when Stephen Harper's Tories won a majority in 2011. A Western prime minister selected a cabinet with a majority of Westerners, and Western MPs dominated the governing Tory caucus. But there were few signs this Western victory put an end to Western alienation. This "victory" of the West was dampened for many by the dismantling of the structures and programs which had provided social and economic shelter to Westerners in the past. For many, it was a victory tasting much like a defeat.

With the triumph of neo-liberalism as the new political consensus, there was a major shift in the dominant ideological orientation and political culture in the West's expressions of grievance. This shift was both caused by, and accompanied by, a political realignment in national politics. Brian Mulroney fashioned an unprecedented electoral alliance between Québec and the West, winning two majority governments and initiating the neo-liberal counter-revolution. When this alliance collapsed in disarray, two sectional movements emerged and grew to dominate politics in their regions, fracturing Canada's traditional party structure and leading to political uncertainty: the Reform party in the West, primarily in an ascendant Alberta, and the separatist Bloc Québécois in Québec.

When Stephen Harper successfully united the right and went on to win a majority in 2011, he did so by gradually building an electoral alliance between the West, rural Canada, and suburban Ontario, and by excluding Québec. The old political certainties were gone. It was unclear how this realignment would turn out. Perhaps more importantly, three decades of political uncertainty and realignment resulted in the disengagement of an increasing number of Canadians from the electoral process — between 35 and 40 per cent of eligible voters failed to vote in federal elections. Similar levels of disengagement occurred in provincial politics, indicating a crisis in Canadian democracy.

In the past, the West was the source of aggressive advocacy in favour of progressive innovations, and of critiques of Confederation and the Canadian political economy from a broadly defined left-wing perspective. Riel, the farmers' movements, and militant trade unions are deeply embedded in the historical political culture of the West. Socialist and social democratic political parties first emerged and won popular support in the West and successfully used this base of support to win a significant following across the nation. Even William Aberhart's Social Credit movement in Alberta began as a radical critique of finance capitalism, especially the banks and mortgage companies, earning Aberhart an early reputation as a wild-eyed, dangerous Bolshevik. For decades, the West remained the most important and reliable base of support for Canada's most successful social democratic parties — first the Co-operative Commonwealth Federation (CCF) and then the New Democratic Party (NDP). Social democratic parties won provincial elections on a consistent basis in three of the four Western provinces and enjoyed only two wins as government in Central and Atlantic

Canada (Bob Rae's one-term government in Ontario, 1990–95, and Darrell Dexter's one-term government in Nova Scotia, 2009–13).

In recent years, the West became the foundation of Canada's right-wing parties. Whether it was the Reform party, the Alliance party, or the new right-wing Tories led by Stephen Harper, the West's electorate reliably delivered to Canada's right from the 1990s on. On a variety of hot-button issues dear to social conservatism — opposition to gun control and gay marriage, support for unfettered free enterprise in free markets, critiques of public ownership, xenophobic fears of immigrants and refugees, and opposition to the welfare state — the West became a loyal base of support. The West's dominant political culture turned sharply right. Though social democratic parties remained competitive contenders for power in Manitoba, Saskatchewan, and British Columbia, they maintained that status by jettisoning traditional social democracy and joining the turn to the right.

There is little doubt a significant cause of this right turn was the chronic economic crises faced by the West, beginning in the 1980s and 1990s as the three main pillars of the region's economic foundation deteriorated. The wheat economy, for all practical purposes, collapsed due to the world wheat wars, farm subsidies in the European Union and the U.S., and the loss of large markets in the former Soviet Union and China. The catastrophic loss of the U.S. market for Canadian beef due to the border closing resulting from the 2003 Alberta BSE scare further deepened the crisis in agriculture, a crisis from which the beef sector never fully recovered. The oil and natural gas industry — despite a bonanza following the deregulation of oil and gas exports with free trade, followed by 911 and the Iraqi and Afghan wars in the first decade of the new millennium — faced an increasingly uncertain future of continuing booms and busts. The West's easily accessible sweet crude in the Western Basin was virtually depleted. Narrow profit margins made non-conventional oil and gas and frontier development less profitable. Many cling to the hope of skyrocketing world oil prices in a post–peak oil world, making Alberta's massive tar sands a future goldmine.

Nevertheless, Westerners knew the easily and cheaply extracted oil and gas were finite and near final exhaustion, and furthermore, that a future based on deep wells, enhanced recovery technology, and the tar sands, in the context of the global climate crisis, was hardly secure. Nor was the U.S. market secure. Formerly it was believed the U.S. market would eagerly take all the oil and gas the West could produce. But new recovery technology, and the hydraulic fracturing ("fracking") process, which opened up large oil and gas pools in shale deposits, quickly turned the U.S. into one of the world's largest oil producers, and Canadian oil faced competition and heavy price discounts in order to gain access to the market. With much of Western oil production shut in, there was a desperate push for dramatically increased pipeline capacity in order to reach alternative markets in Asia and Central and Atlantic Canada.

The forestry industry, promised by Mulroney it would reap great benefits from free trade, particularly for softwood lumber, was hit by a series of never-ending crises due to blocked access to the U.S. market. Further, in common with all resource economies, there is a limit to how far into the future the West can expect the unrestrained exploitation of forests to continue.

These economic anxieties and uncertainties fed the turn to the right, since the old ways of subsidies, government support programs, and public economic strategies were increasingly foreclosed by both ideological choice and the restrictions imposed on Canada's sovereignty by free trade agreements. As the West entered the new millennium, the region began to undergo a process of political redefinition and reconstruction, creating a New West quite different from the Old West. The New West is very conservative and cranky. The West's rural social structure is in decline. Indeed, the West's internal politics are increasingly polarized between largely conservative, declining rural areas and more progressive, prosperous urban areas. The West's economic foundation — the source of extended periods of great prosperity in the past — is cracking and in danger of collapse, feeding these political contradictions. The New West is, therefore, desperately searching for new political and economic strategies, first for survival, and ultimately for security and prosperity. It appears the "new" strategies have been largely inspired by a return to nineteenth-century models of free trade and free markets. This cure for the West's problems was already tested up to the Great Depression of the 1930s, and found wanting.

Faced with recurring crises, the political and economic leaders of the New West returned to the distant past in search of the key to unlock a better future. For a time there was great confidence, but it was cut short by the abrupt economic meltdown in 2008–09, followed by a lingering world-wide recession. Some experts argue this modern economic crisis is far worse than the Great Depression. The West therefore entered the second decade of the new millennium with a deepening fear that the promise of free markets and unregulated capitalism was again betraying the people's trust. Perhaps this explains the Western mood of despair, desperation, and denial, disguised by the shallow boosterism of incumbent neo-liberal politicians, and prominent leaders of the business lobby.

The inescapable reality in the New West is that a triumphal return of the old elixir of free markets and unfettered capitalism bringing prosperity to all has failed abruptly, and the future is both ominous and uncertain.

1

INTRODUCTION: THE WEST IN CANADA

The West, comprising the provinces of Manitoba, Saskatchewan, Alberta, and British Columbia, has always fascinated Canadians in other regions.

In the period leading up to Confederation, the myth of the West as a region of limitless resource wealth was key in persuading the political and economic elites of the established British colonies in North America to support London's plans to found a federated nation state. Exaggerated versions of that myth were later used to lure settlers from Ontario, Atlantic Canada, the United Kingdom, the United States, and continental Europe. As the 1896 wheat boom established the conditions for the irreversible blossoming of the Western dream, wave upon wave of eager farmers, workers, entrepreneurs, and professionals trekked westward to build the lives they wanted but could not have in their home regions. Even today, especially during times of economic boom, the West becomes the embodiment of hopes many thought they had long surrendered to the harsh reality of compromise and making do.

Canada has never really come to terms with the West, nor has the West ever really come to terms with Canada. The West is a region hard to understand, full of contradictions, politically uneasy, economically vulnerable, chronically unhappy. The only armed insurrections in the history of Confederation both occurred in the West — the Riel

Rebellions of 1869 and 1885. Farmers from the West, in alliance with their rural brothers and sisters in Ontario, led the only systematic, mass-supported political attack on the very economic foundations of the nation. Workers in the West at Winnipeg held the only general strike in Canada's history, and long before and long after set a standard for union militancy and political radicalism unmatched elsewhere in the Dominion. Political movements dedicated to a radical remaking of Canada's political economy were spawned in the West and sallied forth to try to win the hearts and minds of all Canadians. The West has never been happy with its lot in Confederation. When times were bad, the West often rebelled openly, challenging the very founding principles of Confederation. When times were good, the voices of complaint and rebellion became only grudgingly more subdued. They were never silenced.

Canada needs the West. But does the West need Canada? Over the years, and even today, there has persisted a strong current of Western opinion that, in wondrously complex ways, has never conceded the West needs Canada. In fact, that's as good a definition of "Western alienation" as any — there is deep doubt among many Westerners about whether they need Canada, about whether Confederation gives to the West as much as it takes from the West. Many Canadians, especially Central Canadians, can't understand that key fact. Westerners are not just complaining about tariffs or about transportation policy, or about oil prices, or about this or about that: the thing that unites all such specific grievances is an abiding Western suspicion that Confederation has been, and continues to be, a bad deal for the West.

Clearly, the West has been central in the Canadian story. Today, just as throughout our history, crises rooted in the West consume a great deal of the nation's political time and attention. This is understandable. The West, though sparsely populated, is a geographically sprawling region endowed with enormous resource riches. The West occupies about 48 per cent of the land mass of Canada, excluding the northern territories. The gross domestic products of the four Western provinces usually make up between 40 and 50 per cent of Canada's total.[1] The West earns about 58 per cent of Canada's farm cash receipts, and 64 per cent of net farm income (2011), produces almost 50 per cent of Canada's metallic and non-metallic mineral production, and contains over two-thirds of Canada's reserves of oil and natural gas.[2] Yet in 2009, average personal per capita disposable income in two of four Western provinces (B.C. and Manitoba) fell behind Ontario's.[3] Thanks to oil, natural gas, and potash, Alberta and Saskatchewan bested Ontario. Between 40 and 50 per cent of Canada's gross domestic product is earned through exports, and about half of these exports are resources, raw and semi-finished. Until the 2008 crash, Canada maintained a long-standing favourable trade balance, two-thirds of which was due to trade in resources, especially oil and natural gas, while one-third was due to the automotive trade.[4] The West, as a major resource region, is therefore central to Canada's economic well-being as a trading nation. The West is clearly geographically and economically vital to Canada. And it has become more so.

In a remarkable reversal of fortunes, the West, particularly Alberta and Saskatchewan, replaced Ontario as the key driver of the national economy.[5] This became particularly pronounced after the 2008–09 downturn, which hit Atlantic and Central Canada hard. The West's oil, natural gas, potash, and to a lesser extent, forestry industries sheltered the West from the worst effects of the economic calamity. Crude oil had become Canada's most important export as oil exports increased ten-fold between 1990 and 2009, falling only slightly after 2008–09 due to the changing U.S. market. Since 2008, 65 per cent of the value of Canada's exports was earned by natural resources, primarily oil and natural gas, up from 45 per cent in 2002. Since 2004 natural resources have been responsible for all the growth in Canadian export earnings. The U.S. market took 99 per cent of all crude oil and oil products. Canada increasingly had the major characteristics of a petro-economy, deeply dependent on large volumes of oil sales to a single market at high prices, resulting in a rise in the Canadian dollar. This hurt all other non-energy exports badly, particularly manufactured goods, which declined all across Canada. Alberta's and, to a lesser extent, Saskatchewan's oil sectors replaced Ontario's autos and auto parts industry as the central driver of the Canadian economy, providing most export value. This reversal of fortunes was reflected by Ontario's unprecedented eligibility for equalization payments from Ottawa — $400 million in 2010–11 and $1.3 billion in 2011–12.[6] Confederation's favourite child temporarily became a have-not province. Of the Western provinces, only Manitoba remained eligible for such a payment. Consequently, the West, particularly Alberta, became more assertive, demanding a key role in shaping national policies. Such demands did not resonate well in the rest of Canada. The prospect of shifting key national policies, especially basic economic strategies, based on an over-heated petro-economy rooted in one region and dependent on one market, seemed flawed.

The West once again faced national economic and political reality. Only just over 30 per cent of Canadians live in the West. Only about 24 per cent of manufacturing sales originate in the West (compared to 46 per cent in Ontario and 24 per cent in Québec).[7] The West elects 94 of 308 members of Parliament, a fair share based on population. During the late Trudeau years, from the mid-1970s to the early 1980s, the West was not significantly represented in the federal government. This lack of political clout at the centre reached its lowest point in the 1980 election, when only two Liberal MPs were elected in Winnipeg to represent the entire West in the governing Liberal caucus. Even during the Mulroney years, from 1984 to 1993, many in the West felt relatively powerless in shaping national policies, despite a large group of Western Tory MPs in the governing caucus and cabinet. This feeling of powerlessness resulted briefly in a consolidation of NDP federal support (32 of 86 Western seats in 1988), but more permanently in a phenomenal growth in support for Preston Manning's Reform party, finally leading to the consolidation of a more right-wing, Western-oriented national Conservative party led by Stephen Harper. With Harper's 2011 win of a majority government, the West expected much, since it now dominated the government — the prime minister, a majority in the cabinet, and a bloc of 72 MPs in the 166 member Tory caucus. But the high expectations hit the brick wall of Canadian political reality. Many in the West reluctantly, and angrily, recognize all parties seeking national power remain deeply dependent on Central

Canada, especially Ontario, for majority governments, and hence tend to ignore the West's deepest concerns and highest aspirations for fear of offending the more populous and seat-rich Ontario. This sense of political alienation and impotence is best symbolized by the fact that the winner of most federal elections is already determined long before Western votes are even counted. Since the rise of the Bloc in Québec, winners of federal elections are determined in Ontario.

Westerners believe the federal government would never have dared to treat Ontario or Québec as the West was treated during the energy crisis of the 1970s. If Ontario had the oil and natural gas, many in the West argue, Canadians would have been forced to pay world prices all along. Had the Crow Rate (the low freight rates fixed by federal law for Western grain) been as significant to Central Canada as it was to the West, it would never have been dismantled. If Central Canada faced a 30-year crisis of the magnitude of the chronic Western farm crisis, a national disaster would have been declared and the necessary political will and economic resources mobilized from the outset, instead of the partisan, politically motivated, cap-in-hand handouts stingily dribbled out to buy elections. When the Ontario automobile industry faced meltdown in 2008–09 Ottawa provided hundreds of millions to engineer a bail-out in co-operation with the United States. Millions were pumped out to rescue Canadian banks. Nothing remotely equivalent was done in response to the U.S. border closures imposed on B.C.'s softwood lumber and the West's beef industries. Ottawa failed to act forcefully and effectively.

These contemporary examples of Western grievance and complaint are seen by many in the West as simply the most recent examples of federal arrogance and Central Canadian self-interest so characteristic of the treatment of the West in Confederation. Therefore, while compromise and concession, and electing a prime minister from the West and winning seats in the House of Commons and at the cabinet table, may temper Western anger, the anger remains today, just as it remained after each of the many concessions made to the West over the years. Such concessions and compromises always stopped short of redressing the structural sources of the West's unhappiness. Clearly, then, what we are dealing with is a contradiction historically rooted in the basic political and economic structures of Canada as the nation was first established and later developed. To understand the West, we must examine the place of the West in Confederation — politically and, more importantly — economically. We must therefore start at the beginning. In order to understand the present, we must come to know the past.

This book provides a short political and economic history of the West in Confederation. It begins with the Riel Rebellions of 1869 and 1885, takes us through the agrarian agitations of the 1920s and the Great Depression of the 1930s, surveys the energy and constitutional wars of the 1970s and 1980s, chronicles the rise of the Reform/Alliance party and the fall of Brian Mulroney in the late 1980s and early 1900s, and ends with the rise of Stephen Harper and the right-wing consolidation of the West's political culture in the new millennium. The story of Western dissent is told through the dramatic events most characteristic of the West's uneasy place in Confederation. Above all, the book documents how Western Canadians repeatedly struggled to reconstruct Canada's political and economic order, not only to redress the grievances of the region, but, Westerners believed, to bring more justice and economic security for all Canadians.

2

"THE LAST BEST WEST": THE WEST IN CONFEDERATION, 1869–1913

Canadians continue to embrace a whole series of myths about Confederation. We talk of the "Fathers of Confederation," politely overlooking the self-seeking motives of the businessmen-politicians who conceived the plan. We speak of the "national dream," focussing on patriotism and other fine sentiments in an effort to elevate the bargaining and trade-offs that resulted in Canada to some higher, moral plane. Our history is "prettified," revised, often completely reconstructed. Even the London *Times* of 1865 revealed a clearer insight into Confederation than most Canadians today have, when an editorial said, referring to Confederation, "Half the useful things that are done in the world are done from selfish motives under the cover of larger designs."[1]

BACKGROUND TO CONFEDERATION
Three great events shaped the essence of Canada long before Confederation was even contemplated. These events ensured that Canada would remain a nation bedevilled by the English-French conflict, characterized by unremitting conservatism, and beset by a deep suspicion of popular movements and aspirations. The conquest of Québec by Wolfe, the immigration of the fleeing counter-revolutionary United Empire Loyalists, and the defeat and repression of the 1837-38 Rebellions all had a great deal to do with determining the essential character of the Dominion which emerged in 1867. As they

approached Confederation, Canada's rulers, encumbered by this legacy, were determined to contain and humble Québec, to resist extreme democracy, and to view popular assertions as seditious. Confederation was never conceived as a plan to address the long-festering grievances of the Québécois, nor was it viewed as an orderly progression to popular democracy, nor, indeed, as a way to fulfill the yearnings of the people for nationhood. The plan was conceived by the business and political elites of the various British North American colonies, inspired by the elite of the colony of Canada, for no other reason than to assure their futures.

To understand the place of the West in Confederation, it is crucial to know the context in which Confederation was finally successfully brought about. The rulers of the united colony of Canada, the merchants and nascent industrialists, had staggered from broken dream to broken dream, from crisis to crisis, emerging each time with the same basic strategy. First, and until the loss of imperial preference, they had striven to build a commercial transportation system to service the great trade between North America and Europe. When American expansion blocked this aspiration, reciprocity with the U.S. was sought and won. Finally, when the reciprocity agreement was abrogated by the U.S. the only option left was Confederation and independence.

Each crisis had increased the public investment in the transportation system, the resulting debt constantly threatening bankruptcy; each crisis and each depression was met with the same response — secure a larger borrowing base, borrow more capital, invest in transportation, accelerate the export of staples, and, only incidentally, establish protection for a modest Canadian industrialization. The single-minded devotion to this strategy finally led to Confederation, the biggest borrowing base of all.

A somewhat reconstituted ruling class, more open to this "political dream of wonderful audacity,"[2] had emerged from the ashes of the 1837-38 Rebellions. Forced reluctantly to grant responsible government, cast adrift by Britain as free trade was embraced in the 1840s, the new ruling class became dominated by the "progressive Conservative" (in Sir John A. Macdonald's words)[3] elements of the hard Tory merchant bloc that had ruled before, a rising group of industrial capitalists, landowners, railway and steamship entrepreneurs, and financial adventurers in the growing Canadian banking and insurance system.[4] This group, and their backers in the British Colonial Office, recognized that some form of federation was the only road to the survival of an independent British fact on the continent, as well as to the establishment of an expanded national economy upon which they could realize their aspirations. In the absence of such a British federation, American hegemony over a growing portion of the continent was inevitable. And in the absence of an enforced east-west national home market, the rising Canadian capitalist class would see their hopes dashed, confined by localism, undercut by American economic competition.

Confederation, therefore, was essential to this new, emerging ruling class in Canada, allied more or less uneasily with the local elites of the other British colonies in North America. Confederation was to be conservative in design and character. The moves toward protection would be modest, as hopes to establish reciprocity with the U.S. were not to be completely surrendered until 1878. The new regime would expand westward by rail and begin the construction of a national industrial economy through protection. This economic design required a political union of the colonies with a strong central government — the final political solution, as Sir John A. Macdonald had so eloquently put it, to "the dead-lock in our affairs, the anarchy we dreaded, and the evils which retarded our prosperity."[5] In one stroke, the union of the Canada's would be dissolved, the reform of representation by population introduced, and a federation established, transferring all the colonies' debts to the new Dominion, which would provide a stronger credit base for further borrowing for westward expansion.

The new union would not go too far down the treacherous road of democracy. As Macdonald had so candidly put it at the 1864 Québec Conference, what was being established was "constitutional liberty as opposed to democracy."[6] The House of Commons would not be elected by universal male suffrage, but tied to British qualifications for electors. Indeed, the principle of adult suffrage was not to be won until women were granted the vote in the context of World War I.

Furthermore, there was to be a Senate, just in case the Commons got out of hand, which would be "the representative of property."[7] As Macdonald said, "A large qualification should be necessary for membership of the Upper House, in order to represent the principle of property. The rights of the minority must be protected, and the rich are always fewer in number than the poor."[8]

As might be expected, these were fighting words to the reformers, and radical democrats resisted the Confederation scheme on the grounds that it threatened the rights of the Québécois and that its structure was too undemocratic and anti-popular. But such arguments were to no avail; the conservative design remained intact. As G. E. Cartier said, "The scheme . . . met with the approval of all moderate men. The extreme men, the socialists, democrats, and annexationists were opposed . . ."[9] The "extreme men" were probably in a majority, had there been a more perfect democracy, but their resistance was futile against the power at the disposal of the "moderate men," backed by the British government. Even with severely restricted suffrage, the elites of the colonies were reluctant to put the scheme to the electoral test. The Confederation scheme was widely popular only in Canada West (Ontario), and other regimes faced political controversy on the issue. Guile, arm-twisting, opportunism, and pressure from Britain were the tactics used most often to effect the union.

When Queen Victoria signed the *BNA Act* on May 29, 1867, Canada, now to be Québec, Ontario, Nova Scotia, and New Brunswick, became the federal Dominion of Canada. It was a new variation on the old theme. The new federal government would borrow capital, or guarantee investments, in order to unite British North America from coast to coast through an expansion of the transportation system westward by rail. Ultimately, in the West, vast quantities of wheat and other natural resources would be extracted to join the similar flow from Central and Atlantic Canada to feed Europe's industrial markets, especially that of Great Britain. Central Canada, especially Ontario, would additionally prosper in a variety of other ways: railway promoters and forwarding interests would move grain and other resources to market and manufactures back, the protective tariff would lead to a growing industrialization to supply the national home market expanded by a vast immigration of settlers to build the West, retailers and wholesalers would benefit through the general commercial boom, financial empires would rise on the growing demand for credit. Atlantic Canada would benefit from a growing demand for coal, fish, and the products of its long-established industries. The strong central government would play the crucial role — it would finance railway development, promote immigration, construct a wall of protective tariffs, and acquire the Prairie West as a colonial possession, while continuing pressure on B.C. to join the federation. The job of the federal state was to "clear and prepare the way for the beneficent operation of the capitalist."[10] The West, especially the Prairie West, was key to the success of the whole project.

THE WINNING OF THE WEST

At the outset a distinction must be made between the Prairies and British Columbia. The Prairie region entered Confederation as a colonial possession of the Dominion government. B.C. negotiated the terms of Confederation as a fully fledged British colony. This distinction is crucial and goes much of the way in explaining why B.C.'s relations with Central Canada have rarely been as tumultuous as the Prairies'. B.C. had to be wooed and won. The Prairies were simply purchased from absentee owners without consultations with the local people. B.C. seriously considered other options to Confederation. The Prairies were not permitted this luxury. Both were viewed by the architects of Confederation as politically and economically vital. London was particularly concerned about B.C. as the opening to the Pacific for both economic and military reasons. Pacific ports would be crucial for trade with the west coast of the U.S. and Asia. London's naval base at Esquimalt was central to British strategic interests in the Pacific. Both the Prairies and B.C. were viewed as potentially rich resource producing regions and as captive markets for Central Canadian industrial products. In that sense they shared a common fate in the basic economic design of Confederation.

Still, the Prairies, a vast underpopulated hinterland, were the cornerstone in the Confederation scheme, politically and economically. The

tremendous economic opportunities envisaged by the architects of
the new Dominion depended upon successful agricultural settlement
of the Prairies. Even B.C.'s eventual place in Confederation depended
upon events on the Prairies. Prior to Prairie settlement, the B.C. colony's production of minerals, lumber, and salmon largely went to
foreign markets, the most important of which was California. The
hopes arising from the increase in B.C.'s population during the gold
rush of the 1850s, hopes that for some included B.C. going it alone,
were dashed when the rush collapsed in the 1860s and B.C.'s population fell to just over 36,000 in 1871.[11] By 1881, development in B.C.
had limped ahead, as even the Northwest Territories and Manitoba
could boast greater populations. Prairie settlement, and the railway
and tariff policies associated with it, became a prerequisite first, for
B.C.'s entry into Confederation and its willingness to stay, and second,
for B.C.'s prosperity in the new national economy. Therefore events
on the Prairies were central. It was on the Prairies that Confederation,
both politically and economically, would succeed or fail. And success
or failure on the Prairies would determine B.C.'s final decision about
Confederation.

The most blunt statement on the place of the West in Confederation
was made by Clifford Sifton, minister of the interior in Laurier's 1896
cabinet. In 1904 he said to a Winnipeg audience:

> *We look in the near future to see upon these western plains, and*
> *in this western province and territories a great population . . .*
>
> *We look forward to other things. We look forward to the*
> *production of natural wealth of all kinds. In this great country we*
> *expect to see the wealth of the field, of the forest and of the mines*
> *exploited in vast quantities . . .*
>
> *What . . . will western Canada do for the Canadian organism?*
> *Sir, it will give a vast and profitable traffic to its railways and steam-*
> *ship lines. It will give remunerative employment to tens of thousands*
> *of men . . . [who] engage in the multitude of occupations which*
> *gather around the great system of transportation.*
>
> *It will do more. It will build up our Canadian seaports. It*

will create a volume of ocean traffic which shall place Canada
in a short time — in its proper position as a maritime nation.
It will furnish a steady and remunerative business to the
manufacturers of eastern Canada, giving assured prosperity
where uncertainty now exists. These are the things the west
will do for the east. In a word, I may say it will send a flood
of new blood from one end of this great country to the other,
through every artery of commerce.[12]

Sifton was speaking at the height of the great expansion of the wheat
boom, the final success of Confederation, and he was speaking primarily of the Prairie West. Yet Sifton was articulating the long-standing
plan regarding the place of the West in Confederation. What he said
applied to B.C. just as much as to the Prairies.

What is now the Prairie West, as well as most of Canada's huge
north, had been granted in 1670 by the British Crown to the Hudson's
Bay Company. For two centuries the fur trade dominated the life of
the region. The Hudson's Bay Company exercised not only an economic monopoly over the region, but ruled the inhabitants politically
as well. There had been, therefore, a long legacy of resistance to all
efforts at settlement — permanent agricultural settlement undermined
the fur trade and threatened the continuing control of the fur-traders.
Settlement was discouraged by a Company policy of outrageously high
land prices combined with a rigid commercial policy that attempted to
enforce the Company's monopoly on all economic activity.

These policies had failed to some extent on three fronts: a Canadian,
Montreal-based fur-trading company, the North West Company, had
emerged to compete with the British concern; the Métis (the offspring
of marriages between European, mostly French, men and Aboriginal
women) had successfully challenged Hudson's Bay Company efforts
to regulate their commercial dealings in the U.S.; and a trickle of white
settlers had continued. Of course, both fur companies were very much
concerned about the advent of permanent agricultural settlement, and
resisted such settlement.

Most dramatically, in 1816 this resistance to settlement had resulted in the North West Company inspired massacre of settlers at Selkirk's colony, established in 1812 on land granted to Lord Selkirk by the Hudson's Bay Company (in which he held a large interest) in order to prove the merits of agricultural settlement in the Red River area. The subsequent merging of the Northwest Company with the Hudson's Bay Company in 1821, and Selkirk's death the year before, ensured that the fur-trading interest in the West was united in efforts to resist permanent settlement. The subsequent persisting decline in interest in settling in the region was not therefore surprising. Meanwhile the U.S. was rapidly expanding westward. The new Canadian government, therefore, was very anxious about a number of problems.

The local population was very small. As the 1871 census later revealed, due to the Hudson's Bay Company's resistance to settlement, as well as the greater attractiveness of settlement in the U.S., there were only about 1,600 white settlers in the region, as well as 9,800 Métis (the largest portion of whom were French-speaking), whose loyalty was suspect among Canadian politicians.[13] Clearly, such a vast territory could not be held with so small a population, especially if the U.S. actively pursued possession of some or all of the territories — and there were real reasons to fear U.S. intentions.

The main economic link from Red River was through the more convenient transportation route south. To the south Minnesota had become a prosperous and well-populated state as early as the 1850s. After the end of the American Civil War, the call for the annexation of the British North West had become popular among many prominent Americans, including politicians and journalists. In fact, in 1868 the Minnesota Legislature demanded the American annexation of the North West. During the Confederation year, 1867, the U.S. had purchased Alaska from Russia, an event that the New York *World* characterized as "an advancing step in that manifest destiny which is yet to give us British North America."[14] This American agitation for annexation, combined with the strengthening of the economic links between Red River and the U.S., caused great consternation among Dominion politicians.

Finally, the region had to be acquired from the Hudson's Bay Company. For many years the Company had resisted Canadian acquisition of the territory, making impossible demands for an agreement. Finally, a new leadership in the Company and vigorous pressure from the British government led to a resolution. In December 1867, Canada's Parliament formally asked Westminster to admit Rupert's Land and the North West Territory to the federation as possessions of the Dominion government. Final negotiations in London between representatives of the Canadian government, the British government, and the Company resulted in an agreement that gave Canada possession of the region in return for £300,000 in cash, one-twentieth of the "fertile-belt" in the region (about 7 million acres), and further land grants around the Company's many posts. In 1868 the British Parliament ratified the agreement and the Canadian government passed the legislation necessary to establish control over the area. In December 1869 a Canadian governor was sent, proclaiming his authority over the West. At no time were the inhabitants of the region consulted.

The local people in the Red River region responded with something less than enthusiasm. The largely French-speaking and Catholic Métis feared for their language, education, and religious rights, as well as the long-term consequences for their nation of Canadian annexation. White settlers and the Métis shared a concern that their rights, particularly land rights, would be over-ridden without prior guarantees. Both wanted some form of responsible government and the prospect of exchanging the unhappy but known dictatorship of the Company for the distant and unknown dictatorship of Canada was viewed with some alarm. The vocal and arrogant agitations of the minority Canada Party, composed largely of recently arrived Canadians from Ontario who enthusiastically called for swift annexation of the district by Canada, did little to placate such fears. As well, a significant, if minority, opinion argued that American annexation of the region was a more logical prospect.

The first confrontation occurred when the Métis refused to permit William McDougall, the Canadian lieutenant-governor, entry into the district. Nevertheless he proclaimed his authority over the West *in absentia.* In response to such threatening arrogance, and under the leadership of Louis Riel, the Métis and a majority of white settlers united to declare a provisional government and to seek further negotiations with the Dominion. The Dominion government was in no position militarily to crush the Red River insurrection, despite a desire to do so. The American giant watched, waiting, it was believed, for the slightest excuse for intervention. Moving an adequate military force quickly enough to engage the rebels was impossible for a number of reasons, besides the obvious geographical and logistical ones. The British government wanted a peaceful settlement. Québec sympathized with the Métis. The prospects of the great First Nations, mainly the Assiniboine and the Cree, allying with the rebels were appalling. And the Métis themselves were well-known as a potentially formidable military foe.

Therefore, the Dominion government negotiated and conceded just enough to reassure the region's inhabitants. In 1870 the province of Manitoba was established with most of the rights of other provinces, including responsible government and representation in the federal Parliament. Guarantees were established for the French language and for largely local control of education. Lands were set aside to meet Métis land claims. Finally, the uncertain land rights of the people on existing farms were guaranteed by an assurance that land acquired from the Hudson's Bay Company would be secure under the new regime.

The Dominion government made up for these humiliations in other ways, finally stealing by stealth what had been a significant victory for the Métis nation and their white allies. In the first instance, the size of Manitoba was tightly constricted to about 10,000 square miles, barely encompassing most of the settlements on the Red and Assiniboine Rivers. It became known as "the postage stamp province" and was the subject of some hilarity among easterners. Alexander Mackenzie, leader of the Liberal Opposition, said, "The whole thing has such a ludicrous look that it only puts one in mind of some incidents in Gulliver's Travels . . . it [is] one of the most preposterous schemes . . . ever submitted to the Legislature."[15] It was really not so preposterous; the remaining territory would be governed arbitrarily as a colonial possession.

Next, one of the most crucial demands of the Red River rebels, control of lands and resources as other provinces enjoyed under the *BNA*

Act, was refused. The denial of such control made it impossible for the province to plan and influence the settlement process, to dispose of, and gain revenues from, timber resources, or, indeed, any resources that began to be developed. Furthermore, the province, powerless over lands and resources, could not ensure fair settlements of outstanding land claims of "old" settlers, Métis or white, or to determine priorities in opening areas of the province either for new farms or the expansion of existing farms. Control of lands and resources was "vested in the Crown, and administered by the Government of Canada for the purposes of the Dominion," in the words of the *Manitoba Act*. As well, the guarantee of 1.4 million acres of land for the settlement of Métis land claims was administratively and politically circumvented by the issue of "scrip," a piece of paper entitling individual Métis to select land later, by deliberate delays in the final settlement of Métis land claims, by refusals to provide a fair census of Métis in the area, and by military and bureaucratic harassment. A heavy trade by land speculators ensured that much of the scrip issued was converted into ready cash, at drastically low prices, by many Métis as they saw their victory turned against them and left the region to move westward.

Finally, Dominion politicians succumbed over-zealously to Ontario opinion, which was outraged at Riel's execution of Thomas Scott, an Ontario Orangeman. (The Orange Lodge, though originally rooted among militantly anti-Catholic Irish Protestants, had become, in Canada, the main Anglo-Saxon anti-French and anti-Catholic lobby.) Scott had defied the authority of the provisional government and had repeatedly attempted to provoke armed civil strife. Had he had his way, Red River would have experienced a blood bath and, in the ensuing military struggle, the West might have been lost for Canada. In what was Riel's only significant strategic political blunder, Scott was tried and executed, becoming a public martyr in Ontario. Riel was hounded into exile, denied the amnesty he was promised and barred from the seat he won in the House of Commons. Thus the leader of the Métis nation, and the man who ought to have been the first premier of Manitoba, had he wanted the job, was driven from his home and his people by the smug opinion leaders of Ontario who, above all else, viewed the West as their own. There was to be no place for rebels who did not embrace Ontario's vision for the West — especially Métis, French, and Catholic rebels. The last vestige of Riel's triumph was to be erased some twenty years later when the Manitoba legislature abolished French, both as an official language and as an acceptable language of education.

This was not an auspicious beginning for the West in Confederation, but the Dominion government had carried the day. The West was theirs, but for the vexation of the postage stamp province. The government moved quickly. Lord Wolseley's military excursion to the Red River district in 1869-70 asserted federal military intentions graphically. The *Manitoba Act* of 1870 was followed quickly by the *Land Act* of 1872, which provided for free homestead land grants as well as preemption rights. The Act creating the Royal North West Mounted Police was passed, establishing a federal paramilitary force to enforce law and order. And finally the *North West Territories Act* in 1875 established Dominion authority over the entire region not included in Manitoba. The stage was now set for the expansion of the Dominion westward, largely on the Dominion's terms.

YEARS OF FAILURE, 1870-1896

The belief was that the establishment of law and order and the clarification of the political status of the region, together with the temptation of free land, would start a huge flow of immigrants to the West. But in the absence of a railway, and in the presence of more attractive alternatives in the U.S., the policy was a hopeless failure. In 1872, there were only 73,000 people (including Aboriginals and Métis) in the entire Prairie region.[16] The year before, in the negotiations that brought B.C. into the federation, the Dominion had promised to complete the railway to the Pacific by 1881. The under-population of the Prairies made that commitment more imperative. And although the 1872 *Land Act* contributed somewhat to settlement, Canada continued to have difficulty retaining the immigrants who arrived from Europe. Canada even had trouble retaining her native born, as settlers came West from the older provinces, took a look around and continued south into the U.S.

The situation became so alarming that by 1890 it was estimated that there were about one million ex-Canadians in the U.S., representing about 17 per cent of Canada's entire population.[17]

In a series of determined manoeuvres, the Dominion government tried to speed up settlement. In 1874-75, a new policy enjoyed some success by encouraging ethnic and/or religious group settlement. This was supplemented by the establishment of Colonization Companies made up of groups of capitalists who bought or were granted blocks of land and proceeded, through sharp practice and propaganda, to entice settlers to their lands. Yet immigration and settlement limped ahead. Success still awaited the arrival of the railway. Ironically, the first railway to arrive was not Canadian; in 1878 a U.S. line connecting Winnipeg with Minneapolis/St. Paul began to bring in the first large flow of settlers.

1878 was an important year for reasons other than the arrival of a U.S. railway in Winnipeg. That year saw the return of Macdonald and his Tories to power with a new mandate, having lost office in 1873 and the election of 1874, largely as a result of the "Pacific scandal." The reasons for Macdonald's victory were clear. Liberal Alexander Mackenzie's transportation policy was failing and discredited; settlement of the Prairie region was dangerously slow; railway routes south through the U.S. were ominously becoming accessible to Canadians who, when they were not using the system to come and go, were using it for their commercial traffic. Macdonald promised to finish the railway and to speed up settlement. As well, Canada had fallen into serious depression in 1873 (together with the rest of the world) and efforts to conclude some kind of reciprocal economic deal with the U.S. were unsuccessful. Therefore Canadian industrial capitalist opinion had finally clearly crystallized around the protective tariff road to domestic industrialization. Macdonald agreed and promised to turn the depression around with a new tariff policy. In brief, Macdonald and his Tories campaigned on what really amounted to a commitment to ruthlessly bring the original design of Confederation to successful if roughshod completion. The architect of Confederation was recalled to continue as its chief engineer.

After victory Macdonald proceeded to erect a formidable tariff wall and to pick up the pieces of his previous railway policies. The tariff wall was begun in 1879, and completed in 1887, imposing a tariff range of 10 to 40 or 50 per cent, depending on the degree of industrial processing. From 1879 onward the primary purpose of the tariff was no longer to generate revenue, but rather to deliberately intervene in the economy in order to foster domestic industrialization.[18]

Such an elaborate tariff wall only made sense if the other two elements of the Confederation scheme — settlement and transportation — were realized. Settlement clearly depended on the railway, and ultimately, the successful settlement of the West was key to the success or failure of Confederation. Macdonald moved quickly on the railway question as well. In October 1880 a contract was signed with a group of capitalists and, after much controversy, the *Canadian Pacific Railway Act* was assented to in February 1881. In exchange for building and operating a transcontinental railway, the CPR entrepreneurs received a massive Western empire, which laid the basis for the company's position today as one of the largest conglomerates in Canada. The terms of the contract still enrage Westerners.[19] In addition to about $38 million worth of completed railway, the CPR received a $25 million subsidy and 25 million acres of prime Western land. Of enormous significance, the company was given the power to locate the main line through the Prairies, as well as branch lines. This ensured that the CPR could locate rail lines in ways to enhance the return on their vast land holdings. Significant tax exemptions were granted and the CPR was guaranteed an effective monopoly for 20 years. It was the kind of deal usually only realized in the dreams of railway promoters.

The agreement ensured that a prominent, powerful, and international group of capitalists had a profound interest in the successful settlement of the region. Patriotism and nation-building were given dollar signs. The West must be filled not only to expand the domestic market for protected industrial capitalists, but also to make the CPR viable and increase the value of the vast tracts of land held by the Hudson's Bay Company (7 million acres) and by the CPR consortium (25 million acres). The railway interests, with the power to choose where to locate the rail lines, were able to manipulate the value of land in any settlement region. But hopes of vast returns on a protected, largely public, investment given outright to a group of economic adventurers, awaited the arrival of an elusive population. Although the line was completed from Montreal to Vancouver on November 7, 1885, the population still didn't come. America continued to be more attractive to settlers for a host of reasons.

British Columbia had watched the Prairie drama unfold with growing concern. There had earlier been great worry among Canadian politicians, and their London masters, about the penetration of American settlers in the valleys of the Fraser River. This concern increased with the gold rush after 1856, especially because the huge Pacific coastal region was virtually empty of white population. However, by the mid-1860s the gold rush was over and concern abated. In preparation for Confederation, the separate colonies of Vancouver Island and British Columbia were united in 1866 into one colony. Yet the B.C. colonial regime was not enamoured of Confederation and resisted it until the death of the anti-Confederate governor in 1869 allowed London to send a pro-Confederate replacement. The new governor succeeded and his Executive Council (there was no responsible government in B.C.) finally petitioned for admittance to Confederation. When the B.C. delegates arrived in Ottawa in the aftermath of the Red River fiasco, Dominion officials generously embraced the new province.

On July 20, 1871 B.C. joined Confederation as a full province, controlling its lands and resources (except for the railway right-of-way). Canada agreed that a transcontinental railway would be completed by 1881. The depression of 1873, the failures associated with the Pacific syndicate, and Mackenzie's equivocal performance all upset the province. In 1876 the Legislature petitioned the Queen complaining of Canada's incompetence, threatening secession. This secessionist agitation continued throughout 1877 and 1878 and played no small part in Macdonald's return to power. B.C. was finally won over by Macdonald's apparent successes associated with his new tariff policy and the establishment of the CPR. But B.C. uneasiness continued.

The promised results had not materialized as quickly as expected.

The railway had not been completed in 1881. The settlement policies on the Prairies had failed to bring the waves of farmers to stimulate B.C.'s lumber and fish industries. The absence of a railway meant that even the small Prairie market had remained closed to B.C. In 1881 products of the mine still accounted for 60 per cent of B.C.'s exports, and foreign markets remained predominant.[20] B.C.'s great staple industries — mining, forestry, and the fishery — grew disappointingly slowly. This increased the province's restiveness. The colony's "Fathers of Confederation" had been very blunt when they decided to enter Confederation. As one of them had said in 1870:

> *No Union between this Colony and Canada can permanently*
> *exist unless it be to the mutual and pecuniary advantage to*
> *this Colony to remain in the union . . . The people of this*
> *Colony have, generally speaking, no love for Canada . . .*
> *Therefore no union on account of love need be looked for.*
> *The only bond of Union outside of force — and force the*
> *Dominion has not — will be the material advantage of the*
> *country and the pecuniary benefits of the inhabitants.[21]*

Even the completion of the CPR main line in 1885 brought only disappointing results, as the Prairies remained largely unsettled. By 1891 B.C.'s population had only grown to just over 98,000, still less than either Manitoba or the Northwest Territory.[22] B.C. 's vast treasure house of natural resources needed the labourers, the investors, and the booming markets promised by the new Dominion. These all awaited success on the Prairies.

FINAL SUCCESS: THE WHEAT BOOM, 1896–1913

It was not until the United States' massive westward expansion was virtually completed that the immigration tide turned in Canada's favour. Macdonald did not live to see the final success of his efforts, dying in office in 1891. The Tories did not live to see it either, at least not in office. The continuing depression into the 1890s, the failure of the grand plans to bear profitable fruit, the controversies surrounding the giveaways that had been indulged in behind the patriotic screen of nation-building, the death of their leader — all these conspired to replace them in office in the election of 1896 with Laurier's Liberals.

In 1896 the Laurier Liberals inherited a Dominion government heavily in debt, with over one-half of the government's current outlay committed to debt charges and new development programs. The same held true for all provincial governments, except Ontario. This had occurred due to the prevailing, if dubious, political wisdom of the proper role of government — "the traditional role of government in British North America as an agency for creating conditions in which private enterprise might thrive"[23] was assumed by all but a few politicians, according to the Rowell-Sirois Commission report of 1940. The fly in the ointment was that vast sums had been expended on creating conditions, yet private enterprise had refused to thrive. The mood abroad was anything but hopeful and, according to the Rowell-Sirois Commission, there were "forebodings about the success of Confederation."[24]

In 1896 prosperity began to dawn as the "wheat boom" of 1896–1913 began.[25] The key to the boom lay in declining transportation costs and rising prices for wheat, which overnight made the production of Prairie wheat profitable. Free and cheap land further stimulated the process, providing a strong magnet for the land hungry from around the world. Add to this the fact that the American frontier was for all practical purposes settled, and the conditions for a massive jump in population and wheat production on the Prairies were amply fulfilled.

The subsequent speed of settlement and agricultural development was unprecedented in Canadian history. In 1896, 140 million acres were available for settlement — 60 million open for free homestead, the rest for sale from private owners such as the CPR, the Hudson's Bay Company, land combines, and private entrepreneurs. From 1896 to 1913, over 1 million people moved into the three Prairie provinces, occupied lands increased by 7 times, and wheat produced leapt by more than 10 times.

For the first time the Confederation design was functioning as it ought to have from the beginning. By 1913 the value of wheat and flour exports alone were greater than the value of all exports in 1896. The Prairies filled up as population moved in and followed the railway to every corner to produce the new gold — wheat. In the 1896–1913 period it would not be an overstatement to say, as the Rowell-Sirois Commission did, "the settlement of the Prairies dominated the Canadian economic scene."[26]

But the production and export of wheat, and the resulting east-west railway traffic, was only one cornerstone of the original design. Out of the boom one element of the original capitalist designers of Confederation gained much — the investors in transportation, the speculators in land, the middlemen who dealt in the international grain trade, the banks and trust companies, the commercial wholesalers and retailers who dealt in commodities for consumption and production, all these benefitted. However that was only one segment of the eager group who watched the final fruition of their long-postponed dreams. The other major segment was made up of the industrial capitalists who had tied their star to a strategy of industrialization through protective tariffs. The role the West played here, too, was crucial — the immigration brought a vast new captive market. In 1903 Wilfrid Laurier said, "The best way you can help the manufacturers of Canada is to fill up the prairie regions of Manitoba and the Northwest with a prosperous and contented people, who will be consumers of manufactured goods of the east."[27]

In 1905, he elaborated,

> They [the Prairie settlers] will require clothes, they will
> require furniture, they will require implements, they will
> require shoes . . . they will require everything that man has
> to be supplied with. It is your ambition [he was speaking to
> the Canadian Manufacturers' Association] that this scientific
> tariff of ours will make it possible that every shoe that has to
> be worn in these prairies shall be a Canadian shoe; that every
> yard of cloth that can be marketed there shall be a yard of
> cloth produced in Canada; and so on and so on.[28]

Again, the industrial component of the original design was working beautifully, as the net value of manufacturing production almost tripled between 1890 and 1910. However, the largest proportion — 80 per cent — of this massive industrial expansion occurred in Central Canada. This fact, combined with the tariff policies, was to figure large, then and later, in Western grievances about Confederation.

Wheat brought the long-awaited boom to B.C. The province's population almost quadrupled from 1891 to 1911, to just under 400 thousand.[29] In 1900 76 per cent of B.C.'s lumber exports had gone by sea. In 1913, 90 per cent were leaving the province by rail.[30] B.C. had joined the new Dominion economy. Stimulated by Prairie demand, the production of lumber doubled between 1908 and 1911 alone.[31] Mining — especially coal and copper — boomed in response to the hunger of the expanding Canadian market. The fishery, especially the canned salmon sector, burgeoned. Growing industrial production, primarily in wood products and fish canning, attracted a vast immigration of workers. The fantastic growth in demand for lumber and mine products led to a boom in settlement and economic activity in B.C.'s newly opened vast interior. The vision promised by Dominion politicians to the colony in 1871 was finally realized.

By 1913, when the boom ended, the pattern was established irreversibly. B.C.'s place in Confederation was to exploit her treasure house of resources for national and international markets. The Prairie West's place in Confederation was to produce cereal grains, primarily wheat, for export to an international market. Any and all commodities derived from "the wealth of the field, of the forest and of the mine," as Clifford Sifton put it, were also to be "exploited in vast quantities" as development went forward. But then, wheat was king, wheat had made Confederation work.

The population, which had been begged, cajoled, lured, and even deceived, into coming to provide the labour, to settle the prairies, to raise the wheat, therefore, served other purposes of which they were initially unaware. They were, behind the walls of the protective tariff, the captive market for the manufactures of Central Canada. The agricultural population and the essential, if small in number, wage earners who settled and rendered productive the Prairies, and the wage earners and entrepreneurs who opened the mine and lumber camps of B.C., were all a commercial capitalist's dream come true. They were forced to buy dear and sell cheap.

This was particularly rankling for Prairie farmers, the most decisive element in the final success of Confederation. The protected manufactures they needed for production, for consumption, and even for amusement, cost them up to 40 or 50 per cent above what they would have paid had there been free trade. At the same time, the commodities they produced for a cash income — grains, especially wheat, and livestock — had to be forwarded through middlemen, each of whom took a share of the final price ultimately gained on the world market, as well as transported vast distances. From the Prairie farmers' point of view, in terms of their share of the final price, they were forced to sell cheaply indeed. Add to this the cost of credit needed to buy land, to purchase machinery, and to erect buildings, and even the ability and right to produce was subject to a tariff in the form of interest.

Granted, but for the small Prairie working class, the Prairie settlers were small capitalists who embraced the basic tenets of the system of private enterprise and extolled individualism and entrepreneurial ability. But they had been brought into being by big capitalists — the railway interests, the grain trade, the retailers and wholesalers, the industrialists, the banking, trust and insurance interests — for purposes beyond their control. Almost immediately there was a clash of interests.

In the first instance, some of the best lands of the vast region had been alienated to the Hudson's Bay Company, the CPR, colonization companies, and many other individual friends of the Dominion government. Hence they found that in order to expand and develop their holdings, they must purchase lands already owned. Indeed, the land sold exceeded the land acquired by free homestead in the West. As well, on a national basis four out of ten free homesteads failed from 1870 to 1927. And in Alberta from 1905 to 1930, 46 per cent of homesteads failed, while in Saskatchewan from 1911 to 1931, 57 per cent failed.[32] Clearly, the myth of the Prairies as a land of free homesteaders is false. Second, they were at the mercy of a legislated railway monopoly, which charged excessive freight rates. Third, they were forced to buy all their manufactured necessities at prices mercilessly inflated by the tariff. More generally speaking, they were involved in a highly sophisticated capitalist agriculture concerned with the extensive industrial cultivation of cash grain crops for a distant market — a market to which they could gain access only through the railways and grain middlemen, and which paid prices over which they had no control.

Still, Confederation had worked and wheat had made it work. Yet it was to be precisely the underpinnings, the very economic foundation of Confederation — a transcontinental railway, a protective tariff, the settlement and land policies — and the special economic place assigned to the West in the newly constructed national capitalist economy, from which the settlers' grievances began to spring. And the grievances had been given expression by early settlers long before the wheat boom, and continued long after that boom had become a fond memory in the cruel cycle of boom and bust that came to dominate their lives.

3

AGITATION AND REBELLION: RIEL AND THE FARMERS IN THE 1880s

The acquisition of the Prairie West by the Dominion, which set the stage for the great wheat boom of 1896–1913, was not viewed with enthusiasm by many Westerners during the continuing depression. The agitations that had resulted in the 1869-70 Rebellion continued among agrarian settlers and Métis alike, though now the focus was on the effects of incorporation by the Dominion and the ongoing grievances of the region, rather than on the principle of incorporation itself. Indeed, angry echoes of discontent reverberated among Prairie settlers from the beginning. Part of the popular historical mythology of the Prairies holds that much of the complaining can be attributed to the harsh environment the settlers confronted and conquered. Nothing could be further from the truth. A close examination of the record shows that from the outset, the farmers' agitations had more to do with senators than seasons, with railway charges than grasshoppers, with land policies than frost, with tariffs than poor yields — indeed, with the many man-made calamities wrought by a distant political and economic system than with the natural disasters faced and overcome.

The Manitoba and North-West Farmers' Union had this to say to the Canadian people at their December 1883 convention:

> *We have hopefully faced the hardships of isolation and of a*
> *vigorous climate, and have been and are still willing to contend*

manfully with the natural disadvantages of our new location.

Now, however, that we have for the first time, a surplus of grain, we have discovered that the prices we obtain are not sufficient to cover the cost of production, and that we are face to face with the fact that notwithstanding all our labour and outlay we can barely subsist.

No doubt a combination of unfavourable circumstances such as early and severe frosts, together with imperfect arrangements for saving and marketing grain, have this season aggravated the farmers' condition and contributed to his discontent. Yet the fact remains that those of us whose crops were untouched by frost and who were at the same time most conveniently situated as to markets, realized little or no profit on our produce.[1]

The organized farmers of Manitoba had other grievances: "excessive charges of a railway monopoly," "an oppressive tariff which, however beneficial . . . to the manufacturing Eastern provinces, cannot fail to be inimical to the interests of a purely agricultural country such as this," and "the improper and vexatious . . . administration of the public lands in Manitoba." The convention issued a Declaration of Rights with the following demands:

- provincial rights to charter railways to break the CPR monopoly and speed up branch line construction;
- Manitoba be given "absolute" control of lands and resources;
- abolition of tariffs on agricultural implements;
- a rail route to Hudson Bay;
- legislation granting authority to municipalities to construct grain elevators and warehouses, and mills; and
- establishment of government grain inspection.[2]

These last two demands represented an early effort to begin to take the storage, handling, and grading of grains out of the hands of the private grain trade.

The convention was trying to address the issues confronting settlers daily in their efforts to prosper. Federal settlement policies were a dismal failure — immigration was a trickle, emigration a real problem. The tariff cruelly inflated production and living costs. There were serious marketing problems as a result of a lack of adequate grain storage and of railway branch lines (many settlers were from 50 to 300 miles from the railway).[3] And when the farmers got their grain to market after bone-shaking wagon hauls, they found the grain merchants imposed fixed, low prices, and unreasonably low grades on the grain. Finally, land problems persisted as many settlers found Dominion control of lands frustrated their desire to expand their holdings. But these grievances were hardly novel.

Matters were brought to a head, stimulating the outbursts of sustained agitation in the 1880s, when serious economic problems crippled the early success of the farmers. As early as the 1870s, the superiority of Manitoba wheat was recognized. In 1878 over a million bushels were harvested and the first shipment of Manitoba wheat reached Great Britain. By 1885 almost 7 million bushels were harvested, and in 1890, over 16 million. Manitoba's share of Canada's wheat production leapt from 3 per cent in 1880-81 to over 38 per cent in 1890-91.[4] There had been a significant, even startling, increase in settlement in Manitoba and the Territory. By 1881 Manitoba boasted a population of over 62,000, by 1891, over 152,000. The North-West leapt from over 56,000 in 1881 to over 99,000 in 1891. Occupied farms in the region grew from just over 10,000 in 1881 to over 31,000 in 1891. Acres under crops grew 5 times — 250,000 to 1. 3 million.[5] This general success in settlement and grain production, though far from the wildly optimistic hopes of federal politicians, was crushed by a fall in grain prices that set in almost as soon as the growth began.

The decade began well.[6] In 1881 a bushel of No. 1 Northern wheat brought a Fort William price of $1.34. By 1885 the price was 84 cents — a 37 per cent fall. This sharp fall in prices was heart-breaking for settlers who had only just begun to have some modest success. Their very success was being stolen by the price system. But the depression in prices was only part of the story. There was a general rise in the costs of production and living, some of which was due to deliberate federal action. For example, in 1883 tariffs on agricultural implements were upped from 25 per cent *ad valorem* to 35 per cent. Nature also took an additional toll — drought or early frosts hit every crop from 1883 to 1886.

But what rankled farmers most was the pricing system, which robbed them, and the freight rates, which squeezed them. In 1886 wheat sold for 81 cents at Winnipeg, 83 cents at Fort William, and $1.00 at Liverpool. At Brandon, the farmer could only get 53 cents. Grain middlemen who bought the wheat at Brandon could make a profit of 30 cents at Fort William, 28 cents at Winnipeg, or 47 cents at Liverpool. In 1886, it cost just under 20 cents to transport a bushel of wheat from Regina to Fort William, or just over 35 cents from Regina or Liverpool. Clearly the full blame for the big difference between the Brandon price and the other prices could not be completely laid on either transportation costs or the mysteries of international competition. The grain middlemen were taking a handsome share on each bushel, leaving less and less for the farmer. Clearly, too, the CPR was imposing excessive charges when, in the same year, it was possible to use the U.S. rail system to get a bushel of grain all the way from Duluth to Liverpool for between 12 and 18 cents a bushel. The grain merchants and the railways were clearly fleecing the farmers.

Prairie farmers were from the outset most angry at the policies and shady practices that deprived them of a just return on their crops: the prices they obtained, the tariff they were forced to pay, the excessive railway charges, the land policies, the lack of branch line construction, the absence of adequate storage. In summary, the problem was the lack of a responsible and responsive government that would serve and defend, or even take marginally into account, the farmers' real interests. The 1880s, therefore, witnessed a period of sustained and serious agitation on the Prairies. In the Saskatchewan region, the agitation culminated in the Riel Rebellion of 1885. In Manitoba, the agitation bordered on insurrection, as the settlers and their provincial government defied the federal government and the CPR. The settlers were definitely not listening to the advice of editorial writers, like that of the

Saskatoon *Sentinel* who, on August 9, 1884, warned, "We want men of pluck and spirit out here, able to do lots and give their tongues a rest."[7]

In Manitoba, agrarian grievances crystallized around the demand for the right of provincial governments to charter railways. Such a focus challenged not only the hated monopoly of the CPR, but federal authority in general. Indeed, the Manitoba government could not act on most of the other grievances since they were in federal jurisdiction. A provincial government could, however, speed up the construction of railway branch lines, an essential part of a solution to the farmers' marketing problems. The Manitoba government therefore incorporated the Manitoba South Eastern Railway. In 1882, the Dominion government disallowed the legislation. There was a local uproar at the "paralyzing policy of disallowance," as the Winnipeg *Free Press* described it.[8] Further provincial railway charters were passed and disallowed in a cat-and-mouse game between the province and Ottawa. Finally, backed by an aroused public opinion, the Manitoba government decided to build, as a public work, the Red River Railway from Winnipeg south to West Lynne, near the U.S. border, regardless of the consequences. The CPR threatened to withdraw its workshops from Winnipeg. There were rumours that federal troops would be sent in to stop construction. There were counter-rumours that local farmers were arming themselves. There was talk of insurrection, of annexation by the U.S., of secession, if the Dominion government and the CPR did not yield. The troops were never sent and the railway was begun in open defiance of the Dominion government and its laws. The CPR monopoly was finally broken a few years later.

Like the farmers of Manitoba, settlers in the Saskatchewan region began to organize and agitate. In 1883, a Settlers' Union was formed just east of Prince Albert. Their initial grievances included complaints about federal land policies and political corruption. Blocks of land had been granted to the Prince Albert Colonization Company, an Ottawa consortium of speculators, including a senator. This was done by the Dominion government without regard to the rights of the settlers who had already settled there, on or near the reserved land."Old" settlers, as they were called, wanted guarantees that the farms they possessed would become theirs; some near the lands in question wanted to expand their holdings but the reserved land stood in the way. Other practices that outraged the settlers, white and Métis, had to do with timber. Officials from the East, usually friends of the government, received contracts for cordwood for the Hudson's Bay Company for around $8 a cord, which they then subcontracted out to locals for from 50 cents to $1 a cord. Even more rankling, settlers had to pay dues for the right to harvest timber for their own use for fuel, construction, and fencing.[9] Whites and Métis alike wanted the right to harvest timber and to contract directly. As meetings were held, however, the grievances and demands of the Settlers' Union went far beyond these initial annoyances to encompass those of their Manitoba brethren and more.

Meanwhile the Métis were agitating for a settlement of their land claims. Ever since the Territory had been annexed by the Dominion, the local Métis had petitioned Ottawa for a settlement of their land entitlements. As the years went by, and as many Manitoba Métis moved to live in the territory, concern grew because of what had happened in Manitoba, where armed confrontation had been necessary to secure the most meagre and unsatisfactory of settlements. In addition to demands for land guarantees, the Métis had regularly petitioned Ottawa for capital to help them begin farming to join the new economy being established in the West. They were ignored, and, as a result, their agitations became more and more frantic. Increasingly, the white settlers and the Métis recognized that they shared similar concerns and that united action might succeed where separate pressure had failed.

Thus a new movement, uniting Métis — French and English — and white settlers, emerged, largely led by the Settlers' Union. On February 25, 1884 a full platform was adopted encompassing all popular grievances in the Territory, including those of the Aboriginals, who, as a result of a policy of deliberate neglect, faced starvation in the midst of appalling living conditions. A later meeting in the spring determined to invite Louis Riel back from exile to lead the agitation. Pleas from the Settlers' Union, in addition to those of Métis leaders, had a great deal to do with Riel's decision to return. Support for the agitation was overwhelming: the press supported it initially and even the Prince

Albert Tories toyed with the idea of adopting the platform as their own. The agitational meetings took on the character of a prairie fire, as they spread throughout the Saskatchewan territory and into the Alberta region. By December of 1884 the demands had been exhaustively discussed and codified into the Bill of Rights sent jointly to Ottawa by the Settlers' Union and Riel. The demands were not unreasonable and had been made many times before: better treatment for the Aboriginals, land settlement for the Métis, provincial status, representation in the federal Parliament, control of land and natural resources, changes in the homestead law and regulations, vote by secret ballot, tariff reductions, and a railway to Hudson Bay.

The federal government did not respond. They did not issue the expected invitation to send a Western delegation to Ottawa to negotiate. Macdonald claimed he never saw this petition; the overwhelming historical evidence is that this was a bold lie. Macdonald clearly wanted a confrontation. An election was looming, and he was in trouble. The CPR giveaways were again provoking serious public opposition. The continuation of the depression had turned his 1878 promise of prosperity into ashes. In order to take the additional steps necessary to finish the CPR and to silence his opponents, a crisis in Manitoba and the North-West Territory served his purposes very well. Perhaps, too, Macdonald sought revenge on Riel for the Manitoba crisis: had it not been for Riel Macdonald would not be facing continual harassment by that small province. Whatever his motives, he wanted a final showdown. Officials in Ottawa and on the scene pleaded with him to negotiate — to no avail. He awaited the inevitable.

As the ominous silence from Ottawa made clear, the movement in Saskatchewan would have to move beyond petitioning and negotiation. The petitions had been ignored. No one from Ottawa had offered to negotiate. Confrontation was in the air. Riel's arrival had already frightened the territory press, and many moderates among the white settlers, into silent neutrality, inactive sympathy, or open hostility. Only the bravest and most militant among the white settlers continued to support the movement. Even many English-speaking Métis had been scared off. Riel continued to beg for such support, so essential for final success of the campaign. On one occasion Riel sent a message to a Prince Albert meeting of settlers saying, "Gentlemen, please do not remain neutral. For the love of God help us to save the Saskatchewan."[10] Riel's subsequent declaration of a provisional government, and the determination of the Northwest Mounted Police to put a stop to the rebellion, frightened off most remaining white settler support. Riel and the Métis, supported by a few Aboriginal allies and a handful of white settlers, stood alone against the Dominion.

Riel had never wanted an open military conflict. Throughout the agitations he had expected negotiation. He had refused to make serious military preparations. When military action began, Riel refused to give Gabriel Dumont, the military commander of the Métis forces, a free hand to use hit-and-run tactics to harry the police and the troops.[11] As the final conflict approached at Batoche, the Métis capital, Riel insisted on staying in fixed position rather than scattering to begin a guerrilla war. Faced with inevitable defeat in a battle of fixed positions with the Canadian troops, Dumont nevertheless organized an admirable defence. Had Dumont been free to organize a serious military campaign from the outset, the Métis forces may well have been able to inflict sufficient casualties, as well as to prolong the conflict for weeks or perhaps months, putting further pressure on Ottawa to negotiate. In the event, the movement was decisively militarily defeated at Batoche and the Métis nation was crushed. Riel and eight Aboriginals went to the gallows. Many others went to prison, while others, including Dumont, fled to sanctuary in the U.S. Still others trekked northward, where their descendants today live. Two white settlers, prominent leaders of the Settlers' Union, were acquitted. Canada, from sea to sea, had exacted its first payment in blood.

The results sent a crystal-clear message. The Dominion government would not tolerate opposition to its plan for the West. Central Canada's vision, especially Ontario's, of the opening of the West would remain Canada's. The Aboriginals were brought to heel by the executions and by the imprisonment of some of their proudest leaders. The Métis nation was defeated, their homes burned and looted, their people, especially their leadership, dispersed in what can only be described as an act of attempted genocide. In the ensuing hysteria, the farmers' movement was discredited as Macdonald blamed the Rebellion on their ceaseless agitations. Although responsible government and provincial status was refused to the Northwest until 1905, some small concessions were made. The CPR monopoly was broken and provincial involvement in constructing branch lines was won. The crisis spurred the CPR to speed up branch line construction. Federal representation was won for the region in the House of Commons. But all this was really a pittance. The main issues raised were brushed aside and ignored as the Dominion relished its triumph.

Macdonald won his 1887 election, an election most observers believed he must inevitably lose before the uprising. Canada paid a heavy price for this cynical victory. The settlers in the West were deeply embittered by what happened — it was the beginning of a distrust of the federal government that was never to be extinguished. The people of Québec were deeply embittered by Macdonald's pitiless and blind determination to hang Riel though, as he himself said, "every dog in Québec bark in his favour."[12] Macdonald saw his chance to win solidly in English Canada and he was sure Québec would forgive and forget, as it had forgiven and forgotten so often before. This time Québec did not and for decades to come the Tory party paid the price for what was, in fact, a legal political murder.

The CPR speedily got the funds it needed, thanks to the Rebellion. Van Horne, CPR general manager and vice-president, jested that the CPR should erect a monument to Riel.[13]

Meanwhile, the farmers on the Prairies redoubled their agitations.

4

"THE MAN BEHIND THE PLOW": AGRARIAN POPULISM AND THE FARMER GOVERNMENTS

As the crisis of the 1880s unfolded in the West, the federal government, the CPR, and the private grain trade were taking the necessary steps to ensure the orderly and privately controlled export of Prairie grain. In 1883 the CPR mainline arrived at Winnipeg and the company completed its first lakehead terminal at Fort William. In 1884 the first shipment of Prairie wheat through the Canadian transportation system reached Europe. In 1886, federal government grain inspection was established at Winnipeg and Port Arthur. In 1887 the Winnipeg Grain and Produce Exchange began operations.[1]

Due to serious problems getting the 1888 crop speedily to market, the CPR offered local monopolies in grain handling to anyone willing to build modern grain elevators at key points on rail lines. These line elevator companies pursued their advantage through deliberate undergrading, unfair dockage, high storage charges, suspect weigh scales, and low prices. As well, farmers saw the speculators in the Grain Exchange filching their profits as prices were often depressed in the fall, when most farmers had to sell, and high during other times of the year when grain moved from storage to market. Government inspectors harshly suppressed farmers' grades and seemed to act more as agents of the grain merchants than public officials. Terminal elevators mixed low and high grades, selling the mixture at the higher price, in which the farmer did not share.[2] Such abuses led to deep anger and bitterness among the farmers. As W. R. Motherwell, first Territorial Grain Growers' Association president and later a federal Liberal minister of agriculture, put it:

> *While this sort of thing continued for twenty years it so calloused and hardened the people against everybody and anybody in authority that the farmers were willing to do almost anything to obtain redress . . . There are few . . . who know how near the people were to resorting to violence . . .*[3]

The farmers, temporarily disoriented by the hysteria after the Rebellion, re-organized quickly. The Patrons of Industry, already long active in the U.S. and in Ontario, began to organize at Portage la Prairie in 1891. Their official aim was clear and blunt: "to protect both farmer and employee against the over-powering influences of the financial and commercial classes."[4] The Patrons' 1892 Brandon convention endorsed the now-familiar demands of Prairie farmers, but added some new ones: farmer ownership of grain elevators and flour mills, provincial banks to loan money at five per cent, and farmer representation on the Grain Standards Board. In that year their Prairie membership reached 5,000.[5] Of great significance was the fact that the Patrons in the West were allied with Ontario's organized farmers, active since the 1870s, and aspired to build a national organization from the outset. The Patrons made other innovations: they established consumer co-operatives for twine, coal oil, and coal; they unsuccessfully tried a binder twine production co-operative; they published their own newspaper; and they went directly into politics. In 1896 two of seven Patron candidates in the Manitoba election won office. In 1894 the Ontario Patrons had won 17 seats. As well, in the 1896 federal election the Patrons fielded 29 candidates, winning 3 seats; and in 1897 they won a federal by-election. Most significant, in terms of what was to come, the Patrons pioneered organized grain growers' co-operation by establishing a grain elevator at Boissevain in southeast Manitoba. They were the first farmers' organization to do so, although by 1898 individual local groups of farmers cooperatively owned 26 of the 447 elevators in the West. The Patron decision to go into politics deeply split the organization and it disintegrated almost overnight — but they had shown the way.[6]

This continuing agrarian agitation gained some quick concessions from the new Laurier Liberal government. The Crow's Nest Pass Agreement of 1897 was a landmark. In exchange for building a rail line from Lethbridge through the Crow's Nest Pass to Nelson, B.C., the CPR, as usual, got a generous public subsidy. However, the new Liberal government demanded that the CPR help redress some of the farmers' grievances through significant freight rate reductions on grain and flour moving eastward, as well as on crucial industrial agricultural inputs, such as machinery and fuel, moving westward. This agreement established the principle of some statutory regulation of freight rates on the movement of grain. Most importantly, at the time, grain production became more viable by cuts in transportation costs. In 1899 a Royal Commission on the Shipment of Grain was appointed, reporting with amazing speed in 1900 that the farmers' grievances were well founded. Again, the federal government acted quickly, passing the *Manitoba Grain Act* that year. The Act, hailed as the "Magna Charta" of the grain producer, proclaimed what the farmers wanted. But the Act failed completely. Its provisions for farmer access to load their own cars and fairer grading practices were ignored with impunity by the CPR and the private grain trade. This growing disappointment was hardened on the question of the tariff. During the 1896 campaign Sifton had promised tariff relief: "Free coal, free oil, free clothing, and free implements you shall have if the Liberal party are returned to power."[7] Indeed, he had gone further at one point, no doubt in response to the cheering enthusiasm of his rural electors, promising that a Liberal government in Ottawa would "wipe off the statute book the villainous protection policy" that had "taken the heart's blood out of the people of Manitoba."[8] The Liberals declined to deliver this promise, even reneging on the limited list of free items. Only in 1907 were some small reductions made on certain items in response to Western demands. As a result, the farmers continued to view both parties with suspicion. A Tory government refused to act at all; while the

Thompson-Nicola Regional District Library System

new Liberal government, after great promises, only pretended to act in ways that were increasingly seen as either hesitant or useless.

Therefore the early years of the 20th century witnessed great changes in the agrarian agitation. The small victories squeezed from Laurier were viewed with contempt and, despite the wheat boom, the abiding conviction among Prairie farmers remained that a fair share of the return on their crops systematically failed to reach their pockets. The farmers quickly learned that many of their earlier specific demands had little to do with the structural problems they confronted. They had agitated for branch lines: now they had branch lines. They had agitated for better grain handling facilities: these were now available. They had agitated for government terminals: a small breakthrough had been made. They had wanted fairer grades: now they increasingly had these.

Inevitably they came to see more clearly that the primary sources of their grievances lay with the whole grain marketing system itself, as well as with the general economic policies of the federal government. As a result the agitation developed two distinct if related thrusts. On the one hand, the farmers fought for changes in the marketing and handling of grain. On the other, the organized farmers developed a sustained populist offensive against the economic terms of the National Policy, the basis of Confederation, as well as against aspects of modernizing capitalism. It was in this context that new grain grower organizations were founded.

Thanks to the CPR and the private grain trade, the organizing went extremely well. In 1901 the farmers again experienced great difficulty getting their grain to market, due, they were convinced, to the CPR's manipulations and inefficiency. This year they publicly denounced it as the "Blockade of 1901," and went on the offensive, successfully taking the CPR to court at Sintaluta, Saskatchewan. The Territorial Grain Growers Association (TGGA) was founded that year at Indian Head. The Manitoba Grain Growers Association (MGGA) was founded in 1903. And with the creation of Saskatchewan and Alberta in 1905, the TGGA became the Saskatchewan association (SGGA), while competing farmer groups in Alberta finally united into the United Farmers of Alberta (UFA) in 1909. That year all three Prairie associations joined the Canadian Council of Agriculture (CCA), uniting with the 9,000 farmers in the Dominion Grange of Ontario (later the United Farmers of Ontario). By the summer of 1910, when Laurier visited the Prairies, the Prairie organizations had over 23,000 members: 9,000 in Manitoba, 6,000 in Saskatchewan, and 8,500 in Alberta.[9] (In 1911, there were just over 40,000 occupied farms of over 50 acres in Manitoba, almost 95,000 in Saskatchewan, and about 60,000 in Alberta. The organized farmers were weakest in Ontario, where there were just over 148,000 such farms in 1911.[10]) Nationally, they now commanded a formidable organized force in excess of 30,000 farmers, and their influence was growing. In response, the private grain trade organized the North West Grain Dealers' Association and began to engage in price-fixing, as well as lobbying against the increasingly militant farmers.

The conflicting agitations, the claims and counter-claims, led to the establishment of yet another Royal Commission on the Grain Trade in 1906, which once again sustained the farmers' case. But the organized farmers did not rest on their laurels. Rather, they began a detailed inquiry into the Winnipeg Grain Exchange and the whole private grain marketing system. The conclusion of this investigation was a shock: rather than demanding legislative controls and penalties on the private grain trade, the farmers decided to organize a farmers' co-operative grain company to engage in marketing from farmgate to international market. In 1906, the Grain Growers' Grain Company (GGGCo) was founded and went to work to win farmers to a new and radical solution to their problems. Success was phenomenal — by 1910, 9,000 farmers marketed their grain through the company.

In efforts to maximize the return to the grain grower, the farmers were on the march to eliminate the grain middle-man through the construction of farmer-owned marketing companies to gain control of the storage and sale of the harvest. This struggle ultimately led to the establishment in the 1920s of the great Wheat Pools, which culminated in final victory. Until their privatization in the 1990s, the Prairie Wheat Pools were among Canada's largest corporations and dominated the domestic grain trade. The pooling idea, whose seeds were planted by the GGGCo, finally ensured that farmers got the full market return for their crops, less a fair cost for marketing. The successes obtained by the organized farmers in the marketing area contributed to the self-confident thrust of their more political agitation. This agitation was nothing less than a national effort to reform the party system, to hold in check the advance of industrial capitalism, and to transform the root economic policies of the whole nation. Its focus was the protective tariff and it took on the character of a crusading class struggle.

THE AGRARIAN CRUSADE, 1910–1930

In December 1910 the Canadian Council of Agriculture brought over 800 delegates from Ontario and the West to a "Siege on Ottawa." Parliament and the nation were presented with the Farmers' Platform of 1910, the clearest expression of organized agrarian thinking to that point, marking the opening salvo in the general political agitation. The demand for free trade was the centrepiece of the document. The petition also expressed the deep concern among farmers at advancing rural depopulation as industrial capitalism marched relentlessly forward:

> *Believing that the greatest misfortune which can befall any country is to have its people huddled together in great centres of population, and that the bearing of the present customs tariff has the tendency to that condition . . . the greatest problem which presents itself to Canadian people today is the problem of retaining our people on the soil, we come doubly assured of the justice of our petition.* [11]

The platform also called for a series of specific reforms and government interventions, most of direct interest to farmers.

Laurier was impressed with what he had seen in the West in the summer of 1910, and this early winter seige helped convince him to make some concessions to the farmers. In 1911, with one eye to the farmer agitations and the other to eastern industrial capitalist opinion, Laurier determined on a course of limited reciprocity with the U.S. in an effort to strike a politically judicious balance between what were contradictory claims. In late January 1911, the federal government announced a new trade agreement with the U.S. The agreement was complex, establishing free trade in natural products and on a number of semi-processed industrial commodities, as well as schedules involving mutually agreed lower tariffs on specific items, especially farm machinery. The overall impact was nowhere near what the farmers wanted, but as a result of the implacable opposition of prominent capitalists, the agreement caused a political furor, which led to a Liberal defeat in the famous 1911 Reciprocity Election.

The farmers saw the agreement as the first step in dismantling the hated tariff economy. The Canadian Manufacturers' Association (CMA) agreed, and saw it as the prelude to more serious free-trade policies. The debate became near hysterical: supporters of the policy were accused of disloyalty, of treason, of selling out to the Americans. The opposition from commercial, banking, and industrial capitalists in Toronto and Montreal was so effective that prominent Liberals deserted Laurier. Even Clifford Sifton, that erstwhile Manitoban champion of free trade, broke with Laurier, joining the opposition. The Liberals reeled under the onslaught, failing either to confront the issues directly or to mobilize free-trade opinion effectively.

The results of the election were not only a defeat for Laurier but, it was thought, a final staggering blow to free-traders. The Tories swept Ontario, 73 seats to 13. The Liberals only narrowly won Québec, 38 seats to 27. The parties split Atlantic Canada. The agrarians rewarded Laurier's small efforts, with 8 of Saskatchewan's 10 seats and 6 of Alberta's 7 seats. Yet Manitoba, under Sifton's influence, went Tory 8 seats to 2. And B.C., always solidly behind the National Policy in these early years, sent 7 out of 7 Tories to Ottawa. Of 221 seats, the Tories took 134. Once again Canada had voted for the National Policy. Free-trade, even the limited policy of Laurier, had failed to convince capitalists or workers.

Even the staunch free-trading farmers were deeply split, as the Manitoban results attested. Clifford Sifton's argument that free trade in natural products would hurt the farmer had been as effective there as similar arguments had been among B.C. farmers, fishermen, miners, and lumbermen. Sifton had painstakingly documented that prices gained by Canada's farm products in the U.S. would be, in many instances, far lower than those prevailing in Canada. Furthermore, he suggested that the Canadian meat packing industry would be destroyed, allowing U.S. packers to pay as little as possible for farm products in the future. Most importantly, he argued that the destruction of the autonomous, east-west Canadian grain market would deliver Canadian farmers forever into the hands of the U.S. grain merchants. In B.C. the suggestion that the loss of the Canadian east-west market in fish, minerals, and lumber would, in the long run, lead to lower prices and less industrial development in canning and wood products, was just as compelling.[12] Yet the 1911 results did not discourage the organized farmers; on the contrary, they urged themselves on to greater efforts. As Edward and Annie Porritt, in a 1913 anti-tariff polemic published by the Grain Growers' Guide, declaimed:

> *The victory of the Conservatives . . . forms the best possible*
> *proof of the immensity and difficulty of the task of education*
> *and liberation which still lies before the grain-growers of the*
> *West and the common people of Canada who do not belong to*
> *the small and privileged class which profits from protection.*[13]

The farmers learned three clear lessons in 1911. First, they could not effectively influence either federal party when in power. Second, those who had all along argued for a peoples' party had won their point, though it took some additional time to win the argument. Third, the sources of the 1911 defeat sharpened the farmers' understanding of the powers ranged against them: the Canadian Manufacturers' Association, the banks and financial interests, the railways, the commercial interests. Further, the British nationalist hysteria generated during the anti-Laurier election showed farmers just how far their foes would go to secure victory. Politically the defeat furthered the discrediting of the two old parties, already well-advanced, by showing the Tories at their worst and by revealing that Liberal equivocation even in marginal efforts did not serve the farmers' cause well. Rather than retreating, therefore, the organized agrarians went on a new political offensive, staging a Second Siege on Ottawa in December 1913, and declaring, *in 1913 it is still the manufacturers of Ontario and Québec, who through the power conferred on them by Conservative Governments, and continued after 1897 by the Liberals, levy toll to the full statutory limit on this population west of the Lakes; and likewise on the rural populations in Ontario and Québec and the Maritime Provinces.*[14]

For reasons other than Laurier's defeat, 1911 was an important year for the farmers. It was a census year and the figures portended the decimation of rural Canada and the final triumph of urban industrial capitalism. The "greatest misfortune" that the 1910 Platform had so feared was on the immediate historical agenda. Nationally, rural population had fallen to just over 54 per cent.[15] More significantly, more and more of the labour force, about 66 per cent, were involved in non-agricultural occupations.[16] Moreover, the number of occupied farms had fallen dramatically in the older parts of the country, especially Central Canada.

Even on the Prairies, where the number of occupied farms continued dramatic increases, the rural share of population had fallen from 75 per cent in 1901 to 65 per cent in 1911.[17] These trends were bitterly lamented by the organized farmers and they blamed the tariff unreservedly. The 1916 version of the platform attributed "the declining rural population . . . largely to the increased cost of . . . everything the farmer has to buy, caused by the Protective Tariff, so that it is becoming impossible for farmers . . . to carry on farming operations profitably."[18] Further, the sheltered industries in the cities served as magnets, drawing population to the higher wages and shorter hours made possible by the tariff. Clearly, the farmers believed, the abolition of the tariff would lead to a return of people to the countryside where work on the land or in the villages awaited as the unnaturally supported industries declined in the absence of protection.

The related themes of the economic injustice of the tariff and rural depopulation became cornerstones of the 1911 to 1921 agrarian political offensive. The sharpness and vigour of the movement surprised many. The political and economic critique of the forces oppressing the farmers, and all common people, was generalized. The two old parties were dismissed, increasingly seen as indistinguishable in their loyal service of vested interests. The critique turned to capitalism itself and parliamentary democracy, very much from the point of view of the small agrarian capitalist. Condemnations of the capitalist plutocracy, of the money power, of special interest, and of the New Feudalism became wide-spread.[19] Add to these the repeated attacks on the corruption of "partyism" as an enemy of true democracy and it becomes clear just how extensive the organized farmer critique became.

The farmers, in the words of one of their polemicists, supported measures that would "revolutionize the whole established commercial system" and denounced those "parasites" who took for themselves an "Unearned Increment." Demands that politicians support the proposals, and the politicians' refusals, led to denunciations of the "nose-pulling game of Party Politics." "A pitched fight between capitalistic groups and the people at large, led by the farmers" was envisaged. The farmers would triumph."What chance will Special Privilege have against the public desire for Equal Rights?" Songs like "The Day of Right" (to the tune of the "Battle Hymn of the Republic") reverberated in community halls across the Prairies:

The farmers of the prairie lands are massing in their might,

Exulting in a Principle, a Cause for which they fight: The sacred cause of Justice, the establishment of Right And Equal Rights to all.

CHORUS: *Oh! 'Tis time to get together You will help us get together; Pledge we all to stand together, For the days of Peace and Right. The farmers of the prairie lands have right upon their side;*

Their platform is the people's, democratic, nationwide;

Their cause, the ancient cause for which brave-hearted men have died — Of Equal Rights to all.

The farmers of the prairie lands know well the foe they fight,

The Profiteers of Privilege, full armed with legal right; Against that giant bluff we aim to solidly unite For Equal Rights to all.[20]

The ultimate goal became "the establishment of GOD'S KINGDOM upon earth."[21] If the national leadership of "the Man behind the Plow"[22] were embraced by all, it was asserted, "in the place of the deep furrows of dissension will be the level seed-bed of greater unity among men."[23]

The intensity of the agitation, and the success of the agrarian organizations, both accelerated with the bust of 1913, the war of 1914–18 and the post-war depression of 1920–23.[24] The wheat boom broke in 1913, beginning an unexpected depression. Wheat prices collapsed and drought slashed the crop of 1914. General industrial and construction unemployment skyrocketed. The export prices of other natural resources fell. Investment contracted. The depression showed signs of becoming deep, general, and long. Only the arrival of World War I saved Canada from economic calamity. Overnight the depression was replaced by a war-induced boom. Prices for Canada's natural resource exports rose — in the case of wheat, astronomically. Industrial production spiralled.

There was, however, a dark side to the boom for the agrarians, as manufacturing's share of the value of exports grew from 13 per cent in 1913 to 31 per cent in 1918, while agriculture's share fell from 55 per cent in 1913 to 48 per cent in 1918. There were other dark portents as the boom inflated farm production costs, pushed up the cost of credit, and ballooned the public debt. Generally farm prices, though good, zigged and zagged as production costs marched steadily upward. Yet the farmers achieved some remarkable successes, moving Canada from its pre-war place of third among world wheat exporters, to second by 1918, to first by 1923. Prairie acreage in field crops increased by 84 per cent between 1914 and 1920, while the Prairie population went up another 19 per cent.

Although the Prairies did well out of the war, Central Canada, as the focus of capitalist industrialization, did even better as industrial and finance capitalism grew to maturity. Growing urbanization confirmed the worst fears of the organized farmers when Central Canada emerged from the war as the industrial heartland of the nation. Paradoxically, the war therefore laid the basis for an aggravated sense of grievance and disillusionment. War profiteering, inflation, high interest rates, the unequal sacrifices demanded of agriculture (price controls were imposed on wheat), combined with cynical calls for patriotism, all were viewed as further evidence of the abject dishonesty and hypocrisy of the political system and the two old parties. The demands for a farmer-led peoples' party became irresistible. In 1916 the Grain Growers' Guide declared,

> The time has come when the Western representatives should represent Western people and Western views and cut off connections with the privilege-ridden, party blind, office-hunting Grit and Tory parties that make their headquarters at Ottawa.[25]

In 1916 another edition of the Farmers' Platform was issued by the CCA and it appeared that the farmers would enter the next election. The 1917 conscription election nipped the move in the bud, as the Union Government walked to an easy victory. With the war's end the agrarians again went on the offensive. In 1919 a further edition of the Farmers' Platform was submitted to member organizations of the Canadian Council of Agriculture, and finally revised for the 1921 election. The document, called "The New National Policy," was more far-reaching and complete in its proposals than earlier editions.[26]

The tariff still occupied centre stage, standing accused of fostering combines and trusts which engaged in shameful "exploitation," of causing rural depopulation, of making "the rich richer and the poor poorer," of being the "chief corrupting influence . . . in national life," and of lowering "the standard of public morality." Free trade was the principled panacea. The document also advocated a reformed tax system, a series of political reforms to deepen democracy, a more sympathetic approach to returned soldiers and trade unions, and public ownership of transportation and energy resources.

Armed with this policy the organized farmers marched into political action federally as the Progressive party. A large part of their arsenal was the postwar depression, which ravaged the Canadian economy. Between 1920 and 1923, wheat prices collapsed by 67 per cent. Real incomes dropped dramatically, exports fell off, and industrial unemployment almost tripled. Very quickly the organized farmers won some notable victories. In the 1919 election the United Farmers of Ontario (UFO) won the largest bloc of seats and formed a minority government. In 1921, the UFA swept to 14 years of secure majority rule in Alberta. And in 1922, the United Farmers of Manitoba won majority power as well.

Most significant, however, were the national results of the 1921 federal election.[27] The Progressives won 65 seats with 23 per cent of the vote. They swept the Prairies: 11 of 12 seats in Alberta, 15 of 16 in Saskatchewan, and 12 of 15 in Manitoba (with popular votes of 57 per cent, 61 per cent, and 44 percent respectively). In B.C. they won 2 seats and 9 per cent and in Atlantic Canada, 1 seat with more than 10 per cent of the vote in each province. No seats were won in Québec. The Ontario results marked the Progressives' most impressive political achievement, 24 seats with 28 per cent of the vote. Thus the Progressives' biggest single bloc of seats and of votes came from Ontario, a fact often overlooked by those who focus on the massive popular support won on the Prairies in efforts to paint the Progressive movement as a regional rather than a national movement. The fact is that in 1921 there was no section of the nation, except Québec, where the Progressives had not made a presentable showing, certainly enough to form the electoral basis for a new agrarian-led peoples' party with the ultimate capacity to govern. It was the organized farmers' finest hour in politics and they appeared to have reached the threshold of political success in turning the nation around. Yet the party faltered and collapsed almost overnight. Why?

Probably it is correct to say that the Progressive refusal of the chance to become the Official Opposition in Ottawa and thereby to adopt the party system ensured its failure. Yet no one should be astounded at that principled decision given the previous 20 years of agitation. It would have quite simply been impossible for the Progressives to have embraced the party system, having denounced it for years as a main source of evil and corruption in political life. Such a decision would have broken the Progressives on the day after the election. The problems were much deeper and were exhibited by the farmer governments in the provinces.

The federal Progressives were a loose coalition of the various provincial farmer organizations. There was no coherent, separate and united, national political organization. The federal agrarian Progressives were solely united around the New National Policy document, and there was little unity on other policy matters. Urban labour had only returned a handful of Progressive MPs, and they found little real sympathy for labour's plight among the more numerous agrarian MPs. The provincial farmer governments were wholly independent, able to pursue their courses with little or no input from either the federal organization or other provincial organizations.

After winning office, federal Progressive MPs, and the farmer provincial governments, rode off in all directions in a spectacle of disunity and policy incoherence that discredited them in the eyes of the electorate. In Ontario, the minority farmer government behaved as a typical party government and, when the rank-and-file organization refused to broaden out to include membership from other popular classes (like workers and teachers) to increase its base of support, its fate was sealed. The United Farmers of Manitoba government, always reluctant violators of political norms, despite its majority, gradually edged back into the Liberal fold, unclear about just what a farmers' government should be doing. In Alberta, the farmer government, its comfortable majority and tradition of militancy providing no excuse, imposed rigid cabinet government and party discipline on MLAs, failed to respond to demands for reform from its membership, and governed unimaginatively until 1935.

The organized farmers had no clear idea about what to do with power after getting it. There was no agreement on how to win the necessary support of the working class. Even the Labour MLAs invited into cabinet in Ontario and Alberta failed to influence the governments to become more generally responsive on labour, minimum wage, and social welfare policies. There was no agreement on the principles needed to guide practical political organization. Survival of the organizations in politics required that they move toward becoming general political organizations of farmers, workers and other sympathetic classes, with a more broadly responsive political program and an effective mechanism for continuing policy development. Such sentiments were unsuccessfully expressed by a minority.

The farmer governments, and the federal Progressive party, decided to remain decisively farmer oriented. There was no agreement on the role of the government in the economy. There was no real policy worth the name, except the principles and polemics of the New National Policy and vague notions of the need for sound, business-like, honest government. Before going political the organized farmers' coherence had had its source in their critique and lamentations; after going into politics, especially after notable victories, there was no coherence. During the federal elections of 1925, 1926, and 1930 their disintegration was as remarkable as their rise, and almost as speedy.

The Progressives had been truly a meteoric political phenomenon, entering and exiting the effective political stage in five years. Yet they had a significant impact: they wrung some significant concessions from the Liberal government and Canadian politics were never as certain as they had been prior to the agrarian onslaught. Most importantly, they won significant concessions for their agrarian base, which helps explain their demise.[28] In 1922 they won the restoration of the Crow's Nest Pass statutory freight rates, suspended in 1919. They also won significant tariff relief on agricultural implements and motor vehicles, some federal farm credit assistance, and the re-establishment of the Wheat Board (suspended in 1920). As well, the Progressives, especially their urban labour members, pushed the government toward the first hesitant steps in constructing the modern welfare state. Such concessions may have taken the edge off their popular support, but the fact is that the crisis in the Progressive party and in the farmer governments merely revealed a crisis at their base.

The united farmer organizations reached their peak in members in 1921, followed by rapid declines in the next year or two: in Ontario, 60,000 members to 30,000; in Alberta, 38,000 to 15,000; in Saskatchewan, 29,000 to 21,000; in Manitoba, 16,000 to 6,000.[29] The decreases were greatest in those provinces where power was won. It is ironic that at the height of what appeared to be their greatest political hour, the organized farmers were disintegrating. The farmers very quickly left overt political action. By 1923 the United Farmers of Ontario declared its withdrawal from politics, devoting itself to educational and cooperative work. And the Canadian Council of Agriculture withdrew support for national political action, leaving politics to provincial organizations, thus removing the national focus for the Progressives. These decisions ended the brief intrusion of the organized farmers into national politics, indeed, into provincial politics, except for the farmer regime in Alberta, a lonely shell that, in its rigid conservatism and unrelenting lack of imagination, reminded everyone of the failed promise.

There is no doubt that the return to prosperity after 1923 undercut the agrarian political offensive. Wheat production and exports regained and surpassed wartime highs. Prices were good, though still unstable from year to year. Nature wrought no general disasters. There was money to be made and hard work to be done. The boom of the 1920s accelerated the mechanization of Prairie agriculture as well as witnessing the final completion of the settlement process. The organizational skills of the farmers after 1923 were focused on building voluntary wheat pools at the provincial level, necessitated by the Manitoba Legislature's refusal to go along with the Wheat Board legislation passed by Ottawa, Saskatchewan, and Alberta. Increasing the return to the farmer through cooperative marketing seemed a more sensible expenditure of time than ceaseless political agitation. Great success rewarded the farmers' efforts when by 1930 the three Prairie Pools had almost 56 per cent of Prairie farmers under contract and controlled one-third of total Prairie elevator capacity.[30]

But it must be said that the most important grievances of the organized farmers remained unaddressed. True to its increasingly sophisticated political habit of granting just enough concessions to blunt the sharpness of any troublesome agitation, the federal government had astutely avoided conceding anything of real importance to the farmers. The tariff, despite modifications, remained essentially intact. The near-complete reliance on grain production remained to plague Prairie prosperity. Rural depopulation continued, and industrialization and urbanization accelerated remorselessly. Control of natural resources was denied the Prairie provinces until 1930, when settlement was completed. What security had been gained had been won by the self-organization of the Prairie farmers into co-operative pools. Control over the costs of production continued to elude the farmer. High interest rates continued to take much of the cream of any profits. Railways continued to impose their freight rates with impunity, save for the small measure of relief granted by the Crow Rate. Grain merchants made up for their setbacks in the domestic market by clinging to their shrinking share of the market, and diversifying their investments. The political clout of agrarian Canada, and of the Prairie West, continued to be virtually ignored but for this or that gesture of conciliation flung by the federal government. The prosperity of the 1920s turned out to have the substance of a house of cards.

During the first round of Prairie agitations, Riel and his efforts had won great sympathy in Québec and deep hostility in Ontario. In this second round, the farmers had won significant support in rural Ontario and indifference in Québec. The pattern of Canadian politics seemed ominously set. And Prairie grievances, once again, were locked up west of the Lakes.

5

SOCIALISM AND SYNDICALISM: THE RISING OF THE WORKING CLASS, 1870–1919

As the farmers' agitations developed and matured, those of the West's working class led inexorably to the 1919 confrontation at Winnipeg and the aftermath of repression. The agrarian movement believed in small capitalism, yet yearned for basic reforms, and mounted a near-effective challenge to the party system and the National Policy. The Western workers' movement generally embraced varieties of socialism or syndicalism, anticipating the final overthrow of capitalism. The farmers dreamed of a society based on co-operation, reason and com-promise, free of class conflict and special privilege. The workers agreed that this was a dream, asserting that co-operation, reason, and com-promise had never got the workers anywhere. The farmers owned land, which they wanted to keep, expand, nurture, protect. The workers had no land, nor any hope of getting any; all they had was their labour to sell for a wage. The capitalist plutocrats may have coveted the farmers' land, imposed low prices on grain, charged high interest and freight rates, and squeezed them with the hated tariff. From the worker, all the capitalist wanted was labour, as much as could be had at the lowest possible wages, regardless of the risks to health or life for the workers.

The Western working class provided the vital labour essential to the settlement of the West.[1] They came in hundreds of thousands to take the jobs in the booming West. They worked in coal and hardrock mines. They built the towns and cities, the homes, schools, and hospitals. They dug the sewers. They laid the track for two transcontinental railways. They cut the trees, sawed the lumber, processed the pulp. They provided the year-round labour on the farm as well as joining the harvest trains for the few weeks of hard work each fall to bring in the Prairie crop. The jobs they found were in resource extraction, construction, transportation, manufacturing, and agriculture. Many of them were migrant, moving to where there was work, and, when the job was finished, moving on to the next mine, construction project, or logging operation. The same worker might cut pulp wood in Western Ontario in the winter, dig sewers in Winnipeg in the spring, mine coal in Alberta in the summer, join the Prairie harvest in the fall, and move on to a B.C. logging camp for the next winter. The "lucky" ones settled into the permanent jobs running the railway, working in the new cities in sundry occupations, digging in the more prosperous among the mines in Alberta and B.C. Many had come with great expectations of a better life with more opportunity and prosperity, some even dreaming of owning a farm. What they found was low wages, high living costs, appalling living conditions, dangerous jobs, and ruthless employers. The coal mines of B.C. and Alberta were the most dangerous on the continent: from 1889 to 1908, 23 men died for every million tons of coal extracted in B.C. — the North American average was six fatalities per million tons. Things in the coal mines barely improved from 1908 to 1918, when over 12 men died in B.C. and Alberta for every million tons, while just under five per million died in the U.S.[2]

Many mines, coal and hardrock, were remote company towns or camps where workers were charged exorbitant fees for family shacks or space in a bunk-house. Charges were deducted for weigh services, for non-existent medical services, and for blasting powder. Often miners were paid in scrip, acceptable only at the expensive company store. Frequently miners were paid a contract price that fluctuated with world prices and took no account of increases in the cost of living. Ten- or twelve-hour days and six-day weeks were commonly necessary to earn a living wage. Railway construction camps were often worse, work often harder, demanding 12 hours a day in a seven-day week. Workers arrived at the job site in debt for transportation charges and saw their

pay packets reduced by costly room and board and high prices at the
company store. Some foremen enforced work discipline with fists and
threats, and some railway camps kept armed guards to protect railway
property. Remote lumber camps were just as bad. Ten-hour days and
six-day weeks were the norm and, again, workers frequently arrived
in debt for travel costs. No matter how bad conditions were, workers
were forced to work at least as long as it took to pay off the debt and to
accumulate enough to travel on. Such camps and company towns were
notorious for their poor food, their vermin-ridden quarters, and lack of
even minimal sanitation. Those who escaped death or maiming in the
dangerous work were often at risk as epidemics of typhoid fever and
other infectious diseases attacked bodies already weakened by hard
labour and poor food. Conditions in the working-class districts of the
new Western cities were not much better. High rents, overcrowding,
and minimal services turned such districts into ghetto's of impoverished humanity.

Resistance and rebellion, therefore, were not simply matters of justice, they were frequently matters of survival. Safer conditions, a living
wage, decent food and living quarters, and security for the families
of those maimed or killed, became matters of great concern. Workers
from the mines of Vancouver Island to the manufactories and skilled
trades of Winnipeg began to organize trade unions. By today's standards their demands were modest. The right to collective bargaining,
decent wages, safer conditions, shorter work days, a day off in seven,
workers' compensation for injured workers and the families of those
killed on the job, were what they asked. The employers' opposition
to unions was implacable and ruthless, buttressed by politicians and
governments. Union sympathizers were fired and blacklisted. Strike
leaders were jailed. Spies and detectives reported on union activities
as well as acting as agents provocateurs. Strikes were met by machine
guns and militia, and governments colluded with employers to bring
immigrants in to scab. Striking railway workers lost their pension
rights. Striking miners and their families were driven from their homes
in company towns. The near-universal response among employers was
that unions were seditious and treasonous, threats to the Canadian

way of life, a short step away from flagrant insurrection. Government officials and politicians agreed, and lent their weight to the employers' side in what was already an unequal battle. An examination of the events surrounding two strikes, one in Winnipeg in 1906 and one on Vancouver Island in 1912, illustrates this unyielding attitude of business and government to trade unions in this era.

In March 1906, the Winnipeg Street Railwayman's Union went on strike against the streetcar company, demanding higher wages, shorter hours, improved safety measures, and union recognition.[3] The strike had been provoked when the company arbitrarily fired two members of the union's negotiating committee. The company brought in scabs to run the streetcars, and private detectives to protect company property, resulting in widespread demonstrations of public support for the union. The demonstrations continued, disrupting the operation of the streetcars, and a number of instances of violence and property damage occurred. The company's subsequent demand that the militia be called out was acceded to by civic authorities. The militia was brought in, the *Riot Act* read, and the crowds dispersed by troops armed with rifles with unsheathed bayonets and at least one machine gun. Public support, a boycott of the streetcars in working-class districts, and mediation efforts by the clergy brought the strike to a speedy end. The workers were granted some of what they asked, but not clear-cut union recognition. And union recognition was the first demand in all early trade union struggles because not only did such recognition mean that employers would have to bargain for formal collective agreements, but union organization and activity among workers could not be punished by firings and blacklisting.

The 1912 strike of miners in the Nanaimo coal fields was merely another in a series of sharp clashes between capital and labour that began there as early as the 1850s. The Dunsmuir coal empire had been the major protagonist for capital, the United Mine Workers of America for labour. James Dunsmuir, a one-time B.C. premier, had publicly declared, "I object to all unions . . . I want the management of my own works, and if I recognize a union, I cannot have that."[4] His remedy for all union activity among his miners was simple: he "fired the heads of the union," "every time," as he himself admitted.[5] The mine workers had been defeated in strikes in 1903 and 1905, and union organization had disintegrated. However, continuing problems with dangerous and poor working conditions, and low pay, combined with persisting repression of union activity to precipitate a strike in 1912, this time against Canadian Collieries Ltd., which had bought out the Dunsmuirs.[6]

The strike began with over 3,000 miners out, but quickly spread to involve over 7,000 miners in a two-year strike (September 1912 to August 1914). In efforts to continue production the companies brought in immigrant labour to strike-break, had martial law declared in the district, and imported special police to protect the scabs. Several incidents of violence between strikers and scabs justified the final decision to bring in the militia in August 1913 to begin what was to be a 15-month military occupation. The strike was finally broken: 256 strikers were arrested, five were sentenced to two years in jail, 23 to one year, and 11 to three months. One striker died in Oakalla prison due to a lack of medical attention. Although a public campaign finally led to the pardoning of 22 of those convicted, the battle had confirmed the deep chasm separating capital and labour. As one of Dunsmuir's partners had put it:

> The battle . . . is one of principles. It is labour versus capital, and . . . the question is: How far labour is to be supported in lawlessness?. . . Surely there can be no question whether the Government should support the law or not so long as capital has the law on its side, about which surely there is no doubt.[7]

Such implacable attitudes, and repeated defeats did not deter the struggle for trade unions. Indeed the workers in the West persisted, as they did all over the world, and continued to organize and to agitate, confronting the great myths and promises of their society with the dreary reality of their labour and their lives. On the Prairies, however, the polarization was muted by the farmers. Capital and labour frequently squared off in polarized confrontation, especially in Manitoba and Alberta, but the farmers, often critical of both sides, set the tone of Prairie politics. Both workers and employers had to defer to the agrarian umpire on the Prairies. This was not the case in B.C.

THE WORKING CLASS IN B.C.

The Western working class made its biggest mark in B.C. The farmers there were too few to be significant, and always conservative. The B.C. working class therefore became the real opposition in the province, the sole repository of a vision of an alternative, more just society. Even as early as 1870 wage workers in mining, trade, and manufacturing made up almost 69 per cent of the labour force, agriculture accounting for the rest. In 1872 products of the mine made up 75 per cent of B.C.'s exports, falling to 60 per cent in 1881.[8] B.C. was and remained a province of workers, and their bosses, not of farmers. By the 1931 census only six per cent of B.C.'s adult male wage workers were involved in agriculture (there were only just over 26,000 farms), while nine per cent were in forestry and fishing, six per cent in mining, 20 per cent in manufacturing (most resource-related in the wood, pulp and paper, and fish-canning industries), and the rest in transportation, trade, finance, and service jobs.[9] It was, therefore, a province polarized between the capitalists, who owned the economy and dominated the political parties and the government, and the workers, who were virtually powerless.

The first trade unions in B.C. began to organize in the 1850s in what remained a bitter struggle. Employers showed no quarter, forcing the unions to re-double and intensify their agitations. In response to the implacable opposition of employers, and the seeming hopelessness of orderly change, B.C. workers became increasingly radical. Notions of revolutionary socialism emerged. The only solution to the workers' plight, it was argued, was political education and action until a majority of workers voted socialist. Although as early as 1882 trade unionists ran for office, it was not until 1898 that the Socialist Labour Party emerged, followed by a series of organizations, often working at cross purposes, until the Socialist Party of B.C. emerged. In 1900 the first socialist labour MLA was elected in Nanaimo. In 1903, three were elected, one Labour and two Socialists, giving them the balance

of power between contending business groups. By 1912, two MLAs
elected by the Socialist Party became the Official Opposition for a
time. Despite repeated failures to find a third reform road, real politics
in the province remained polarized between capital and labour. Out
of this polarization there developed two thrusts in B.C. labour politics
— radical socialism and syndicalism.

By 1904 the Socialist Party of B.C., as a result of its electoral successes, had been convinced to become the core for the Socialist Party of
Canada (SPC). It was Marxist, militant, and revolutionary and it dominated socialist politics for almost a decade. The SPC propounded the
doctrine of "impossibilism" in response to the bosses' intransigence.
Their views could not have been more blunt and direct: capitalism
could not be reformed, trade unions were largely useless efforts, and
the only solution was to build working-class consciousness leading
to concerted political action and revolutionary change. The SPC were
unique in the history of socialism, even of revolutionary socialism,
demanding and wanting no reforms. Many B.C. workers flocked to
the SPC banner because "impossibilism" explained the daily dismal
reality — bosses granted no concessions and ought to be given none.
Practically, however, SPC members and supporters were in the forefront of winning reforms and concessions of real significance to workers. For example, their early efforts led to the eight-hour day in mines
and improved safety conditions. In terms of the ultimate goal, they
remained impossibilists — capitalism had to be entirely overthrown.

Another stream of working-class thought emerged in B.C., more
attuned to the reality of trade union struggle, and less directly politically oriented — syndicalism. The syndicalists were just as radical as
the impossibilists, perhaps more so. In its purest form syndicalism
conceived a coming together in one big union of all wage workers
whereupon a general strike would bring down capitalism and the
state in preparation for a genuine socialist democracy. They were
militant, courageous, uncompromising. And they had great success
because they began to win some immediate results — improved
food, more adequate quarters, better pay. Pure syndicalism gave way
to a more pragmatic variety — the general strike became not a tool

of revolutionary transformation, but an industrial strategy to bring employers to their senses; the sympathetic strike became not a prelude to a general struggle for an anarchist Utopia but a practical means of supporting fellow unionists on strike. As a result, syndicalism in Western Canada became an intelligent way to fight bosses unwilling to grant even the least concession of union recognition. Syndicalism in B.C. ceased to be solely a vision of the final revolutionary apocalypse. The general and sympathetic strike became tactics in the industrial guerrilla war that emerged between bosses who refused to recognize the unions which refused to disappear.

Unions like the Knights of Labour, the B.C. Loggers' Union, the Western Federation of Miners, and the United Mine Workers, as well as a series of unions in the construction trades and crafts, waged a series of bitter struggles for union recognition and collective bargaining rights. Though often ineffective in winning long-term recognition, such struggles forced employers to improve conditions. Effective strikes often hit employers hard, undermining their profits and giving their competitors an edge. Therefore, while often declining to deal directly with the unions, employers slowly began unilaterally to respond to what they decried as a wave of industrial terrorism. The union most feared by employers was the Industrial Workers of the World (IWW), which began organizing in Western Canada in 1906, obtaining an estimated membership of 10,000 by 1911.[10] The IWW's influence spread far beyond its own membership — their devotion and attacks on the "pork-choppers" of the older unions inspired workers, while impelling less militant union leaders to respond to persistent challenges for leadership.

Wherever there was a dispute, a strike, a particularly rotten boss, the IWW's organizers, sort of itinerant preachers of pure syndicalism, would appear. Few mines, logging camps, construction sites, or harvest trains of the era failed to contain at least some adherents of the IWW, if not a leading organizer. Miraculously mattresses and sheets appeared in bunkhouses, food became better, wages improved, coal scales became less dishonest. But these were small victories often won at great expense, and the basic rights of collective bargaining still eluded most unions in the West.

Yet failure and repression seemed not to discourage the workers, but only to push them further down the road of militancy and revolutionary thought. Commitment to the need for independent working-class political action, and to at least a modified form of syndicalism, became characteristic of virtually all Western trade union activists. Some were moderate labour supporters, others social democratic reformers, others revolutionary socialists, still others revolutionary syndicalists. But on a number of things they began to unite to form a coherent Western bloc in Canada's trade union movement: the need for independent working-class political action, the need for militant strike tactics, the need to organize on an industry-wide rather than a craft basis, and the utility of syndicalist forms of strike solidarity and struggle — the general and the sympathetic strike.

The Trades and Labour Congress of Canada (TLC) was a moderate and conservative trade union central based in the more traditional craft unions. These craft unions represented workers with the traditional skills such as carpenters, plumbers, painters, and plasterers — and argued that organization should be primarily along craft lines. Thus on a large construction site, or in a large industrial plant, many unions representing the different skills would be active. The problem this posed for most Western workers was simply that it was irrelevant to the realities they faced, except perhaps in the larger Western cities where craft organization made some sense. However, this left out the masses of unskilled and semi-skilled workers in the West.

Western trade unionists therefore were among the first in Canada to push industrial unionism — the need to organize all workers on a job or in a factory into one union, or, indeed, all workers in an industry (miners, loggers, labourers) into one inclusive union. Their experience had been that only a complete shutdown served the workers' cause. They also argued that a general strike in a whole industry, like coal mining, might be necessary to win concessions. At least, they argued, workers in various locals might want to support the actions of striking brothers through a series of sympathetic strikes, putting pressure on an employer from other employers.

The TLC did not like this talk of general and sympathetic strikes.

Increasingly committed to continental or international unions, the TLC wanted all its members to affiliate with American unions, most of which were deeply conservative and anti-political. Not surprisingly, the TLC was highly critical of independent working-class political action. This would divide workers, they argued; the best political strategy was to act as a pressure group on the existing parties and to throw labour's support to the candidate or party expressing most sympathy for labour's case. Generally, the TLC leadership became increasingly nervous about the growing militancy and revolutionary sentiment among their Western comrades. As a result, TLC conventions became scenes of increasingly fractious clashes between radical Western delegates, led by B.C., and the more moderate Central Canadian representatives. This polarization finally resulted in a deep cleavage in the TLC.

THE PRAIRIE WORKING CLASS

On the Prairies the working class was outnumbered by the farmers. In fact, Prairie farmers were the employers of thousands of workers, permanent and seasonal. For example, in 1913, there were an estimated 200,000 farmers on the Prairies, 49,000 farm wage labourers, 50,000 non-agricultural wage workers, and as many again involved in trade, finance, clerical, service, and professional work.[11] In 1921 B.C. may still have been a rural province, but it was not a province of farmers. By 1931, B.C. had become a decisively urban province and the farm sector remained very small, employing only 14 per cent of the gainfully occupied. On the Prairies agriculture remained dominant, employing a huge share of the gainfully occupied — in Saskatchewan and Alberta, a decisive majority. All other Prairie occupations, as Table 5-1 demonstrates, remained overshadowed by agriculture. The opposite was the case in B.C. Manitoba was the most working-class province on the Prairies, but even there agriculture remained the leading sector of employment. The Prairie working class therefore found their complaints constantly drowned in the clamour for reform from agrarian organizations.

As a result, only in Manitoba, especially Winnipeg, and in Alberta, was the working class able to assert itself with anything approaching general influence. In Winnipeg, working-class leaders were moderate and restrained in comparison to their B.C. counterparts, and were quite successful in putting forward labour's case, sending the first labour-oriented MP to Ottawa in 1900. But even moderation did not save Winnipeg's trade unionists from the same fate as the B.C. militants. Employers were just as implacable in their refusal to recognize a moderately led trade union as they were one led by militant syndicalists. As we have seen, the government in 1906 lent the same complete support against unions in Winnipeg as they did in the Nanaimo coal fields in 1912. In Alberta, the miners shared the militancy of their B.C. counterparts, and, in common with Manitoba and B.C., established an early independent socialist political presence. Strikes in Alberta's mines were regularly suppressed by police, and Alberta governments typically supported employers in their refusals to deal with the unions. In Saskatchewan, the working class was weakest and had no significant impact on the province's politics until the founding of the CCF in 1932.

The working class in Saskatchewan more completely faced the problems shared by all Prairie workers. The Prairie working class was very dependent on the prosperity of the Prairie farmer. Wage-work in virtually every sector — except perhaps industrial and construction work in Winnipeg and mine work in Alberta — was directly or indirectly related to servicing agriculture. Good times in agriculture meant jobs; hard times, layoffs. Furthermore, unlike B.C., which was more or less polarized between workers and employers, Prairie politics were increasingly dominated by the farmers. Prairie workers, therefore, not only had to contend with traditional employer hostility to unions in the daily economic struggle, but also with the political necessity of winning their case among the grain growers. Furthermore, as small employers, grain growers, who relied on seasonal labour, and often some year-round labour as well, did not generally support ideas like universal minimum wages and reduced work days. Indeed, when such concessions were finally made, rural and small-town labour were excluded in the legislation.

Grain-grower organizations often complained of the high cost of

TABLE 5.1

Urban and Rural Population Percentages, Number of Occupied Farms and Distribution of Workforce* in the West, 1921 and 1931

	Manitoba		*Saskatchewan*		*Alberta*		*B.C.*	
	1921	1931	1921	1931	1921	1931	1921	1931
Population								
Urban	43%	45%	29%	32%	38%	38%	47%	57%
Rural	57	55	71	68	62	62	53	43
No. of Occupied Farms	53,252	54,199	119,451	136,472	82,954	97,408	21,973	26,079
Occupations								
Agriculture	40%	35%	65%	60%	53%	51%	16%	14%
Mining	0.1	1	0.1	1	4	3	5	3
Forestry, fishing and trapping	0.3	2	0.3	0.2	0.4	1	8	7
Manufacturing	8	8	3	4	5	5	11	11
Construction	5	5	2	2	3	3	6	6
Transportation	7	8	4	5	5	6	8	10
Labourers	7	10	3	5	5	6	12	14
Clerical	9	7	4	3	5	4	7	6
Trade, finance and services	24	26	17	19	20	21	26	28

*Per cent of gainfully employed (aged 10 years and over) by occupation group.

Source: *Census of Canada*, 1931. All percentages are rounded to the nearest whole number except those under 0.5 per cent.

labour in the same breath as they complained of high freights and low grain prices. As well, Prairie farmers were appalled and disturbed by the deep class conflict that was emerging, usually denouncing both sides, while presenting themselves as the great re-conciliators between antagonistic capitalists and strike-prone workers. Furthermore, the working class' main weapon — the strike — provoked deep hostility among farmers. Strikes in transportation, grain handling, meat packing, flour milling, and so on, were seen as direct threats to the prosperity of the farmer. Strikes in all branches of industry were viewed as at least indirectly increasing the farmers' costs of goods as manufacturers were forced to pay higher wages. The grain growers were highly ambivalent, therefore, in their attitudes to the working class and its trade unions. While often sympathizing with the plight of the exploited worker, the grain grower could not unreservedly support general working-class demands.

Yet there was a significant minority opinion within the grain growers' organizations supporting thoroughgoing farmer-labour unity. Even the early Grange in Ontario had called for an alliance between the "toilers of the field" and the "toilers in the city." But this fine sentiment did not prevent the Grange from rejecting support for an 1886 TLC call for an eight-hour day by saying, "It would be impracticable on the farm, a waste of valuable time, and must necessarily lead to an increase in the price of the products of labour."[12] In Alberta, the Society of Equity, a radical agrarian group that helped to create the UFA in 1909, had long supported the need to unite farmer and worker in the same organization to fight the "Special Interests." Yet in the UFA they remained a minority if active opinion. Henry Wise Wood, who later became the dominant leader of the UFA and its major ideologue, explained farmer hostility to labour in 1907 by saying, "the farmer was an employer and a capitalist."[13] That view expressed the majority sentiment. Later the Nonpartisan League, which forced the UFA into direct politics, abandoned its advocacy of a coalition of farmers, workers, and returned veterans, and of an "open door" to labour to join the UFA, without too much fuss.

Trade unions and labour political parties on the Prairies therefore found themselves reduced to generally supporting the farmers' major demands in exchange for dubious and uncertain support on only a few of labour's demands. This was understandable. The interests of farmers and workers were quite different. Farmers were small capitalists who owned land and engaged in commodity production for a capitalist market. It was in their interests to have high prices, low freight rates, low input costs, as well as low wages and long hours for farm wage labour. Further, farmers were deeply concerned about the growth of unions among urban labour, fearing that higher wages for fewer hours of work would inevitably push up the costs of things they needed — consumer goods, machinery, fertilizer, and transportation. Farmers also had a deep affection for high prices for products of the farm — eggs, milk, wheat, beef, and hogs. Workers wanted cheap food, the cheaper the better. Further, workers wanted higher wages, legal limits on the daily hours of work, legal minimum wages, new social welfare benefits, union recognition, and the right to strike to win their demands. Consequently, the uneasiness of relations between farmers and workers was to be expected. Certainly, farmers and workers began to co-operate, but it was hesitant, sometimes hostile, always distant.

The tariff question was a case in point. On a national basis working-class opinion was deeply divided on the tariff. Central Canadian workers were generally pro-tariff since they believed that protection created industrial jobs. Prairie workers, who derived little direct benefit from the tariff in the form of jobs, tended to support the farmers' case for free trade. The tariff increased the Western worker's cost of living. Yet Prairie workers did not go the whole distance on the tariff that Prairie farmers went — for Prairie farmers the tariff became the center of their complaints, for Prairie workers it remained a significant but still minor grievance. Agrarian calls for fairer freight rates, better grain prices, and orderly marketing, all were supported by Prairie working-class organizations. In exchange they got very little — Prairie farmers remained leery of minimum wages, the eight-hour day, trade unions, and strikes. Western workers and farmers did unite on more general Western grievances — the control of natural resources, a bigger voice for the West in national affairs, complaints about the failure to diversify the Western economy, and so on. But many of the workers' employers also echoed such complaints.

As well, Prairie workers and farmers agreed about the need to stop unrestricted immigration — again for different reasons. The workers saw immigrants used repeatedly as scabs to break strikes and knew from experience that the presence of immigrants could only push wage rates down. The farmers saw unrestricted immigration as putting severe strains on the land base and the local government infrastructure. Prairie workers and farmers also united on demands to dismantle the system of "Special Privilege." But each group meant something quite different. For the farmer, dismantling "Special Privilege" meant tariff abolition and a return to free trade, small capitalism. For the worker it meant trade union rights, an end to government intervention on the side of the employer in labour struggles, and, ultimately, for many, the achievement of socialism. As well, farmer and worker united on the need for the political reform of the party system to ensure a deeper, more responsive democracy, as well as on the need to begin the construction of the welfare state — the establishment of a "social wage" in the form of a minimum social, educational, health, and economic security net for all. But again, the trade unions and the labour parties pushed the idea of the welfare state more persistently and further, while for the agrarian organizations such reforms were incidental to getting rid of the hated tariff. As a result, efforts at farmer/labour unity generally foundered in attempts to bridge the great gaps that separated the immediate and long-term interests of both groups. There was, therefore, never a marriage, not even one of convenience, of the two groups; rather there were a series of temporary liaisons, usually leaving both groups dissatisfied.

UPSURGE, DEFEAT, AND SMALL VICTORIES

The coming of World War I temporarily dampened the growing general agitation among Canadian workers, except in the West. Western Canadian trade union leaders, as well as labour and socialist political leaders, did not stampede to embrace the patriotic appeals for a united war effort. Some opposed the war on the grounds of international solidarity among workers, others on the grounds of principled pacifism, and still others out of the pragmatic fear that the few gains made by labour might be stolen during a war crisis, screened by calls to patriotism. Many Western workers, much more ethnically diverse than those in Ontario and Atlantic Canada, were less willing to answer the calls to patriotism from the same groups who were willing to describe some of them as "alien scum."[14] For many among the non-British Western working class there was little eagerness for this British war.

Central Canadian trade unions were more divided on the issue, especially as the war-induced boom in industry saw the growth of many jobs at good wages. The war boom was less directly beneficial to the Western working class. Prairie workers shared in the general increase in agricultural prosperity, but they did not share in much of the industrial growth. B.C. workers hardly benefitted from the war boom at all. Unemployment in B.C. remained high, layoffs remained commonplace, and many B.C. workers joined the line to enlist more out of desperation than patriotism. Indeed, during the war, many B.C. workers receiving layoff or termination notices in their pay envelopes, also received the following note, "Your King and Country need you — we can spare you."[15]

As the war continued, and as the human carnage in the trenches of Europe mounted, it became clear that conscription would be necessary to fulfill Canada's military obligations. Western workers, especially those in the trade unions and the labour and socialist political parties, were deeply opposed to conscription, in common with Québec. Western farmers were not enamoured of conscription, though less deeply hostile to it. In fact, Western labour and farm organizations had mounted a general criticism of war-profiteering, of incompetence in the administration of the war, and of the evil consequences of a party system that was unable even to meet a national crisis without conniving to exploit it in favour of the Special Interests. They had called for the conscription of wealth before the conscription of men.

This Western sentiment, which doubtless would have found reflection in independent farm and labour candidates in the coming federal election, was a large part of the reason for the formation of the Union government. The prospect of Liberals and Tories splitting the pro-conscription vote in English Canada, especially in the West, perhaps thereby allowing the election of a large number of independent farm and labour MPs in the West, as well as Laurier's determination to continue as Leader of an anti-conscription Opposition, even if it reduced his Liberal representation to Québec, would make a war-time conscription election uncertain.

Determined to avoid such uncertainty, Prime Minister Robert Borden asked Laurier to join a war-time coalition based on Borden's conscription policy. Laurier refused, and refused again when Borden tried to sweeten the deal by a promise not to proceed with conscription until after an election. Therefore the Union government was formed uniting the governing Tories and only the anglophone Liberal opposition, and the 1917 election was called. Just before calling the election, determined to leave nothing to chance, Borden had Parliament pass the *War Time Elections Act*. This Act disenfranchised all Canadians naturalized since 1902 and all war objectors, while giving the vote to adult females in the immediate families of men in the armed forces and to all men stationed overseas.

The outcome was inevitable — the Union government swept to power, decimating the opponents of the government's war policies, including conscription, in English Canada. Laurier won decisively in Québec and clung to significant popular support in the rest of the country, thanks to a deep popular fear of conscription. Borden and the Union government swept the country in terms of seats, but the civilian vote had only given him a majority of 100,000 votes. The addition of the military vote increased this to 300,000. It was a decisive parliamentary victory, but still an uncertain popular one (much of the farm vote, for example, had been won from opposition to conscription by a last-minute Order-in-Council exempting farmers' sons).[16]

Despite Borden's win, Western labour leaders did not cease their opposition to conscription. There were demonstrations and riots. Many were fired from their jobs. Some went to prison for draft violations. One prominent B.C. labour leader was shot in the back by Dominion police in his efforts to evade the draft. As inflation shot up, strikes and trade union agitations continued unabated in an effort to stop the decline in real wages. Western delegates took resolutions to the TLC convention calling for opposition to conscription, up to and including a general strike. They were defeated, denounced as strongly by other trade unionists as they were by over-zealous patriots from coast to coast.

As the war ended, Western trade unionists found themselves on the defensive. Increasingly, with the victory of the Bolshevik Revolution in Russia in 1917, an event they cheered publicly, they faced not only the ongoing hostility of employers and governments, but they also confronted the accusation that they were proponents of a Bolshevik Revolution in Canada. The end of the war also brought depression, unemployment, and wage cuts. This situation was to the employers' advantage — and they pressed this advantage. But the trade unions refused to yield, and polarization and confrontation increased. In the last year of the war, 1918, there were 169 strikes, more than there had been in the three previous years.[17] Most of the big strikes occurred in the West. The Union government responded with regulations under the *War Measures Act* banning strikes and a number of left-wing organizations.

Trade unions, having won such sparse victories, had nothing to lose in pushing their case, even during the post-War depression. Employers, fresh from the war boom and the political victories over conscription, saw even less reason why unions ought to be taken seriously. Indeed, they argued, pointing to Russia, unions were the harbingers of socialist revolution. Therefore, employers redoubled their efforts to defeat the trade unions, deepening the absolute polarization between capital and labour. The economic conditions of the time would today have under-cut unions. Then, they spurred unions on to greater efforts. Returned veterans found little work, leading to growing disillusionment. Trade unions had two choices: fight or surrender. They intensified the struggle. In the West, more radical leaders came to leadership, even in traditionally moderate unions. Such leaders at least had some kind of strategy for struggle. More and more of the traditional craft unions in the West voted for industrial unionism. With the war's end therefore, Western trade unions — the longstanding syndicalist as well as the traditionally moderate—became increasingly radical politically and increasingly militant industrially. Even Winnipeg, long the bastion of the moderates among Western workers, elected a more radical leadership to the local Labour Council.

These events culminated in the March 1919 Western Canada Labour Conference convened at Calgary. Almost every Western Canadian trade union was represented. A decision to secede from the TLC and to form a Western labour central, the One Big Union (OBU), was passed overwhelmingly. The conference endorsed industrial unionism, the tactics of the general and the sympathetic strike, as well as making a series of immediate demands to be met under threat of a June 1, 1919 general strike. Politically the conference endorsed socialism, calling for the abolition of capitalism, and applauded the Bolsheviks in Russia and the Spartacists in Germany.

The scene was obviously set for a serious confrontation between capital and labour, particularly in the West. Though the battle could have been fought out in any of the major cities, especially Vancouver, events determined that the confrontation occurred in Winnipeg.[18] The story of the Winnipeg General Strike has been well told. In early May 1919, the metal and building trades went on strike for union recognition, the eight-hour day, and improved wages. The employers refused to bargain. The strikers asked the Winnipeg Labour Council for support, whereupon the Council held a general strike vote among all Winnipeg trade unions asking for a living wage, the eight-hour day and union recognition backed up by signed collective agreements. A strong majority voted to strike. The walkout started on May 15; 24,000 trade unionists went out on strike. Soon thousands of Winnipeg's non-union workers joined them. It became truly a general strike. Across the country tens of thousands of workers joined in sympathetic strikes — involving 80 strikes and over 88,000 workers, mostly in the West, This general support for the strike was solid, even startling, yet it was far short of the general strike of syndicalist dreams. Many workers were supporting the strike, but not enough. Soon thousands of veterans were on the march in support of the strike, over 10,000 on one occasion in Winnipeg. This active and growing support among veterans, who were, as a group, deeply divided by the strike, gave great cheer to the strikers. Among government officials, however, it created dread. If the veterans were to go over to the strike, actively and *en masse*, many officials believed, the situation could become seriously out of control.

The federal government therefore was convinced they faced revolution and acted accordingly. RCMP, regular military and militia reinforcements were brought to Winnipeg, including at least one armoured car and over a score of machine-gun squads. The entire Winnipeg police force, with the exception of the officers and two constables, was dismissed because of sympathy for the strike. They were replaced by special constables (largely recruited from among Winnipeg's middle and upper classes, anti-strike veterans, and farmers) whose inexperience and zeal created confusion and unnecessary violence. Firings of strikers began to spread, especially among civil servants.

In Ottawa a series of legal measures were put in place to aid authorities in efforts to break the strike on the grounds that it was seditious, including an amendment to the Criminal Code to allow the deportation of foreign-born agitators, which was passed in less than twenty minutes (this law affected all who were not Canadian born, including those from the UK). Later, Section 98 was added to the Criminal Code defining "unlawful associations" as those that advocated violence as a means of economic or political change and imposing Draconian prison sentences of up to twenty years for membership in such organizations. Attendance at a public meeting was considered evidence of membership. Section 133 of the code was repealed, erasing any guarantee of freedom of speech. On June 17 six of the most prominent strike leaders were arrested, as well as a number of other militants from various organizations, 11 men in all, and charged with sedition.

After the arrests the expected collapse of the strike did not occur. Indeed, protest and support increased in the West and began, ominously, to grow across the country. Now demands included the release of those arrested. Even violent police baton attacks on peaceful demonstrators had the effect of redoubling support for the strike. On June 21 a silent parade to protest the arrests and the police violence was called. The *Riot Act* was read and the parade of men, women, and children was attacked by RCMP and Specials on horseback, swinging baseball bats. When this brutality failed to disperse the demonstrators, the police drew their guns and began firing into the crowd without discrimination — two were killed, 30 injured, 100 arrested. Military rule was imposed on the city, as armed military patrols and machine-gun nests became commonplace on the streets. The strike was broken and as the defeated, but still defiant, workers went back to work they faced severe, wholesale economic reprisals. The workers had been taught that employers, backed up by the government, were prepared to use all the force necessary to break the strike. Further resistance would have led to yet more bloodshed.

This suppression of the strike in Winnipeg was buttressed by authorities with a series of night-time raids of offices of trade unions and ethnic associations, and of homes of trade union and socialist leaders. This occurred not only in Winnipeg; the authorities settled accounts all across the Dominion, breaking in doors, searching homes, taking records, files, books, papers, membership lists, and correspondence. These actions were justified by the authorities as necessary for the collection of evidence to be used at the sedition trials. But the vehemence with which they asserted their police state powers over trade unionists and left-wingers indicated a desire to intimidate and to avenge. Eight strike leaders were charged with seditious conspiracy. Seven of eight were found guilty: one was sentenced to two years, five to one year, one to six months, another was found not guilty. The message was clear: determined industrial action by the trade unions, especially if it became generalized, would be repressed by all means possible. Agitations for a living wage, for an eight-hour day, and for collective bargaining rights were declared to be seditious. The OBU reached its peak in membership during and immediately following the strike, with some 50,000 members (there were only about 380,000 trade unionists in all of Canada in 1919, out of a work force of over two million).[19] Yet it was clear to all that the one serious application of industrial syndicalism had failed — the general and the sympathetic strike was ineffective when confronted by severe and determined state reprisals. And contrary to the federal government's claims at the Winnipeg show trials, the major leaders of the OBU were not Bolsheviks and revolutionists, since none had advocated meeting state violence with revolutionary violence, the only real alternative to final surrender. Indeed, the leaders had, throughout the strike, counselled moderation, peaceful demonstration, and orderly protest; in fact, when the police attacks began the leaders had advised against further demonstrations.

The labour movement, therefore, despite the momentary strength of the OBU, in the aftermath of the Winnipeg defeat, saw a re-assertion in the West of moderate labourism and traditional, business union-ism, replacing the radicalism of syndicalism. A concerted coalition of government officials, employers, and moderate trade unionists very quickly isolated the OBU. Unable to win any gains in the face of gov-ernment harassment and employer refusals to bargain with OBU-led unions, the OBU saw its membership returned piecemeal to modera-tion as more conservative unions won recognition and contracts with surprising ease. As well, advocates of moderate socialist politics made great gains in elections immediately following the strike. In 1920 in Manitoba Labour elected 11 MLAs, including three imprisoned strike leaders, and in 1922, six Labour MLAs were returned. In Winnipeg, Labour candidates won three seats on the school board and three on the council. In 1921 in Alberta Labour elected four MLAs and a Labour member was appointed to the UFA cabinet. In B.C. Labour took three seats in 1920 and 1924. Federally, two strike leaders were elected in Winnipeg as MPs, one in 1921, joined by a colleague in 1925.

Hence, radical syndicalism, though itself defeated, had set the stage for some modest working-class victories. More moderate trade unions began slowly to win recognition and collective bargaining rights. More moderate labour political parties established themselves permanently in the politics of the country. These working-class organizations kept alive the reform sentiment to replace the earlier militancy, which continued to be husbanded on the sidelines of the working class by the declining OBU and the newly formed Communist Party. The repression of the Winnipeg General Strike, the police raids across the country, and the punitive show trials had defeated the insurgent Western working class as the boom of the 1920s replaced the post-war depression. The road to workers' rights through the militant tactics of syndicalism appeared to be permanently blocked. More modest approaches to union recognition, and the establishment of a moderate working-class political presence, seemed to be the only way out of the defeat after the confrontation.

As well, the strike and its aftermath enhanced the problems of building a serious alliance between the farmers and labour. Farm organizations were deeply disturbed by the confrontation at Winnipeg and its aftermath. Their hostility and suspicion of the working class and its main tools of struggle — the trade union, the strike, the socialist party — deepened. Although labour was given a seat in the 1921 UFA Cabinet, this gesture was not repeated in 1926 or 1930. In Manitoba, labour MLAs and UFM MLAs had great difficulty co-operating — which only increased after the UFM won government in 1922.

A year after the Winnipeg strike the UFM President said, "The seeds of Bolshevism . . . are like wild oats — they will only grow when all the conditions are favourable . . . If we are disposed to criticize the labourman . . . much of the criticism is just, in fairness we should remember that men and women have wrought and toiled under the worst possible conditions."[20] This reflected the organized farmers' deep ambivalence toward labour. A year later, in an effort to distance farmers from Labour's repeated calls for socialism, he said, "There is . . . a very distinct limit beyond which it is not wise to go in the direction of state control of industry and commerce."[21]

Federally, the basis for farmer/labour unity laid out for the Progressive party in the run-up to the 1921 federal election was a bitter disappointment for labour. All the manifesto could reluctantly bring itself to advocate was that a "spirit of co-operation" ought to guide negotiations between capital and labour. Unemployed veterans were further offended by a section of the platform that suggested that men be kept in the army until work could be found. And the Farmers' Platform Handbook, published by the *Grain Growers' Guide*, laid out a very self-interested basis for farmer support of workers' demands for better pay, "An underpaid worker is a detriment to the farmer for he is a potential customer who cannot buy."[22] On the big issues facing the working class the farmers remained silent. Indeed, where the farmers won power in the West, Alberta and Manitoba, provincial government policy of hostility to trade unions and strikes remained largely unchanged.

The rising of the Western working class was massively defeated. Radical ideas, revolutionary socialist politics, and militant industrial tactics had been largely discredited, if only because of fear of ruthless state repression. Moderation had triumphed, but in its moderate triumph the working class had been granted some apparent concessions, if only to further discredit radicalism and to inoculate the working class against its return. Trade unions, collective bargaining, and some social reforms slowly began to be gained. A moderate socialist political presence had been permanently established. Farmers and workers had learned more clearly what to expect from each other, resulting in less ambitious efforts at unity in the future.

Most significant of all, trade unions gradually came to be accepted as an inevitable fact of life in Canada; but the structural problems confronting the Western working class remained — dangerous work in uncertain industries at unsatisfactory wages. And the establishment of trade unions and collective bargaining rights remained an uphill struggle against resisting employers and unsympathetic governments. The defeat at Winnipeg forced the Western working class to accept a smaller share of the boom of the 1920s than they had appeared prepared to accept in 1919. Yet finally the beating and shooting of innocent marchers, and the imprisonment of strike leaders, had merely instructed the Western working class on the limits set on what they would be allowed to have. Such events did not stop them from yearning for a life better than the one employers and the authorities were willing to permit. The legacy of the Western upsurge and the events at Winnipeg became a permanent fixture in Canadian politics — haunting the employers with the worst to be feared; inspiring workers to contemplate what again might have to be done.

6

DEVASTATION AND PROTEST: THE DEPRESSION IN THE WEST

No one expected the collapse on Wall Street in the fall of 1929 to begin a decade of economic hardship. Indeed, it was not until the Depression was two years old that people, citizens and experts alike, began to realize how serious the situation had become. No one was prepared for the bleak years of the 1930s, especially farmers and workers. The farmers' organizations had withered throughout the 1920s and were, therefore, ill prepared to lead a fight for economic security and justice. The trade unions, and labour-based social democratic parties, had declined seriously in membership and influence throughout the 1920s and were in no position to recommence a general offensive to fight the Depression. But then, as the 1920s came to a dramatic end in 1929, few believed there was any need to worry.

The Great Depression was a world-wide disaster. Canada, as a predominantly resource-exporting nation, was particularly hard hit. Between July 1929 and December 1932 the prices for Canada's 17 major exports fell 53 per cent, export prices for farm products fell a full 70 per cent, industrial production fell 48 per cent, and employment fell 33 per cent.[1] The national average per-capita income fell 48 percent.[2] It was an economic downturn of unprecedented proportions. Canada's world markets contracted and the prices for her principal exports fell rapidly.

But if the Great Depression was a disaster for Canada, for the Western provinces it was cruel calamity. It was especially so since it followed so quickly on the heels of a brief period of prosperity, which had begun to heal earlier wounds. And it was cruel because the incidence of the Depression was even more unevenly experienced in Canada than all previous depressions had been. The West, almost exclusively a producer of resources for export, felt the full force of the collapse. The declines in average provincial per-capita incomes between 1929 and 1933 were greatest in the four Western provinces: Saskatchewan, down 72 per cent; Alberta, down 61 per cent; Manitoba, down 49 per cent; B.C., down 47 per cent (Québec and Ontario each experienced a 44 per cent decline). Prairie agriculture was the worst hit, suffering a 94 per cent decline in net money income from 1929 to 1933. The fisheries, crucial to B.C. and Atlantic Canada, were not far behind, suffering a 72 per cent drop in net money income. Most importantly, although the prices of all Canadian exports fell an average of 40 per cent from 1929–33, resources from the West fell further, faster.[3]

Meanwhile, the net money incomes of those employed in the protected manufacturing industries fell 37 per cent, while those who earned interest income from bonds, life insurance, and farm mortgages actually increased their net incomes by 13 per cent. Although most groups experienced sharp income declines, some groups improved their relative positions because they experienced less sharp declines. Canada's farmers' share of the national income fell from 15 per cent in 1929 to 7 per cent in 1933, whereas the share of the national income won by wage and salary earners in the tariff-protected industries improved marginally (1929, 14 per cent; 1933, 15 per cent). As well, salaries and wages in the so-called "naturally" sheltered industries and occupations (transportation, communication, merchandising, government, education, banking, insurance, and the professions) markedly improved their relative positions: earning 29 per cent of the national income in 1929 and 35 per cent by 1933.[4]

In other words, the Depression struck hardest at farmers, farm workers, fishermen, lumbermen, and miners, less hard at those in protected central Canadian industry, still less hard at those in the middle class professions, while actually initially benefitting finance capitalists. Clearly, the unemployed across the country, conservatively 25 per cent of the wage labour force, along with the Prairie farmer and farm worker, faced the brunt of the economic collapse. But even here there was a regional inequity as the collapse of the Western resource industries, the very heart of the Western economy, created a much higher level of Western unemployment. Certainly, no part of the country was unscarred, but the scars in the West went deeper than elsewhere.

The impact of the Depression was so much greater in the West as a result of the West's overdependence on those industries that were the most immediately and hardest hit — resource industries. Saskatchewan and Alberta suffered most due to their overdependence on wheat, the prices for which fell farther and faster. In 1925 almost 76 per cent of Alberta's net value of production came from agriculture, most of that from wheat (in 1926, 67 per cent of Alberta's field crop was in wheat). Saskatchewan was even more dependent on wheat. In 1925 almost 93 per cent of Saskatchewan's net value of production came from agriculture, mostly from the new gold, wheat (in 1926, 69 per cent of Saskatchewan's field crop was in wheat).[5] From 1920 to 1943 fully 70 per cent of the total income in Saskatchewan was earned directly from the sale of wheat.[6]

Manitoba, less dependent on agriculture, did not share the depth of the collapse in the other two Prairie provinces. But Manitoba was dependent on the Western market for its small manufacturing sector, and on the general regional commercial activity, which flowed through Winnipeg eastward. With the Depression in the rest of the West, "the economic support of nearly 40 per cent of Manitoba's population virtually collapsed," according to the Rowell-Sirois report.[7]

B.C.'s dependence on a greater variety of resources, and resource processing, merely ensured that the downturn was not as steep as on the Prairies. The export prices for B.C.'s main products were cut by almost 40 per cent from 1929 to 1933. The value of timber production fell by 62 per cent, mineral production by 59 per cent, and fish production by 63 per cent. The total value of production fell 55 per cent. Unemployment reached almost 28 per cent in 1931, the highest in the Dominion.[8]

Dependence on resource production meant calamity; near exclusive dependence on one resource meant complete collapse. The problem of indebtedness exacerbated the situation. The problem of debt was general. To finance its rapid expansion during the wheat and war booms, and then during the boom of the 1920s, Canada borrowed heavily abroad through the massive import of foreign capital. Much of this money had been borrowed at boom-time interest rates. With the Depression, servicing this debt became difficult: in 1932-33 fully one-third of Canada's total export receipts was required simply to service the debt. But the problem of debt was bigger in the West. The 1920s boom saw the virtual completion of the settlement process in the West. A large part of this expansion was financed through borrowing, often at high interest rates, which, when added to the cost of earlier expansions, created a large debt load. Again, Saskatchewan and Alberta, the most recently settled provinces, were the deepest in debt. Farmers went into debt to begin, expand, and develop their holdings. Workers went into debt to build homes. Provincial and local governments went into debt to finance the basic infrastructure required by a rapidly burgeoning population. Even during the height of the boom of the 1920s the West echoed with loud complaints about the gouging interest rates of the financiers. With the Depression the debt load became quite simply unsupportable. In 1932, debt interest charges took 29 per cent of the Alberta government's total expenditures, nearly equal to combined expenditures in education, public health, and welfare.[9] In 1937 it was estimated that all interest and debt charges in Saskatchewan took 52 per cent of provincial revenues.[10] In 1935-36, 42 per cent of the Manitoba government's expenditures were on interest charges.[11] As early as 1933 B.C.'s credit as a province, and of its municipalities, was declared exhausted.[12]

The debt load of individual Prairie farmers was staggering. For example, a conservative estimate of Saskatchewan farm debt in 1936 was $525 million. To meet the interest payments alone would have required 50 per cent of the value of the total 1935 crop — another 17 per cent would have been required to meet tax obligations.[13] Needless to say, these obligations could not be met and hundreds of farmers were forced to abandon their farms, or were driven out by foreclosure. Urban workers lost their homes. Whole towns and cities, indeed provinces, in the West teetered on the precipice of bankruptcy.

On the Prairies these problems were compounded by the drought, which became so severe and general in Saskatchewan that the average yield per acre of wheat fell to 8 bushels in 1936, then, in the worst drought year, to 2.5 bushels in 1937.[14] The top-soil of whole farms, indeed whole crop districts in areas that ought never to have been put to the plough, simply blew away. But often too much is made of the drought. Had the price structure been normal, the drought would have meant a few bad years for those areas hardest hit. The fact is that, throughout the Great Depression, the prices paid for wheat would not pay for the costs of production even for those farmers who continued to harvest crops. In Alberta, which did not suffer heavily from drought, fairly good crops from 1930 to 1935 could not find a price to make their planting worthwhile. For those also afflicted by drought, a heart-breaking situation was therefore made soul-destroying.

The situation in the West became increasingly desperate as each year failed to bring the turn-around to prosperity promised repeat-edly by incumbent government politicians. By 1937 fully two-thirds of the total rural population of Saskatchewan was on relief,[15] joined by more than 1 in 5 urban residents.[16] From 1930-37, nearly two-thirds of the total revenues of Saskatchewan's municipal and prov-incial governments were consumed for relief expenditures. Over 13 per cent of total 1930-37 provincial income was required for relief, representing almost four times the average national relief burden.[17] Saskatchewan's per-capita income fell from $478 in 1929 to $135 in 1933.[18] Things were somewhat better in Alberta where, in 1938, over 52,000 people (in a population of about 775,000) were on relief.[19] Alberta's per-capita income fell from $548 in 1929 to $212 in 1933. In B.C. the situation was as bad, perhaps worse. By March 1933 there were about 120,000 people on the relief rolls (out of a total population of about 700,000).[20] This figure did not include the many transients who flocked to B.C. only to find themselves ineli-gible for the meagre handouts that passed for relief. B.C.'s per-capita income fell from $595 in 1929 to $240 in 1937. Manitoba, the senior

Western province, combined the problems of the Prairie farmer with mass industrial unemployment in Winnipeg. Manitoba's per-capita income fell from $466 in 1929 to $240 in 1933. Despair, degradation, fear — such words cannot begin to communicate the loss of hope among a whole generation of Western Canadians.

GOVERNMENT RESPONSES

The responses of the federal and provincial governments were appallingly inadequate. All of them — with the exception of the Manitoba Liberal-Progressive hybrid — were ultimately defeated as a result of their record of indifference and neglect. Levels of relief were designed to provide the thinnest possible margin of simple survival to people who often literally could not feed themselves. Access to relief was a difficult and degrading process. Governments were niggardly in the amounts of relief they paid. Recipients were initially told they would have to repay the government's generosity, particularly farmers obtaining agricultural relief to continue production. Often relief was cancelled in the summer months to force men to look for work at any wage. Relief recipients were frequently compelled to provide at least one day's work a week on public projects. Some were paid small wages by government to provide labour to farmers. Thousands of recent immigrants, who became public charges, were deported. Transients, searching for work, were refused relief when no work was found.

Two of the many letters sent to Prime Minister R. B. Bennett, one from Lambert, Saskatchewan and the other from Sayward, Vancouver Island, portray the desperation of many. The Lambert letter, from the wife of a labourer, written in 1934, complained of the inadequacy of relief:

> *I am writing you regarding Relief. Will you please tell me if we can get Steady relief and how much we should be allowed per week we have three children . . . one boy is going to School. Some day's he can't go to school as we have no food in the house & I won't let him go on those day's . . . everytime I go up to ask the Mayor here in Lambert for any*

assistance he always Says he can't help us as the town is
broke . . . there are times we live on potatoes for days, at a
time & its lasting So long I don't see how much longer it can
last . . . I am five months pregnant & I haven't even felt life
yet in my baby . . .[21]

The Sayward letter, from an old-timer, part-time worker and part-time homesteader, written in 1935, raised similar concerns:

Please pardon me for Writing you. but I am In Such a
Circumstances That I Really don't Know What to do. When
Will This Distress and Mental Agitation Amongst the People
come to an End. & how Long Will This Starvation Last. I am
on The Relief & only Git 4 days Work on the Public Road
. . . That are not Sufficient for both of us to Live on . . . Next
Came My Land Taxes . . . If I don't Pay it This year. Then
The Government of B.C. Will Have My 40 acres Cancelled.
& I & My Wife Will be on The bear Ground, is That Way
The Government Will Help the Poor Men.[22]

Provincial and municipal governments, responsible for relief but without the funds to meet the huge demands put upon them, had to beg for federal support. In exchange for such support, provincial governments were forced to retrench even more deeply than they already willingly had — further cutting services, sacking more employees, rolling back wages and salaries in the public sector even more, raising the taxes few could pay even higher. This cap-in-hand approach to Ottawa only made the situation worse, as inadequate government services became even more so. And the political price of federal support had the effect of deflecting the provinces from demanding more government intervention and yet more generous support from Ottawa. Incumbent politicians, federal and provincial, were unable to think of the Depression as long-term and therefore satisfied themselves with simply dealing with the situation as if it were merely a temporary disaster requiring only patience, hope, and just enough help to get through to the next year, which was going to be better. Indeed, government politicians, businessmen, and experts repeatedly claimed that prosperity was just around the corner — and each additional year of Depression only served to mock the people with this continuing chorus of optimism.

The initial response of Western Canadians to the calamity was groping. They had been disarmed during the previous decade. The farmers' offensive had been defeated, divided, contained. Agrarian organizations were shadows of their former selves. The workers' revolt had been defeated at Winnipeg and in the subsequent wave of repression. The early promise of moderation in advancing the workers' cause had evaporated as trade unions during the 1920s declined amid the combination of prosperity and business unionism. Labour parties were unprepared for the disaster and, having abandoned militancy, found it difficult to cope with the enormity of the collapse. Unable to win further concessions during the years of prosperity, traditional farm and labour leaders initially abandoned any hope of winning concessions during the Depression. Bargaining and strikes became halfhearted affairs centered, not on advances, but on minimizing defeats as employers rolled back wages and laid off workers with impunity. Farm organizations reflected their impotence as their standard appeals and petitions were ignored by banks, mortgage companies, and municipalities foreclosing on defaulting farmers. The unemployed and the relief recipient did not even have these weak voices to speak for them.

The Communist Party (CP) filled this initial leadership vacuum through the Workers' Unity League (WUL) and the Farmers' Unity League (FUL). Although national in scope, these organizations had their biggest impact in the West. The WUL, a new militant trade union central, advocated aggressive trade union tactics to deal with the Depression. They proposed that efforts by employers to cut wages and to refuse to bargain with existing unions had to be met by strikes, tough picket lines, and even sit-ins. They also launched a concerted organizing drive among unorganized workers, especially in industries of large-scale, low-paid employment. Although most successful among miners, lumber workers, and agricultural workers in the West, and the textile industry in Central Canada, the WUL also began to make inroads in the new mass industries (automobiles, steel, and rubber).

The WUL led a series of bitter strikes over wage-cuts and layoffs, as well as over union recognition and collective bargaining rights. They also organized relief recipients and the unemployed, an activity which made government officials uneasy. Under WUL leadership, or inspired by their example, the unemployed held "hunger marches," organized sit-ins, established picket lines, led strikes on make-work projects, and even held "relief strikes," demanding only, with the utmost simplicity, "work and wages," or failing that, adequate and dignified relief.

The FUL similarly organized farmers to demand better relief, to picket, and often to prevent, mortgage or tax sales of the property of evicted farmers. Even more disturbing to the authorities, they mobilized farmers to physically prevent the eviction of defaulting fellow farmers. For a time it appeared that the mass militancy of the farmers and workers of the 1914–1920 period would be re-ignited by these organizations.

The response of governments to these events was not unlike that applied in Winnipeg in 1919. Concerned with the growing unrest, Prime Minister R. B. Bennett vowed to crush Communism under "the iron heel of ruthlessness."[23] This the federal government, and all provincial governments, proceeded to do with a zeal they could not mobilize to cope with the people's despair and deprivation. Eight of the CP's top leadership were arrested under Section 98 of the Criminal Code and imprisoned at Kingston Penitentiary. (Section 98, passed shortly after the Winnipeg General Strike and used primarily against the Communist Party, made membership illegal in an organization advocating the use of force to change the existing system.) Suspected communists, strike leaders, and agitators among the unemployed were frequently arrested under Section 98, often to be released when the back of the strike or demonstration had been broken.

Concerned with the volatility of the situation, the federal government, at the urging of many provincial governments, established remote relief camps across the country for single unemployed men, under the authority of the military. Single unemployed men found themselves faced with the "choice" of starvation and homelessness in the city, or "voluntarily" entering such camps. The WUL organized the camps, leading strikes and sit-downs to protest the conditions and to demand improvements. By the time of the cancellation of the program in 1936 over 170,000 of Canada's single unemployed had had a taste of life in what the WUL dubbed "slave camps." Hunger marches were dismissed as "red" plots, picket lines of unhappy relief recipients as "red" agitators, the demands of the unemployed for work as "seditious conspiracy." Strikes, demonstrations, and picket lines were smashed by police armed with tear-gas and clubs, backed up by machine guns.

In a peaceful demonstration emanating from a bitter coal strike at Bienfait, Saskatchewan three miners were shot and killed in cold blood by the RCMP. Participants in a 1932 hunger march in Edmonton were beaten indiscriminately by baton-wielding RCMP officers. The famous 1935 On To Ottawa Trek of unemployed men from B.C. relief camps was stopped at Regina in a bloody Dominion Day riot. The principal leader of the 1938 sit-in at the Vancouver Post Office was beaten almost to death in a savage dawn raid by police. The response of the authorities was to act as if insurrection was imminent. The hungry, the unemployed, the relief recipient, the striking worker, the dispossessed farmer, if they dared to organize and to protest, met clubs, tear-gas, machine guns, and prison.

History records that, in Canada, during the initial years of the Depression, the Communist Party (CP) articulated the complaints of the afflicted and organized their resistance. It was the CP's finest hour. The courage and perseverance of the CP militants, and those who were inspired by them without embracing their ideology, rekindled the fighting spirit of Canada's working class, setting the stage for the emergence of militant industrial unionism in the 1940s. The example of the FUL also helped to inspire Western farmers to confront the self-evident failure of a social and economic system that had betrayed them. And though the authorities were most deeply disturbed by the activities of the CP, they experienced deep consternation at two more successful, less militant, movements of mass protest that emerged in the West. Just as the hunger marchers, these movements were labelled as "communist" and "revolutionary." But unlike the CP, these movements drove irresistibly to power in two Western provinces, and threatened to spread across the nation. The movements were rooted, once again, in the farmers of Western Canada and, once again, new principles of political economy and of Confederation were advocated and won broad support.[24]

THE FOUNDING OF SOCIAL CREDIT AND THE CCF

The arrival of the Great Depression simply completed popular dis-enchantment with the UFA government in Alberta, a process under-way since the 1921 victory. The UFA government had systematically betrayed every important principle on which it had been elected, with the exception of its promises to provide "business-like" government and to decrease dependency on government among the people. These latter two principles came to dominate the regime as it pursued parlia-mentary and fiscal orthodoxy and elevated parsimoniousness in gov-ernment spending to a veritable secular religion. Upon the 1921 vic-tory, the UFA rank-and-file had expected immediate, dramatic results and annual conventions became a battleground between demands for action from the membership and the government's refusals to act. A particularly bitter quarrel emerged between those committed to mon-etary and credit reform to relieve the burden of public and private debt and the UFA Cabinet, determined to avoid any reckless innovations that might annoy investors and damage the credit standing of the province.

By the time the UFA won its second term in 1926, the will of the Cabinet had been imposed and the organization withered, becoming a loyal rubber stamp of the regime's views. With its easy 1930 victory, the government became even more remote, convinced of the correct-ness of its previous ten years of uninspired rule, unbothered by any thought that there might be more that could be done. Even the arrival of the Depression failed to change the regime's attitudes as it marched forward to complete defeat in 1935.

The UFA regime proved to be as neglectful as all other governments of the day. In fairness the UFA did not do any less than other govern-ments, but neither did it do any more. For this the farmers who elected it never forgave it. Relief was hard to get and insufficient, besides being degrading. Strikes and marches in Alberta met the same repression as elsewhere. Labour demonstrations were red-baited. Once the Premier even advised the unemployed on a Hunger March to be "moderate" and "prudent." The 1932 Speech from the Throne exhorted the population to embrace "the spirit of the pioneers and have determination, fortitude and courage to meet and overcome emergencies."[25] At the 1932 UFA Convention the Premier declared the government's Depression policy: "The only course . . . to follow in these times is with all the courage we can command to look for the best, but prepare for the worst."[26] This was to be done without too much help from the government: the UFA regime, in common with all others, proceeded to cut services, lay off civil servants, roll back wages and salaries, and raise taxes. In fact the regime did exactly what it did from 1921-23 to deal with the earlier depression: severe retrenchment. The depression of the early 1920s gave way to prosperity; the Depression of the 1930s got worse each year and traditional policies of retrenchment merely contributed to a further deterioration of the situation.

The UFA rank and file became only slightly less angry with the government than the Alberta Federation of Labour (AFL). Two basic Depression remedies emerged and were hotly advocated by growing numbers of UFA members. One remedy involved massive monetary and credit reform, including calls for a debt moratorium, for a suspension of bank interest, for the recognition of new currencies like "wheat dollars," for the issuance of credit at cost by the government, as well as often including the more thorough-going Social Credit proposals of men like William Irvine, a Labour and then a UFA MP since 1921, who was totally committed to the whole Social Credit package. The other remedy, finally officially endorsed by the 1932 UFA Convention, the "Cooperative Commonwealth," was defined as "a community freed from the domination of irresponsible financial and economic power, in which all social means of production and distribution, including land are socially owned and controlled."[27]

The UFA organization voted to affiliate with the newly established national Co-operative Commonwealth Federation (CCF). The UFA

government, however, largely ignored this fact, refusing to contemplate the implementation of CCF measures, while expressing deep
dismay at the continuing Social Credit agitation in its ranks. Indeed,
the government studiously ignored pursuing either set of remedies
vigorously, contenting itself with continuing to govern in accord with
its record. This was a serious error. People wanted and needed solutions. The federal government's long-standing strategy of repression
of organizations advocating revolutionary change, encouraged people
to look for less costly, more painless solutions to the crisis. Both the
CCF and Social Credit promised such solutions — more or less painless methods of radical but peaceful social change. Of the two, Social
Credit came to appear the more painless, at least in Alberta.

The new national CCF, founded in Calgary in 1932, was really a
federation of existing farm organizations and labour political parties.[28] The ground had been prepared for the emergence of the new
party by the work of a group of Fabianesque intellectuals, who established the League for Social Reconstruction in 1931, and the famous
Ginger Group among the remnants of Progressive MPs who had survived the upsurge of the 1920s, largely composed of four Labour MPs
and a handful of UFA MPs from Alberta. The Western Conference of
Labour Political Parties, held in Calgary in 1932, had invited various
farm organizations to send representatives, and that meeting created
the Co-operative Commonwealth Federation. The original groups
included the UFA and the Canadian and Dominion Labour parties
from Alberta; the Socialist Party of Canada from B.C.; the United
Farmers and the Independent and Cooperative Labour parties from
Saskatchewan; and the Independent Labour party from Manitoba.
Only one trade union attended, the Canadian Brotherhood of Railway
Employees, which decided later not to affiliate.

A year later, in Regina, a comprehensive national program was
adopted, the "Regina Manifesto" with its concluding promise to
eradicate capitalism. The new party almost immediately obtained a
political presence in Ottawa through its handful of MPs, as well as
representation in some provincial legislatures where affiliated Labour
parties held seats. But most important of all, despite the Alberta UFA

government's hesitancy about acting on CCF principles, the affiliation of the UFA had brought into the party an organization currently in government. As the organization matured, the policies of the new political federation must inevitably come to be expressed in Alberta government policy. But an event just a few months after the founding of the CCF determined that the UFA government had neither the leisure nor the time to work out how it ought to govern now that it was an affiliate of the new national CCF.

In the autumn of 1932 the Social Credit movement in Alberta was launched by school teacher and part-time evangelist William Aberhart. This was not a particularly unusual event. Ideas of monetary and credit reform, the Social Credit system most prominent among them, already had a mass following thanks to the agitations of the organized farmers, and were rapidly becoming a popular panacea to the Depression crisis in Alberta. As hundreds of farmers were forced to appeal to the Debt Adjustment Board for some compromise to avoid foreclosure, many others experienced foreclosure. Yet agricultural production remained high, prices impossibly low. The result was that the fruits of the farmers' production were siphoned off to finance and re-finance debts acquired for expansion during earlier, more prosperous times. This "poverty in the midst of abundance," a Social Credit aphorism used to good effect by Aberhart, was increasingly seen as unjust, as the result of the "despotic sway of the money kings."

Aberhart was able to use a crude re-interpretation of Social Credit doctrine, which addressed the very real crisis of debt and depression, to march irresistibly to office. Almost overnight Aberhart was able successfully to challenge the UFA for the political leadership of Alberta's farmers. More, he also won the political support of Alberta's conscious working class from the Labour party. He even won significant elements of the urban and small-town middle class. By 1934 Social Credit ideas dominated Alberta's politics. In a 1934 Calgary by-election the CCF-Labour and the Communist candidates endorsed Social Credit ideas, while the successful Liberal expressed sympathy for the notion. The UFA was riddled with prominent supporters of Social Credit. Increasingly what distinguished Aberhart from all other Social Credit supporters and sympathizers was his insistence that a plan could be implemented in Alberta alone with existing provincial powers, a contention he held to with blind tenacity against all gainsayers. It was in this context that mass defections of the UFA rank-and-file to Aberhart's Social Credit League occurred.

Aberhart has been variously painted as a demagogue, an opportunist, and an unprincipled and ambitious power-seeker. All this is beside the point. Such contentions can be proved or disproved by selective evidence. And often we revile in those with whom we disagree precisely those qualities we admire in those with whom we agree (Aberhart was a demagogue and a bible-thumper; T. C. Douglas was a great orator and a preacher). Whatever Aberhart's motives may have been, the way in which he approached his agitation for Social Credit endeared him to Alberta's farmers. His was a non-partisan movement, against the old-line parties, to win Social Credit to benefit all the people (and, of course, free or cheaper credit was particularly attractive to the farmer). He was not a seeker of office but a seeker of Social Credit. He went to the UFA, at Convention and in the Legislature and at countless local meetings, to beg them to take up the cause. He asked the same of the Tories and the Liberals. He dragged his feet when his supporters pleaded for political action. In 1935 Aberhart himself was not a candidate, awaiting the call to be MLA and Premier when his victorious supporters clamoured for his leadership. The point is he was *seen* to be non-partisan, politically reluctant, and resistant to the siren call of high political office, all postures (if postures they were) which only enhanced his reputation among an electorate dominated by agrarian crusaders for 14 years.

Like the UFA of 1921, when Aberhart spoke of the problems of debt, depression, unemployment, despair, and degradation, he was reflecting the real concerns of the farmers and workers, aggressively, angrily. In contrast, the UFA government seemed to counsel passivity and patience due to constitutional constraints. In short, Aberhart articulated the grievances of the people and offered to lead a struggle for a better, more humane social and economic system. Above all else, he said something could de done, and done now.

In the run-up to the 1935 election Aberhart published his *Social Credit Manual*, in which he described his "wondrously simple plan."[29] His basic premise was: "It is the duty of the State . . . to organize its economic structure in such a way that no bona fide citizen . . . shall be allowed to suffer for the lack of the basic necessities . . . in the midst of plenty." So bad was the situation that this premise proved to be electrifying. Aberhart argued that the root of the trouble lay in the fact that people lacked purchasing power, that "wildcat profiteering" was occurring, and the "flow of credit" had been retarded by high interest rates imposed by "the Fifty Big Shots of Canada." Social Credit was the answer. Basic dividends would be distributed to all, solving the purchasing power problem.[30] A price control system would be established, ending wild-cat profiteering. Credit would be socialized and made available at administrative cost, breaking the Fifty Big Shots' stranglehold on the economy. Once Social Credit was in place, the most urgent problems would be solved. Just Prices would be paid to producers and exacted from consumers. A minimum economic security would be assured by the basic dividend. All would have the opportunity and leisure to pursue self-development. Unemployment would end. Credit would be available at cost. Gradually debts would be paid off. Just Prices and Just Wages would, on the advice of experts, climb with productivity and abundance. Economic justice would be firmly, irrevocably established. This solution to the basic problems of deprivation, want, idleness, and insecurity would prove the solution of other vexatious problems as well. "Contentment and happiness will lead men and women from debauchery." The abuse of alcohol would decline if not cease altogether. Wasteful advertising would end. Women would be more independent with the result that "there would . . . be more wholesome marriages contracted, [women] would not need to marry for a meal ticket." Young people would get all the education they wanted. Taxation would inexorably decrease. Ceilings on incomes would be imposed, no one would be "allowed to have an income . . . greater than he himself and his loved ones can possibly enjoy, to the privation of his fellow citizens." "Crime would be reduced. There would be no need for theft. "

Social Credit was, therefore, such a basic solution to the root problems of society that inevitably other problems, caused ultimately by neglect, deprivation, and insecurity would begin to disappear. This was heady stuff. This was the stuff of dreams in the dark days of the Depression. Above all else Aberhart was promising hope, hope now, not at some vague, future, more prosperous time.

SOCIAL CREDIT IN POWER

On August 22, 1935 the people of Alberta embraced Aberhart. The electorate, still 63 per cent rural and including residents on over 100,000 farms, poured out to the polls in an unprecedented 83 per cent turnout.[31] The UFA failed to win a seat. Labour was decimated. The Liberals won 5 seats, the Tories, 2. Social Credit won 56 seats with over 54 per cent of the popular vote, taking all but one rural seat and nearly sweeping the towns and major urban centres. The *Financial Post* (FP) described it as "a popular mandate for a complete transformation of the political and economic system." The problem was, the FP went on, "Alberta is only a province . . . with none of the powers that its new political leader will require . . . so instead of a social revolution Alberta faces only chaos."[32] Before the week was out Alberta's bond market collapsed. Yet this did not prevent the Alberta electorate from electing 15 Social Credit MPs (and 1 Liberal and 1 Tory) in the October 1935 federal election, completing the decimation of the once-proud UFA.

The farmers and workers of Alberta seemed to agree that the "chaos" was caused by the Fifty Big Shots of finance capital, rather than by Aberhart. The financial crisis, it was hoped in orthodox circles, would deter the Social Credit government from any rash action. It did not. Aberhart's Social Credit regime embarked on a course of sustained constitutional defiance of the federal government, complemented by a frontal assault on finance capital. It resulted in a chain of events without parallel in Canadian politics, before or since.

The events began, in a serious way, in 1936 when the Alberta government defaulted when a 1916 issue of provincial bonds fell due by simply refusing to pay off those holding the bonds. This sent shock waves through the federal government and financial institutions, since default might prove an attractive option for other beleaguered provinces, not to say municipalities and school boards. This action was followed by a unilateral cut in interest rates on all of Alberta's public debt to one-half the previously agreed rate, with a floor of 2 per cent. Alberta refused to pay any more until a settlement was reached some years later. The calls from across the country for a re-negotiation of all public debt at lower rates of interest now became deafening.

The federal government and the financial community scrambled to oblige, setting in process negotiations that proved surprisingly generous, though Alberta refused to yield (other provinces did and took good advantage of the consequences of Alberta's initiative). The Alberta government proceeded to enact a series of Social Credit laws to establish the system in the province. These measures were first greeted with derision, then with horror. This thrust was supplemented by a more practical, and more serious, attack on finance capital, as the government began to pass debt adjustment legislation that made foreclosure for default virtually impossible.

As the confrontation deepened, the government passed laws to license banks and to force them to carry on business in accordance with Social Credit laws, issued its own currency, imposed punitive taxes on banks and all other corporate opponents, and even tried to squeeze fairness out of the province's daily press by drafting a law to force newspapers to print the government's side in an atmosphere that became increasingly hysterical.

The pro-business opponents of the Social Credit government became almost frenzied. At one point the *Financial Post* said,

> *Alberta's brand of Social Credit is [a] thin disguise for Communism . . . there is underway in Alberta an effort at social revolution which may thrust Canada into a major . . . crisis . . . [It] is an unprecedented attack on private capital . . . akin to the confiscation of private property. It strikes at the very root of commerce, business and finance in a way which characterized the early stages of the Russian revolution.*[33]

The Montreal *Gazette* echoed,

> *[The Aberhart government] has now run amok through a field*
> *of radical legislation that is without precedent in any country, civi-*
> *lized or savage. It has legalized theft. Having attempted to exploit*
> *the banks, to muzzle the press, and to tie the hands of the courts,*
> *and having been frustrated in these efforts, it has proceeded to the*
> *enactment of laws which are equally if not more vicious.*[34]

Aberhart's government countered with mass rallies, radio broadcasts, and an endless stream of printed propaganda to keep the people
on side. One Social Credit leaflet was so extreme that the Social Credit
MLA and an employee of the government who drafted and authorized
its release went to jail for criminal libel. While one side listed nine
prominent Albertan enemies of the Social Credit government, the
other said ominously,

> *My child, you should NEVER say hard or unkind things about*
> *Bankers' Toadies. God made Bankers' Toadies, just as He*
> *made snakes, slugs, snails and other creepy-crawly, treacher-*
> *ous and poisonous things. NEVER, therefore, abuse them —*
> *just exterminate them!*[35]

Naturally virtually every controversial piece of legislation was challenged in the courts. And frequently when the government lost, the
legislation was redrafted and re-passed. This was especially true for the
debt adjustment laws, since as long as the law in question was before
the courts, foreclosure could not occur. Therefore, no sooner was this
or that aspect of Aberhart's debt laws found *ultra vires*, then the Alberta
legislature re-enacted it in a cat-and-mouse game that went on for
years. The laws in question unilaterally cut interest rates, declared a
moratorium on debt collection, imposed a general reduction in debts,
prevented foreclosure for debt, and tried to transform banks into little
more than community-controlled credit clearing houses.

Of course the laws were struck down. Eleven provincial statutes were disallowed by the federal Cabinet, while the Albertan Lieutenant-Governor refused to sign three duly passed bills into law. Countless others were taken to court in a series of legal battles, all of which the Social Credit government lost. The whole package of Social Credit laws was finally declared *ultra vires* by the Supreme Court in 1938. Three years later the Court struck down Aberhart's elaborate debt adjustment legislative edifice. A further unsuccessful appeal to the Privy Council only delayed the inevitable a further two years. Out of this near-complete constitutional defeat, Aberhart snatched political victory. The will of the people of Alberta was being subverted by the Fifty Big Shots, he declared, supported in a most sinister way by the federal government and the courts. This declaration was widely believed in Alberta, largely because it appeared indeed to be the case.

While most attention was focused on the fight over credit and debt, the Social Credit government was proving a sensitive regime during the Depression. Past indebtedness of farmers to the government for relief was gradually and regularly forgiven. Relief was made more generous and easier to get. The government, by putting a limit on how much it would pay on the public debt, freed up funds for other, more needed services. The most progressive, pro-labour trade union act in the Dominion was passed. Legislation on co-operatives was revamped in accord with farmer suggestions. Modernization and reform of the educational system was begun. Aspects of health care were "socialized." And on most day-to-day matters the government proved as competent as its predecessor. Such measures deepened support for the government. Furthermore, although the government failed to establish Social Credit or to distribute dividends, it had tried to do so only, Aberhart argued, to be blocked and blocked again by the superior powers of the federal government. And the government's debt adjustment legislation struggle was proving enormously helpful to farmers and workers, many of whom faced foreclosure. Emergency relief from foreclosure was provided as the court battles raged.

Even in those cases where foreclosure could be pursued, financial institutions hesitated to pursue such an option vigorously because of the political atmosphere. And, then, finally, when even Aberhart's debt laws were struck down, some discovered to their general rejoicing that the statute of limitations on debt collection had passed, making their debts virtually uncollectable. Despite his defeat in the courts Aberhart had provided, when the whole thing was over, five or six years of debt protection through the worst Depression years. Afterwards, doubtless softened up by the battle, banks and other financial institutions were reasonably generous in working out voluntary debt adjustments with victims of the Depression. (They claimed they would have been just as generous before the battle, but we will never know, and neither Aberhart nor the people of Alberta at the time were prepared to sit back and find out.)

In the run-up to the 1940 election, and despite the arrival of World War II, things continued to boil in Alberta. Aberhart's opponents were determined to defeat him, pulling out all the stops. Liberals and Conservatives formed a coalition and when they weren't accusing Aberhart of being a Nazi they were accusing him of being Communistic. The provincial and national daily press continued their shrill attacks on the Social Credit "Frankenstein, " as the *Financial Post* once described the controversial regime. But Aberhart continued to stand firm, as the Throne Speech before the election made clear:

> *We are determined to provide food, clothing and shelter for*
> *the people to the limit of our financial ability, and we will*
> *continue our unrelenting fight for monetary reform and social*
> *security with the determination to relieve unemployment and*
> *banish poverty from Alberta . . . No person should be allowed*
> *to lose his farm or home . . .*[36]

Aberhart and his colleagues pointed to the five year record without apology. He even turned the attack on him for failing to give the promised dividends against his detractors when he said:

> *I can stand all the abuse heaped upon me when men whose*
> *farms I have saved by my debt legislation grip my hands in*
> *thanks . . . Never mind the dividends, let them go. After get-*
> *ting 95 per cent, are you going to pluck me on that?*[37]

One telling Social Credit election slogan was, "Keep Aberhart In and Keep the Sheriff Out."[38] Although Aberhart lost a lot of his urban middle class support, and even some working-class strength, the farmers kept the faith as Social Credit won 36 of 57 seats with 43 per cent of the vote. The *Financial Post* complained that the "most sinister aspect of the result is the Social Credit success in undermining the simple fundamentals of business morality."[39] The farmers and workers who elected Aberhart had clearly confirmed their rejection of "business morality" not so much in favour of Social Credit as in favour of a new economic morality which would free them from fear, deprivation, and degradation. Most important of all, for the farmers, Aberhart had exhibited remarkable ingenuity in using the limited powers of a province to help them keep their farms.

THE CCF IN SASKATCHEWAN

While the arrival of the Depression in Alberta divided and then destroyed the organized farmer government there, in Saskatchewan the calamity finally drove the organized farmers into politics. Saskatchewan's farmers' decade of resistance to going political crumbled almost overnight as the Depression began. A decade of confusion, division, followed by reorganization and consolidation ensured that the farm movement was amply equipped to deal with the disaster when it struck. Unlike the organized farmers in Ontario, Manitoba, and Alberta, the Saskatchewan Grain Growers Association (SGGA) had not earlier gone directly into provincial politics. Agrarian-dominated but formally separate political organizations had been established for the work of the federal and provincial wings of the Progressive party. The SGGA, divided on the issue of going into politics, containing strong pro-Liberal elements, left the Liberal regime in the province, in power since 1905, intact.

The SGGA's indecision, moderation, and notorious cosiness with the Liberal party had offended many more militant agrarian activists, resulting in the establishment of the Farmers' Union of Canada (FUC) in 1922. The aggressive FUC, adopting a farmer version of the One Big Union's constitution, called for a "class struggle" to advance the interests of "the great Agricultural Class."[40] It strongly opposed the party system and was totally hostile to involvement in electoral politics. The organization struck out aggressively at capitalism, especially finance capitalism, often borrowing Social Credit ideas freely. Radical debt protection and compulsory debt adjustment to the advantage of the debtor-farmer, as well as socialized credit at cost, were demanded.[41] In 1923 Clifford Sifton denounced the FUC as "an out and out radical deadbeat organization, appealing directly to the impecunious and those who are so loaded with debt that they do not ever expect to get out of debt."[42]

What pushed the FUC onto center stage in spite of its strong rhetoric was the marketing issue. Farmers had been enamoured of orderly marketing for their grain ever since the success of the Wheat Board during the war. The failure to establish a post-war compulsory wheat marketing board, as well as the SGGA's hand-wringing on the marketing issue, created a leadership vacuum that the FUC filled with the contract, wheat pool plan. Farmers were asked to commit themselves for five years to market their wheat cooperatively. The idea caught fire and even the more staid SGGA joined the FUC in the resulting Wheat Pool campaign. By 1926, 45,000 Saskatchewan farmers had signed contracts, encompassing 73 per cent of seeded acreage. Because of this success, the FUC became enormously influential and pushed agrarian opinion leftward on all manner of issues. As well, the success of the joint FUC/SGGA Wheat Pool campaign convinced the organizations to amalgamate into the United Farmers of Canada (Saskatchewan Section). The FUC gave up its class struggle constitutional rhetoric in exchange, as it turned out, for domination of a united organization of all organized farmers.

The United Farmers proved to be more like the Farmers' Union than like the SGGA, and former Farmers' Union militants ultimately won control of the new organization when in 1929, George Hara Williams, a former Farmers' Union organizer, won the presidency. Williams brought a more militant, class struggle, and a broader political and economic, orientation to the new United Farmers of Canada (Saskatchewan Section). No longer content to act simply as a pressure group, though still strictly non-partisan politically, and still absolutely opposed to direct political action, the new organization took radical political stands on a whole range of issues. Underlying every position paper and every proposed reform was a central commitment to the principle of co-operation applied to the social structure as a whole as the road to a much improved social system. Final success in redressing the grievances of the farmer, and of the people, was seen as ultimately dependent on a successful reconstruction of the social system, especially its economic foundation, according to the co-operative principles so long advocated by the organized farmers. In retrospect, everything the United Farmers did, particularly after Williams' victory in 1929, seemed a preparation for plunging directly into politics. With a membership fluctuating between 20,000 and 30,000, with an increasingly well-developed and clear program, with a president who had earlier been fired from the Farmers' Union for his efforts to steer it toward political action, the United Farmers could not have long remained a mere pressure group going cap-in-hand to discredited politicians. The Depression merely sped up a decision that was inevitable.

The United Farmers' decision to go political was further abetted by a decade of increasingly abysmal politics in the province. The earlier failure of the SGGA to go political at the height of the agrarian upsurge had left those opposed to the party system somewhat at sea. A separate provincial Progressive party organization had been set up and contested some seats in provincial elections during the 1920s, regularly winning a handful of seats. However, the provincial Progressives failed to capture the political leadership of Saskatchewan's farmers since the party proved unable to reflect the farmers' growing radicalization. Apparently oblivious to events around them, the Progressives remained moderate, incapable of taking relevant or distinctive positions on most important issues.[43]

In desperation a large bloc of Saskatchewan's electorate, won over to the critique of the party system, had started voting independent. Consequently the political situation in Saskatchewan became an unpredictable morass of confusion and contention during the 1920s. Although the, Liberal party stayed in power, it did so only by shrill partisanship and judicious patronage, dropping all pretense of being a

farmers' party. The Opposition, composed of a confused conglomera-
tion of Tories, Progressives, and Independents, was united only by an
overriding passion to oust the Liberals. And as the economy improved
in the 1920s the issues on which the Opposition assailed the government became increasingly confused. Since all political groupings
rhetorically supported the general demands of the agrarian crusade,
clear political distinctions could not be drawn on agrarian issues.
Increasingly, therefore, the issues that came to dominate public debate
became religious and racial.

The Opposition, under the leadership of the Tories, was aided
by a new and dramatic extra-parliamentary force: the Ku Klux Klan
(KKK).[44] The Klan emerged as a frontal attack on Catholics, continental European immigrants (especially Eastern European), Jews,
Orientals, the French language, indeed, upon any forces that tended
to erode true morality, patriotism, British institutions, and the Anglo-
Saxon "race." Such groups were attacked in language that can only
be described as violent, abusive, and potentially dangerous. The KKK
received enormous support: the Grand Wizard was a prominent Tory;
Anderson, the Tory leader and 1929 Premier, helped the KKK organize
Saskatoon by providing membership lists; many Protestant clergymen
joined. Members of all political parties joined the KKK, but the Tories
led the field with the Progressives close behind. At its height the KKK
had between 20,000 and 30,000 members. In other words, the KKK
appealed to the sentiments of a wide section of the population. The
KKK was decisive in electing aldermen to city councils, had a big effect
on who became mayor in the larger centers, and, in the 1929 election,
aided in unseating the Liberal government.

In fact, in the 1929 election the Tories and the Progressives tended to
win in those areas where the Klan was best organized. The KKK episode
brought into sharp relief the political bankruptcy of the provincial
Progressives. Unable and unwilling to gain the blessing of radicalizing
elements among the farmers, confused about what kind of alternative
to offer, uncertain about what issues to push, the Progressives degenerated to the point where they submerged themselves in a parliamentary
alliance with the Tories and damaged themselves by benefitting from

the KKK agitation. Desperate in a search for issues upon which to defeat the Liberals, the Progressives joined the Tories in a determined exposure of Liberal patronage. Yet this same desperation led them to pander to the Klan campaign of racial and religious intolerance, which painted the Liberal government as puppets of the Pope, diluters of pure Anglo-Saxon blood through unrestricted immigration, and therefore unfit to govern a British society.

In 1929 the newly resuscitated Tories won 24 seats, the Progressives 5, and the Independents 6. The Liberals took 28 seats. There was no doubt that there was active co-operation between the Tories and the Progressives: their platforms were very similar and only 12 of 63 fights were three-way. Very quickly the Tories and the Progressives, with the support of the Independents, formed a coalition and replaced the Liberals as government. They called themselves the "Cooperative Government."[45] But the farmers of Saskatchewan felt that a Tory government by any other name was still a Tory government.

The Tory-led coalition government of 1929-34 was a defeated government when it took office in September, 1929. Less than two months later the Depression collapse began. The government's response was typical of the day — retrenchment, higher taxes, wage rollbacks, staff cuts, and reduced services. For this they were bitterly attacked. On other issues the government behaved like a ping-pong ball, now trying to appease business interests, now trying to appease the farmers. The government's behaviour on two crucial issues exemplifies this: the compulsory pool and debt adjustment. The 1929 crop had been good and the Wheat Pool, expecting good prices, had made an initial serious overpayment to its members. As a result the Pool was almost bankrupted. One result of this crisis was a strong farmer agitation for a legislated 100 per cent compulsory wheat pool. The government acquiesced, passing the legislation and thus offending business interests.

Yet while passing the law the government washed its hands of it, failing to stand behind the law as it was inevitably challenged in the courts, thus offending rather than appeasing the farmers. The law was finally declared *ultra vires* and the government, in its attempt to get the best of both worlds ended up getting the worst of both. In the case of debt adjustment the government began to respond to demands for debt protection and adjustment from the farmers with a weak and unsatisfactory law and was gradually pressured, as the years of Depression went by, to make the law stronger and more intervention-ist on the side of the debtor. The resulting law finally offended busi-ness interests because it went too far down the road of intervention, and offended farmers by not going far enough. Clearly, most agreed, the government would have to go. For the organized farmers, however, there was no alternative.

It is therefore understandable that the 1931 United Farmers con-vention decided to enter politics almost unanimously and virtually without debate. A series of resolutions was passed laying the basis for political action, and the convention committed itself to seek an alliance with labour. Negotiations were successful, and a joint convention of the United Farmers and the Independent Labour Party (ILP) founded the Farmer-Labour party (FLP) in 1932 and affiliated with the national CCF. This formal fusion should not cloak the fact that the new FLP was essentially a farmers' party — there was no doubt that the UFC (SS), with 27,000 members, was the senior partner in the fusion. The ILP never had more than 500 members. And although the United Farmers continued to function as a farm organization, the new FLP political structure resulted from a tremendous overlap of United Farmer leadership and member-ship. Clearly the farmers of Saskatchewan had learned from earlier mistakes by founding a party committed to "broadening out" to include workers, teachers, small businessmen, and professionals, as well as farmers. But farmers remained the dominant group in the alliance and the new movement.

The progressive elements among Saskatchewan's organized farmers, long frustrated by a lack of unity on the question of political action, had finally won the opportunity to stop behaving primarily as a pressure group to defend the interests of farmers and instead to put on display their vision of a new society. The Depression provided the justification for the need for a new society and the new political party provided the vehicle, now more or less free of the constraints of the older agrarian organizations. The "ultimate objective" of the new party was bluntly stated:

> the present economic crisis is due to inherent unsoundness of the capitalistic system, which is based on private ownership of resources, and capitalistic control of production . . . We recognize that social ownership and co-operative production for use is the only sound economic system.[46]

In order to achieve this objective, the public ownership of all natural resources was proposed. Agricultural land would become publicly owned under a voluntary perpetual "use-lease" system by which the land would continue at the productive disposal of the farmer, who was also assured of the right to pass the farm on to his heirs. In the meantime, foreclosure would be prevented. Compulsory co-operative marketing of agricultural commodities would be established. Social security and public insurance of all kinds would be put in place. Work at decent wages was promised. Federally, the first order of business was the socialization of currency and credit.

Such ideas were finally formulated into a 15-point program. The first three points were key: "a planned system of social economy"; "socialization of the banking, credit and financial system" and "the social ownership . . . of utilities and natural resources"; and "security of tenure . . . by perpetual 'use hold' on home and lands . . . when requested by . . . present owner or dispossessed owner . . . The prevention of immediate foreclosures by an exchange of provincial non-interest bearing bonds." The other points promised social security, socialized health, educational reform, workers' rights, and so on. But the centerpiece of the program was the economic planks, on which the new party would rise or fall: planning, public credit, publicly owned resources and utilities, and protection of farm and home from foreclosure.

Socialist rhetoric notwithstanding, this was not socialism. This was a program designed primarily to defend the people of the province, and most particularly the farmers, from the ravages of the Depression.

Its implementation would take key economic sectors out of the private sphere, and generate larger public revenues, but it would most significantly keep small property-owners on their land with their rights to individual commodity production unimpeded.

This was key: the program would protect the small agrarian capitalists from losing their farms through debt protection and public ownership of farmland, while ensuring that all their other rights as small capitalists — production for a market for profit; entrepreneurial freedom; guaranteed control of the land, including the right to pass it on to their heirs — would remain intact. The program clearly would dramatically tip the scale of the relationship under law between finance capital and the farmer in the latter's favour. The fact that the program promised to save the wage worker's home and to provide work and wages to the unemployed does not in any way lessen the qualitatively greater benefits the program would bring to the farmer.

The new party was immediately attacked by the politicians of the old parties and the press. The Minister of Public Works called the FLP a "union of socialists, communists, and men of all shades of radicalism."[47] The press carried on an uninterrupted campaign against socialism and radicalism, increasingly focused on the FLP. The efforts of the old parties and the press to label the new party communist were legion and unrelenting. Ironically, almost simultaneously the Communist Party, through the FUL's newspaper, *The Furrow*, mounted a vigorous left-wing attack on the FLP. The FLP responded to such attacks with a program of ceaseless agitation and education.

The most savagely attacked FLP policy was the public ownership of farmland and the use-lease system of tenure. The simple defense that the proposed program was purely voluntary, and that no one would be forced to enter the program, did not placate hysterical critics, who likened the policy to forced state expropriation. G.H. Williams' repeated assurances that "the basis of the CCF land policy was a recognition of the family farm as the fundamental unit,"[48] and that the use-lease proposal was merely a way to prevent confiscation by financial interests, had not dented the widely held belief that the FLP wanted to collectivize agriculture. Both the Tories and Liberals had good reason to nurture and broadcast such distortions of the FLP program: the Liberals, because they recognized the FLP as the real challenger to their return to power; the Tories, because the FLP had already destroyed the future of their coalition by winning much of the Progressive and Independent electoral base.

In the 1934 election the Liberal party pulled out all stops, promising everything to everybody: work and wages, adequate relief, debt protection, and moves to state medicine. Indeed, they stole much of the FLP's thunder, rhetorically at least. The Tory government was a nonstarter; few took it seriously. Both Tories and Liberals accused the FLP of being communistic, of wanting to confiscate farms and businesses, putting the FLP on the defensive. The FLP election policy therefore was more directed against "the financial interests" than against capitalism in general, promising true "economic freedom" if elected. The results were disappointing for the FLP, winning only 5 seats with 24 per cent of the vote, compared to the Liberals' 50 seats with 48 per cent. The Tories and Independents won no seats. All 5 FLP seats were rural, clustered in better-off agricultural areas. In fact the FLP did best in the prosperous rural areas, worst in the poorest areas. Most disappointing, the FLP failed to win a single urban seat, trailing both the Liberals and Tories in urban popular vote. Clearly the FLP emerged as the Official Opposition and the major challenger to Liberal domination among the more economically advanced farmers. Among the poor farmers the FLP ran a poor third behind the Liberals and Tories.[49] This should not be surprising: the FLP was primarily the creation of the organized farmers with deep roots among the "middle sort" of farmer, the better-off though not rich, the ones with a viable stake to defend and extend, those with sufficient self-confidence to fight to improve their position in the economic system.

The election of the Liberal party brought no change — the Depression continued and worsened. The next political test of the provincial CCF (the FLP name was dropped after the 1934 election) occurred in the October 1935 federal election. Alberta's massive endorsation of the Social Credit depression remedy had rekindled the attractiveness of Social Credit doctrine, long a central part of the beliefs of the organized farm movement in Saskatchewan. Things went so well that the Social Credit party in Saskatchewan ran in 20 federal seats, winning two rural seats, and outpolling the CCF in eight other rural seats, with 18 per cent of the popular vote. The CCF also won two rural seats with 21 per cent of the vote — but both had been won with Social Credit co-operation. In Weyburn the victorious T. C. Douglas was a joint CCF-Social Credit candidate and, in Rosetown-Biggar, M. J. Coldwell received the unsolicited blessing of the local Socreds. Of the four seats with significant urban components, the CCF was outpolled by the Socreds in two. The CCF was badly shaken. Clearly the advanced farmers of Saskatchewan were seriously split between CCF and Social Credit depression remedies. Had the two reform movements co-operated, at least 11, and perhaps more, instead of four seats, would have been wrestled from the old parties.

This double political crisis — the 1934 failure and the Social Credit challenge — was met by a wide-ranging debate in the CCF regarding program changes and co-operation with other reform groups, most notably Social Credit. Although those committed to retaining the organizational integrity of the CCF by refusing formal co-operation with other groups won the debate, it was not certain that, on the hustings, the CCF could retain its leadership of the reform-minded among the farmers. The Social Credit party had made much of the CCF "use-lease" land proposal and general commitment to public ownership, while the CCF pointed to the futility of focussing solely on financial reform as the way out of the Depression. Aberhart's failure to deliver Social Credit in Alberta helped the Saskatchewan CCF immeasurably as the 1938 election approached. At the same time, the CCF modified its platform significantly while, as Official Opposition, dominating reform politics on a day-to-day basis.

The 1936 convention of the Saskatchewan CCF replaced the old FLP program with a nine-point platform. Gone were ringing declarations about socialism and eradicating capitalism. In their place were calls for the co-operative commonwealth and attacks on trusts, monopolies, and big business. Gone was the use-lease land program, in fact, gone were any overly complex policies. In their place was a simple direct, moderate, pragmatic platform: "security to farmers on their farms and to urban dwellers in their homes," "drastic reduction of debt," "socialized health services," "public works with wages at trade union rates and. . . adequate relief," "equal educational opportunity," "increased social services," "the national issue and control of currency and credit," "a Growers' National Marketing Board . . . to . . . fix . . . a price which will return . . . the average cost of production plus a decent standard of living," and "the maintenance of Peace and . . . extension of . . . Democratic rights."[50]

The decisions to moderate the platform and to retain the CCF's organizational integrity, were supplemented by a rather confused campaign against Social Credit ideas. On the one hand, the CCF attacked the soundness of Social Credit doctrine and emphasized provincial constitutional constraints. On the other hand, the CCF began more and more to emphasize those policy areas — such as foreclosure prevention, debt reduction, and socialized credit — that were close in content to Social Credit policy. As a result, the exchanges between Social Credit advocates and CCF advocates became sharper and sharper.

The 1934 program and manifesto of the CCF had made much of its policies on finance and credit. It had called for the socialization of credit; it had promised to "protect the farmer from foreclosure or eviction"; it had promised debt relief "by reduction of existing debts"; it had promised a "publicly owned rural credit system"; it had promised to protect the homes of workers from foreclosure and to provide work to all on "socially useful public works . . . financed by public credit."[51] Such themes continued to occupy center stage in CCF policy declarations, as did rhetoric about purchasing power, the money power, and the slavery of debt and interest. Increasingly, the CCF, to set itself apart from the Socreds, also pointed to those policy areas that complemented such guarantees from the cruel ravages of finance capital: social ownership through co-operative and public enterprise; orderly marketing; the construction of a comprehensive public health and welfare system. Yet the promise of security of tenure — of farmers on their farms and the workers in their homes — continued to be the central feature of the CCF agitation as the Depression deepened and threatened even this small but tangible evidence of economic security. Again and again, the CCF promised security of tenure, real debt adjustment, adequate welfare, and work and wages as the basis of its total program.

The 1938 election, following on the heels of the worst year of depression and drought, was shaped by an invasion by Social Credit. Aberhart, facing total opposition from the federal government, the courts, and business interests, recognized the need to win Social Credit by winning the country, province by province if need be. Saskatchewan was the obvious place to start, especially since the Social Credit party had done well there on short notice in the 1935 federal election. Social Credit organizers streamed into the province from Alberta. CCF efforts to arrange an informal "saw-off" were rebuffed by Aberhart — Social Credit was out to win the province for the cause. Other reform groups were active as well, further muddying the waters. Independent Labour, the Unity movement, which advocated united action by all reform groups, and the CP all ran some candidates. The CCF therefore fought for sheer political survival rather than facing the problem of winning against what ought to have been a thoroughly discredited and vulnerable government. The CCF decision to run in only 31 of 52 seats was a public admission that they could not hope to form a government. The problem was simply to survive the Social Credit onslaught by concentrating on areas of known strength.

The Liberal party also saw Social Credit as the major threat in 1938. This was not surprising. Aberhart had swept Alberta provincially and federally, decimating all political parties. Aberhart's legislative program was the talk of the country and the nightmare of the business community. The prospect of the Social Credit party, now entrenched in Alberta, adding Saskatchewan to its victories was appalling to Ottawa, the old parties, and business interests. Such a success would transform the movement overnight from a dangerous effort at experimentation in Alberta, to a potentially disastrous national force. As a result the Liberal party virtually ignored the CCF and, again promising nearly everything to everyone, opted for an hysterical anti-Social Credit campaign. One Liberal pamphlet proclaimed, "Communism is the Threat, Do you want Alberta's Stalin regulating your daily life?"[52]

Aberhart's broken promises were detailed, his "misuse of public funds" lamented, his "futile debt legislation" ridiculed. Aberhart was accused of establishing a "dictatorship" in Alberta, "in active cooperation with the Communist party and other subversive forces." If Aberhart won, "Saskatchewan's industrial development will be sacrificed to pay . . . dividends in Alberta." Aberhart and other Alberta Socred notables plunged into the campaign, with Aberhart regularly out-drawing the Premier at rallies throughout the province.

The CCF was caught in the squeeze and had to fight hard just to keep its program on public view. The crisis was so serious that the CCF did not even attempt a break-through in urban areas, focussing its efforts on keeping its farm base. The CCF tried to make the Liberal record the issue — to no avail. Attention was rivetted on the Social Credit invasion. Therefore, the CCF joined in the attack on Social Credit, dubbing it "the last illusion of capitalism."[53] The Social Credit invasion would "split the reform vote" and keep the Liberals in power. The CCF claimed that "Social Credit has failed to give the things it promised in Alberta" and "those things it has done were CCF platform, not Social Credit platform."[54] While thus rebuking Social Credit, however, much of the CCF campaign mixed co-operative commonwealth and Social Credit rhetoric to good effect, promising to do virtually everything to save the farmer and worker from finance capital that Aberhart was doing, and to do it more effectively.

> *The CCF is determined that Humanity will come first . . .*
> *and will . . . use this power to protect the people . . . and*
> *will keep on using it against the imposition of usury, until*
> *the powers of entrenched finance give a square deal to the*
> *Farmers and Home Owners of this province.*[55]

Aberhart could hardly have said it any better.

The 1938 results were a further disappointment for the CCF. The failure to run in urban centers made the CCF claim to be a farmer-labour coalition more myth than fact. The CCF won ten seats with 19 per cent of the vote, while the Social Credit party won two seats with 16 per cent (one of these seats was won for Social Credit by the 1934-35 President of the United Farmers). Two Unity candidates won seats and their votes together with the other reform currents reached almost eight per cent. The 1934 decimation of the Tories was re-confirmed with no seats, while the Liberals took 38 seats with 46 per cent of the vote.

The CCF had defeated the Social Credit threat, holding its base among the province's reformist farmers and retaining its position as Official Opposition. It was a bitter-sweet success, for had the various reform currents, especially the CCF and Social Credit, united, the Liberal government would have been defeated. Interestingly the 1934 pattern of support for the CCF was repeated in 1938 — the CCF did best among the more prosperous farmers.[56] All ten CCF MLAs were successful farmers and CCF support was effectively concentrated, as the leader put it, "in that portion where crops have been harvested,"[57] no insignificant fact in the worst Depression year. Indeed, the CCF claimed that Liberal threats that federally supported relief payments would end if the Liberals were not returned had been used to frighten less secure farmers.

Although the arrival of World War II and the end of the drought slowly began to drag the province out of depression, the social and economic burden of the depression legacy lingered on: debt remained, instability remained, indeed, all the basic structural problems that had brought the CCF into existence remained. Despite constant attacks on its loyalty and silly efforts simultaneously to equate the CCF to Communism and Hitlerism, the CCF continued to flourish in Saskatchewan. A good test of the CCF's growing support was provided in the March 1940 federal election. Liberals again accused the CCF of being communists, Nazis, and disloyal pacifists. The tactic failed — the CCF won five of Saskatchewan's 21 seats with nearly 29 per cent of the vote. This election also announced the end of the Social Credit upsurge in Saskatchewan — no seats with just over three percent of the vote. The support pattern continued. The CCF won no urban seats. In rural areas the story was different. Four of the five rural seats won by the CCF were won with more than 50 per cent of the vote, including one seat in which Social Credit took over eight per cent. Three of the victories were two-way fights with the Liberals. In the seven rural seats the CCF failed to win, CCF candidates came a strong second. Election victories in Saskatchewan were still decided on the farm in 1940, and the federal results made clear that provincial power for the CCF only awaited the next provincial election.

Both the CCF and Social Credit movements saw themselves as more than merely agrarian, sectional movements. Although they had their greatest successes in the West, hardest hit by the Depression, both movements believed that they had uncovered new principles of political economy that ought to be applied nationally. Indeed, the CCF in Saskatchewan always maintained that the achievement of the cooperative commonwealth required federal power. The Alberta Social Credit movement, after failing to implement its ideas provincially, reluctantly agreed on the need for federal power after the federal cabinet and the courts repeatedly slammed the door on Alberta initiatives. Therefore both movements sallied forth to win the whole Dominion to their ideas. The CCF had considerably more success since, from the outset, a national movement was envisaged and a significant group of Labour and Progressive MPs supported the new party. As well, almost every provincial section of organized farmers affiliated with the CCF, giving the new party a good organizational toehold across the country. The Alberta Social Credit movement had less luck, forced to build a national organization outward from Alberta with no significant indigenous core to incorporate in other provinces, and often facing resistance from more orthodox Social Crediters.

The CCF believed it had made the biggest breakthrough when the Alberta UFA affiliated with the national group. As we've seen, this was a short-lived triumph. In Manitoba, the new provincial CCF was able to win seven seats with 12 per cent of the vote in the 1936 election, yet failed finally to become a serious contender for provincial power until the 1960s. In Alberta the CCF was gradually extinguished after the UFA's massive defeat in 1935. The CCF tried to make a breakthrough in Atlantic Canada with little luck. In Québec the party was humbled from the beginning. In Ontario the CCF won one seat with seven per cent of the vote in 1934, only to be rolled back in the 1937 contest. Federally, in 1935, the CCF won all seven seats and most of its nearly nine per cent of the national vote in the West. And in 1940 the pattern was similar — seven of eight seats were won in the West, as was the bulk of its national popular vote. In the West the party did well, though not as well as many had hoped. In 1935, the CCF won 19 per cent of the federal vote in Manitoba (two seats); in Saskatchewan 21 per cent (two seats); in Alberta, 13 per cent; in B.C., 34 per cent (three seats). In 1940, the party again took 19 per cent in Manitoba (one seat); 29 per cent in Saskatchewan (five seats); 13 per cent in Alberta; and 28 percent in B.C. (one seat). And the situation worsened as the Depression dragged to an end. In 1935, only 43 per cent of the CCF's national vote was won in the West. By 1940 this figure reached 78 per cent. Clearly, the CCF failed to win the nation to its vision of the co-operative commonwealth.

Yet the CCF did come close to winning B.C.[58] In fact, second to Alberta, the greatest hopes were held by the new party for early success in B.C., particularly after the 1933 election when the new B.C. section of the CCF won seven seats with an astonishing 32 per cent of the vote and became the Official Opposition. This result was astonishing first of all because the 1928 Labour vote in B.C. had collapsed to just under five per cent and only one MLA had been elected. The trade unions and labour parties in B.C., in common with the rest of the West, indeed of the Dominion, were in disarray, apparently on the threshold of extinction when the Depression struck.

The economic downturn revived the Independent Labour Party which, as it grew, changed its name to the older Socialist Party of Canada, and attended the 1932 Calgary meeting. The new party grew with incredible rapidity. The 1933 electoral result was astonishing too because of the disputes that had marked the founding of the provincial CCF in B.C. The Socialist Party tended to be more radical in its approach to socialism, many of its members were intellectual adherents of Marxism. A variety of more moderate groups — a whole series of independent CCF clubs (which amalgamated into the Associated CCF Clubs of B.C.), the more softly socialist League for Social Reconstruction, the Reconstruction party — clamoured for affiliation to the CCF. After much controversy and debate, a founding convention including the Socialist Party, the CCF Clubs, and the Reconstructionists was held. The policies adopted tended in the more radical direction of the Socialist Party, which remained the dominant influence in the B.C. wing of the party. Almost overnight, therefore, the B.C. CCF organized itself, settled old battles by uniting warring factions, established a platform and ran in a general election, which returned it as Official Opposition with almost a third of the popular vote. The party seemed on the road to victory.

However, an unprecedented campaign of vilification, red-baiting and scare-mongering by the press, combined with the new 1933 Liberal government's efforts to help the victims of the Depression, broke the party's momentum. A re-emergence of even more divisive internal squabbling took an additional toll. The CCF's vote fell to 29 per cent in 1937, returning the same number of MLAs, but losing Opposition status to the Tories. The subsequent revival of the party at the beginning of World War II, when in 1941 the CCF won more votes than either the Liberals or the Tories, and permanently became the Official Opposition, convinced the two old parties to form a coalition to keep the CCF out of office. The coalition was successful and, when it was near collapse, Tory back-bencher W. A. C. Bennett formed it anew in the 1952 election under the Social Credit banner. The tactic of uniting the so-called free enterprise vote to keep the CCF out of power remained effective in the province until the early 1970s. In fact the B.C. CCF (and later NDP), throughout the 1940s, 1950s, and 1960s, seemed destined to remain in perpetual opposition, victory often just slightly beyond its grasp.

The Social Credit party did not go anywhere in its efforts to organize beyond Alberta. Certainly they dominated federal and provincial politics in Alberta, but failed to convince other Canadians. The Socreds had their best results in Saskatchewan until the CCF finally beat them back. Except for the two seats won in Saskatchewan in 1935, the Social Credit party went nowhere in the other provinces in federal elections. Results in provincial elections were just as bad. In 1937, B.C. gave

Social Credit just over one per cent of the vote. In Manitoba, Social Credit picked up five seats in 1936 with nine per cent of the vote, but collapsed thereafter. Outside the West, the story was worse. In the 1935 federal election, all Social Credit votes were cast in the West, 67 per cent of those in Alberta. In 1940, 91 per cent of Social Credit votes were cast in the West, 75 per cent of those in Alberta.

By the beginning of World War II, and as the Depression began to end, it appeared that these new movements with their outlandish ideas had been effectively bottled up in the West. Their challenge had been met and rolled back, their influence, it appeared, largely confined to their Western roots. Canada was not about to establish either a Social Credit system or the Co-operative Commonwealth. The farmers and workers of the Prairies had presented two visions of a new basis for the national economy. The visions were defeated and rejected by the rest of the country, just as the vision of the Progressives of the 1920s had been. This time, however, the two new movements did not disintegrate. Rather they began to consolidate their Western power bases and to continue to demand concessions to deal with the grievances of the farmers and workers they represented. The Depression ended, painfully slowly in the West, but the agitations did not.

7

CONCESSION AND COMPROMISE: THE WAR AND AFTER, 1940–1960

While Canadians outside the West may have rejected the doctrines of social credit and the co-operative commonwealth, they increasingly agreed with many of the complaints of the two movements. The burden of public and private debt was unbearable. Unregulated capitalism in crisis created widespread human suffering. State repression was not the best way to deal with the demands of the unemployed, the striking worker, or the evicted farmer. The absence of adequate systems of relief in times of economic crisis took an appalling toll not only in material suffering but in degradation and humiliation. Governments had an obligation to intervene in times of crisis to help those who, through no fault of their own, could not help themselves. Increasingly all politicians were compelled to accept these as truisms and to begin to develop policies to deal with the crisis. Liberal and Tory alike, in or out of power, began to accept and advocate selected aspects of the basic social security programs of both the CCF and the Social Credit. As they did, Canada, in common with all capitalist nations, slowly began to construct the modern welfare state.

Furthermore, the unevenness in the effects of the Depression revealed even more starkly that the economic crisis was also a crisis of Confederation. It was clearly a crisis partly resulting from the economic tasks assigned to the various regions. The West, a region overwhelmingly dependent on the extraction and export of resources, was obviously highly vulnerable. At the same time, Central Canada, the designated region of industrial concentration, though still devastated, enjoyed a more secure and resilient economic base even in depression times. But it was also a more general political crisis emanating from the division of powers between federal and provincial governments. The economic crisis therefore revealed the basic constitutional crisis that has beset Canadian politics ever since. The economic crisis simply brought the constitutional crisis to a head in a way which could not be avoided. Events were making it clear that a country that tolerated such grave regional economic inequities was in danger of disintegration in times of deep crisis. Furthermore, a federal political system that based its unity on the brutal assertion of the superior powers of the federal government could not long survive.

The disallowances and reservations of the Alberta Social Credit measures were only the latest examples of an unbridled use of federal power to keep the provinces in line. From 1867 to 1946, 122 provincial statutes were disallowed by the federal cabinet: 86 of these, or 77 per cent, were statutes passed by the four Western provinces. During the same time, there were 69 reservations by provincial lieutenant-governors, and 36 of these, or 52 per cent, were bills passed by Western legislatures.[1] Such an approach to governing a federal system could not long survive in the 20th century.

Indeed, due to the extremity of the situation, separatist sentiment had again emerged in the West just as it had during the railway agitations in Manitoba in the 1880s and during the agitations leading up to the 1885 Saskatchewan Rebellion. The famous "Wilkie Charter" in Saskatchewan, a document circulated among agrarian activists in the early 1930s that figured large in the early formulation of the policies of the United Farmers as it went political, had threatened secession. And the legislative program of Aberhart was separatist in all but name. Clearly, the estrangement of the West was deepening — one of the few measures we have of how deep this estrangement went was a poll conducted in 1938 by the Regina *Leader-Post* that found 42 per cent in favour of secession, 47 per cent against and 11 per cent undecided.[2] Separatist sentiments could only grow in the absence of some accommodation.

The United Farmers in Saskatchewan had presented a vision of a more just system of political economy and of Confederation in the following terms:

> We desire to build up in Canada, a well-rounded Dominion,
> where the best of feeling prevails between class and class,
> province and province, and believe that this can only be done
> by treating fairly all classes and parts of the country, and
> eliminating all special privileges to any class or section.[3]

The Social Credit government in Alberta put it less eloquently in 1938:

> Successful confederation cannot continue when benefits and
> burdens of national policies are unequally distributed. The
> benefits of policies instituted for the general good should not
> in practice be restricted to particular groups or areas. Where
> national policy, deliberately or by force of circumstances,
> impinges unequally on various groups or areas, there should
> be some corresponding compensation.[4]

There ought to be, according to Social Credit, at the very least, "a nation-wide minimum standard of living." Such ideas were not completely novel, but the depth of the economic crisis, and its increasingly ominous political accompaniments, made it clear that the issues at the heart of the crisis — regional economic inequality and the federal-provincial distribution of powers — would have to be addressed. A failure to do so could fracture the nation, or worse, from the point of view of the establishment, lead to the more basic and radical restructuring proposed by the new Western movements.

The old-line parties, especially the Liberal party after its return to federal power in 1935, began to search for an accommodation significantly short of the simplistic and outrageous financial Utopia of social credit or the more dangerously radical and popular notions of the co-operative commonwealth. The Rowell-Sirois Royal Commission on Dominion-Provincial Relations was established in 1937 with a wide mandate to look into the crisis, reporting in 1940. The Report documented the depth of the economic crisis and the accompanying crisis of Confederation. Apart from the regional inequities structured into Confederation, the report also confirmed the incapacity of existing federal-provincial arrangements to cope with the situation.

The *British North America* (*BNA*) *Act* had been drafted to establish a strong central government to play the key role in nation building. Therefore the federal government had been granted the major economic powers, as well as unrestricted taxation powers. Provincial governments were placed in a very subordinate position, concerned mainly with "generally all matters of a merely local or private nature in the provinces," according to the Act. Consequently, the provinces' economic powers, in the context of the 19th century, were weak, and the tax fields left to them small and restricted. But the provinces were given strong social powers: education, health and social welfare. In the 19th century, such areas were not central, there was little government involvement in such activities. As well, the federal government, by 1869, was committed to providing annual grants or subsidies to supplement weak provincial revenues. In the 20th century the social powers of the provinces took on a new importance as the population began to demand more public programming and spending in health, education, and welfare.

The provinces, despite having the responsibility for these areas of growing expenditure, did not have the taxing powers to finance them. The Depression therefore brought what was already a growing crisis onto the center of the political stage, as the Rowell-Sirois Commission recommended a series of reforms to deal with the problem. The Commission recommended a re-distribution of some important powers, a clarification of taxation areas, as well as a coherent program of federal grants to provinces to ensure a basic minimum, common level of social services in each province. Opposition from the provinces vetoed the Commission's specific proposals, but, politicially, the report had vindicated the complaints, especially those from the West.

THE WAR

The coming of World War II began to pull the country out of the

Depression. National unity for the war effort initially appeared to deflect people's attention from the political and economic agitations of the previous decade. The 1940 election results revealed that the CCF and Social Credit challenges had been locked up in the West with little growth in support. Increased responsiveness by governments of the old parties, as well as the growing public recognition of the need for some reform of Confederation, seemed to augur a return to political stability, despite Aberhart's re-election in 1940.

They did not. The turn to a degree of prosperity, the view that WWII was a battle of world progressive forces against those of fascism and reaction, actually raised expectations and intensified demands for change. The 1941 B.C. election had returned the CCF to Official Opposition status with over 33 per cent of the vote.[5] The 1941 Manitoba election had seen the CCF increase its vote to over 17 per cent. The 1941 Nova Scotia election had seen the CCF win three seats with 7 per cent of the vote. In February 1942 a local CCF candidate defeated federal Conservative leader Arthur Meighen in a by-election in Ontario. And a 1943 Gallup Poll showed that CCF support had tripled since 1940 — to over 25 per cent.[6] The growth of the party seemed irresistible. The declaration of the Canadian Congress of Labour that the CCF was viewed as the political arm of labour continued the momentum.

Most dramatic of all, because it suggested that the CCF was breaking out of the West, the 1943 Ontario election saw the CCF win 34 seats with 32 per cent of the vote (only four seats fewer than the victorious Tories). And in 1944 the CCF swept to power in Saskatchewan, winning 47 of 52 seats with over 53 per cent of the vote. While Social Credit had been securely blockaded in Alberta, the CCF seemed on the verge of a national breakthrough. The 1945 federal election, therefore, took on great significance.

The CCF failed to make the expected breakthrough. Although winning 28 seats with 16 per cent of the vote, the only seat won east of Manitoba was in Nova Scotia. The dramatic showing in the 1943 Ontario election did not spill over into the federal election. Indeed, a provincial election in Ontario one week before the 1945 federal vote had reduced the CCF to eight seats and 22 per cent. In the 1945 federal vote the CCF was humbled in Ontario. In the West the story was different. The CCF swept 18 of Saskatchewan's 21 seats with 44 per cent; five Manitoba seats with 32 per cent; and four B.C. seats with 29 per cent. Even in Alberta, though winning no seats, the CCF got a respectable 18 per cent of the vote. Therefore, 27 of 28 seats and more than 55 per cent of all CCF votes were won in the West. This was an improvement over 1940, but hardly sufficient to claim a national breakthrough. For Social Credit the situation was worse: all 13 seats won were won in Alberta, as were 53 per cent of all votes. In the West as a whole, Social Credit won fully 68 per cent of its national vote (which had fallen to four per cent).

Yet the CCF and Social Credit had obviously had a significant impact during their first ten years on the political stage. Thanks to their agitations, and the ongoing political threat they posed, Tories and Liberals increasingly joined them in the advocacy of the welfare state, and the Liberals began to embrace a watered-down version of the CCF's call for economic intervention and planning by governments. The CCF's surge in the 1940s had decisively pushed the Liberals in this direction.[7] Prime Minister Mackenzie King called upon the basic resiliency that had earlier allowed him to win the support of the Progressives for his minority government in 1925 by implementing old age pensions. Early in the war, the federal Liberal government negotiated the transfer of responsibility for unemployment insurance to federal jurisdiction and, in 1944, established a federal family allowance scheme. Recommendations prepared by senior Ottawa civil servants urged the establishment of a federally funded and administered comprehensive social insurance program, including health insurance, family allowances, unemployment insurance, and workers' compensation. This would have required a massive transfer of provincial powers to Ottawa and provincial consent was therefore unlikely. As well, the federal government was urged by some advisors to declare its commitment to government economic planning to encourage full employment. A federal Department of Health and Welfare was established. The principle of additional federal transfer payments to provinces in urgent need was approved, providing fiscal security to provinces faced with serious economic difficulty.

Therefore the federal government, in preparation for the 1945 election, and haunted by the CCF, had responded to the great public fear of another post-war depression by putting in place a modest start on a social insurance scheme, while adopting the rhetoric of government initiatives to guarantee near-full employment. Although the federal government did not move on the other features of a general social security program it convened a conference with the provinces to discuss the issue and appeared to be moving, albeit slowly, in the direction advocated by the CCF. Simultaneously, convinced they were on the upswing, CCF national strategists had moderated the party's policies sufficiently that, in fact, much of the rhetoric of the CCF and of the federal Liberal government was indistinguishable on many questions. Clearly a corner had been turned in Canadian politics — all major parties, at least rhetorically, now conceded that it was the responsibility of governments to ensure a basic social and economic security for all. This principle, and its articulation, had been central to the CCF and Social Credit successes in the West. But this moral victory was small consolation: the two movements remained stymied West of the Great Lakes, merely a decreasingly ominous presence to keep the old parties on their toes.

PROVINCIAL CONSOLIDATION: SOCIAL CREDIT IN ALBERTA

The failure to break out of Alberta combined with the repeated failures to establish social credit and radical debt protection, turned the Social Credit government increasingly inward. The government continued its gradual improvement of the social welfare, health, and educational systems that had characterized it during the Depression. The government held fast to its refusal to settle with the financial interests holding Alberta's public debt, insisting on a low adjustment and declining to pay more than the low rate of interest fixed by Aberhart. Supports and aid to farmers continued the process of agricultural diversification. But the inspiration was gone, save for conspiratorial speeches and pamphlets warning of the "hidden hand of Finance which rules the world."[8]

With the death of Aberhart in 1943, even this continuing agitation against the tentacles of finance capital disappeared.

Ernest Manning, the new premier, after some further expansion of the welfare state and a promise of "Social and Economic Security and Freedom for All,"[9] sought his own mandate on August 8, 1944, less than two months after the Saskatchewan CCF victory. The main enemy of the 1944 Social Credit campaign was no longer the "Fifty Big Shots" of finance capital, as it had been in 1935 and 1940. This time it was a fight against "socialism" and "bureaucratic regimentation"[10] embodied in the CCF, "this pinkism,"[11] "these Socialistic soap-box orators."[12] Certainly Manning promised to continue to fight for financial reform, but given the last nine years of struggle such reform awaited federal power, an increasingly unlikely prospect for the Social Credit party. And, it was clear, after the June 1944 victory in Saskatchewan, that the CCF was the only serious contender to replace the Social Credit government. As a result the Social Credit party pulled out all stops to beat the CCF, especially since the CCF was accusing the Manning regime of having sold out to the capitalists. The CCF argued that the election of the CCF was the next logical step in the progressive movement's evolution in Alberta, noting that the Social Credit government had accomplished a good deal but the CCF would "take up where Social Credit left off, and continue more speedily."[13]

Manning swept the province, winning 51 of 57 seats with 52 per cent of the vote (the CCF won two seats with 25 per cent). The press, which had never had a good thing to say about Aberhart, cheered Manning's victory. As the *Financial Post* said, "the monetary reformists . . . have proved harmless in their efforts to achieve their monetary policies, but at the same time have given nine years of good government."[14] The *Edmonton Journal* praised Manning for "the decisive rejection of the CCF, which was desirable above everything else."[15] Upon victory, Manning settled the outstanding issue of Alberta's public debt by offering a new 33-year bond to debenture holders. Alberta thus returned to the fold as a safe investment for finance capital.

Manning, with unseemly haste, took the advice offered to Aberhart in 1936, to become, as the *Financial Post* had so delicately put it to

Aberhart, "a socially minded conservative of deep human sympathies."[16] As well, Manning heeded the combined threat and promise, spurned by Aberhart, when he was promised that millions in oil capital were "poised to enter promising fields" in the province "if Premier Aberhart swings away from the left."[17] Manning swung very speedily. The sudden transformation of the Alberta Social Credit government from the champion of the common people of the province against finance capital and its corporate and federal government allies into a pro-business, anti-socialist provincial management team was disturbing to some. In fact, Alf Hooke, a long-time Social Credit cabinet minister under both Aberhart and Manning, said in his 1971 memoirs that under Manning "politics in Alberta took a strange turn, with the result that people even today are confused."[18]

Manning presided over a government that increasingly became an orthodox, "socially aware" conservative government, with little reflection of the earlier confrontation with finance capital, though it was not above standing up for Alberta against the federal government. Indeed, Manning later advocated a political realignment that would have fused the Social Credit party with the Tories. By 1970, after his retirement, Manning had become a director of the Canadian Imperial Bank of Commerce — an ironic turn of events for the party that had decried "Bankers' Toadies." The Alberta agrarian populist crusade for a new Canada, for a new National Policy and a reconstructed political economy, ended with Manning's victory in 1944. His ascension to power marked an end of the use of provincial government power in Alberta as an instrument for political mobilization and confrontation in order to fight for structural political and economic reform. Manning's anti-socialist, frequently hysterical, rhetoric led Alberta away from any meaningful state intervention in the economy and permanently placed the Alberta electorate on the right wing of Canadian politics.

Yet Social Credit still had a province to govern and the party wanted to continue governing it. A reasonably sensitive approach to social welfare, health, and education was not, in itself, enough. The government required increasing revenues to deliver its version of good government. Furthermore, economic diversification was crucial in order to decrease the province's deep dependence on agriculture, particularly wheat. In the 1935 election, the Social Credit party had assumed that the establishment of its financial Utopia would automatically lead to rapid diversification."Why not have machines in Alberta, save all freight and expense, letting us manufacture the finished article in Alberta, giving our producers a Just Price for their raw materials?" they asked.[19] Social credit and dividends were therefore only the first steps in the dawning of a new and abundant industrial order that would see new industries mushroom — woolen and leather goods factories, brick factories, pulp and paper mills, food processing plants — followed by a mass immigration of skilled and useful people. Alberta's new industrial order would be a magnet "to draw the inventors, the manufacturers, and the people who follow them, and [the] standard of living will be lifted to higher planes."[20] Obviously, this did not happen as Aberhart's dreams were struck down, but still something had to be done to encourage economic diversification.

Unwilling to use the provincial government directly in the economy as initiator, organizer and entrepreneur, Social Credit relied upon attracting private capital investment to create new economic activity. The provincial government was active, through aid and supports, to facilitate and encourage agricultural diversification. As well, the government proceeded to modernize the province's infrastructure to attract new investment. But the most dramatic event was the 1947 Leduc oil strike, which transformed Alberta from an agricultural province with some oil and natural gas to an oil province with some agriculture.

Although the Alberta government was extremely generous to the oil industry, taking only quite modest royalties and allowing virtually unregulated development and expansion, the new revenues still proved vast enough to silence serious opposition. This, then, was the extent of Alberta's economic diversification — to the basic economic foundation of a diversifying agriculture was added the boom in oil and natural gas development. The resulting prosperity seemed endless enough that the population was largely content to believe their Social Credit leaders' claims that Alberta had solved her problems. The Social

Credit government became virtually unassailable, as election after election returned comfortable majorities until the regime's defeat in 1971 by the Tories.

PROVINCIAL CONSOLIDATION: THE CCF IN SASKATCHEWAN

The 1944 "CCF Program for Saskatchewan"[21] was the most detailed manifesto yet presented to the electorate, revealing the nature of the coalition built from 1938 to 1944 among progressive farmers, urban workers, and progressive elements of the professions, especially teachers. The first section of the program, and clearly the new CCF government's first priority, was the "provision of security," "farm security," and "urban security." "Farm security" took pride of place in this most agricultural of Canadian provinces.

A CCF government would "stop foreclosure and eviction from the farm home"; prevent the seizure for debt of sufficient of the crop to provide for the livelihood of the farm family; and "force loan and mortgage companies to reduce debts" and "prevent accumulation of new debt." More, a CCF government would "encourage the development of the cooperative movement" with a view to replacing capitalism "by community ownership." As well, a CCF government would deal abruptly with the institution most hated by progressive farmers: the government would "press for the closing of the Winnipeg Grain Exchange." Finally, the CCF would pressure Ottawa to obtain "parity prices for agricultural products." (Parity prices simply meant that the price farmers received would fairly reflect the costs of production and a reasonable profit for their labour and skill.) Clearly the CCF program crystallized the major demands of the organized farm movement, developed over decades of agitation. Gone were such proposals as "use-lease," instead, the CCF stood four-square for protected individual private ownership of farm land and denounced the Liberal government because of the lamentable increase in the percentage of rented lands in the province.

The CCF's 1944 "urban security" package was in marked contrast to its simple "work and wages" labour programs of 1934 and 1938. To bring about security for urban workers, the CCF promised fairer

laws to permit the development of trade unions and to make collective bargaining compulsory for employers organized by a trade union.
Higher minimum wages, the 44-hour week, and stricter enforcement
of such laws were promised, as was a more adequate system of workers' compensation.

By far the greatest portion of the manifesto had to do with social
services and educational reform — an attractive package of general
social security measures. Commitments were made to socialized health
services, increased old age pensions, pensions for "all who are unable
to care for themselves," increased mother's allowances, improved child
protection, and so on — the list seemed almost endless. A massive
reform of the educational system was proposed: larger school units
to provide a bigger tax base to finance improved services; improved
teacher earnings; provincial government grants in aid to school units
to speed up the construction of modem facilities; free textbooks.

It was the final section of the manifesto that stirred the most controversy — "planning, public ownership and finance." In an effort to
explain where a CCF government would get the revenues to pay for its
ambitious program, the party was exceedingly blunt.

> *The lion's share of the wealth of the province has been*
> *stolen from the people who produced it. This must cease . . .*
> *The CCF maintains that our natural resources must henceforth*
> *be developed in the public interest and for public benefit. They*
> *cannot continue to be exploited in a hit-and-miss manner. The*
> *CCF stands for the planned development of the economic life of*
> *the province and the social ownership of natural resources.*[22]

It was this commitment to public ownership and planning on which
the CCF's enemies focused in efforts to smear the party as communistic. The proposed CCF measures to raise revenues for its programs
were just as deeply upsetting to business interests. A CCF government
would: "refuse to pay the high interest rates currently levied to service
the provincial debt" thus freeing "a large sum of money" for other
expenditures; establish a Fuel and Petroleum Board to market wholesale

petroleum products; expand the electrical system, generating more revenue; establish government marketing boards for the distribution of "staple commodities, say food or machinery"; and develop resources under public ownership. All these measures, the CCF argued, as well as "the elimination of graft . . . in the public service" and more aggressive demands on Ottawa, could provide more than enough funds to carry out the CCF program. CCF critics pointed out that such measures would not simply generate more government revenue, but would make the government the principal economic actor in the province.

The program was repeated throughout the election in long and short versions, in versions especially for farmers, others designed for workers, still others for housewives, for teachers — no group was ignored as the CCF carried its general message in the 1944 election. And as a final touch, the CCF issued a pamphlet listing all its candidates and their occupations in an effort to show that its coalition represented a cross-section of the province. The 52 candidates included 29 farmers, eight teachers, seven industrial workers, three professionals, three merchants, and two housewives.[23] The professionals were a doctor, a lawyer, and a preacher (T. C. Douglas). Clearly, if one goes by candidates nominated, a rather crucial indicator of the vital middle leadership, the party was a farmers' party that had successfully developed alliances with other key sectors of the population: workers, teachers, small merchants, some professionals. And the 1944 victory reflected this coalition; the CCF won 47 seats with 53 per cent of the vote. A somewhat more detailed breakdown is significant: the CCF won over 58 per cent of the rural vote while its urban wins in working-class areas were even more decisive. The CCF heavily won the farmers and the working class, while the Liberals took the majority of the urban and small-town middle classes.[24] No matter how one examines the results, the CCF had won a convincing mandate to carry out its detailed and controversial program.

In the heady years of 1944-48 the CCF moved aggressively to implement its program. The promises made to the farmers were implemented quickly and thoroughly (although the crop failure clause of the *Farm Security Act*, which freed farmers from mortgage payments during years of crop failure, was later ruled *ultra vires*). Marketing boards were to be set up if over 50 per cent of farm producers voted in favour. (Marketing boards act on the same principle as the Canadian Wheat Board: all producers market through the Board and earn the full final price obtained in the marketplace, less a fair cost of administration.)

Massive relief debts incurred by farmers during the Depression were written off. Aggressive government support of farmer efforts to re-fund outstanding debt was provided. Rural Saskatchewan was modernized as the CCF strove to deliver the amenities of urban life to the farm. Programs of support and aid to agriculture encouraged farmers to modernize and diversify to lessen the great dependence on the monoculture of wheat. Almost as quickly, the promises made to the workers were delivered: the most pro-labour *Trade Union Act* in Canada, higher minimum wages, paid annual vacations, the 44-hour week, a more generous workers' compensation system. For the general benefit of farmer and worker, dramatic steps were taken toward the construction of a comprehensive system of social security in health, education, and welfare. An economic planning agency was set up. Crown corporations in insurance, power, fur marketing, timber, cardboard box production, fish filleting, wood products, leather products, bricks, and bus transportation were established. With the exception of insurance, power, bus transportation, and telephones (which had long been largely publicly owned), the public enterprises were all modest operations. But they did indicate, initially, a certain seriousness in the government's determination to strive to diversify the province's economy by means of publicly owned industries closely linked to Saskatchewan's natural products. In 1946 Premier Douglas outlined the CCF's vision of growing economic diversification:

> First, it is to process . . . by means of private industry, public enterprise or co-operative development, our agricultural and other primary products . . . to turn our wool into clothing, our leather into shoes . . . to process the by-products of the farm, and . . . the forest . . . and so on. In other words, instead of being exporters of base primary products, wherever we can,

> *to carry those primary products one stage farther along the*
> *course of economic development, with small factories in vari-*
> *ous communities turning these primary products into more*
> *saleable commodities. [This will] provide employment for the*
> *people . . . on these prairies. I do not think that the people . . .*
> *are prepared, for ever and a day, to be hewers of wood and*
> *drawers of water . . .. [Then] we should use those industries*
> *. . . to produce revenue to give our people a certain measure of*
> *social security . . .*[25]

The vision that motivated the CCF program, and the government's initial moves, was clear. The Cooperative Commonwealth was viewed as a society founded firmly in the family farm. The provincial government, within the constitutional limits (federal power was essential for the full construction of the Commonwealth), would use its powers to defend and extend small agricultural production and its socioeconomic basis, the productive enterprise of the working farmer. However, the social ownership of selected areas of the economy was essential. Social ownership was conceived by the CCF in various forms: cooperative ownership, municipal public ownership, provincial public ownership, and federal public ownership. The CCF also, with some twists and convolutions, insisted that the private ownership of farms by family farmers was a form of social ownership since the land was disbursed, not monopolized or concentrated. The provincial government would use its powers and resources to support, encourage, and even to subsidize, co-operative ventures of all kinds.

Further, the government would enter into the ownership of utilities, insurance, and natural resources: the first two were seen as essential public services that would be unwisely left to private planning for private advantage; the last was seen as the people's birthright. As well, due to Saskatchewan's economic vulnerability, the government would proceed to do some of those things the private sector refused to do: it would embark on a modest industrialization program, linked directly to the natural products of the province, in order to widen the province's economic base. Wage workers, with the exception of farm wage-labour, would be accorded an unfettered right of combination and collective bargaining, buttressed by strong labour standards and a higher minimum wage. But it would remain wage-labour and traditional relations of production would obtain in the public as well as the private spheres. Finally, health, education, and welfare services would be improved, expanded, and gradually extended into new areas of public good. This was the vision of 1944-48.

But in the run-up to the 1948 election the CCF government had already begun to abandon its commitment to develop natural resources under public ownership. Indeed, the hysterical red-baiting attacks by the Liberal Opposition, and the growing Cold War mood, also convinced the government to back off from its program of modest industrialization under public ownership. More and more the government pointed proudly to the advances made by the Crown corporations in power, telephones, insurance, and transportation, less and less at the more controversial public industries in blankets, shoes, boxes, fur, fish, and clay. These latter enterprises were not doing too well, as they found the capitalist marketplace largely closed to them. Convinced by the growing mood of anti-communism, as well as its own belief that a provincial government did not possess the capital and the expertise essential to a full-scale and rapid development of the province's natural resources, the CCF government increasingly opened the door to private investors to develop the new resource growth industries. By the pre-election budget speech in 1948 the CCF government had made it flatly clear that it did not intend to pursue public ownership in natural resource development. That task would be left to private capital under the watchful eye of the government.

The general decline in support for the national and Ontario CCF found its reflection in Saskatchewan. As the old parties pursued their policy of a judicious adoption of aspects of the core CCF program, combined with an anti-CCF campaign of vilification and smear in the context of the growing Cold War mood, the CCF, even in its Saskatchewan bastion, faced a decline in support. The 1948 provincial election results revealed some significant erosion of CCF support. The erosion might have been even more serious had the Saskatchewan

Liberals learned to be more moderate than they proved to be. In 1948, the Liberal party failed to articulate its alternative version of the social welfare state, contenting itself with a near-hysterical red-baiting campaign against the CCF. The government was re-elected with 31 of 52 seats and about 48 per cent of the vote, reflecting a loss of over five per cent in popular vote and 16 seats. The biggest loss came in rural areas, which returned 19 Liberals and 24 CCFers. The CCF urban, working-class support remained solid, but there was a serious erosion and had the CCF faced a united free-enterprise alternative, in the context of the red-baiting that took place, the government might well have been defeated. The federal election a year later confirmed that erosion. A drop of less than four per cent in the popular vote reduced the CCF from 18 federal seats in the province to just five seats in 1949. Nationally, the CCF's total number of seats fell from 28 to 13, its popular vote to just over 13 per cent. Again, the CCF was corralled in the West — 11 of 13 seats and almost 53 per cent of all the votes polled by the CCF. Clearly, the federal results confirmed the need to take stock.

Although the *Financial Post* believed that the 1948 results revealed that the "socialists" had been "unmasked" and that the "virtual defeat" suggested that the electorate saw the CCF as "a narrow socialistic class party,"[26] the CCF government saw it differently. The government believed that the results confirmed the correctness of the policy of a continuing moderate consolidation of its basic 1944-48 program. No dramatic new initiatives were contemplated. The legislative program of the government, as well as its annual budgets, from 1949 onward reflected this fact. There were no new experiments in public enterprise and the government continued to place its emphasis upon the crown corporations in power, telephones, insurance, and transportation. There were no new adventures in publicly owned industrial plants and those that existed were increasingly put on the rear shelf of public display, and most were finally allowed to die more or less natural deaths. Resource development — especially of the new mineral riches — was to be carried out by private capital.

After considerable internal party debate, as well as careful and moderate analyses of the possibilities of a public ownership strategy

of resource development, the government had irrevocably decided
to go with private development. This decision was motivated partly
by an uncertainty about whether the government of a small province
could mobilize sufficient capital and expertise, as well as develop
secure international markets, to ensure the success of large-scale public
resource development. As well, the decision was motivated by deep
political doubts about whether the growing political conservatism in
Canada would accept serious public ownership beyond basic essential
services. The commitment to public ownership of resource development was, therefore, unceremoniously dropped, not to be picked up
again until the initiatives of the NDP government in the 1970s.

Advances in welfare, health, and education were slowed down to
allow increasing balanced economic growth. As well, the CCF continued its aggressive advocacy of government programs to aid and
further agricultural development and the establishment of cooperative
enterprises. Largely gone were ringing declarations about the ultimate
establishment of the co-operative commonwealth, gone were denunciations of capitalism as a system. In their place was the rhetoric and
practice of a sound, Western-oriented, business-like administration,
careful management of the province's affairs, a commitment to social
security, a dedication to obtaining a decent share of resource profits
through taxation and royalty schemes, and a clear intention to provide
all essential aid necessary for agricultural prosperity and stability.

This moderation and consolidation paid off in handsome electoral
dividends as the CCF government easily retained power throughout
the 1950s, a remarkable feat that boggled the minds of the Liberal
Opposition, completely confounded by the fact that Saskatchewan's
farmers continued to elect those "reds" and "socialists." Only in 1960
did the CCF make a dramatic move to extend the welfare state by
campaigning for re-election on a promise to implement a universal
medicare system. Easily re-elected, the CCF moved to implement the
program, the first in Canada, against the wishes of the medical profession, supported by the province's despairing right-wing forces. The
resulting doctors' strike of 1962, and the incredible right-wing political
agitations that accompanied it, finally united the CCF's political foes

sufficiently that in 1964 the 20-year-old regime was defeated by the long-suffering Liberal Opposition.

THE QUIETING OF THE WEST

The moderation and consolidation of the CCF and Social Credit regimes and their undeniable success in providing good government, contributed to a quieting of the agitation in the West. Clearly denied the chance to apply their remedies nationally, both the CCF and Social Credit governments retreated to provincial strategies, focussing on establishing all-class political coalitions by providing solid, competent, reasonably sensitive, and business-like government. Both movements had begun by advocating an aggressive restructuring of capitalism, and of Confederation, in favour of the common people — most particularly, in favour of the Prairie farmers they represented. Thwarted in such efforts by a failure to win national power, and by the evolution of a less harsh welfare-state capitalism, the two movements more and more focused on becoming competent provincial administrations defending their people in battles with the federal government in the growing morass of federal-provincial gamesmanship.

This consolidation of the two movements in Alberta and Saskatchewan was accompanied by relatively poor results in the other two Western provinces. In Manitoba, the Liberal-Progressive government continued to survive by moving sufficiently on basic reforms. The CCF, but for a strong showing in 1945 (34 per cent of the vote), retained its third-party status, a fate that seemed sealed when the more "progressive" Tories gained office in 1958. The Manitoba Social Credit party failed to gain any credibility at all.

In B.C., the CCF continued to be electorally outflanked by the free enterprise coalition. A near CCF win in 1952, when the old Tory-Liberal coalition collapsed and was replaced by W. A. C. Bennett's Social Credit party, was not repeated. In 1952 the CCF gained the most votes of any party and missed forming a minority government by just one seat (the CCF won 18 seats; Social Credit, 19 seats; Tories, four seats; Liberals, six seats). Bennett's minority government of 1952 was returned with a solid majority in 1953 when sufficient additional

Tory and Liberal voters finally agreed that Bennett alone could save the province from socialism.

Social Credit had done very poorly in the province previously, for example, only winning just over one per cent of the vote in 1949. But Bennett's party, the control of which he wrested from orthodox Social Creditors, had nothing to do with Social Credit doctrine, except for the odd bit of florid populist rhetoric that Bennett indulged in from time to time. The party had most to do with making Bennett premier. Bennett's more favoured rhetoric was anti-socialist and anti-communist, and the need to unite the free enterprisers against the socialist hordes. But this extremely reactionary rhetoric did not deter Bennett from pursuing the construction of a reasonably generous system of social security in the province, if only to steal at least some of the CCF's thunder. As well, Bennett picked up a lot of the federal bashing, anti-Central Canada rhetoric that had characterized the earlier Alberta Social Credit and the Saskatchewan CCF. As a result, the movements, especially the CCF, were denied decisive success anywhere but in their original fortresses.

The two movements were therefore not just locked up in the West; they remained locked up in Alberta and Saskatchewan, unable even to win the hearts and minds of sufficient people in the other two Western provinces to join either crusade. This failure helped speed up the process of moderation of the movements. In the case of the CCF, the process was sped up by a conviction that the old socialist remedies for harsh times had to be modified to meet the new situation. In the case of Social Credit in Alberta, the process was sped up by the government's conviction that fortress Alberta required careful tending as the sole province with a genuine Social Credit government, indeed, the sole province with a genuine and significant Social Credit party.

The federal government helped subdue the expression of grievance through a series of significant concessions, gradually, often reluctantly, but inexorably. In recognition of the growing expense of programs in areas of provincial jurisdiction, the federal government conceded the need to generously supplement provincial revenues. As well, the federal government completely took over particularly expensive areas of social security. Unemployment insurance, old age pensions, family allowances, and, later, a general pension plan, all became federal responsibilities. Major cost-shared programs in hospital insurance, post-secondary education, and medicare committed the federal government to massive injections of revenue into programs established and administered by provincial governments. Regular federal equalization payments to needy provinces established a guaranteed minimum provincial revenue base. New tax fields were opened to the provinces and vacated by the federal government; other lucrative tax areas were increasingly shared between the two levels of government.

Federal support and aid to agriculture helped the West, as did the continuation of the Canadian Wheat Board and the Crow statutory rate. John Diefenbaker's federal regime proved especially sensitive to the West. Price supports for a whole range of agricultural products were established. Massive amounts of federal funds were contributed to the modernization and diversification of Prairie agriculture and rural society. Economic development grants to areas targeted as needy were put in place to try to deal with the problems of regional disparity and the need for general economic diversification, especially in areas dependent on natural resource exports. Increasingly the voices of the Western provinces were simply four voices among nine and then ten clamouring for more and more from the federal government — more tax powers, more shared-cost programs, more direct federal spending.

The election of the Diefenbaker government in 1957, and his sweep in 1958, rooted partly in his flamboyant populist rhetoric, had deeply undermined the two Western movements. Diefenbaker, the first truly Western prime minister, seemed to promise that he would redress Western grievances by action in Ottawa. His "northern vision" foresaw an era of growth and prosperity which would not only diversify the Western economy but elevate the West to its proper place of influence in the nation. His rhetoric, denouncing the corruption, arrogance, and indifference of the federal Liberal government as well as its smug corporate backers, electrified the West. In 1958 the West had rewarded its man electorally with all 14 seats and 57 per cent of the vote in Manitoba; 16 of 17 seats and 51 per cent in Saskatchewan; all 17 seats and 60 per cent in Alberta; and 18 of 22 seats and 49 per cent in B.C. In Alberta, the Social Credit party was wiped out as a federal presence — for the first time since 1935 Social Credit ideas would not be heard in the House of Commons. The Saskatchewan CCF's federal wing did not fare much better, winning only one seat. The CCF nationally was reduced to eight seats and just under ten per cent of the vote — and, again, five of eight seats and 52 per cent of the total vote was won in the West. As a result the CCF, as a national force, came close to being extinguished, even its major remaining role as the Western voice of reform threatened by Diefenbaker's populist rhetoric.

Poised on the threshold of national extinction as the 1960s began, the CCF and Social Credit movements were victims of their own successes. As the latest expressions of Western grievance, an expression that began with the first Riel Rebellion, the movements contributed significantly to winning the great concessions that helped shape modern Canada. Indeed, the Western agitation had a long legacy of concessions to which it could lay some claim of authorship: the establishment of the province of Manitoba; more adequate federal political representation; an end to the CPR monopoly clause; some freight rate relief; the regulation of the grain trade; public involvement in the storage and handling of grain; some selective tariff relief; direct federal agricultural assistance for a whole range of programs; debt adjustment; regular and guaranteed federal equalization payments; the Bank of Canada; the Canadian Wheat Board; the Farm Credit Corporation; and so on.

The greatest general gain, for which authorship must be shared with victims of the Depression all across the Dominion, was the growing federal financial commitment to the construction of a welfare state through programs to ensure a minimum level of well-being for all Canadians regardless of place of residence in the country. There is no doubt that the fundamental character of capitalism had been softened. Furthermore, the growing federal commitment to the notion of "co-operative federalism" altered the practice of federal-provincial relations by conceding more and more ground to the provinces.

But, in fact, though muted, the West's structural grievances remained.

This was reflected in the continuing strength of the CCF and Social Credit movements in the politics of the four Western provinces in spite of the Diefenbaker sweep. The grievances remained because the basic structure of Confederation and the West's political and economic place in that structure continued fundamentally unaltered. Cap-in-hand petitions to Ottawa, even proud outbursts, brought modifications, but modifications on the terms and at the pleasure of the federal government. What the federal government could give, the federal government could take away — and the federal government frequently had its own ideas of what it should give, ideas often at variance with provincial governments. Though the federal government neglected to use them, the overriding federal powers of disallowance and reservation remained at the disposal of Ottawa, to be used should a provincial government get out of hand again.

Economically, the West remained a hewer of wood and drawer of water —a source of diversifying natural resources for export. Certainly, the list of resources to be exploited for export grew, but the fundamental vulnerability of the West's resource-based economy remained. Despite all the significant concessions made to the West, no concessions were made to what Vernon Fowke called the political and economic terms of "national integration."[27] The structure of Confederation and the economic role of the West in the national economy remained as in place as it had been when Clifford Sifton called for the exploitation of "the wealth of the field, of the forest and of the mine . . . in vast quantities." The concessions muted and quieted the agitations. But the basic grievances remained, festering below the surface of the decorous federal-provincial conferences.

8

OF RESOURCES AND CONSTITUTIONS: THE RISING OF THE NEW WEST

As the Western provinces moved into the 1960s they found themselves still structurally destined to remain most importantly producers of primary resources for export. Certainly diversification had occurred, but it had occurred in the resource sector and, of course, in common with all other advanced capitalist societies, in the growing service and construction sectors. Agriculture had been greatly diversified on the Prairies as new cash crops and expanded livestock production were added to the backbone of wheat and other grains. But there had been costs associated with this modernization: there were far fewer farms, farm land had concentrated, and the rural Prairie social structure was in steep decline, as more and more people left the land to take jobs in the growing towns and cities.

As well, farmers as a class had been deeply divided — the days of a single agrarian organization speaking with one voice for the majority of farmers in a province were irrevocably over. New farm organizations emerged to reflect the special interests of different commodity groups — stockmen, cow-calf producers, rapeseed producers. Even the wheat growers were increasingly divided between conservative and progressive wings. Conservative groups, like the Cattlemen's Association and the Palliser Wheat Growers, tended to advocate the return to pure, competitive free enterprise in the marketplace, while more progressive groups, like the Cow-Calf Association and the Saskatchewan Farmers'

Union (later joining in founding the National Farmers' Union), fought to retain and extend the reforms won for agriculture over the years like marketing boards, the Canadian Wheat Board, the Crow Rate, federal price supports, and so on.

Land concentration had resulted in the growth of a class of very large, very rich grain or cattle barons who looked to new non-agricultural investment opportunities. Farmers with small- and medium-sized farms were increasingly insecure, and for thousands survival became possible only through off-farm wage work, often for both farmer and spouse. The overwhelming direction of government aid to agriculture seemed to speed up the process of modernization and concentration — smaller farmers discovered that rather than keeping them on the land, such programs seemed more designed to hasten their exit from farming. Government agencies and their programs were increasingly committed to the idea of the economically viable farm unit — and farmers whose farms were considered to be too small were encouraged to exit from farming so their farmland could be used to increase the size of other units.

In the absence of general economic diversification, the Western provinces found themselves forced to take the only road left to them — an opening of their provinces to virtually unrestricted resource development. Indeed, the provinces were forced to compete with each other for scarce investment by offering increasingly favourable terms to largely foreign capital eager to open the new West. Tax incentives, low royalty schemes, few environmental regulations, government guaranteed loans — the incentives offered to lure such new investment seemed endless as the provinces competed in a desperate gamble to maximize development.

It became the era of the resource mega-project, of rapid and uncontrolled development, based on the premise that such activity would inevitably have spinoff benefits for the economy as a whole. The argument was that the province would not only benefit from the jobs, temporary and permanent, in the development itself, and in the generation of revenues through taxes and royalties, but in the multiplier effects as economic activity to service such projects would create jobs for workers and economic opportunities for entrepreneurs. This doctrine became increasingly fiercely held as the few industrial jobs located in the West, especially in the Prairie West — in railway shops, in meat packing, in flour milling — began to disappear as these industries modernized and centralized.

Even Manitoba, the Ontario of the West, with its well-diversified economy rooted in agriculture, forest, and mineral resources, and a strong manufacturing sector, could not escape the pressure. Manitoba's manufacturing sector was, and remains, rooted in the dual tasks of food processing and of servicing the limited Western market. Unable to break into national or international markets with new manufacturing activity, the province joined the scramble to diversify by opening its virtually undeveloped north to forestry and mining development on terms favourable to private capital. The biggest debacle in this effort resulted in the disappearance of about $40 million in public funds. In 1966 the Tory government announced the Churchill Forest Industries project at The Pas, a community about 760 kilometres northwest of Winnipeg.[1] The project, organized by a Swiss company, was to consist of a $100 million unified complex involving pulp, paper, and lumber mills. Great promises were made: 2,000 new jobs directly; another 2,000 indirect jobs; good opportunities for employment for native people; the beginning of an industrial turn in Manitoba. Ultimately the provincial government put up $92 million, the federal government $15 million, as almost daily the costs of the project spiralled. There were to be no pollution controls. Timber concessions of a size equal to the area of Portugal were to be granted. The Pas forgave most of its local taxes. The owners and investors, whose identity initially was kept secret, were able to develop the project without investing a cent, in fact, they were able to walk away with a great deal of public funds. The project collapsed and was scaled down: less than 1,000 jobs were created, public money had disappeared in a complex maze of interlocking foreign companies, and the government was finally forced to take the project into receivership and to begin to seek legal remedies. The whole thing turned out to be a disaster and a rip-off — for which the taxpayers of Manitoba paid.

The Saskatchewan CCF's open-door policy to investors in new resource development in oil and potash, and later in uranium, was extended even more aggressively by the 1964 Liberal regime. Potash mine after potash mine was allowed to come on stream in efforts to increase production to the limit. Further oil exploration and production were encouraged as the Liberals expanded on the CCF's policy of following Alberta's lead in oil development policies. Efforts were made to encourage pulp production, again through generous incentives to foreign capital.

The pulp decision proved to be among the more politically costly for the Saskatchewan Liberal government. Desperate to diversify the province's economy, and thereby to show the superiority of free enterprise over socialism, the provincial Liberal government entered into an agreement with an American-based firm, Parsons and Whittemore, to construct two pulp mills in the province — one at Prince Albert, about 220 kilometres north of Saskatoon, and one farther north, at Meadow Lake.[2] The province agreed to assume virtually all the risks by guaranteeing almost $160 million in loans, for a 30 per cent equity in the mills. As well, the government agreed to build a gas pipeline, a bridge, and a new road, as well as 320 kilometres of roads every ten years in the Prince Albert district to facilitate the harvesting of wood. Again, no serious pollution controls were put in place. Although the project went forward, the deal caused a political furor that helped defeat the Liberal government in 1971.

In Alberta, the Social Credit government continued its virtual "hands-off" approach to oil and natural gas development. The doctrine was simple: let the industry do it, and have its way, and Alberta would prosper through royalties and spinoffs. The low royalty revenues gained were, it was believed, offset by the maximization of exploration and production activities and, of course, the resulting general stimulus to those servicing the industry. The Alberta government continued to approach oil and gas production as if they were limitless sources of wealth. In fact, oil and gas development was and remained Alberta's mega-project, the star to which all else was tied.

B.C. was the master of the resource mega-project strategy. Martin Robin's two-volume political history of the province, *The Rush for Spoils* and *Pillars of Profit*, both subtitled *The Company Province*, records the massive give-aways that occurred in B.C. from the beginning.[3] The government was, in its early days, seen simply as the mechanism for providing the right to exploit resources, and for building the infrastructure necessary to do so. Mineral and timber rights on a vast scale were given to entrepreneurs without the slightest concern for adequate returns to the public treasury. In addition to granting these concessions, the B.C. government concentrated on providing access, publicly funded, to the resources: roads, bridges, port facilities, railways. The Bennett government of 1952 simply raised this basic economic strategy to an art form with a massive program of highway and bridge construction and resource give-aways. Such give-aways, low tax and royalty schemes, and a virtual absence of government regulation, continued to be the approach of the government as it strove to maximize economic spinoffs by maximizing resource production — which, of course, meant to let the entrepreneurs have their head. Bennett, in the 1960s, added to his name as a road and bridge builder that of a dam builder as he harnassed B.C.'s great rivers for cheap hydro-electric power. The basic strategy of the government remained simple: give away the resources; build the infrastructure to allow their exploitation; and watch the province grow.

As a result, the basic vulnerability of the West's resource economy continued. A collapse in grain prices would devastate the Prairies. A collapse in potash prices would hurt Saskatchewan deeply. A collapse in lumber prices would be disastrous for B.C. And, for Manitoba, a downturn in any of the Western provinces would create difficulty for its manufacturing sector. Clearly the Western economies were no longer as vulnerable as they had been in the Great Depression. Each had a more diversified resource base, and, it was hoped, a collapse in one sector would be offset by continuing strength in other sectors. Should agricultural prices decline, Saskatchewan could fall back on potash, oil, uranium, and a range of other minor resources being developed; Alberta had its oil; and Manitoba had its manufacturing base, as well as growing forestry and mining developments in the north. B.C., however, despite high levels of prosperity, remained extremely vulnerable to events in the forestry and related industries.

THE RE-EMERGENCE OF UNREST IN THE 1970s

As the 1960s came to a close, a series of events indicated that people in the West were increasingly uneasy with this economic strategy. Simply stated, the strategy was just not working. Workers were not enjoying growing employment opportunities. Local business groups found that there were not the expected golden investment opportunities in spin-offs from large resource developments. The new environmentalist lobby was exposing the terrible implications arising from such uncontrolled and unregulated growth. Conservationists were increasingly listened to as they warned that resources, non-renewable as well as the theoretically renewable (like forestry), were being seriously depleted and resource exhaustion was on the relatively near historical horizon. This latter concern was particularly strong in Alberta, as the end of sweet, conventional oil reserves was predicted to be surprisingly imminent, and in B.C. where the forests and the fishery were being ravaged at a pace that could not possibly be sustained. Even the Prairie soil was being mined for the wheat economy to such an extent that serious soil problems would be confronted in a generation or two.

During the 1960s the relationship between Ottawa and the Western provinces began to harden again. The eternal federal search for a way to patriate, and provide for the amendment of, the constitution, including some kind of charter of rights (especially language rights), intensified. Ottawa, faced with the Quiet Revolution and the disconcerting evidence of the *Report of the Royal Commission on Bilingualism and Biculturalism*, which vindicated Québec's complaints, was determined to deal with Québec's grievances, at least partly, through constitutional change. The other nine provinces, including the four in the West, were mainly concerned about a way to protect existing provincial powers from future erosion through an unacceptable amending formula. Simultaneously, the federal government, especially under Pearson, moved quickly on a number of generous concessions, not only to Québec, but to all provinces: shared cost agreements on medicare, post-secondary education, social welfare, as well as a federal pension plan.

The Western provinces were not overly active in the constitutional process in the sense of pushing for enhanced provincial powers, but they were eager for further federal economic concessions. W. A. C. Bennett took a cavalier attitude to federal-provincial meetings, often dismissing them as irrelevant to B.C. Ernest Manning was committed to the traditional view out of the Depression, that more should be squeezed out of Ottawa. Meanwhile, Premier Ross Thatcher of Saskatchewan, eager to put some distance between himself and the Ottawa Liberals, contented himself with vague fed-bashing in the absence of a coherent alternative approach to federal-provincial relations. Premiers Duff Roblin and then Walter Weir of Manitoba shared the views of Manning — the federal government ought to be putting up more money for the programs the provinces were forced to put in place.

There was, therefore, no new Western initiative on constitutional reform, except for a determination to safeguard existing provincial powers. There was a lot of Western concern about favouritism to Québec, but this was eased somewhat by federal largesse in other areas. Further, the Western provinces had nothing new to say about a national economic strategy — they were largely content to go with the foreign investment, expanded resource extraction, mega-project strategy and only demanded that Ottawa, through measures like the Department of Regional Economic Expansion, further support this thrust by sweetening provincial give-aways to such investors with federal grants as well. In the event, the near agreement on the constitution at Victoria in 1971 went the way of the earlier 1964 Fulton-Favreau proposal — Québec vetoed it.

In general, then, the Western provinces during the 1960s were not overly worried about the constitution. What they wanted from Ottawa was more financial concessions and they appeared prepared to go along with Ottawa to satisfy Québec as long as it didn't cost anything. There was almost a certain contentment, despite the raised voices demanding concessions from Ottawa from time to time, because the West was prosperous and the programs from Ottawa, though never quite enough, were buttressing that prosperity. The West, especially B.C., even shared a bit of Central Canada's enthusiasm for Trudeau in 1968. The Western provinces seemed to be saying, let's keep Québec happy; yes, let's have a just society; but, more importantly, let's keep the economic boom going and let's continue to pump more federal money into the public infrastructure. The carping voices of left-wing critics, trade unionists, environmentalists, and noisy students were minor discordant notes in what was, or appeared to be, a booming symphony of prosperity and growth. But this didn't last — the boom of the 1960s staggered and then fell.

The relatively high level of Western prosperity was replaced by a general recession, as incomes began to contract and unemployment rose. In 1968-72, B.C. 's average per-capita income fell to the lowest point, relative to the national average, in over 17 years, and unemployment began a steady climb in 1966.[4] Alberta's average per-capita income, having reached the national average in the late 1960s, stalled and fell slightly in relative terms in the early 1970s. Manitoba continued to limp along at about the same level of prosperity. A severe recession in agriculture in the late 1960s and early 1970s plagued the Prairie economy. Saskatchewan was particularly hard-hit as its 1969 and 1970 average per-capita incomes, relative to the national average, fell to the lowest ebb since the 1959-61 recession. A collapse of the potash market further deepened Saskatchewan's difficulty and contributed to deep doubts about the wisdom of all-out development of resources as the road to diversification and prosperity.

Aggressive agrarian agitations re-emerged on the Prairies, led by the National Farmers' Union, complaining that federal and provincial policies were destroying agriculture. The 1969 Federal Task Force on Agriculture report particularly incensed Prairie farmers by advocating a deliberate policy of massive acceleration of land concentration as marginal farmers were forced to leave agriculture. In fact, the Task Force's report advocated programs to bring about the ultimate exit of about two in three of Canada's farmers.[5] This enraged Westerners. The federal Lower Inventory For Tomorrow (LIFT) program, designed to discourage wheat production to overcome world oversupply and low prices, was assailed as the Lower Income For Tomorrow program (the farmers turned out to be correct — those who participated in LIFT found themselves without a surplus of wheat to sell when demand and prices went up). Such developments contributed to some rapid and astonishing political upsets in the Western provinces.

In 1969 the Manitoba NDP, led by Ed Schreyer, went from third-party status to government. A large part of this upset can be attributed to the NDP's critique of the Tory government's resource give-away approach to development, particularly growing public uneasiness over the Churchill Forest Industries mega-project. In 1971 the Saskatchewan NDP, led by Allan Blakeney, swept the province. Again, significant in the campaign had been an NDP critique of the Liberal approach to resources and agriculture, and, again, scandals around some of the government's largesse to foreign capital played a role in its defeat. In 1971 the newly revitalized Alberta Tories, under Peter Lougheed, won office. His drive to power had almost exclusively focused on the Social Credit failure to use the oil and gas boom either to capture sufficient revenues from these depleting resources, or to use the boom as a base to create significant economic diversification. In 1972 Dave Barrett led the B.C. NDP to a surprise victory after nearly 40 years as Official Opposition. The B.C. NDP victory, although mostly due to divisions among free enterprisers (Liberals and Tories joined the fray against the Socreds), was also rooted significantly in the NDP's ongoing critique of the B.C. government's irresponsible approach to resource development.

Without exception, although there were clear differences between the Alberta Tories and the three NDP governments, the new regimes promised a bigger role for provincial governments in planning and pacing resource development, as well as aggressive new tax and royalty schedules to increase returns to public treasuries. Although the NDP regimes, especially those of Blakeney and Barrett, promised a significant public role in resource development through crown corporations, the Lougheed Tory government in Alberta proved also to be surprisingly interventionist.

The Blakeney, Barrett, and Schreyer victories reflected most clearly a defeat of the local business elite, which had tied its star to the mega-project, trickle-down strategy for economic enhancement. As well, the argument that the old strategy was ill-serving the West in its efforts to carve out a decent economic niche in Confederation proved compelling.

The Lougheed victory amounted to a defeat of the farmer-rooted Social Credit by a growing and more aggressive urban business elite, convinced that provincial powers could be used much more effectively both to maximize economic opportunities for local businessmen and to steer and stimulate economic diversification through capturing a bigger share of the oil and gas wealth for provincial use.

The common denominator aiding the election of the four regimes was dissatisfaction with the resource strategy of the 1950s and 1960s. Everyone in the West wanted economic diversification, new development, jobs, and prosperity — but they began to question the price. Clearly, resource development by external, largely foreign, capital was not doing the job. Tremendous give-aways, concessions on taxes, pollution controls and conservation rules, faith in the magical expertise of international capital — all had not paid off. Quite simply the provinces were being ripped off, and the rip-off was less acceptable because the promise of general prosperity had not been realized. In different ways, the electorates of each of the Western provinces had said clearly: there had to be a better way. Surely the Western provinces could control resource development so that Westerners would retain more benefits. Surely sensible pollution controls and reasonable conservation measures would be a long-term boon to both businessmen and the public.

The election of the four regimes marked a new era in the West's struggle for a place in the sun in Confederation and in the national economy. The older agitations had won the West significant concessions, but had not overcome the basic structural problems. Content with the victories in Saskatchewan and Alberta, the traditional movements on the Prairies, largely reflecting agrarian interests, had rested on their laurels. Indeed, they had won much and done much, but the problems persisted while the concessions simply softened the reality. The Social Credit and CCF governments had initially proven to be surprisingly aggressive in their use of provincial powers to defend the farmer, their basic constituency, but had failed to recognize that these same powers could serve the interests of the province further. Just as the great social powers conferred on the provinces by the *BNA Act* had allowed the movements, upon victory, to push for the construction of the welfare state in the era of the Great Depression, the provinces' control of natural resources could be used to push for a better economic deal for the West. This power was all the more vital in the modern era both because of the growing range and diversified richness of the West's resources, and because of a continuing national dependence on the export of resources as a foundation of the national economy.

This realization of the growing potential power of the West because of its resource riches was magnified by an increasing sense of Western alienation from the federal government. The defeat and degradation of Diefenbaker, the failure of the CCF/NDP to make a national breakthrough, and the Pearson government's growing pre-occupation with Québec all tended to increase a Western sense of political distance from Ottawa. The brief hope contained in Trudeau's election in 1968 was quickly replaced in the West by an ever-growing alienation from and hostility to the federal Liberal government.

Trudeau's pre-occupation with Québec separatism, his clumsy policy initiatives in the West, like LIFT and the Federal Task Force on Agriculture, and his lack of sympathy for Western concerns about resource development, began a process of Western political estrangement that saw the Western Liberal party, federally and provincially, virtually annihilated in a decade. Indeed, the once-proud Liberal party in the West, which in 1969 could boast 27 MPs, 56 MLAs, and the control of the Saskatchewan provincial government, had been reduced, by 1979, to three MPs, and one MLA.[6] Trudeau's conviction that a large part of the Québec problem, indeed of the growing crisis of Confederation, had to do with an excessively weak federal government and his consequent commitment to strengthen it, ensured a further confrontation with the West. The West was happy enough to see Trudeau flex federal muscles against the Québécois, such as during the 1970 October crisis, but did not appreciate a similar flexing against the West on the issue of resources.

Two contradictory forces ensured a deep confrontation: the growing sense of power in the West and a determination to use provincial powers aggressively to maximize provincial benefits from resource development; and a growing conviction on the part of the Trudeau regime that federal power, atrophied by lack of use during the Diefenbaker and Pearson years, had to be re-asserted. Ottawa found itself fighting a constitutional battle on two fronts: to the East, the Québec separatists, who won provincial power in 1976; to the West, the growing assertion of provincial powers over natural resources.

THE WESTERN RESOURCE BOOM

In the early 1970s the recession plaguing the West began to turn around. Agricultural prices improved steadily, lifting the industry out of its temporary trough. Potash prices began to rise, leading to great hopes for the industry in Saskatchewan. A boom in international demand and prices for uranium spurred significant developments in Saskatchewan. But overshadowing everything else was the phenomenal increase in the world price for oil. Western industrial capitalist nations had become deeply dependent on cheap oil from the Middle East; indeed, they had become nearly exclusively dependent on oil for their energy supplies. Cheap oil was the secret of a mass auto market, of a view that central heating for all in detached homes was a right, and, most significantly, of a competitive edge in the markets for manufactured goods. An endless supply of cheap oil had become a basic necessity for the economic prosperity of Western Europe and North America.

Canada was doing very well out of oil. Exports of Western oil and natural gas to American markets had mushroomed as Alberta and Saskatchewan scrambled to reap the benefits of the U.S.'s insatiable need for energy. Although Canada was forced to import oil to fulfill demand in eastern Canada, the massive exports from the West made the country a net earner as exports offset the costs of imports.

In the early 1970s the picture began to change. Oil-supplying countries had organized themselves into a cartel, the Organization of Petroleum Exporting Countries (OPEC), determined to reap a greater share of revenue from oil for the producing countries. Sporadic pressures to increase the world price of oil continued until 1973, when OPEC began a series of unilateral moves which doubled, then tripled, and then quadrupled world oil prices. The major oil companies joined the crusade for higher prices by drastic revisions downwards of their estimate of recoverable, conventional oil and gas reserves in North America, especially Alberta, suggesting that oil exhaustion was disturbingly imminent.

The "oil crisis" was upon us, creating a bonanza for the oil-producing countries and for the major international oil companies. The crisis was a disaster for the oil-consuming countries. The industrial sectors of the advanced countries, deeply dependent on cheap oil, found themselves in a crunch. The costs of home heating and auto fuel deeply cut into the disposable incomes of families, while oil-price-related spiralling inflation and interest rates further contracted incomes. Third World oil-consuming countries were dealt a staggering blow in their efforts to modernize and develop. And in Canada, the oil crisis created a further Confederation crisis.

The Western energy provinces — led by Alberta, more or less supported by Saskatchewan and B.C. — moved aggressively to capture the windfall profits associated with the oil price rise (which also stimulated a rise in the price for natural gas, as consumers and industries rushed to convert from oil).[7] The federal government moved aggressively as well. Ottawa imposed an oil price freeze in the fall of 1973, slapped on a federal oil export tax to capture increased revenues, and decided to deny resource companies the right to deduct provincial royalty charges before computing federal taxes. These moves markedly diminished the extent to which the energy provinces could capture the windfall. They were supplemented by a 1974 law granting Ottawa the power to fix oil prices. Further, Ottawa threatened to impose a federal tax on natural gas exports and resisted dramatic increases in natural gas prices in Canada.

Alberta and Saskatchewan moved quickly as well, revising their royalty schedules upward and, in the case of Saskatchewan, taking into public ownership all non-crown oil and gas rights and imposing a surcharge on oil production (the surcharge was later ruled *ultra vires*). Alberta similarly moved to establish technical public ownership rights over its oil, though hesitating to go as far as Saskatchewan, through a marketing commission mechanism and by declaring that the royalty share of oil going through the marketing commission was publicly owned.

These legislative moves, as well as a host of other technical enactments and amendments, were designed to buttress provincial control over all aspects of oil and gas development — production, marketing, and pricing. By asserting their ownership rights over oil and gas after they were out of the ground, the provinces were, they believed, less likely to be seen to be interfering with trade and commerce, an area of clear federal jurisdiction. These moves were supplemented by aggressive new royalty and taxation schemes to increase the share of the oil and gas wealth collected by the province. By 1975, an impasse was reached with both levels of government sharing the wealth in the context of hostility and confrontation.

This atmosphere of contention was increased by the Saskatchewan NDP government's 1975 decision to nationalize a significant portion of the potash industry. This decision was taken as a result of the industry's efforts to resist the government's taxation policies (which had dramatically increased potash revenues flowing into provincial coffers), the government's general efforts to plan and pace the development and expansion of the industry, and the government's desire to participate on an ownership basis in future potash expansion.

The potash industry, largely supported by the federal government, consistently challenged the constitutional right of the province to take the potash measures it was determined to take, taking the province to court repeatedly. The outcome of such challenges was sufficiently uncertain to convince the province to nationalize a portion of the industry — ultimately about 50 per cent. As the challenges dragged through the courts, the potash experience simply confirmed the oil experience — the provinces had only very imperfect and uncertain authority over natural resources. Furthermore, it was clear that the federal government, through its superior taxation powers and its control over trade and commerce, could easily frustrate every provincial move. As well, federal disallowance and reservation powers could ultimately be used in any serious showdown, nor was there anything preventing the federal government from invoking the "general advantage" clause of the constitution by declaring the oil industry to be in the vital national interest and therefore subject exclusively to federal control.

As the 1970s continued, both Blakeney and Lougheed won two renewed and convincing mandates from their electorates by declaring their intention to continue to fight for provincial control of resources against the arrogant intrusions of the federal government. In 1979 Saskatchewan's Premier Blakeney clearly articulated a general view of the Western resource rich provinces, a view more or less shared across the West:

> *Now, we feel, resource development potential . . . finally offers us a chance to diversify our economic base. But, like any farmer, we're a bit cautious. Saskatchewan isn't called Next Year Country for nothing. Being intimately aware of what happens in a high-risk, single resource economy [wheat], we ask ourselves the question: how can we manage this promised development of other resources [oil, potash, uranium], each of them individually just as risky, so that we move closer to our number one goal: economic stability?*
>
> *The best way to minimize the risks inherent in a primary resource economy, we feel, is to utilize our short-term wealth in order to create long-term benefits. By taking the substantial revenue from our rapidly depleting oil reserves, for instance, and investing it in potash which, at current rates of production, has a life of several thousand years. Perhaps a more enduring method of achieving this kind of stability . . . is to use part of our short-term wealth to initiate and support a vigorous manufacturing sector in this province. We may have to export some of our primary resources, but we do not want to export all the jobs with them.*[8]

Premier Lougheed outlined a similar approach:

> *I believe it [Alberta's approach to development] means building on strengths such as our energy potential . . . to*

*be self-reliant, getting away from the idea that there are so
few "have" provinces and so many "have not" provinces.
Processing our resources up stream to the extent that we can
do so to spread job opportunities . . .*[9]

For his part, such arguments notwithstanding, Trudeau made it clear
that he had no intention of letting the Western provinces hold the
nation to ransom over energy pricing.

The West had a strong case. Resources were clearly an area of exclusive provincial jurisdiction. Yet when the *BNA Act* was drafted, its authors had in mind such resources as timber and land, as well as the apparently insignificant mining sector. Resources were seen as incidental to
the great effort of nation building and the construction of an east-west
economy where the wealth to be made most importantly lay in agriculture, commerce, and manufacturing. Furthermore, the resource control
concession was essential to win the quasi-independent British colonies
in North America to agree to Confederation. Finally, superior federal
powers were ample and the federal government in the 19th century
had exhibited no hesitation in using them.

As the new resource wealth of the West was developed, since most
of it was for export, federal powers over trade and commerce had easily contained the situation. However, Western provinces' efforts in
the 1970s to extend their control over resources involved new aggressive departures. No longer simply content to sell the rights to exploit
resources to investors, and then to collect royalties as the resources
were extracted and exported, the provinces were now trying to control
the whole process — production, marketing, and pricing. The federal
government, faced with losing all say in resource development, felt
obliged to defend its prerogatives from the provinces, particularly in
oil and natural gas.

The West's unanimity on the question of resources was surprising.
The Tory Lougheed regime, the Blakeney NDP regime, the Barrett NDP
regime (replaced in 1975 by the Bennett the Younger Social Credit
regime) and the Schreyer NDP regime (replaced in 1977 by the right-
wing Tory Lyon regime), all agreed on the need to enhance provincial

control of resources, including the provinces' rights to determine the development of resources and to derive the lion's share of the benefits from such development. They all agreed that the West's resource boom was an historic opportunity for the region to use this new wealth as a basis for economic diversification, as well as a revenue source.

At this point the unanimity broke down. The NDP regimes, representing political coalitions of progressive farmers, workers, and elements of the middle class, argued that the provincial government must not only establish firm control on the direction, development, and revenue flows in resource development, but also use public ownership to capture additional profits, jobs, and to increase decision-making authority. Public ownership would not just win additional revenues, but would ensure that as many jobs as possible were retained in the province.

The Lougheed Tory regime (supported by Bennett in B.C. and Lyon in Manitoba) rejected such socialistic talk, while agreeing that an interventionist government could capture large shares of revenue to be judiciously used as loans to the private sector to help diversify the economy. Further, the government could use its powers to encourage the participation of local businessmen in economic activity associated with the boom. Lougheed, whose province's boom rested on a rapidly depleting resource, went furthest down this road, establishing a Heritage Fund out of the revenue windfall to aid provincial diversification. Blakeney's NDP regime followed suit with its own more modest Heritage Fund, though much of its disbursement of funds went to support the further development of public participation in potash, oil, and uranium, as well as a range of other public industrial investments. Despite these obvious differences in ideology and strategy, the Western provinces were one on the issue of provincial control of resources and were united in their determination to push provincial powers in the area to the maximum limit.

For its part, the federal government also had a strong case. The oil crisis had driven up the price for oil to the point where Central and Atlantic Canada were in deep trouble. Forced to pay burgeoning world prices for much of Canada's needs in the east, the federal government tried to soften the impact on these areas through enforcing a low domestic price for oil. The difference between the world price paid and the administered domestic price had to be made up, the federal government argued, at least partly by the greatly expanded revenues being earned for Western exports of oil and natural gas. By 1975, Canada was in a serious deficit position in the oil trade — its imports of oil at world prices outpaced the revenues from exports of Western oil. The resulting dislocation and inflation would be a disaster for the national economy. Furthermore, the rise in oil prices had worsened the growing crisis in Central Canadian industry, which required, to help it out of decline, cheaper than world price energy sources in order to sustain a competitive edge. Therefore, the federal government argued that it was in the interest of the national economy, in this case the industrial heartland of the nation, to establish energy policies to protect Canada's manufacturing sector. It was, the federal government argued, in the national interest to shelter Central and Atlantic Canadian consumers and industries from the full negative weight of world oil prices.

The Western provinces largely agreed with such arguments in principle. The debate centered on how much of the bonanza the West ought to give up in the national interest. The West argued that it was not fair that it should again be exclusively called upon to bear the full cost of Canadian nationhood. The wheat boom in the West had set the stage for the realization of the idea of a viable and successful east-west economy cementing the Dominion. The West had largely paid, through land grants, mineral rights, and a period of monopoly, for the railway that first bound Canada together. The West's captive market had helped make Central Canada's industries successful. Now, once again, Canada was calling on the West to give up the energy resource boom to help salvage the viability of the nation. Many in the West felt that too much had been asked in the past, and too much was being asked again. As Premier Blakeney put it:

> As a provincial government, we intend vigorously to protect
> what is constitutionally ours — in particular the revenue
> from our natural resources — but we understand that in

order to reap the benefits of Confederation, we must be will-
ing to give a little . . . And in recent years, that is just what
Saskatchewan has done. For the good of all Canadians, we —
and Alberta — have accepted substantially less than the world
price for our oil. We have, therefore, deflected the blow of ris-
ing oil prices from the rest of Canada. And that deflection has
cost us dearly [$283 million in 1979 alone, or $300 per cap-
ita, in Saskatchewan]. You will find few Western separatists
in Saskatchewan. You will find people who believe that for too
long Saskatchewan has not had its fair share of the benefits,
those who are tired of the West being considered a hinterland
for the industrial triangle of the St. Lawrence valley.[10]

Out of the negotiations, the federal and provincial governments
agreed on a policy of a gradual move of oil prices upwards, though
the federal government refused in principle a commitment to a rapid
move toward world prices. Further a complex formula for federal-
provincial-industry revenue sharing was negotiated. There was also
an agreement providing for federal-provincial-industry involvement
in the development of unconventional oil — the tar sands and heavy
oil upgraders. (Heavy oil upgraders transform thick, gummy heavy oil
into a lighter synthetic crude, which can then be refined.) The compromise was almost completely unsatisfactory to the West, which continued to insist that the region was being asked to surrender too much
of the boom to aid the nation. Acrimony and bitterness increased.

It was in this context that Joe Clark's Tories won the May 1979 federal election. The West delivered to Joe Clark, the second Western Prime
Minister. Liking his decentralized vision of Confederation as a "com-
munity of communities," the West gave him 57 of 77 seats.[11] Atlantic
Canada was less enthusiastic, yet still gave him 18 of 32 seats. The key
to victory however was Ontario, where the Tories won 57 of 95 seats.
Although a minority government (136 Tory, 114 Liberal, 26 NDP, six
Créditistes), the West was significantly represented in a federal govern-
ment for the first time since John Diefenbaker. And very quickly the
West got some major concessions in the proposed budget presented by

the Tories in late 1979 — a $4 a barrel increase in oil prices in 1980 (representing what Trudeau was only willing to concede over two years), followed by equally dramatic increases in subsequent years. This would have been a bonanza for the West, especially Alberta. This energy decision was received with deep concern in Ontario, a province that, above everything else, wanted cheap energy.

The demands of Tory Alberta and Tory Ontario were just too contradictory for the Clark government. Atlantic Canada was concerned, too, though Newfoundland's Brian Peckford was happy because Clark had agreed to Newfoundland's claim for substantial control of offshore resources. The concern in Ontario might have abated with time, but time was something that Prime Minister Clark did not have. A series of other unpopular measures in the budget, combined with Clark's serious political miscalculations (he was determined to govern as if he had a majority!), brought about the defeat of the government in the House of Commons over the budget on December 13, 1979.[12] The government had lasted less than seven months. The ensuing election, and its aftermath, sparked the most serious confrontation between the West and Ottawa in the twentieth century.

CONFRONTATION WITH OTTAWA

Joe Clark's 1979 defeat occurred when the crisis of Confederation had reached a watershed. The hopes of the West for obtaining major concessions from Ottawa on resources were dashed. And the hopes of Newfoundland to obtain federal recognition of provincial control of offshore resources were similarly undercut. The contradictory demands of Canada's regions had reached a point where conciliation and compromise seemed out of reach. Québec had elected a separatist government, which was moving confidently toward a referendum on sovereignty association. Atlantic Canada wanted a strong central government in order to ensure a continuation of equalization payments and of federal support of the region's weak revenue base. Yet Newfoundland also wanted significant provincial control of the fishery and offshore resources. The West wanted confirmation, and a firming up, of provincial control over natural resources, as well as concessions to allow the Western provinces to increase their share of the resource boom. Yet the West also wanted continuation of federal participation in shared-cost programs. Ontario wanted a strong federal government to assert and impose a new national economic strategy to help industry out of its deepening stagnation.

The West was seriously isolated, since all other regions wanted lower energy prices than the West wanted. The rest of Canada generally supported federal initiatives to regulate energy prices and to capture a share of the boom from Western energy exports to help off-set the spiralling costs of energy in the consuming provinces. The West's complaints received less and less sympathy in the rest of Canada. Earlier Western complaints, especially during the 1920s and 1930s, had received significant support in Central Canada, most notably Ontario. But these earlier complaints were presented by movements of farmers and workers advocating a new and more just vision of what Canada could and should be. The Western complaints of 1979-80 were presented by provincial governments, and resource entrepreneurs, demanding more revenue — a demand that would inevitably increase the cost of living for consumers as well as exacerbate the industrial stagnation of Central and Atlantic Canada. No new vision of a more just Canada was offered by the West. Understandably, many Central and Atlantic Canadians saw the demands of the West as motivated by greed and sectionalism.

Hostility to the claims of the West was exaggerated by the deepening recession in Central Canada at a time when the West's resource-powered economy was booming. The facts seemed to confirm this. Alberta became the national income leader in 1979, replacing Ontario. Wages in the West became better than those in Central Canadian industry. Alberta and Saskatchewan boasted near-full employment while Ontario, Québec, and the Atlantic provinces were facing dramatically rising unemployment. While most provincial governments and the federal government were facing budget deficits and cutbacks, Alberta and Saskatchewan were buttressed by the resource revenues filling their Heritage Funds.

An exaggerated view of the booming West was purveyed by the Central and Atlantic Canadian press and politicians, rendering the West's complaints unconvincing to most Canadians. The headlines, while based on fact, created an image of a rich, arrogant, and selfish West. "Alberta pay nation's best, figures show," yelled a page one head-line in *The Globe and Mail.*[13] Another, on the first page of the *Financial Post*, proclaimed: "Only Alberta stays ahead."[14] Another announced, "Alberta's provincial taxes about half those facing Ontario."[15] Another asserted: "Growing oil wealth spawns a Bay Street West."[16] Ontario's historic economic lead had never received as much breathless atten-tion as Alberta's lead of only two or three years. Alberta, and the West as a whole, became the bad boys of Confederation, needing a sharp rebuke.

The hard facts of the continuing vulnerability and instability of the West's economy were forgotten in the temporary boom. At the height of the boom, in Alberta, the biggest single portion of investment capital still went into oil and gas. Most of the province's budget, over 55 per cent in 1980, was derived from taxes and royalties on natural resources, most importantly oil and gas. Despite the boom, about 44 percent of Alberta's gross domestic product (GDP) was derived from minerals, another eight per cent from agriculture.[17] Hence over half of Alberta's annual GDP was based on minerals (mainly oil and natural gas) and agriculture. Alberta's efforts at diversification had only made a few gains in the petrochemical industry, some in food processing, and some in non-conventional oil projects. Agriculture and oil remained Alberta's main sectors of real wealth production. Alberta's per capita income from 1950 to 1980 had reached or exceeded the national aver-age in 18 years, and had never reached Ontario's until 1979, when the boom had pushed Alberta into the position of national income leader.[18]

In Saskatchewan the situation was similar. Saskatchewan's economy was deeply dependent on its major resources: wheat and other agri-cultural products, oil and natural gas, potash, and uranium. Although not as dependent as Alberta on a single mineral sector, Saskatchewan remained a resource economy. About 51 per cent of the province's GDP in 1980 was still generated in agriculture and minerals. And agriculture remained Saskatchewan's biggest economic sector, account-ing annually for between 40 and 50 per cent of total value produced, while mining was the next biggest sector. In the years 1950 to 1980, Saskatchewan's per capita income exceeded the national average in only four years, never matching Ontario's. Indeed, Saskatchewan's per-capita income continued to fluctuate wildly from year to year, largely reflecting booms and busts in the wheat economy.

Despite its apparent wealth, B.C. had always been plagued by a fragile economy. Always considered a rich province in Confederation due to a strong industrial base, which comprised about 39 per cent of GDP in 1980, and a very active resource sector, 13 per cent of GDP in 1980, B.C. had been haunted by uncertainty. B.C.'s industrial production was mostly related to the forestry industry — in fact, the forestry industry remained the biggest single sector in the province — and rose and fell dramatically with world (especially American) market conditions. And although B.C.'s per-capita income from 1950 to 1980 consistently surpassed national averages, it exceeded Ontario's in only 12 of those years.

In 1980 Manitoba had the most diversified Western economy. Only 22 per cent of the province's GDP was derived from agriculture and minerals, while a healthy 35 per cent was earned in industrial production. Yet Manitoba's manufacturing sector continued to be largely related to processing the West's natural products, and in servicing the limited Western market, rendering the province highly dependent on general levels of Western prosperity. In the 1950 to 1980 period, Manitoba's per-capita income exceeded the national average only during two years, and had remained chronically behind that of Ontario.

But such a complicated assessment of the nature of the Western economy was drowned by all the boom talk that swept Canada. The West's continuing complaints were not taken seriously, particularly in the context of the deepening recession plaguing Central and Atlantic Canada. Indeed, the West was seen as selfish and unreasonable.

It was therefore not surprising that Trudeau was re-elected with a majority government in the February 1980 election. There is no doubt that the victory can be largely attributed to Trudeau's promise to Central and Atlantic Canadians that he would keep the lid on the West's demands for increased oil prices and that he would continue to

#550   26-07-2016 1:05PM
Item(s) checked out to p10572119.

TITLE: The rise of the new West : the hi
DUE DATE: 23-08-16

Thanks for using Clinton Library.
TEL: 250 459-7752 WEB: www.tnrdlib.ca

frustrate Western efforts to gain unimpeded jurisdiction over resources, especially energy resources. The Liberals won 19 of 32 seats in Atlantic Canada, 74 of 75 seats in Québec, and 52 of 95 seats in Ontario.[19] In the West the Liberals were decimated, winning only two seats in Manitoba. Clearly what had won the election for Trudeau was the shift in Ontario, largely as a result of his energy promises and with the clear support of the premier of Ontario, a province increasingly desperate for cheap energy. Trudeau had promised to slow down the rise in the price of oil and natural gas and to continue federal moves to share significantly in the revenue windfall generated by Western exports. For this, the Ontario electorate rewarded him.

The impasse between the West and Ottawa therefore deepened. Alberta refused to accept a new oil price agreement anywhere short of that promised by the Clark government and warned that a federal export tax on natural gas, the price of which was rising rapidly in the U.S., would be viewed as little short of aggression. In preparation for a drawn-out struggle, Alberta enacted legislation giving the Cabinet the power to determine levels of crude oil production (if they couldn't get the price they wanted, they could stop selling oil).

In October 1980 the federal government brought down its budget, which included the National Energy Program (NEP).[20] This program unilaterally imposed federal authority over energy resources and established new price and revenue sharing regimes in the absence of consent from the West. The price regime involved a complex calculation of a "blended" price determined by the world price and the domestic price. Prices for domestic oil were to go up $2 a year per barrel from 1981 to 1983; $4.50 in 1984 and 1985; and $7 per year thereafter. However, the domestic price would never be allowed to go above 85 per cent of the world price in order to ease the burden on Canadian industries and consumers.

The new price regime was not the issue — it did, after all, go a long way in meeting the West's demands for significant increases. The revenue-sharing regime, however, provoked deep anger in the West. Traditionally oil and gas revenues had been distributed as follows: 45 per cent to the province, 45 per cent to the industry, and ten per cent to the federal government. By 1979 this had changed to: 49 per cent to the province, 39 per cent to the industry, and 12 per cent to the federal government. The NEP revenue formula for 1983 changed this drastically: 41 per cent to the province, 31. 6 per cent to the industry, and 27. 5 per cent to the federal government. NEP also established policies, mainly incentives, to encourage the Canadianization of the oil and gas industry (the goal was 50 per cent by 1990), as well as to push non-conventional developments and frontier exploration in order to reach energy self-sufficiency. A greatly expanded federal government role directly in energy development, through Petro-Can, was also promised.

The complicated formula for determining generous federal incentives in order to encourage frontier exploration, besides encouraging Canadianization, also determined that the focus of exploration would shift to areas controlled by the federal government — in the north and off the east coast. Some aspects of NEP were clearly in the public interest — like the bigger public role in the oil and gas industry and the effort to carve a Canadian-controlled industry out of what had hitherto been the near private, monopolistic preserve of the foreign-owned major oil multinationals. In the West these good points were lost in the anger over the federal effort unilaterally to determine the shape of the industry and to grab a huge share of the wealth being produced. Indeed, the view in Alberta, shared with more or less intensity by Saskatchewan and B.C., was that this was nothing more than a naked federal effort to take over control of energy resources and to appropriate an increasing, and unjust, federal share of the revenue. As Premier Lougheed declared, "They'd like to siphon off western resource money that will be gone in a few years."[21] Lougheed expressed a view of Ottawa's approach to the West, a view increasingly shared in the West generally: "Let's make sure the West is suitably subservient and we continue to get cheap food and cheap oil and the tax revenue flows."[22]

This confrontation over energy resource policy was deepened by Trudeau's declared intention, with the support of only Ontario and New Brunswick, to proceed with the patriation and significant amendment of Canada's constitution.[23] Western provincial governments viewed this determination as a blatant attempt to increase the power of the federal government at the expense of provincial powers. The federal government, it was felt widely in the West, was determined to get through naked power what it couldn't get through negotiation — control of Western resources and a growing share of the wealth realized from these resources. Even Premier Blakeney, usually circumspect and careful, became exceedingly blunt during a spring, 1980 tour of Central Canada:

> For Western Canadians the reasons for the push towards constitutional reform are not difficult to understand. Ever since Alberta and Saskatchewan became provinces in 1905, people on the prairies have been struggling against the dominant forces in Confederation — the political, business and financial interests in Central Canada — for a say in national policy, for a fair share of the economic and social benefits of this country. We in Saskatchewan thought that resource wealth would finally help us achieve our place in the sun. But as prices of western resources began to rise, and substantial revenues began to accrue to our provincial treasuries, the federal government stepped in. With price controls; an export tax on oil; a unilateral decision to declare provincial royalties nondeductible for income tax purposes. And the Supreme Court of Canada, in the CIGOL and Central Canada potash cases, began to interpret "indirect taxation" and the federal trade and commerce power in ways that threatened to undermine provincial power to manage and tax resources. Those developments have led us to demand constitutional changes that will confirm and strengthen provincial powers over resources.[24]

Overall, the view widely held in the West was that these two federal initiatives — the NEP and the unilateral patriation of the constitution — were nothing less than another concerted effort to make the Ontario perspective on Confederation the "national" perspective through the use of Ontario's considerable political and economic strength. Ontario had won the election for Trudeau, now he was rewarding that province.

In return, Ontario's support of unilateral patriation of the constitution was vital to provide Trudeau what little credibility his initiative had.

Western anger and alienation grew incredibly. Suddenly Western separatism, a long-husbanded dream of a tiny minority of Westerners, became nearly respectable. Meeting halls across the West filled to capacity as the formerly isolated voices of Western separatism found eager listeners. Long cherished as a dream by elements among the traditional agrarian movement, Western separatism found receptive audiences among what commentators variously dubbed "blue-chip separatists"[25] and "the silk stocking crowd."[26] Oilmen, professionals, executives, entrepreneurs, academics, as well as farmers, were reported to be swelling Western separatist ranks. Separatist organizations — Western Federation (West-Fed), Western Canada Concept, United West, Unionest — were growing across the West and making exaggerated membership claims. During the early spring of 1980 the separatists gained their first elected members of a legislative assembly in the West when two Saskatchewan Tory MLAs left the party and founded the Unionest party, committed to Western separation and annexation to the United States. As events unfolded dramatically, the various separatist organizations began to discuss unification.

The debate became more and more heated. Tory Opposition Leader Joe Clark made a series of speeches across the nation in which he argued that Prime Minister Trudeau and his policies were driving Westerners to consider separatism. During a speech at a Calgary dinner Ernest Manning (now a senator) warned of violence should Western separatism become a serious threat. Lougheed expressed the fear of a loss of control of the separatist mood should Ottawa rebuke the West any further. The respected and non-partisan Canada West Foundation suggested that separatist sentiment could explode in the West if the polarization continued and worsened. Blakeney expressed a fear of a separatist surge in 1981. Even Québec's Premier René Lévesque joined the debate, accusing Ottawa of having "ravaged Alberta's resources."[27] Trudeau provided much grist for the Western separatist mill with his explicitly contemptuous dismissal of the movement, warning the West not to use separatism to blackmail the federal government.

The publication of a series of public opinion polls documenting the growth of Western separatist sentiment further deepened the debate. The *Financial Post* reported a secret Alberta government poll that found over 20 per cent support for separatism among Albertans.[28] A joint *Edmonton Journal–Calgary Herald* poll found 23 per cent support for separation in Alberta.[29] In Saskatchewan, a poll conducted for the CBC in summer 1980 found that ten per cent would vote for a separatist party if one appeared on the hustings.[30] A poll conducted by Edmonton publisher Mel Hurtig found 14 per cent pro-separatist sentiment in Alberta,[31] and a similar figure was reported by a later CBC poll in the West as a whole.[32]

Needless to say, 1980–81 will go down in history as years of Western anger of unprecedented depth. The crisis, in fact, deepened.

In February 1981 Lougheed warned Albertans to "prepare to suffer and bleed"[33] in the battle with Ottawa. The four Western premiers met and began to revive traditional grievances regarding the tariff and freight rates. B.C.'s Premier Bennett claimed that the West contributed, between 1973 and 1980, almost 45 per cent of Canada's total economic growth, while Ontario, 25 per cent larger in population, contributed only 28 per cent in the same period.[34] He alleged a massive and unjust transfer of wealth from the West to Central Canada. On March 1, 1981 Alberta cut the flow of oil eastward by five per cent, or 60,000 barrels a day, an unthinkable act just a year before. In April, an Alberta cabinet minister accused Ottawa of "bare-faced aggression" against Alberta.[35] Ontario worsened the situation by an arrogant proposal for a national sharing of resource revenues.[36] In May, Lougheed accused Trudeau, "mandarins" in the federal civil service, and the eastern-based media of orchestrating a "conspiracy" against the West to end its boom.[37] On June 1, 1981, Alberta cut the flow of oil eastward by a further five per cent.

Western support for Confederation was at an all-time low. A Gallup Poll conducted in early 1981 found that 25 per cent of people in the Prairie provinces, and 20 per cent of the people of B.C. believed that Canada would break up.[38] A poll conducted by the Canada West Foundation in the spring of 1981 obtained some rather ominous results.[39] No less than 36 per cent of Westerners agreed that "Western Canadians get so few benefits from being part of Canada that they might as well go it on their own." Forty-nine per cent of Albertans agreed. Fully 84 per cent of Westerners agreed that "the West usually gets ignored in national politics because the political parties depend upon Québec and Ontario for most of their vote," and 61 per cent agreed that "Western Canada has sufficient resources and industry to survive on its own." Such results were the cause of deep foreboding since they indicated a growing, general disaffection among Westerners.

This general disaffection was fertile ground for the firm 10 per cent separatist sentiment in the West as a whole (17 per cent in Alberta). The depth of alienation and accompanying political crisis is well illustrated by two events that occurred in Saskatchewan during that period. In January 1981 the biggest rally ever held in the small city of Weyburn took place, sponsored by the separatist organization, West-Fed. Anywhere from 900 to 1400 people attended, depending on whose count you believe.[40] In May 1981, in Yorkton, another small Saskatchewan city, a pro-federalist group, annoyed at the growing separatist agitation in the region, organized a meeting in support of Canadian unity. They were modest in their expectations. Only 200 chairs were put out. Nine people came.[41] Needless to say optimism about the viability of Confederation was rare indeed in the West.

UNCERTAIN VICTORIES

The same day (June 1, 1981) that Lougheed staged in his second five per cent cut in the flow of oil eastward, Trudeau finally made a significantly conciliatory speech at Fredericton, New Brunswick. In that speech, Trudeau said he foresaw "improved regional representation as the next issue for constitutional reform" recognizing "a common perception that legitimate regional representatives do not exercise enough influence in the Canadian parliament and therefore in the national Government."[42] Gestures of conciliation recurred from both sides largely because the impasse was creating an impossible situation for both Trudeau and the Western premiers. Constitutional opinion was divided, but many experts argued that Trudeau could not hope to gain the patriation and significant amendment of the constitution with the consent of only two of ten provinces. There was no consensus in appeal court decisions in Québec, Newfoundland, and Manitoba. The Supreme Court confused the issue further by ruling that "substantial" provincial consent was required for such moves by convention but not by law. Therefore Trudeau could act legally in a unilateral fashion, but such action would be conventionally improper. In order to obtain patriation and amendment without more deeply dividing the nation, Trudeau clearly needed to win some of the eight dissenting provinces over. It would be a seriously divisive outcome if all the provinces of one region, like the West, continued in opposition.

The Western premiers, especially Lougheed and Blakeney, were deeply worried about the developing separatist sentiment. Clearly a continued impasse could only encourage this trend. Lougheed's decision to turn down the flow of oil eastward had led him to the precipice: if he continued the shut-down Ottawa would eventually assert federal power to stop him, perhaps completely taking over regulation of the energy sector, justified on the grounds of defending the national interest from Lougheed's sabotage. Such an event would lose what gains Alberta had made and obviously provide an incredible stimulus to separatist sentiment. Lougheed needed a way out or he risked disaster. Therefore the needs of Lougheed and Trudeau came together, setting the stage for a compromise on both oil-and-gas policy and the constitution, a compromise out of which both sides could claim victory. By yielding a bit on oil and gas prices and revenues, and on resources in general, Trudeau could hope to woo the Western provinces to his constitutional package. By yielding a bit on oil and gas prices and revenues, Lougheed could hope to extricate himself from an increasingly dangerous political stance.

In September, 1981 Ottawa and Alberta announced a new energy-pricing agreement to be in place until 1986. Alberta agreed to accept a slightly modified NEP in principle and to accept the principle that the domestic oil price would never rise beyond 75 per cent of world prices. Finally, Alberta agreed to the maintenance of a low domestic price for natural gas. In exchange Alberta obtained substantial price hikes for oil — more than double the increases earlier agreed to by Ottawa. Additionally, Ottawa promised not to impose an export tax on natural gas going into the lucrative American market. A revenue sharing agreement was also approved: 30.2 per cent to the province, 25.5 per cent to Ottawa, and 44.2 per cent to the industry. The proposed price hikes had increased the revenue pie considerably — to a projected $212 billion by 1986. Lougheed and Trudeau toasted the agreement as a victory for both sides — an intelligent compromise that judiciously balanced the interests of Alberta and of the nation.

In early November 1981 a First Ministers' Conference reached agreement on the constitution with the blessing of all provinces except Québec. The Western provinces made some significant gains in wringing concessions from Trudeau. The amending formula — constitutional amendments require the agreement of the House of Commons and at least seven of ten provincial legislatures representing more than half of the population of Canada — gave the West an effective veto. If all four Western provinces were united against an amendment, the amendment would not pass. Additionally, equalization payments and special programs to overcome regional disparities were written into the constitution. Thus the principle of sufficient revenue from the federal government being made available to provinces to maintain a minimum level of services and well-being became a constitutional right. Finally, the new constitution granted the provinces clearer jurisdiction in natural resources, including exploration, development, production, and inter-provincial trade. Furthermore, the provinces' resource taxing powers were made unlimited ("any mode of taxation").

These were clear victories for the West, constitutionally redressing for the first time some of the most basic political grievances of the region. These concessions did little to change the basic economic structure of the West's place in the national economy, but they did give the West, potentially, some of the political powers necessary to extract the maximum benefit from its resource strength. Trudeau had his constitution. The West had its resources. Now the Western regimes could get back to work using the resource-powered boom to encourage diversification, work that had been interrupted by the battle with Ottawa.

It was not to be. The Western boom began to collapse in 1982. The NEP's effects had already cut conventional oil and gas exploration activities in Saskatchewan and Alberta by more than half. The reasons for these cuts were complex. The revenue sharing proposal resulted, the industry declared, in a loss of cash flow of at least $2 billion in the first year of the NEP, thus reducing the funds available for conventional exploration.[43] The NEP itself, because of the generous subsidies and write-offs available, attracted exploration funds to frontier and offshore exploration. The NEP's Canadianization incentives encouraged a rash of take-overs, or buy-ins, of foreign firms by Canadian interests, further reducing the cash available for exploration (this accounted for $5.1 billion in 1981 alone). The continuing uncertainty of the situation, as well, encouraged many in the industry to engage in a kind of "capital strike," to force further concessions from Ottawa and the provinces.

President Reagan, while attacking Canada's NEP, opened up U.S. exploration areas on generous terms to drillers who had been active in the Canadian oil patch. Wells drilled in Saskatchewan fell from 1498 in 1980 to 807 in 1981. By August of 1982 only 147 of the 465 oil rigs once active in the West were drilling.[44] With the new year the recession that had plagued the rest of Canada finally caught up with the West. World oil prices began to fall, and continued to fall. The combined effects of conservation and high prices had deeply cut into consumer demand for oil and gas, and this, together with maximum production from new sources (North Sea oil particularly), resulted in a glut on world oil markets. The 1981 OPEC price stalled at $34(US) and spot prices, which in 1980-81 had reached as much as $40(US), began to fall. By 1983 the OPEC price was $29(US) and the average spot price was $26(US).[45] Potash, uranium, and grain prices all softened. Western unemployment figures rose dramatically.

Alberta and Saskatchewan had enjoyed near-full employment during the boom, and had often complained of a shortage of skilled labour. Alberta's unemployment figures more than doubled between October 1981 and October 1982 (40,000 to 97,000). By March 1983 Alberta's unemployment figure had reached 146,000 — almost four times the number in 1981, representing 11 per cent of the labour force. Similarly, Saskatchewan's number of unemployed doubled in the same period, from 18,000 in 1981, to 28,000 in 1982 to 37,000 in 1983, reaching almost seven per cent of the labour force. Unemployment insurance commission payments in Alberta went up 89 per cent from January to May 1982. While such unemployment figures were less than the national average, they were dramatic because they came about so quickly. One year, Alberta and Saskatchewan had very little unemployment, the next year they suddenly faced double the number of unemployed.[46]

The boom was over. Saskatchewan, two years before the economic leader of the nation in terms of growth, plunged to the predicted lowest growth rate in the country in 1983.[47] And the Conference Board predicted that Alberta, the envy of Central Canada during the boom, would enjoy virtually no growth in 1983.[48] In 1983, for the first time in history, all four Western provincial governments simultaneously faced serious deficits.[49] Contrary to general perception the boom had never been general in the West. B.C. had already long faced unemployment levels higher than the national average — indeed higher than anywhere but Québec or Atlantic Canada — due to a collapse in the lumber industry. In fact, in August 1982, B.C. had set a record of sorts — the unemployment rate reached 13.8 per cent, the highest since 1946.[50] The revenues from B.C.'s small oil and gas industry had simply helped prevent a bad situation from becoming worse. Manitoba had not directly shared in the boom at all — the province had experienced the national recession from the beginning. Manitoba's oil-and-gas and potash industries remained fond hopes as the province encouraged exploration, begging any capital, foreign or otherwise, to get to work. The fact was that the so-called "boom" had been limited to Saskatchewan and Alberta. But in 1982 even that limited, narrow Western boom began to fizzle, as world prices for the provinces' resources began to fall. Alberta's share of $212 billion in oil and gas revenues became a piece of paper.

The massive investment coalitions to develop the tar sands and heavy oil fell like houses of cards.[51] Oil from the tar sands in Alberta could no longer be as profitably produced. Syncrude, a tar sands project started in 1978, producing about 100,000 barrels per day, shelved a $2 billion expansion plan. The smaller Suncor, established in 1967, abandoned a more modest expansion. The Alsands consortium (Shell, Petro-Canada, Amoco, Hudson's Bay, Gulf, and Dome), involved in a tar sands project slated to cost over $13 billion, abandoned the project, claiming that they might proceed in the indefinite future with a scaled-down version. Imperial Oil's $11 billion Cold Lake project was stalled, to be picked up again on a much more modest scale in 1983 to produce mainly asphalt for the U.S. market. Studies for a new tar sands project by a Petro-Canada and Nova partnership stopped. The proposed $35 billion Alaska highway gas pipeline was forgotten.[52] The proposal of a consortium (Husky, Gulf, Shell, Petro-Canada, and Saskoil) to develop a $1 billion heavy oil upgrader in Saskatchewan was abandoned.[53]

The West had lost again. First, large pieces of the boom were stolen by the federal government. Then, the boom was stolen by world market conditions. The West's great victories, at least temporarily, seemed hollow and meaningless. And even Ottawa began to hurt, as expected oil and gas revenues from the NEP agreement fell by a full two-thirds and the costs of frontier exploration incentives became enormous[54] — in 1982, the total bill for all exploration on northern Crown lands was $1.6 billion, $1 billion of which was paid by federal grants.[55] So, Ottawa was sharing some of the pain.

The political results of the collapse were fairly immediate. 1982 elections were held in both Saskatchewan and Alberta. In Saskatchewan, in April 1982, Blakeney's apparently unassailable regime was defeated. It was more than defeated: the once-proud NDP government was thoroughly humiliated by the Tories. The Tories won 55 seats with 54 per cent of the vote, while the NDP was reduced to 38 per cent and nine seats, their worst showing since 1938.[56] The Saskatchewan separatists won only about three per cent of the vote.

The Tories swept the province on two issues: a promise, in a recession context, to put "money in the pocket" of the electorate to help deal with the crisis; and an attack on the NDP government for having betrayed the West, first, in the defeat of the 1979 Clark government (for which federal NDP MPs had voted), second, in the constitutional accord that had been largely authored by Saskatchewan's Premier Blakeney and Deputy Premier Romanow. The NDP in the West, the Saskatchewan Tories argued, were just a bunch of closet Liberals, always eager to defend federal Liberal initiatives in the crunch. Upon victory, the Saskatchewan Tory government began to dismantle the edifice built by Blakeney during the resource struggle. The role of the crown corporations in resources was downplayed and their right to join any new investment was curtailed. Further, three months after victory, the new Saskatchewan Tory government gave the oil industry in the province a massive tax break: a one-year tax holiday on new conventional wells and a five-year holiday on deep wells.[57] Top employees of the crown corporations, and scores of civil servants, tainted with the socialist stigma, were fired. Arms were opened to private investors, apologies were made for the years of NDP socialist abuse, and Saskatchewan was declared unreservedly open for business.

In Alberta, the once-proud Lougheed, who had campaigned in two previous elections against the federal government's arrogance, was forced to fight the November 1982 election locally. He was no doubt haunted by the speed with which the Alberta electorate had turned against the Liberal government in 1921, the UFA government in 1935, and the Social Credit government in 1971. Blakeney's fate in April no doubt further concerned him. Lougheed campaigned on four issues: the use of the $11 billion Heritage Trust Fund for current expenditures like mortgage interest relief, his record, his eminently constructive views on Canada, and his economic recovery program. There was no fed-bashing, indeed, Lougheed was on the defensive as his critics argued that his oil-price agreement and support of the constitutional accord represented a caving in to Ottawa. Lougheed won his greatest victory — 63 per cent of the vote and 75 of 79 seats,[58] but, ominously the separatists won almost 12 per cent of the vote (though they won no seats, losing the seat won in a by-election in February 1981 in Olds-Didsbury). The Western separatists, plagued by a reactionary ideology (Trudeau was a communist, the social welfare system had to be dismantled, pure free enterprise was the way to go),[59] lost much of the confidence they had among the electorate. No matter how large the victory, Lougheed was on the defensive — about the oil agreement, about the constitution, about the recession, about his April gift of $5.4 billion to the oil industry in tax breaks.[60] The re-elected premier was a chastened man.

So ended the historic confrontation of the West with Ottawa over resources. Alberta, driven to the wall by a steep fall in world oil prices, was forced to go cap-in-hand to Ottawa to beg that the 75 per cent world price rule not be imposed, if this would lead to a steep fall in domestic oil prices. As the so-called "energy crisis" ended, Alberta found it difficult to sell its natural gas to the U.S. — the gas had become too pricey, according to the Americans. In Saskatchewan, the oil collapse had been accompanied by a fall in prices for uranium, potash, and wheat, confirming Blakeney's worst fears. The Blakeney government was replaced by a government willing to do virtually anything private capital demanded in order to sustain development.

This general conservative turn in the West was dramatically confirmed in B.C. with the re-election of the Socred government on a platform of severe restraint and accelerated, large-scale resource development. NDP leader and former Premier Barrett's election campaign promising work and wages through a large-scale public works program, as well as his promise to back off from the heavy-handed wage controls Premier Bennett had imposed on public sector workers, failed to bring about what everyone initially believed would be an NDP victory. The 1981 re-election of the NDP in Manitoba clearly had not represented a trend, but rather had resulted from Tory Premier Sterling Lyon's harsh program of cutbacks and restraint.

The circle was now complete. The West once again was forced to seek development on any terms. Uncontrolled development, resource give-aways, foreign financed mega-projects were all again in fashion. Unbridled free enterprise again had become the solution to the crisis. The West, despite the great victories, was back where it had been in the 1960s, still destined as Clifford Sifton had so crisply said, to exploit "the wealth of the field, of the forest and of the mine . . . in vast quantities." The West's economic place in Confederation, in all essential respects, remained unchanged, despite the constitutional victory on the resource question. The West was still a hewer of wood and drawer of water — now and for the foreseeable future.

Ottawa proceeded to rub salt into the West's wounds with an announcement that would have been unthinkable during the West's boom. On February 1, 1983 federal transport minister Jean-Luc Pepin announced that Ottawa was determined to dismantle the Crow Rate,[61] long a symbol of the West's struggle for concessions from Ottawa. First won in 1897, the Crow Rate, put into federal statute in 1926, cheapened the cost of transporting grain out of the West. In fact, in 1983 Western farmers paid only about one-fifth of the actual cost of shipping grain to market by rail. The National Farmers' Union estimated that dismantling the Crow Rate would result in a half-billion dollar loss to Western grain farmers. The Crow Rate was first put in place in recognition of the West's contributions to building Canada — the giveaways to the railways, the tariff protected prices paid for Central Canadian industrial goods, and the vital importance of wheat as one of Canada's principal exports. Ottawa was determined to end that concession or, as it turned out, at least drastically to erode the Crow benefit (by 1993 farmers were paying about one-third of the cost). Once again, the Western provinces confronted the reality of federal power — Ottawa can give, but Ottawa can also take away. Ottawa had given the West what it wanted in the constitution on resources. But Ottawa was determined to take away the Crow Rate.

Not very much had really changed.

9

THE RISE AND FALL OF THE NEO-LIBERAL PARTIES, 1982–1993

When Brian Mulroney swept aside Turner's Liberals on 4 September 1984, few Canadians realized what had been set in motion. The new prime minister set a series of records: with 211 of 282 seats, the Tories enjoyed the largest parliamentary majority in Canadian history; with 50 per cent of the popular vote, they had the largest sweep since Diefenbaker won 53 per cent in 1958; with 29 per cent and 40 seats, the Liberals were reduced to the lowest popular vote and smallest parliamentary caucus since Confederation; with 50 per cent of the vote in Québec, the Tories won their first popular majority in that province since 1891. Further, the Tories won the largest popular vote in every province, and a decisive parliamentary majority in all regions: 58 of 77 seats in the West, 18 of 32 seats in Atlantic Canada, 67 of 95 seats in Ontario, 58 of 75 seats in Québec, and 3 of 3 seats in the North. The West, however, remained ambivalent about Mulroney and his reconstructed Tories, giving him a popular vote majority (and all 21 seats) only in Alberta. Many voters in Manitoba, Saskatchewan, and B.C. remained loyal to the NDP, giving them 35 per cent of the vote and 8 seats in B.C., 38 per cent and 5 seats in Saskatchewan, and 27 per cent and 4 seats in Manitoba.[1] Nevertheless, the West was rewarded, obtaining 13 seats in Mulroney's first cabinet. No longer could Westerners complain that they were excluded from power at the centre, as they had been during the Trudeau period.

Mulroney was a man of profoundly conservative views, and a politician with few scruples.[2] His rise to power in the Tory party, generously greased by funds from powerful corporate backers, was a case study in dirty tricks and nasty deals. Mulroney's close links to the corporate sector were important. His successful career as labour lawyer and miracle negotiator on the management side had brought him to the attention of key figures in the Canadian corporate establishment, the most important of whom was Paul Desmarais, who controlled the Canadian-based international conglomerate, Power Corporation. Mulroney's performance so impressed Desmarais and others that doors were opened for him that finally led to his appointment as president of the Iron Ore Company, a billion-dollar firm employing 7,000 workers.

By the time Mulroney finally won the leadership in 1983 on the heels of a well-financed campaign to destroy Clark, he was on the boards of directors of ten leading companies, including Provigo and the Canadian Imperial Bank of Commerce, and counted as personal friends people like Conrad Black as well as Paul Desmarais. His corporate credentials were, therefore, impeccable, yet remained those of a loyal servant to capital, a reliable lieutenant on whom the captains of industry and finance could rely. He had got where he was not because he had made a fortune on his own, but simply because he had performed brilliantly on behalf of those he served. He had rolled up his sleeves and got labour settlements. He had fired those he was ordered to fire. He had closed down Schefferville, Québec, when the owners of the Iron Ore Company told him to do so.

The new prime minister openly embraced the neo-liberal agenda from the outset and, despite artful zigs and zags required to reassure the public, proceeded with its loyal implementation. Armed with the pro-business, pro-free-market policy proposals generated by the $21-million, three-year-old Macdonald Royal Commission on the economy, which Mulroney enthusiastically characterized as "some excellent ideas" with an analysis "essentially the same as our own,"[3] and the new government's shorter, more succinct *A New Direction for Canada: An Agenda for Economic Renewal*,[4] issued two months after the election and which clearly laid out the government's intentions, the Mulroney government went to work. The business lobby was delighted, and the alliance between the Mulroney government and corporate Canada was cemented. As Laurent Thibault, former president of the Canadian Manufacturers' Association, said, "They began with a basic agenda, and they stuck to it."[5] Thomas d'Aquino of the Business Council on National Issues was equally pleased, endorsing the government for successfully achieving "a very strong public acceptance of what I call some of the very fundamental values important to business."[6]

The key ingredients of the Mulroney's neo-liberal agenda have been well documented.[7] The agenda included cutbacks in social spending, including the significant erosion of Canada's social security net; an assault on the incomes and living standards of wage and salary earners, while the total share of wealth flowing to capital and its privileged servants was increased; a weakening of federal power *vis-à-vis* the provinces; a program of deregulation and privatization and a move to free market forces as the engine of social and economic development; a free trade deal with the U.S. as a prelude to the establishment of a continental free market encompassing Canada, the U.S., and Mexico; and a deliberate process of discrediting and disabling government as a popular democratic tool available to the people to shape the economy and society. This last item was achieved largely by burdening governments with huge annual deficits and a crippling debt, and by shifting the increasing tax burden from the rich and the corporate sector to those in the middle income category.

Taken as a whole, this amounted to an ambitious agenda. It involved a major re-structuring of Canadian society and the economy and a rewriting of the post-Depression, post-war political consensus of Canada as a society based on a mixed economy, generally committed to incremental increases in a universal social security net, a humane regulation of the worst features of unregulated, free enterprise capitalism, and slowly advancing standards of living for wage and salary earners. The neo-liberal agenda was an effort to overturn that consensus and to set the clock back fifty years and more to the era of the unregulated free market and a modified Social Darwinism as the basic creed governing interventions to assist the weak, the afflicted, and the vulnerable. Ironically, Mulroney enjoyed the enthusiastic support of three provincial governments in the West, the region where the universal social security net and the interventionist government had been pioneered and successfully tested by the CCF and Social Credit movements.

The neo-liberal counter-revolution in the West evolved through three distinct stages: 1982 to 1986 was a period of hesitation and uncertainty; 1986 to 1990 was a period of arrogant ascendancy, clarity of purpose, and sweeping implementation; 1990 to 1993 was the period of collapse, accompanied by unprecedented levels of popular hostility and opposition, amid the unraveling of a host of scandals and revelations of economic incompetence.

HESITATION, 1982–1986

During the period from 1982 to 1986, neo-liberal provincial governments in the West went through some severe tests of political will due to uncertain popular support. In British Columbia the lessons were particularly painful, and in the forefront of neo-liberal thinking was the unmistakable fact that Socred premier Bill Bennett had not fared well. His May 1983 initiative had provoked massive opposition, intensifying the traditional class polarization in B.C., as labour and a variety of pro-labour groups coalesced in Operation Solidarity and organized huge anti-government protests, threatening a general strike.[8] In exchange for Solidarity calling off the strike, Bennett promised a reconsideration of the restraint program and closer consultations in future with labour, putting an end to the elevated confrontations. During the struggle, former NDP premier Dave Barrett stepped down and was replaced by Robert Skelly, considered to be on the centre-left of the party. Polls recorded Bennett's deepening unpopularity, as well as an almost certain victory for Skelly and the NDP in the next election. In May 1986 — the third anniversary of his neo-liberal initiative — Bill Bennett announced his retirement after more than a decade as premier, a victim of the unpopularity he had earned. The people of B.C. flatly rejected the new agenda.

On the Prairies, despite clear victories, uncertainty prevailed in neo-liberal circles. Premier Lougheed's massive victory in November 1982 — 63 per cent of the vote and 75 of 79 seats — had been blemished by the 12 per cent won by the separatists and the defensive, almost apologetic campaign Lougheed was forced to run. Further, after the election the recession in Alberta continued due to low world prices for oil and grain, falling natural gas prices, and chronic drought reducing the harvest. Lougheed's decision to retire, and his replacement by his old Edmonton Eskimo teammate and former energy minister, Don Getty, increased that uncertainty. Getty was widely viewed as less than competent and inspiring.

In Manitoba, Tory premier Sterling Lyon's effort at neo-liberalism had turned him into a one-term wonder, resulting in the NDP's return to power under Howard Pawley in 1981. Though there was little doubt about the free enterprise commitment of the Alberta electorate, Manitoba's voted against the neo-liberal experiment.

The Devine sweep in Saskatchewan in 1982 — 55 seats and 54 per cent of the vote — reduced the NDP under Blakeney to 9 seats and 38 per cent, the party's worst showing since 1938. Seats held by the party since 1934 were lost, and even the party's citadels of working-class urban support largely went Tory. The party was virtually annihilated in rural areas, feeding speculation about the party's ability to reconstruct the farmer-worker alliance which had kept the CCF/NDP in power from 1944 to 1964 and 1971 to 1982.

As a result, Saskatchewan remained a beacon of hope for neo-liberalism.[9] The humiliation of the NDP in the cradle of Canadian social democracy was seen by many as a watershed in Canadian politics. But Devine hesitated. The recession continued and deepened. Once asked at a press conference what would happen if all resource sectors in Saskatchewan experienced a downturn at the same time, Blakeney had commented, "that would be an economic nightmare." By the mid-1980s, Devine lived that nightmare. Oil prices continued low, potash prices and sales fell, uranium was pushed back in the doldrums after Chernobyl. Agriculture faced a long-term crunch as one-third of Saskatchewan's farmers teetered on the brink of bankruptcy. No incumbent government had ever survived such an economic collapse in Saskatchewan. The recession that helped elect Devine became in fact a full-scale provincial depression.

Compared to what was to come later, the Devine government only played cat-and-mouse with the neo-liberal agenda during its first term. The civil service was purged of socialists and NDPers, but there were no cuts in its size. The province was "open for business," and the government catered to the business lobby with deregulation, a legislative attack on trade union rights, and a host of tax breaks for corporations, resource companies (especially the oil and natural gas sector), and the affluent. Government support for free enterprise was made manifest by an endless stream of public cash and loan guarantees to help big and small entrepreneurs develop projects, from barbecue briquettes and shopping carts to pork plants and oil up-graders. Many of these schemes were foolish, others were self-evident failures from the outset, others were simply fiscally irresponsible. But all had the effect of mortgaging the future of the province through deepening debt and appalling future financial liabilities through loan guarantees.

The Devine government attacked Saskatchewan's large Crown sector — the Crowns were curtailed, bled of revenues, hamstrung with hostile boards and CEOs, and deprived of their public policy role. Yet there were only a few privatizations and a sell-off of blocks of government shares in a variety of key enterprises. The government denied that it intended to privatize the Crowns, while preparing the way: "participation" bonds were sold in SaskOil, and eventually one-third of the oil Crown's shares were sold off at low prices; bonds were sold in the utility Crown, and small pieces of SaskPower's assets were sold off. The Crown-owned Prince Albert Pulp Co. (Papco) was sold back to Weyerhaeuser, and created considerable controversy if only because the original pulp deal had been instrumental in the fall of the Thatcher government in 1971.[10] Meanwhile the government's accumulated deficit grew — as a result of a combination of the continuing depression, uncontrolled spending, and irresponsible cuts on the revenue side — from nothing to over $1.7 billion in four years.

Despite these efforts to steer a "moderate" right-wing course, while carefully preparing the ground for the future, public support for the Devine government collapsed, as by-elections revealed that the urban NDP vote was coming home in an unprecedented way, just as Tory rural support was slipping out the back door largely to the Liberals.

It was in this context that Premier Devine opted for his rural strategy. The strategy was simple and brutal — write off the urban centres as NDP strongholds, where Tory support was soft in the first place, and concentrate on rural and small-town Saskatchewan. In pursuit of that strategy the Devine government encouraged an unprecedented political polarization between rural and urban Saskatchewan. Welfare recipients were attacked, social support programs for urban residents were slashed, trade unions were bashed. The premier railed against outside labour big shots and red-baited the NDP as Marxists. Tory labour minister Grant Schmidt, a small-town lawyer, attacked trade unionists and city professionals as unduly affluent and charged that their outlandish wage and salary demands were made at the expense of poor farmers and rural residents.

While attacking urban residents, especially wage earners and welfare recipients, and ignoring the plight of the urban poor, the Devine government tended to Saskatchewan's crisis-ridden farmers. Devine personally took over the agriculture portfolio to deal with the farm crisis. Whirlwind trips to Ottawa by the premier squeezed concessions from the feds. The premier dashed off to meetings in the U.S. and Europe to plead for a stop to the wheat wars. More concretely, he promised to put the provincial treasury at risk to save rural Saskatchewan — and he did so, mounting a series of programs from cheap money to production cost relief, from hog incentives to farm purchase support, and from loan guarantees to tax relief. These were estimated by the premier's own officials to amount to $36,000 per farmer for a total of $2.4 billion.

An examination of the numbers — Saskatchewan was divided almost equally between rural and urban voters but a rural vote counted much more than an urban vote — as well as the massive NDP victory in Regina North East, suggested a rather ominous possible outcome. It was conceivable that, given a strong NDP sweep in urban areas with large majorities, and a tighter Tory-led race in rural areas, the NDP could emerge as the Official Opposition despite having the largest popular vote.

ASCENDANCY, 1986–1990

Although it started off badly in March, 1986 eventually proved a good year for neo-liberalism in the West. The setback in March was the victory in Manitoba of NDP premier Pawley who won the closest election in the province's history, an election many expected him to lose.[11] Brian Mulroney punished Manitoba a few months later by awarding a $1.8 billion CF-18A fighter aircraft maintenance contract to the Montreal-based Canadair rather than to the Winnipeg-based Bristol Aerospace, despite recommendations to the contrary by a panel of 75 experts.

Two months later, on May 8, 1986, Premier Getty led the Alberta Tories to yet another victory. But it wasn't comparable to the easy victories won by Lougheed in the past. The depression had taken its toll,[12] and the electorate punished the Getty government while re-electing it: Tory support fell to 51 per cent and 60 of 83 seats (in 1982 Lougheed had won 62 per cent and 72 seats) and six cabinet ministers were defeated. More ominously, the NDP came from virtually nowhere to win 29 per cent and 16 seats, becoming the Official Opposition, an unthinkable event in Alberta just a few years before. The NDP's strong showing in Alberta caused deep concern among Tories in Saskatchewan and B.C., where elections were also imminent.

Elections were held in B.C. and Saskatchewan in October 1986. In B.C., two factors defined the election — the return of William Vander Zalm to politics and the opening day fumble of NDP leader Robert Skelly. Vander Zalm had been the lightning rod of public hostility as Minister of Human Resources in the early days of the Bennett government, when he played the leading role in dismantling much the Barrett government had accomplished in social program innovations. After being sidelined to less controversial ministries by the premier, he had voluntarily left politics under a cloud in 1983, branded as a right-wing yahoo, and had been further rebuffed in his political aspirations by his defeat by the NDP's Mike Harcourt for the Vancouver mayor's position.

In an incredible rebirth, Vander Zalm, now an outsider on the right-wing fringe of the Socred establishment, took the Socred leadership two months before the election. During the election, there was another rebirth — Vander Zalm campaigned as a fresh face who would listen to the people and do politics differently and better than the discredited Bennett government. The past was forgotten and forgiven.

The NDP's campaign never fully recovered from Skelly's 30-second anxiety attack in the full view of the media at the press conference convened to kick off the NDP campaign. Fighting hostile media and a well-financed Socred machine, and hampered in the two-way fight by repeated media replays of his election kick-off fumble, Skelly managed to improve the NDP's popular vote. But it was not enough. The NDP lost the election many expected them to win — Vander Zalm's new-age Socreds took 49 per cent of the vote and 47 seats, the NDP took 43 per cent and 22 seats.

In the more pivotal Saskatchewan election the Tories carried out the most deceptive campaign in the province's history. Devine invoked the ghost of Tommy Douglas and claimed the traditional CCF populist turf now belonged to him. The government lied about its post-election intentions regarding privatization and social spending. The public accounts were kept under wraps, while Finance Minister Gary Lane predicted a deficit of under $400 million. After the election it became clear he had "underestimated" the deficit by over $800 million. Further, there was an orgy of spending promises to buy the rural vote and, for good measure, hundreds of millions in subsidized mortgages, low-interest home-improvement loans, and matching grants to woo urban voters. Still unsure of victory, Devine begged Mulroney for help. Mulroney intervened at the last moment with a billion-dollar deficiency payment to western farmers, half of which was earmarked for Saskatchewan farmers.

Premier Devine's rural strategy paid handsome dividends on October 20, 1986 when 33 of 36 predominantly rural seats were won by Tories. The last-minute Tory effort to buy some of the urban vote netted 5 of 26 urban seats, 4 of which were middle class seats in Regina and Saskatoon. The Tories won their rural seats with about 53 per cent of the vote and their few urban seats with 37 per cent. The NDP, on the other hand, swept the major urban centres with 21 seats and 52 per cent of the urban vote, while being decimated in the countryside where they had 2 seats and 38 per cent of the vote. The outcome of the election was deeply disturbing. Devine proved that the farm vote could be bought. Granted, at over $3 billion, it was an expensive purchase, but it was still a purchase. Worse, Devine won that rural support after his government, over its four-and-a-half years, took public pride in its harsh approach to the poor, urban workers, trade unionists, and the urban unemployed.

Even more ominous, for the first time in its history, the province was clearly cleaved along urban and rural lines. The urban wage and salary earner largely went NDP, while the rural vote went Tory. This tension was increased by the fact that the NDP won the election by over 3,300 votes, but didn't win enough seats to form the government. For the first time in the province's history there was a government with a large majority of seats in power in spite of winning less of the popular vote than the major opposition party. This failure to win a plurality of votes immediately called into question the legitimacy of the Tory government. Many urban voters believed the election was stolen from them by the Tories with their bought rural vote.

The period from 1986 to 1990 was an ugly political era in the West as the three neo-liberal premiers proceeded to implement their agendas, now finally revealed to the public. The last holdout against complete neo-liberal hegemony in the region fell eighteen months later when the government of Manitoba premier Pawley was brought down in 1988.[13] Despite the relative health of the provincial economy, Pawley had been caught up in the fiscal hysteria promoted by his colleagues, Ottawa, and the business lobby. He opted for some sharp fiscal corrections, including a sudden 24 per cent rise in AutoPac rates, large tax increases that hurt the working and middle classes, as well as a nagging policy of underfunding health, social welfare, and education. He also allowed himself to be badgered into supporting the Meech Lake Accord in 1987, which became increasingly unpopular in the province. As a result Pawley lost his razor-thin majority in the Legislature when disaffected backbencher James Walding voted against his government and brought it down. In the ensuing election Tory leader Gary Filmon presented himself as "socially progressive" and "fiscally conservative," declaring social, health and education programs safe from the neo-liberal knife. Tory Ottawa tantalized the Manitoba electorate with a wave of patronage just before the election: millions in flood compensation payments, more money under the Western Diversification Program, a microbiology laboratory expansion, and millions for lake clean-up. The unspoken message from Mulroney was clear: remember the CF-18A? These are the good things that could continue to happen if you elect a government friendlier to Ottawa.

In the April 1988 election new NDP leader Gary Doer went down to dramatic defeat — the NDP fell from 30 seats to 12, the Tories dropped from 26 to 25, while the Liberals under the charismatic Sharon Carstairs surged from one seat to 20. Later, former premier Pawley admitted his error in judgement: "We were too impressed with the reports of the technicians and the actuaries. We permitted ourselves to lose our political sixth sense." Due to his uncertain mandate and minority government status, new Tory premier Filmon implemented a diluted version of the neo-liberal agenda while moving slowly and relentlessly in the same direction. Still, the defeat of the NDP had national significance — the NDP's version of moderate, social democracy had been expunged from official political life and there was now no provincial government to show there was an alternative road to take, as the Pawley government had done with modest success since the defeat of Lyon in 1981.

THE FREE TRADE ELECTION, 1988

1988 became a banner year for neo-liberalism with the defeat of the last NDP provincial government in the spring, followed by Mulroney's federal victory in November. The November 21, 1988 free trade election allowed Canadians to pass judgement on only one feature of Mulroney's agenda. The massive cuts to social programs, the biggest downloading onto the provinces, and the major privatization moves were all delayed until after the election. Indeed, had the 1988 election

focused clearly on Mulroney's social program and privatization intentions, the outcome might have been very different. As it was — with
the election virtually exclusively focused on free trade — the popular
outcome was uncertain until the ballots were counted, and the popular
result was close: Tories, 43 per cent and 169 seats; Liberals, 32 per cent
and 83 seats; NDP, 20 per cent and 43 seats. Though Mulroney won a
clear majority in the House of Commons, the public rejected free trade
in what was a single issue election: 52 per cent opposed, 43 per cent
in favour.[14]

As a result of intensive negotiations over a few months, the U.S.
obtained most of what it had been unsuccessfully demanding for 50
years and more. Further, this decision was not based on any clear view
of the long-term consequences for Canada — even the Macdonald
Royal Commission, after expending millions on economic studies and
analyses, argued that free trade with the U.S. had to be a "a leap of
faith." The objectives of the U.S. were, however, clear, and had ominous implications for the West. For years, the U.S. wanted free trade in
energy resources, a free continental market in natural resources generally, and access to Canada's copious supplies of fresh water. On each
and every item the Mulroney government caved in. Many Westerners
knew the obvious immediate dangers of the FTA. Traditional tariff-
protected industrial sectors would die, and they largely did. It was
doubtful if Canada's brewers, packers and canners — indeed, food
processors generally — could survive. Very soon it became clear they
would not. There was no clarity regarding the impact of the FTA on
Canada's diverse and complex agricultural industry, and the worst fears
were quickly realized: two-price wheat ended, oats and barley were
moved out from under the Canadian Wheat Board, and the assault
on Canada's orderly marketing structures continued. It was feared that
many of the branch plants of American parents — now assured by
the FTA of free access to Canada's market — would close and central-
ize production in U.S. plants, or migrate to lower wage areas in the
southern U.S. Many have. Indeed, many Canadians were assured, all
these leaps of faith, these risks, were worth it if Canada could obtain
guarantees of free access to the American market and a reasonable,

mutually binding dispute settlement mechanism. Yet neither of these very limited Canadian objectives was achieved. But at the time those who expressed such concerns were dismissed, in Trade Minister John Crosbie's words, as "security blanket seekers [who] go home at night and put their thumbs in their mouths and worry."[15]

Two words sum up the 1988 free trade election: fear and money. The Liberals and the NDP raised fears regarding the FTA's negative effects on Canada's sovereignty, social programs, and regional development programs.[16] The Tories, in response, linked the FTA to future prosperity. Mulroney made particularly extravagant claims: "Free trade means lower prices for Canadian consumers, better jobs, and greater individual opportunity. Free trade will help the regions of this country and it will do so by creating a broader and deeper pool of national wealth, not just by redistributing existing resources." Trade Minister John Crosbie, not to be outdone, insisted: "Business investment will go up. Canadian exports will increase. Our total Canadian manufacturing output will increase. There will be a net gain of jobs by Canadians."[17]

These were strong claims, but polling revealed that Canadians weren't buying the FTA as Canada's economic panacea and had real concerns about sovereignty and social programs under the FTA. Therefore, the Tories and their allies changed their approach. Mulroney claimed 2 million jobs would be lost if the deal were scrapped. Finance Minister Michael Wilson and Crosbie agreed that the U.S. would rip up the Auto Pact, the dollar would collapse to 70 cents, and interest rates would shoot up to 20 per cent if the deal didn't go through. Saskatchewan premier Grant Devine wondered how his province would be able to sell its hogs, beef, and potash if the deal collapsed. Québec premier Bourassa cited probable U.S. trade retaliation and a flight of capital if Canada withdrew from the FTA. Canada's trade negotiator Simon Reisman foresaw a sombre future Canada where there would be no jobs for our children and grandchildren. Critics of the FTA were maligned. Mulroney accused opponents of fearing change: "They fear change. They fear competition. They, I think, fear the future."[18] Crosbie joined Reisman in smearing FTA opposition as an attempt to "deceive the Canadian people," declaiming that the

Liberals and the NDP were conducting "a negative, twisted, insidious campaign . . . to frighten the Canadian people out of their wits" by spreading "deliberate lies and untruths."[19]

The business lobby commenced an independent economic fear campaign, which included newspaper, radio, and television ads, as well as compulsory meetings with employees for pro-FTA lectures containing dark warnings of economic disaster and massive unemployment if the Tories were defeated and the FTA terminated. Businesses donated over $14 million to the Tories in 1988, representing 58 per cent of the $24.5 million the party raised that year, over double the 1987 figure.[20] Meanwhile, the Liberals were punished, receiving a paltry $1.5 million from business.[21] In fact, in 1988 the Tories raised almost as much as the NDP and the Liberals combined — the Liberals raised $13.2 million and the NDP $11.7 million.[22] Furthermore, the business lobby carried out a $2.3 million ad campaign through the Canadian Alliance for Trade and Job Opportunities, including a four-page newspaper insert which appeared in every daily newspaper in Canada.[23] In August in an effort to destroy NDP leader, Ed Broadbent, the National Citizens' Coalition bought half-page newspaper ads across Canada attacking Broadbent as "very, very scary."[24] Two months later, in the midst of the election campaign, the same group spent over half a million dollars for 700 broadcasts of two radio ads comparing Broadbent to Karl Marx and the Ayatollah Khomeini: "Ed Broadbent, very, very scary."[25] After the election, research by the Royal Commission on Electoral Reform and Party Financing revealed that the pro-FTA business lobby had spent over $6 million on advertising during the campaign and the period immediately preceding it.[26]

Despite his earlier concerns about the deficit, Mulroney put the federal treasury further at risk to buy the election with the public's money. Tory election promises in the period preceding the election amounted to between $12 and $14 billion, ranging from a low of $12 million for water development assistance projects for Western livestock to a high of $6.4 billion for a national child care program, and including $3.2 billion for the Hibernia project, more than half a billion dollars in economic development programs for Québec and $400 million for the Lloydminster oil upgrader in Saskatchewan. Even Mulroney's business supporters were left stunned and speechless by his profligacy.[27]

In the end, Mulroney and his business allies bought the election. But not without a cost. The country was bitterly divided, with a clear majority opposed to the FTA, despite the fact that Mulroney had won a majority of seats in the House of Commons.[28] Every province but Québec and Alberta had voted heavily against the FTA. Besides this regional and linguistic division, there was a clear class polarization — business heavily supported the FTA, while the organized farmers and workers opposed it.[29] Unfortunately, Canada's undemocratic parliamentary system still allowed Mulroney to win a majority government, contributing to growing public despair and cynicism about the political process. Yet Mulroney and the neo-liberal premiers in the West interpreted the election victory as a clear mandate to accelerate their agenda, embarking on a massive privatization program and deep cuts in social spending, provoking widespread public opposition.

After years of conservative rule, neither B.C. nor Alberta had an excessively generous social and health security system, nor an unusually large public sector. The major cuts there awaited the continuing downloading actions of the federal government. Yet, there was still a legacy in B.C. from the Barrett regime and from earlier Socred days when public ownership was a reluctantly accepted, if severely limited, tool of government. Vander Zalm proceeded to increase user fees for residents of long-term and extended care homes by 13 per cent, to raise medicare premiums by 38 per cent, and to slash the prescription drug program for senior citizens. The premier billed these measures as necessary to kill the national view of B.C. as Canada's preferred retirement location.[30] Vander Zalm also continued to sell off public assets: for example, the natural gas division of B.C. Hydro, almost 6 per cent of the Crown's total assets;[31] highway maintenance in 27 of the province's highway districts;[32] and the provincially owned freight railway.[33] Vander Zalm sold off over $ 1.4 billion in public assets in two years. His continuing zeal for program cuts culminated in the premier's violation of the cabinet consensus reached after Bennett's 1983 disaster — to steer away from explicit calls for an ultra right-wing spending restraint program — by raising just such a spectre without even discussing it in cabinet. Coming in the midst of developing economic problems in forestry and in the context of already announced cuts of 6.5 per cent in government department budgets, Vander Zalm's comments appeared to presage another sudden attack similar to the 1983 assault which had pushed labour to the threshold of a general strike and destroyed Bennett's political career.[34] Ignoring the lesson learned that the best and deepest neo-liberal cuts are the quietest cuts of all, Vander Zalm seemed to be thumbing his nose at the public and courting political disaster.

The neo-liberal counter-revolution in the West was most significantly focused on Saskatchewan if only because the long years of social democratic rule had left the province with a comparatively well-developed and expansive social and health security system as well as a large public sector. Further, the counter-revolution was paced in two overlapping phases: first, a process of ransacking the social and health security system, and, second, a program of privatization of public assets. In preparation, the Devine government established a Draconian dictatorship through the *Government Organization Act*, granting the cabinet the power to make sweeping changes without debate in the Legislature. Then in the spring of 1987 — "the year of the cutting knives" — the assault began on Saskatchewan's comparatively elaborate social and health security system, a system described by Social Services Minister Grant Schmidt as "a hammock" in which "a lot of people [are] laying . . . having a good time at the expense of a majority of taxpayers." Schmidt later summed up the government's credo: "If you work hard, you eat. If you won't work, you don't eat. And if you can't work, then we'll take care of you. That's what social programs are for."[35] There was a blizzard of budget cuts issued by order-in-council. Each day brought new announcements coming so quickly that the media found it impossible to keep up: 2,000 civil servants cut one day, school board funding cuts, layoffs of Potash Corporation workers, cuts for municipalities, nursing home fee increases, cancellation of promised construction projects, the closure of the Regina branch of the provincial medical school, a funding freeze on universities, cuts to the large NGO human service and support sector; cuts in legal aid, cuts in the prescription drug program, the cancellation of the children's dental plan, and the sacking of 400 dental technicians. The list went on, as the public watched, first in stunned disbelief, then in anger. Then came the tax hikes on incomes, gasoline, and an end to controls on utility rates — all of which hit hardest at the ordinary taxpayer. The Coalition for Social Justice, a united front of labour and social activists, organized the largest protest demonstration in the province's history.[36]

The Devine government's ambitious privatization plans were implemented by a new department, the Department of Public Participation. Throughout 1988 and 1989 there were a host of privatizations of public assets at firesale prices: a sodium sulphate mine, a peat moss operation, most of what was left of SaskOil, the government printing company, a forest products company, the Crown computer utility, pieces of SaskTel (from the phone book to the computer division), SaskPower's natural gas reserves (worth $1 billion, sold for $325 million), the Crown's vast uranium holdings in existing mines, and the province's huge potash company was put up for half its value. As well, the already well-developed policy of contracting out continued to accelerate. Public support for privatization plummeted, especially after the potash decision, but public opposition became rage after the move to privatize the Crown natural gas utility and the general insurance arm of the Crown insurance company. The NDP Opposition, now under new leader Roy Romanow, provided only desultory resistance until public pressure grew. Finally Romanow acted when the privatization of the gas utility was proposed, boldly bringing the Legislature to a procedural standstill.[37] Devine backed off, shuffled his cabinet, and decided to re-examine his privatization strategy. In the end the big utility Crowns were saved, but not before much else was lost.[38]

Despite neo-liberalism's extravagant promises, the magic of the market and free trade did not bring results. In the West, the depression of the early and mid-eighties showed no signs of abating. It was not without a certain irony that the public very quickly learned that despite the ability of their premiers to articulate neo-liberal economic principles, when it came to performance, the western neo-liberal governments couldn't deliver. By any standards, including those of business, many of the privatizations were either foolish business decisions or deliberate acts of raiding the public treasury to benefit investors and corporations. In many cases, like Papco, the Potash Corporation and SaskOil in Saskatchewan, or BCRIC in B.C., the public assets were sold at a fraction of their real value, frequently because the sale took place during a low point in the relevant market, a time when no rational owner would sell. In other cases, such as the natural gas distribution system of B.C. Hydro, the privatization took place by imposing further financial obligations on the public — a case of lending your own money at low interest to someone to buy your assets at foolishly low prices.[39] The company was worth $741 million and sold to Inland Natural Gas for $291 million in cash, a loan from B.C. Hydro for $300 million, and a provincial debenture for $150 million.

In addition, many of the entrepreneurs given the grants, low-interest loans and loan guarantees were poor risks. In B.C. hundreds of millions were loaned out to businesses that failed to meet even the minimal official guidelines, when Vander Zalm or one of his ministers personally intervened.[40] In Saskatchewan and Alberta, the list of abuses was equally extensive.[41] Finally, many of the megaprojects that came back into fashion under the neo-liberals involved huge public financial risks while posing serious threats to the environment.[42] Increasingly, the entire economic strategy of the neo-liberals in the West, initially perhaps perceived by the public as somewhat over-zealous, came to be perceived as, at best, abysmal incompetence, at worst, malfeasance and an abuse of the public trust.

COLLAPSE AND DEFEAT, 1990–1993

Almost as soon as the neo-liberal counter-revolution reached its apotheosis in the period from 1986 to 1990, public support for western neo-liberal governments began to collapse. The growth in public opposition was complex, a cauldron of contradiction, anxiety, and fear. Partly, it had to do with the economic failures of neo-liberalism, though it was true that much of what caused the West's economic problems was beyond provincial government control — drought, the world wheat wars, low and unstable world prices for virtually all the West's export commodities. Similarly, much of what was needed was also beyond provincial control — provincial governments do not have the constitutional powers to lower interest rates, to pursue new national economic policies, to force Ottawa to reform the tax system or to stop downloading. Yet in democracies governments are routinely blamed for the poor performance of the economy — and this is fair, if only because governments take credit for economic prosperity even if their policies have nothing to do with it. Furthermore, the neo-liberals had raised expectations that their strategy would work, bringing prosperity, diversification, jobs, and growth. Neo-liberal extravagance with public funds for their privatizations, economic development spending, and tax concessions to the rich and to business, and the resulting deficits and debts, only served to increase the blame assigned to the governments in power. The ghosts of Trudeau in Ottawa and the NDP provincial governments in the West could not be blamed forever by neo-liberal governments already long in power.

The economic facts could not be denied. Year after year unemployment rates in the West in the 1980s and early 1990s were the highest in twenty years.[43] Personal per capita income in the West lagged far behind the Ontario average — in 1990, 23 per cent behind in Manitoba, about 33 per cent behind in Saskatchewan, 14 per cent behind in Alberta, and 12 per cent in B.C. — and the brief closing of that gap during the 1970s disappeared.[44] Net farm income continued to collapse while farm debt skyrocketed.[45] Meanwhile, the accumulated provincial debt spiralled. Alberta faced a public debt for the first time since the 1930s, a source of great controversy given the province's political history.[46] In 1979, oil brought almost $9 million a day to the public coffers and there was no debt. By the early 1990s, Alberta was spending about $8 million a day more than it brought in as revenues. A combination of low oil and gas prices, and huge tax breaks to the oil and gas sector, was taking its inevitable toll on the public revenue. The once proud Heritage Fund had been capped at a mere $12 billion, not enough to pay off the province's debt.[47] The debt problem in Saskatchewan was the worst in Canada: by 1988 over $8,000 per capita.[48]

B.C. had remained relatively immune from the worst effects of the depression and growing debt, but it faced other problems. In B.C. the forestry industry drives the economy, with 17 per cent of the work force in jobs related to forestry and one dollar in five from forestry going into government revenues. In 1986-88, the industry was in a boom cycle largely due to strong exports to the U.S. However, anxiety was increasing as the inevitable bust was expected. The industry also faced major restructuring. There was pressure to increase the export of raw logs which earned B.C. forestry companies twice what they earned processing logs in provincial mills. A great deal of the larger, old growth forests available under provincial rules for clear-cutting had been exhausted, and virtually the entire B.C. milling industry along the coast was tooled to process the disappearing giants of the forest: Douglas fir, cedar, hemlock and balsam. Further, the FTA was being used to attack Canada's access to the U.S. market, where the U.S. lumber industry faced a log shortage that had forced many mill closures. The B.C. government was faced with pressure either to increase the export of raw logs, or open up access to the remaining old forests along the coast, like Clayoquot Sound, or assist the industry through a massive retooling so the mills could process smaller, younger, and much less profitable logs. The people of B.C. were clearly not persuaded that the free market and free trade were the best approach for what could be a wrenching adjustment that would reverberate throughout the provincial economy. The fear was that the completely free market would lead to the rape of B.C. 's few remaining old forests, the spiralling export of raw logs, and the collapse of B.C.'s existing forestry manufacturing base.[49]

The growing debt was used by neo-liberals to beat the public into submission. Having run up the debt and clearly willing to continue to tolerate annual deficits, western neo-liberal governments now claimed that they could not afford the expensive social and health safety net. In the context of growing economic anxiety, these claims provoked a deepening of public anger rather than meek submission. It was evident that the origins of annual deficits and burgeoning provincial debt lay, not in spending on social, health, and education programs, since they had been underfunded in real terms since the late 1970s. Rather, the origins lay in uncontrolled spending on economic development, including megaprojects, in spasmodic efforts to buy elections, in the high interest rates of the period (ranging from 9 to 19 per cent), and in deep cuts on the revenue side, particularly tax breaks to corporations, the resource sector, and the affluent. Granted, the continuing depression was now increasing the debt, particularly due to growing unemployment insurance and social assistance payments and federal downloading, as well as annual bailouts for major economic sectors, like the fishery, agriculture, and non-conventional energy. This public perception was confirmed by a suppressed Statistics Canada study which showed that the federal deficit and accumulated debt up to 1990 — some $400 billion — was mostly due to tax breaks (50 per cent) and high interest rates (44 per cent). Only 6 per cent was due to government spending increases, and only a third of that on social spending.[50]

In Alberta, the province's entire debt could be directly attributed to misspending on ill-conceived megaprojects and on tax cuts to the oil and gas industry. This perception was also confirmed in Saskatchewan by *Sask Trends Monitor*, a specialized newsletter issued by independent social and economic analysts.[51] The return to the Saskatchewan treasury from oil sales had fallen from 65 per cent of value of sale in 1981 to 15 per cent in 1989. In fact, from 1987 to 1991, Saskatchewan provincial budgets ran a "program surplus" each year, the growth in debt entirely accounted for by the need to borrow in order to pay interest on the previous borrowings. Almost the entire Saskatchewan debt could be accounted for by the Devine government's spending spree, largely to buy elections in 1982 and 1986.

Besides the economic sources of discontent in the West, there were the constitutional ones — the Meech Lake Accord, followed by the Charlottetown Agreement. In 1987 all four western premiers agreed to the Meech Lake Accord, including the NDP's Pawley. Other than minor concessions to Québec, the key feature of both agreements was to weaken the federal government while enhancing the powers of the provinces. It was a clear victory for "provincial rights" and a clear defeat for traditional federalism. As part of the neo-liberal agenda —

which saw the weakening of government, particularly the fairly intrusive federal government, as vital — it was an effort to constitutionalize key aspects of neo-liberal principles. The four western premiers were immediately caught in a crossfire. On the one side was the bigoted, conservative, francophobe element which attacked the agreement as giving Québec too much, while not going far enough in decentralization. This position was articulated most forcefully by the Reform party and the regional, resource-based business lobby. On the other side was a coalition of traditional federalists and the left which feared the consequences of weakening the federal government, thus crippling its ability to develop and implement universal, national social programs and coherent national economic policies, something that had been very important to the region. Throughout the constitutional process — and for these often contradictory reasons — Westerners had made it clear they did not support either agreement. Those premiers and the prime minister who participated in trying to force the Meech Lake Accord on Canadians against their clearly expressed will were finally driven from office. Meanwhile, premiers who supported the Charlottetown Agreement were somewhat protected from public indignation only by the fact that a public referendum was allowed in 1992.

The scandals which repeatedly rocked three of the four western provincial governments were the final features of the defeat of western neo-liberals. The scandals surrounding Getty unravelled amidst a lot of media attention, largely after the March 1989 election in which the Tory government was returned, but the premier went down to personal defeat in Edmonton-Whitemud. Just days after the election, it was revealed that Getty had hired U.S. consultants to find him the safest Tory seat in Alberta in which to seek re-election in a by-election. The consultants identified Stettler, a rural seat near Edmonton. In the subsequent by-election, and after the premier's re-election, Stettler became the place to be in rural Alberta as a grateful Getty showered the riding with patronage.[52] From then on it was downhill for Getty, when scandal after scandal was revealed: wine boutique licences for cronies,[53] the collapse of the Principal Group amid charges the government had been "neglectful even reckless,"[54] the giveaways to Peter Pocklington's

Gainers,[55] and a secret pulp project.[56] The more personally damaging revelation was probably that Getty had continued to be an active investor in the province's oil lands while in office, holding an interest in 3,240 hectares in the Kaybob field, 300 kilometres northwest of Edmonton.[57] The premier's response was: "So what? What can I do that could somehow benefit me?" He insisted that his active interest did not influence his decisions as premier, yet he had personally made at least $60,000 and doubled his holdings since 1986. Getty hurt himself further by defending his actions with a comment that reverberated across the depression-afflicted province: "How do you put bread on the table? You sell off assets. I was making . . . around six to seven hundred thousand dollars a year [in the oil business] when I came back to government. How's that for a cut in salary? [As premier, Getty earned over $117,000 in salary and tax free allowances.] Tough on my family, very tough on my family. Tough on our standard of living." As of November 1989, Premier Getty's political career was effectively over.

In Saskatchewan, the taint of scandal did not affect the Devine government until after the 1986 election. During the first term there were the usual stories of excessive patronage flowing freely to Tories and friends of the government: a consultant's job for the premier's brother-in-law, government work and contracts granted without tender,[58] the collapse of Pioneer Trust, and the proposed $140 million for the Rafferty-Alameda dam in the premier's riding.

During Devine's second term a number of scandals developed, starting with revelations regarding the true size of the deficit and the reversal of Devine's personal assurances regarding privatization and spending cuts. The juiciest scandal in 1989 involved GigaText Translation Services which received $5.25 million in government investment and loans to produce perfect English-to-French translation by computer. No translations ever took place, but the GigaText hustlers siphoned off the money.[59]

The public money squandered on GigaText paled next to the $140 million for the Rafferty-Alameda dam, which proceeded in 1988 after the release of a much-criticized provincial environmental assessment. Since the project affected both interprovincial and international water flows, a federal licence and environmental assessment were also required. Devine violated federal law by ignoring these requirements. By the time the legal issues had been resolved, the project was a *fait accompli*.[60] The scandal involving the purchase of buses for the publicly owned Saskatchewan Transportation Company (STC) received still-larger headlines. STC's president and vice president of operations were charged with fraud for taking a $50,000 kickback to arrange the purchase of $3 million worth of buses from Eagle International of Texas.[61] Then there was the nearly $60 million in questionable business investments — involving loans and grants — throughout the Devine years.[62] Charitably, these investments revealed equal measures of bad judgement and economic desperation.

Although Devine emerged relatively personally unscathed by the more seedy stories of patronage and scandal, during his second term he was criticized for abusing power, showing contempt for democracy, and violating parliamentary norms and conventions.[63] The premier's contempt for the system became well known and was clear in his behaviour in the Legislature during his first term. This contempt was confirmed by his use of the Charter's notwithstanding clause to legislate striking government workers back to work, a casual and routine use not envisaged by the framers of the constitution. However, commencing with his controversial re-election in 1986 when, with a little help from Ottawa, he bought the rural vote, Devine made no secret that he viewed the system as something to be bent to his personal will and that he would not hesitate to use his power to punish those who defied him, even those fulfilling their statutory duties to the Legislature, including the Legislature's law clerk, the provincial ombudsman, and the provincial auditor.

Devine's most serious attack on the democratic system involved an effort to follow through on his rural strategy in order to stay in power. First, he imposed a legislated gerrymander on the province's electoral boundaries that had the effect of giving a greater weight to the rural vote than the urban vote — as a result of the gerrymander it took 121 urban votes to equal 100 rural votes.[64] The gerrymander was found to be unconstitutional under the Charter by the Saskatchewan Court of Appeal which, in its decision, rebuked the Devine government for "spawning the divisive notion of rural and urban interests." However, upon appeal, the Supreme Court, encumbered with more conservative jurists appointed by Mulroney and increasingly resistant to an overly constructive application of the Charter, reversed the lower court and sustained the gerrymander. To further his rural strategy, Devine also "harmonized" the provincial sales tax with the hated federal GST, projected to raise an additional $150 million annually "to pay for the protection of Saskatchewan farmers," in the government's own words. This was the first time in Saskatchewan history that a specific tax levied on everyone was openly targeted by a government to benefit only one class of citizen. Easily the most controversial measure to assure Devine's rural appeal was the last-minute "Fair Share" program which proposed, without consultation, a Draconian program of decentralization of government services and departments, and 2,000 jobs, from Regina to rural areas.

In Devine's final days, the abuses worsened. Facing mutiny in his own ranks, including the sudden surprise resignation of one of his ministers, and an indication that his own caucus might not sustain him in the Legislature, Devine abruptly prorogued the Legislature, despite the fact that the budget and a raft of proposed bills, many with important fiscal implications, remained unpassed.[65] The premier himself admitted that he might not have been able to get the budget approved. Rather than calling an immediate election, as many expected, he made clear his intention to continue in power. Devine's government began routinely to spend money not approved by the Legislature and continued to act as if the proposed unpassed bills were law. By doing so, Devine violated the principles of responsible government and the rule of law. In Saskatchewan, during the last days of the Devine government, the people suffered under what can only be described as a dictatorship. Granted it was a dictatorship with a time limit, since the premier constitutionally had to hold an election before 12 November 1991. But it was a dictatorship nevertheless.

In British Columbia, many of the problems Vander Zalm experienced during his brief 1,700 days in office can be traced to his inability to manage his own cabinet and caucus and finally his own party. Over the years, the public was allowed to view repeated party rebellions. Three senior cabinet ministers resigned due to the premier's interference in their departments, two MLAs openly refused the premier's offer of parliamentary secretary positions, four MLAs left the party in protest, the party memberships of 15 constituencies challenged Vander Zalm's leadership, and three candidates nominated for the 1991 election rejected their nominations in anger and disgust.[66]

These episodes reflected resistance to Vander Zalm's unwitting if effective dismantling of the free enterprise, anti-socialist coalition established by W. A. C. Bennett in 1952 to keep the CCF/NDP out of office. The coalition had been allowed to atrophy once before due to Bennett's refusal to recognize it was time to step down, resulting in Barrett's victory in 1972. Bill Bennett had negotiated the coalition's repair for 1975, and he had done so by carefully cultivating the business lobby as well as provincial Liberals and Tories. It was a fragile alliance which rested on a fair division of the spoils of office, most particularly access to the government, influence on government policy, and a share in government contracts and patronage. The coalition would put up with colourful, flamboyant and even slightly ridiculous leaders, but it could never long tolerate a leader who ignored advice and behaved irresponsibly. Vander Zalm began to exclude key figures of the coalition from access and influence, he stopped taking much of the advice given to him, and he began to fill his cabinet with sycophants and even fools. Above all else, the coalition could not long tolerate a leader who appeared to be leading the party to defeat at the hands of the NDP. When, after 1983, Bennett's popularity plummeted, he listened to advice, read the polls, and decided to retire. He did not want to repeat his father's mistake. Vander Zalm refused to do likewise, repeatedly promising the caucus and cabinet that he would do things better in the future. And after each rebellion, the caucus backed off and Vander Zalm survived. Even backbencher Kim Campbell, who later as prime minister was to make much of her opposition to Vander Zalm, said after a 1988 caucus rebellion was quelled, "He is the leader, and I am supporting him in what he has pledged to do."[67]

The spectacle that unfolded before the public was one of the premier's tolerance of an unprecedented level of corrupt abuse of office.[68] Seven cabinet ministers were forced to resign for dubious practices, and most were returned to cabinet positions after perfunctory investigations that satisfied the premier. This standard of morality was set by a premier who had difficulty separating his private business interests clearly from his public duties. Vander Zalm appeared to see winning the premiership as a licence to abuse the public privileges and powers of his office for his own private benefit. He was hungry for quick returns and eager to please his business friends regardless of the consequences. He tried to get the government to lease his own building in Kamloops[69] and ordered his environment minister not to impose new tougher and more expensive pollution controls on the pulp and paper industry, thereby saving the industry an estimated $600 million.[70] These two tendencies — seeking immediate personal benefits and helping his business friends — are what finally brought Vander Zalm down.

The "Toigo affair" involved the 1987-88 sale of the provincially owned 84-hectare Expo 86 site in downtown Vancouver, prime urban real estate worth tens of millions.[71] The British Columbia Enterprise Corporation (BCEC) — the Crown company which owned the Expo land — was instructed to accept bids on the Expo site. From April to December 1987 Vander Zalm repeatedly intervened in the process in order to advance a bid made by the late Peter Toigo, a close friend and the chief fund-raiser for his leadership campaign. Despite the fact that Toigo had not entered his bid by the deadline, Vander Zalm took it to cabinet anyway, without informing the minister responsible. Although Vander Zalm was finally unsuccessful — Toigo's bid was rejected and the site went to Hong Kong billionaire Li Ka-ching — the revelations shocked the public and provoked two ministerial resignations and upheaval in the party. The RCMP launched an investigation of the premier to see if there were grounds for charges of influence peddling. No charges were laid.

The Fantasy Garden scandal involved Vander Zalm using his office as premier first to enhance the value of Fantasy Garden and then to engineer its sale for top dollar.[72] In 1984, Vander Zalm bought a 8.5 hectare botanical garden located in Richmond, a Vancouver suburb, for $1.7 million. It was renamed Fantasy Garden World and continued as a botanical garden as well as a Biblical theme park. When he became premier, Vander Zalm assured the public that he had transferred ownership of the business to his wife and from then on he referred to Fantasy Garden as "Lillian's business." In fact, he retained 83 per cent ownership and continued to be actively involved in running the business. In 1988, half of the Fantasy Garden property was removed from the agricultural land reserve regulations, thus lifting development restrictions and greatly enhancing the property's commercial value. Vander Zalm then proceeded to negotiate the sale of Fantasy Garden to Tan Yu, a Taiwan tycoon heading up Asia-world (Canada) Development Corporation. Tan Yu expressed an interest in other business opportunities in B.C., including setting up a bank or trust company, but Vander Zalm's wife informed Tan that the sale of Fantasy Garden must take place before any meetings with B.C. government officials could be arranged. The meetings were arranged for Tan, including a session with the Minister of Finance and his officials, and a state luncheon with the Lieutenant-Governor, and on 7 September 1990 Vander Zalm announced the sale of Fantasy Garden World for $16 million.

An aspect of the scandal revolved around the secret cash payment of $20,000 to Vander Zalm by Tan, made though Faye Leung, Vander Zalm's real estate agent. Leung claimed that Tan wanted to purchase a PetroCan property adjoining Fantasy Garden and he hoped the premier would help him acquire that and other properties. Tan gave the $20,000 to Leung who in turn gave it to Vander Zalm at a late night meeting at the Bayshore Inn. Though Vander Zalm did phone PetroCan's chair regarding Tan's desire for the property, the premier denied the $20,000 was to buy his influence, insisting it was left with him "in trust" and "for safekeeping," and to pay for a jade sculpture.

The full facts gradually emerged over the months. On February 13, 1991, when sealed documents, filed in the B.C. Supreme Court in a quite different case involving Leung, were released on application by the CBC and *The Globe and Mail*, the facts showed without any doubt that Vander Zalm was directly involved in the sale from the beginning. The same day Vander Zalm turned the matter over to B.C.'s Conflict-of-Interest Commissioner Ted Hughes for investigation. On March 21, 1991, Vander Zalm announced his intention to resign after a successor was chosen. On 2 April 1991 the Hughes report was released documenting Vander Zalm's repeated and willful violations of conflict-of-interest guidelines. Vander Zalm announced his immediate resignation, and the caucus chose deputy premier Rita Johnston, Vander Zalm's leadership campaign manager, to succeed him as premier.

In May 1992 Vander Zalm made political history one last time, becoming the first premier or prime minister in British Commonwealth history to face a criminal breach-of-trust charge. The charge related to the $20,000 cash payment and to Vander Zalm's involvement in the Fantasy Garden sale. Vander Zalm chose trial by judge and declined to take the stand, denying the prosecutor an opportunity for an interesting cross-examination in open court. On 25 June the judge found Vander Zalm not guilty. But the verdict was heavily qualified by the judge, who said Vander Zalm's actions were "foolish, ill-advised and in apparent or real conflict of interest or breach of ethics." Yet, the judge found, the prosecution did not prove "beyond a reasonable doubt" that Vander Zalm was guilty of criminal breach of trust.

It was perhaps conceivable that the Vander Zalm. scandals could have been blamed solely on the premier, thus rescuing the party from political culpability. Indeed, there was ample public evidence that many in his own cabinet, caucus and party fought to rein him in before the final disaster. But the 1989 scandal involving former premier Bill Bennett suggested to many among the public that the rot went much deeper than just Vander Zalm's misdeeds. Indeed, coming in the midst of the Vander Zalm scandals, the Bennett scandal did perhaps more deep and lasting political damage, if only because Bennett had been lionized by the party and had almost achieved the status of secular political saint. On January 28, 1989 Bill Bennett, his brother Russell, and Herb Doman, chief owner of Doman Industries, the largest provincially owned B.C. lumber company, were charged with illegal trading by taking advantage of an illegal inside tip in a major stock market transaction to earn a profit of $2.1 million. Though finding the trio not guilty, the judge allowed that it was a "reasonable inference" that the Bennetts had got an illegal insider tip, but the prosecution "failed to prove beyond a reasonable doubt" that such was the case.[73] The damage from both the Vander Zalm and Bennett scandals was to prove irreparable.

The fall in support for the neo-liberal regimes in the West was dramatic and precipitous, both reflecting and contributing to Canada's growing political volatility. In Alberta, Getty's fate was sealed with the results of the March 1989 election, widely described as "a referendum on Getty's future."[74] Though the Tories held onto power, their showing was comparatively poor — 59 of 83 seats and 44 per cent of the vote, while the NDP won 16 seats with 26 per cent and the Liberals 8 seats with 29 per cent. The loss of his own seat, the continuing and new scandals, a push from former premier Lougheed,[75] a November 1992 poll (Tories 36 per cent, Liberals 41 per cent), and the loss of three of four by-elections after the 1989 vote, finally led Getty to resign. Though his successor, Ralph Klein, was able to retain power in June 1993, with 51 of 83 seats and 45 per cent of the vote, while the Liberals took 40 per cent and 32 seats, shutting the NDP out of the Legislature with 11 per cent, the victory had been costly to neo-liberal unity.[76] The Alberta Tories broke formal ties with the federal party in 1991[77] and commenced to resurrect the Central Canada bogey-man, with Getty declaring that Alberta wouldn't be "raped and pillaged" again,[78] and new premier Klein accusing Central Canada of again plotting to grab Alberta's oil wealth.[79]

In Manitoba, where Premier Filmon was plodding a more moderate neo-liberal course, the electorate declined to give him an overwhelming mandate in the September 1990 election — the Tories took 30 seats with 42 per cent, the NDP returned as Official Opposition with 20 seats and 29 per cent and the Liberals fell to 7 seats and 28 per cent.[80] With a razor-thin majority and a combined opposition vote of 57 per cent, Filmon got a clear message not to embark on a wholesale neo-liberal agenda. In fact, Filmon began to pose as the champion of western interests against the increasingly beleaguered Mulroney, attacking him bitterly in public.[81]

But all attention was focused on Saskatchewan and B.C., where the real test of public support for neo-liberalism was fought out. In B.C., support for Vander Zalm and the Socreds plummeted. By 1988 the NDP was 17 points ahead in one poll and 18 points ahead in another. By 1991 the distance was 14 points.[82] Four by-elections, in 1988–1989 were particularly decisive evidence of the collapse in public support for the government. The NDP took all 4 seats, including an Okanagan seat held by the Socreds for over 20 years,[83] a rural seat in the Interior held for 40 years,[84] and 2 upper-middle-class seats in Vancouver and Victoria usually won by the Socreds.[85] The real test, however, of whether this collapse resulted largely from Vander Zalm's antics, or reflected a more general rejection of the Socred's neo-liberal provincial agenda waited the outcome of the general election called by Premier Rita Johnston for October 1991. The outcome was a disaster for the Socreds, who fell to third spot with 24 per cent of the vote and just 7 seats. The NDP won 51 of 75 seats and 44 per cent of the vote. The Liberals — out of the Legislature for 17 years — became the Official Opposition, winning 17 seats and 33 per cent of the vote.[86] The sheer size of the vote for the NDP and Liberals, and the utter defeat of the Socred government, including the personal defeat of Premier Johnston, could not have more clearly conveyed the electorate's decisive rejection of the neo-liberal counter-revolution.

The collapse of support for the Devine government in Saskatchewan was even more spectacular. A poll in 1989 put the NDP ahead 21 points — 54 per cent to 33 per cent.[87] A poll regarding the Tories' privatization program revealed deep public opposition, ranging from a low of 52 per cent opposed to privatizing the Saskatchewan Transportation Company to a high of 75 per cent opposition to privatizing SaskPower. A year later, a poll put the NDP 21 points ahead of the Tories, with the Liberals now in second spot.[88] In May 1991 the NDP was an incredible 44 points ahead — 63 per cent to 19 per cent.[89] This trend was confirmed in three 1988 by-elections.[90] In two urban seats — one in Saskatoon and one in Regina — Tory support

collapsed while NDP support was unprecedented, reaching 77 per
cent in the Regina seat. In the rural seat, formerly held by a Liberal, the
Tories won by a whisker, 44 to 42 per cent. A similar pattern across the
countryside, especially in those many rural areas with a larger base of
traditional NDP support, would result in an easy NDP victory, if not a
sweep, in much of rural Saskatchewan. Wisely the Tories decided not
to hold by-elections in four rural seats vacated later by retiring cabinet
ministers in order to avoid further pre-election humiliations. Until the
October 1991 election, Devine concentrated on the province's rural
areas, not bothering to campaign in the cities. On October 21, 1991
the Saskatchewan electorate badly defeated the Devine government,
granting 55 seats to the NDP and 51 per cent of the popular vote, 10
seats and 26 per cent to the Tories, and 1 seat and 23 per cent to the
Liberals. All 10 Tory seats were rural. The NDP won 58 per cent of the
urban vote and 43 per cent of the rural vote. The Tories were cut to 16
per cent in the urban seats and 36 per cent in the rural seats.[91] The
Saskatchewan electorate, like that of B.C., voted decisively to stop and
to reverse the neo-liberal counter-revolution.

NEO-LIBERAL IMPACTS

At the end of a decade of neo-liberalism, the people of western Canada
were worse off than at the beginning, and the "new reality" was personally tangible for increasing numbers. Not only had real incomes
declined, but the social, educational and health security system, as well
as the whole community infrastructure, appeared to be collapsing. The
health care system was less and less universally accessible, and quality
was in serious decline. The educational system from kindergarten to
university, staggering first from years of underfunding and then from
outright cuts, was increasingly unable to deliver quality education,
with even the huge public investment in the physical infrastructure at
risk from lack of maintenance. Every western city had its share of the
growing army of the homeless, many begging in the streets, as well
as its share of the millions of Canadians in need of help from food
banks. Hardly a family in the region was not directly touched by the
plight of the millions of Canadians on welfare and the 1.6 million

unemployed.[92] Westerners, along with all Canadians, watched as the public infrastructure of roads, and water and sewage systems began to visibly decay after more than a decade of spending cuts — an infrastructure requiring an immediate expenditure of $20 billion for emergency repairs alone.[93]

Despite all this material evidence of cuts and declines in personal and public living standards, by 1993 the national debt had ballooned to $500 billion, the annual federal deficit seemed permanently fixed in the over $30 billion range, and western provinces began to falter under a growing debt load — for example, $15,000 for every man, woman, and child in Saskatchewan, the province hit hardest.[94] Meanwhile, as a result of the free trade agreement, jobs were fleeing south as Canadians began to spend billions each year in cross-border shopping.[95] And, as Canadian incomes and public services were in decline, quarterly reports revealed that business had begun to enjoy a profit bonanza:[96] up 21 per cent in 1987, up 25 per cent in 1989, up 60 per cent in 1993. The profit of Canada's six chartered banks did particularly well — up 37 per cent in 1989 over 1988, up 359 per cent in 1993 over 1992. Natural resource companies also did very well, up 207 per cent in 1993 over 1992, while the profits for companies in non-consumer industrial products went up 1,389 per cent.

The western regional economy limped along — little of the promise of neo-liberal economic magic had materialized and the efforts to diversify the economy had largely failed.[97] B.C.'s more prosperous boom/bust economy, including its very large manufacturing sector, was still rooted deeply in resources, largely forestry. Saskatchewan's economic reality remained defined by agriculture, oil, potash, and uranium. Many of Alberta's local diversification projects — in magnesium, cellular phones, petrochemicals and plastics, meat packing, pulp and paper — had either failed or were at risk at great cost to the public treasury and economic confidence. Alberta remained pre-eminently dependent on oil, natural gas, and agriculture. Manitoba's historic mix of agriculture, mining, and a significant, largely regionally oriented, manufacturing sector remained. Yet the evidence was clear that the West's long-cherished dream of economic diversification, a dream

husbanded by the people and manipulated by politicians from the
founding of the West, was becoming less a matter of merely increasing
stability and prosperity, and more a matter of sheer survival.

Canada could no longer continue to base its long-term economic
strategy significantly on the export of natural resources, and that was
clearly even more true for a major resource-producing region like
the West. The stark option of "diversify or die" plagued the West's
economy. Yet Mulroney's Ottawa had turned its back on significant
regional development initiatives, decreasing funding for sustainable,
long-term diversification projects, while opting for the big splash
approach of megaprojects, largely in energy. The expenditure of billions on megaprojects captured headlines and bought elections, but,
as in the past, did little to diversify the general economy. Such projects
brought very few permanent jobs, overheated local economies during
the construction boom setting the stage for painful contraction after
completion, and did little to diversify the region's economy. In fact,
such megaprojects deepened the region's dependence on traditional
economic sectors.

Pouring billions into megaprojects may have created the illusion
of progress in diversification, but such glamour strategies were no
substitute for the brick-by-brick building of long-term economic
development which truly diversified the region's economic base while
providing permanent jobs. Federal funding for the less glamorous
projects was cut by Ottawa, and replaced by Mulroney's assurance that
a free market and free trade would solve Canada's chronic problem of
regional disparity once and for all, bringing prosperity to a region too
long denied a place in the sun. Unfortunately, not only did neo-liberal
diversification strategies fail the West, but the policies adopted, when
combined with changes in world market conditions, appeared to jeop-
ardize, in different ways, the long-run viability of the three main pillars
of the region's economic foundation: agriculture, energy, and forestry.

AGRICULTURE

In the mid-1970s, the West lost the European wheat market. Historically
one of Canada's prime markets for wheat exports, in 1975 the

European Community (EC), thanks to generous subsidies to its farmers, became a net exporter of wheat, and by 1989 replaced Canada as the second world exporter of wheat behind the U.S. The U.S. began a retaliation subsidy program in 1985, and the "wheat wars" were on. Although the struggle was mainly between the EC and the U.S., western Canadian farmers got caught in the crossfire. By 1989, the developed countries were spending $250 billion to subsidize their farmers in order to keep or win back export markets. Fully 46 per cent of the average Canadian farmer's income came from subsidies, and the value of Canada's exports fell from $7 billion a year before the grain wars, to $4 billion a year in 1990. According to a study done by the Farm Credit Corporation, in 1989 the average grain farmer obtained 50 per cent of his/her income from off-farm wage work, more than 25 per cent from farm program payments, and less than 25 per cent from the actual sale of crops. For wheat farmers, one dollar in every three received for putting in and taking off a crop came from government payments. In Saskatchewan, in 1986, 81 per cent of realized net farm income came from subsidies; in 1988, 67 per cent. In truth, Canadian farmers were increasingly "farming subsidies" rather than farming the land.[98] As prices fell, and farm debt grew, western farmers went through the worst depression since the 1930s, and for perhaps all but the largest and richest farmers, about one farmer in three, government assistance was all that saved them from bankruptcy and foreclosure.

The responses of Ottawa and the provincial governments were to provide a variety of emergency bailout programs, usually through cheap loans and direct acreage payments. Many of these were *ad hoc* programs to deal with the crisis on a year-by-year basis. The key problem with these programs was that they were not targeted to the farmers most in need but were paid out universally, usually on an acreage or commodity basis. Thus, large debt-free, wealthy farmers, who needed no help to survive, got most of the help while the smaller-or medium-sized farmers, who needed a great deal more help, got just enough help to survive.[99] And for many thousands, especially for those deeply in debt, even the government assistance was not enough to stave off final foreclosure. This was clearly irrational and wasteful of public funds.

The billions expended could have been more wisely targeted to those farmers closest to the margins of survival, as well as to re-adjustment programs to respond to the changing world market, rather than paid out to all farmers on an acreage basis. In the 1980s alone these bailouts cost Ottawa and the provinces $6.5 billion. Clearly, the public treasury could not absorb such costs forever.

Finally, after long negotiations between Ottawa and the western provinces, a much-heralded new farm safety net program was announced — a farm version of unemployment insurance.[100] The subsidized insurance scheme rolled safeguards against crop failure in with farm income protection against falls in world prices. The plan — jointly funded by farmers, Ottawa and the provinces — guaranteed farmers 70 per cent of the average price over the previous 15 years and also provided an income-protection feature by which the farmer deposited part of his/her annual income, to be matched by governments, with payouts occurring when a farmer's income fell below the long-term average. Farmers complained that they were being blackmailed to sign up, threatened that if they did not sign on there would be no more bailouts. And increasingly farmers noted that the program, though good in theory, was bad in practice because there had been too many very bad years in the last 15 years, thereby ensuring that the price and income guarantee level was far too low. As opposition grew, farmers began to pull out of the program.

These problems were exacerbated by the determination of the neoliberal governments in Ottawa and the West — now clearly speaking for big agribusiness and the more conservative farm groups, like the Cattlemen's Association and the Palliser Wheat Growers — to commence the dismantling of the marketing protection system first pioneered by the Wheat Pool in the 1920s, and then embodied in the Canadian Wheat Board (CWB) and other legislated marketing monopolies. These agencies were premised on the concept of collective marketing protection rooted in the "pooling" idea. Rather than farmers competing with each other as individuals in seeking buyers in the marketplace, they would all pool their products and sell through one central agency. This gave them greater market clout in dealing with both buyers and other competitors. The central agency marketed the products, and farmers received a full and fair return based on the average price received in a crop year for the harvest.

Agribusiness, many wealthy farmers, and ideologues of free market doctrine fought the concept relentlessly from the outset, but with little success until the triumph of neo-liberalism. With an ideological commitment to free-market-oriented agriculture policies, neo-liberal governments in Ottawa and the provinces moved to slash agricultural support. While blaming the world grain wars, these governments moved more quickly than the U.S. or the EC. Under the free trade agreement, which was used as a pretext for the attack on Canada's orderly marketing system, Canada had agreed to re-examine its entire edifice of provincial and federal agricultural policy, in consultation with the U.S., in an effort to "harmonize" Canada/U.S. agricultural trade, to remove non-tariff import barriers and to ferret out and define unfair trading practices. Two-price wheat — whereby farmers received a higher price for the wheat used in Canada than for wheat exported — was abandoned at an annual cost to farmers of about $300 million.[101] In 1989, oats were taken from the jurisdiction of the CWB and put on the free continental market.[102] In 1993, barley was similarly removed by cabinet order.[103]

Another central focus of the attack was the "Crow benefit" which continued to be paid directly to the railways to subsidize grain transportation costs. The business lobby desperately wanted to dismantle the Crow benefit, which in effect regulated the railways' charges on grain, by paying the benefit directly to farmers and leaving the rest to market forces.[104] Farmers resisted this move, correctly fearing that an unregulated grain transportation system would lead to rising rates, cuts in service through an acceleration in branchline abandonment, the increasing use of the U.S. rail system and, hence, the bypassing of Canadian ports in the export of Canadian grain. There was also a fear that bigger, richer farmers would not only get the lion's share of the Crow cash buyout, but would also be in a better position to bargain for special lower rates due to larger volumes of grain to move. By 1992 the Crow benefit had been whittled down to $720 million a year and

Ottawa, in an effort to pressure farmers to agree to a cash buyout, announced a 10 per cent reduction in 1994-95, as well as threatened a further 15 per cent cut in 1995-96, and 20 per cent cuts each year thereafter. Yet farmers continued to insist that the Crow system remain intact, hoping to salvage as much as possible from their 1897 victory. Ultimately the system of provincial and federal agricultural supports was to be re-examined and tested for interfering in the free market by giving Canadian farmers an unfair advantage. Everything from government subsidies to encourage tree planting to fuel tax rebates were on the table. Indeed, the moves against the big-ticket farm supports, such as the Crow benefit and the proposed insurance scheme, also fit into this long-term drive to a continental free market in agricultural products. Therefore, just at the time of the greatest western agricultural crisis since the 1930s, a time when western agriculture needed new and effective national policies, agricultural policy was increasingly abandoned to the market place — which, in effect, meant that Canada moved toward an absence of agricultural policy. This created anxiety in the West. The wheat economy, which the West had known since settlement, the very key to the initial success of Canada's National Policy in 1896–1913, was ending. The loss of the European market, the emergence of the EC as a major wheat exporter, and the future prospect of the loss of wheat markets in the former Soviet sphere of influence as Russia and the Ukraine finally solved their agricultural problems, made it clear that western Canada needed a new national agricultural strategy and the specific policies to realize that strategy. Instead, western farmers were told that ultimately the final shape of their future would be determined by the free market and their individual entrepreneurial success. Western farmers felt increasingly abandoned by Ottawa and their own provincial governments.

ENERGY

Mulroney was fond of claiming that the Trudeau government's National Energy Program (NEP) was a "burr beneath the saddle of Western Canada."[105] It is certainly true that the oil and gas industry, and those who depended upon it for jobs and economic activity, as well as western provincial governments, particularly that of Alberta, resented the NEP deeply. On the other hand, most Canadians, including most Westerners, supported many features of the NEP — the Canadianization of ownership, a reasonable public share in profits from exploitation, a systematic public presence through Crown oil companies like PetroCan and Saskoil, and some regulation and conservation to secure Canada's energy future. What united Westerners during the energy wars of the 1970s was that the NEP was unfair. It took too much of the wealth, imposing an unfair share of the costs for what was a national energy policy upon the western producing region. The promise of neo-liberalism was that deregulation and a free continental market in energy would both stimulate the expansion of oil and gas production, as well as encourage exploration. An open export policy into the U.S. market, rather than bleeding Canada of a vital non-renewable resource for short-term cash gains to the industry and the producing provinces, would in fact both solve the future security-of-supply problem by stimulating a flurry of exploration and provide jobs, profits and revenues now. Further, Canadians were promised that the deregulation of natural gas would lead to lower prices for consumers.

Upon election in 1984, the Mulroney government moved quickly to deregulate oil and gas exports to the U.S., and in one year crude oil exports increased 70 per cent while natural gas exports increased 17 per cent.[106] But exports of natural gas were still subject to review by the National Energy Board (NEB) which continued to impose the 25-year rule: there had to be sufficient reserves to meet Canada's projected needs for 25 years. The government decided that this was hampering exports and the rule was accordingly changed in 1986 to 15 years, and then further reduced in 1988 to 3 years.[107] Even this period was considered too strict, and in 1989 the rule governing natural gas exports to the U.S. was changed to the "net benefit to Canada" test.[108] Under this test, the NEB would only authorize natural gas exports when it could be demonstrated that the returns on the exports would be sufficient to cover the infrastructure costs for taking the gas to market, and the exploration costs necessary to search for new replacement gas.

Up until the FTA, these changes were merely matters of government policy and could be easily reversed by a new government if they did not work out. Under Chapter 9 of the FTA, however, the move to deregulation and a free continental market became unchangeable unless the entire FTA were abrogated. Articles 901 to 909 forbade minimum export prices, as well as export taxes. Any future restriction on exports to the U.S. cannot reduce the proportion of total Canadian oil and gas production going into the U.S. Differential prices are forbidden; for example, one price for Canadian users and another for American users. Further, export restrictions can never disrupt "normal trade patterns."

The implications of the FTA for the NEB's already weakened regulatory powers were almost immediately tested in 1989-90. In 1989, the NEB took an extremely unusual step since the Mulroney victory by denying four export contracts under the "net benefit to Canada" rule, creating a storm of protest from the industry and the business lobby on both sides of the border. The U.S. distributors successfully challenged the decision under the FTA on the grounds that the test amounted to the imposition of a floor or minimum price on natural gas exports, and was therefore forbidden. Thereafter Ottawa and the NEB caved in and scrapped the test, leaving natural gas exports subject entirely to market forces.[109] The NEB was rendered ineffective and most of its remaining powers were stripped away. In 1990, the NEB lost its regulatory power over electricity exports to the U.S. and over the construction of international power-lines. These were approved routinely without hearings.[110] The next year the shell of the NEB was moved from Ottawa to Calgary, a clear signal that the agency was now fully in the pocket of the oil and gas lobby and the Alberta government.[111] In 1992 the last vestiges of Ottawa's regulation of oil and gas were expunged with the repeal of both the 50 per cent Canadian ownership rule for frontier development north of 60 degrees latitude, and the lifting of all meaningful restrictions on foreign investment in oil and gas. This last change was effected against a chorus of contrary advice from Ottawa's own experts and bureaucrats.[112] The focus of continuing controversy in Canada's energy debate had been on NEB permits for pipeline construction. American proponents of a continental energy policy had long dreamed of a network of pipelines criss-crossing Canada's gas and oil fields in the Western Basin, with tendrils into the north, feeding into the hungry and growing U.S. market. While Americans continued to cap a significant portion of their domestic wells to ensure future security of supply, they dreamed of the unrestricted pumping of as much oil and gas out of Canada as possible. Canada's reluctance to build pipelines without careful consideration of the implications was understandable. Once oil and gas were flowing through an existing pipeline, it would be next to an act of war to turn off the tap. This concern became even stronger after the FTA, since the treaty forbade reducing the U.S. share of Canadian production or disrupting normal trade patterns. Under the FTA, once a pipeline was in place, there was no possible reconsideration. After the FTA, NEB approval for pipeline construction became almost obscenely routine, despite an elaborate ritual of public hearings.[113]

As expected, the insatiable U.S. market took as much oil and gas as the Canadian industry could pump out of the ground and deliver. By 1989, the NEB reported Canada was exporting twice as much natural gas as in the 1970s and projections suggested a tripling by 2000.[114] The demand in the U.S. for Canadian natural gas was skyrocketing because of the abandonment of the nuclear power option in the U.S. in the wake of Three Mile Island and Chernobyl.[115] No U.S. utility had ordered a nuclear reactor since 1978, and 36 new plants under construction had been delayed or cancelled. A new $5 billion plant in New Hampshire, upon completion, had not even been allowed to begin electrical generation. As an alternative to nuclear generation, the U.S. had opted for a two-pronged strategy to supply its energy needs — hydro-electric power imports from Québec and natural gas imports from the West, with Alberta projected to supply 10 per cent of the entire U.S. market. In the case of crude oil, by 1989 Canada's exports out of the Western Basin into the U.S. only barely exceeded the imports of Middle Eastern crude for Central and Atlantic Canada.[116] The next year, Canada became a net importer of crude oil, an ominous portent for the future when, after exhausting the easy conventional oil in the West, Canada will be more and more dependent on imports from the Middle East, the North Sea, and its own frontier.[117]

Anxieties about the future of the energy industry in the West grew due to two issues. As the world price for oil declined, the price for natural gas also declined, leading to a continuation of the recession in the energy sector throughout the 1980s and into the early 1990s. As the world oil price tracked down toward $12 a barrel, non-conventional oil was being produced at a loss, and, at $12 a barrel, the West stood to lose $10 billion a year. Oil royalties to Alberta and Saskatchewan fell dramatically.[118] The only blip in the dismal picture was the 1990 Gulf War, which pushed world oil prices briefly into the $30 to $40 range. But the price fell to previous levels after peace. The oil industry made an excellent windfall profit as a war dividend — profits rose 183 per cent in the first quarter of 1990 over 1989 — which the neo-liberal governments allowed them to keep, failing to tax away a share of the windfall for the public treasury (or indeed to help pay Ottawa's $100 million expenditure on the war).[119] A final accounting in 1991 revealed that the oil companies had made increased profit levels of 81 per cent as a result of the Gulf War.[120]

Many Westerners believed that despite granting the oil and gas lobby everything it had asked for, including complete deregulation and a free continental market, few economic benefits seemed to be flowing to Westerners. Further, in exchange for little real return, the West was squandering a non-renewable resource at fire-sale prices. Finally, the promise that deregulation would bring consumers across Canada lower prices for natural gas proved to be deceptive. Only large industrial users who, due to deregulation and the free market, could cut out the middleman and bargain directly with suppliers of gas, enjoyed a decline in price for gas — down 30 per cent by 1988. Residential and non-industrial customers, especially in Central Canada, enjoyed only an 8 per cent drop, hardly significant, as the Alberta government and suppliers resisted passing on benefits to non-industrial and residential gas users.[121]

The security of future energy supplies became a public issue. In 1988, a study by the Canadian Energy Research Institute indicated that in order to meet Canada's oil and gas requirements, as well as projected U.S. export demands, Canada would have to bring in 6,000 successful wells each year, whereas only 1,600 wells were brought in in 1987.[122] The report further noted that the industry would have to find 5 trillion cubic feet of oil and gas each year in the Western Basin until 2005 and then would need to supplement supplies with oil and gas from the Atlantic offshore, the Arctic and tarsands/heavy oil projects. Canada's exports were projected to increase by 50 per cent in just two years. The next year the NEB reported that Alberta had only a 18-year supply of natural gas in reserve. A year later, the NEB reported that Canada would have to increase imports of crude oil dramatically from 1990 to 2010. Meanwhile, the NEB reported that reserves of conventional light crude in the Western Basin would decline by 45 per cent by 2000 and by another third by 2010.

The Canadian Petroleum Association, hardly a critic of the oil and gas industry, reported that in 1987 Canada replaced only 56 per cent of the conventional natural gas, and 80 per cent of the oil, produced, and that crude oil reserves since 1969 had fallen from 10 billion to 4.9 billion barrels. As a result, Jake Epp, the energy minister, and industry representatives, drew a dark portrait of Canada's energy future. They pointed out that as a net importer of crude oil, Canada was increasingly reliant on expensive frontier and non-conventional oil and gas, and would face an energy short-fall in the future. As a result, huge public investments in upgraders, tarsands projects, the North, and offshore were crucial. The wisdom of a policy, or absence of policy, that allowed the market to suck out Canada's conventional reserves of oil and natural gas at low prices, while leaving Canada a more expensive energy future based upon frontier and non-conventional oil and gas, became increasingly dubious, even to Westerners who benefited in the short term from the rush to increase exports to the U.S. as quickly as possible.

FORESTRY AND WATER

In the early nineties, the forestry industry in B.C. was poised on the brink of a potentially catastrophic readjustment.[123] Though the FTA had exempted raw logs from the treaty, enabling B.C. to refuse "national treatment" to the American lumber industry eager to increase

imports of raw logs, the U.S. industry continued to use the FTA to harass
B.C.'s exports of cedar shingles and shakes, and softwood lumber. The
search for a mutually accepted definition of what constituted an unfair
subsidy had allowed the U.S. industry to claim that B.C.'s royalties on
tree cutting were so low as to constitute a subsidy. Furthermore, the
U.S. raised Canada's superior and largely universal social programs
— most notably UIC and SAP payments, as well as medicare — as
indirect subsidies of workers' wages in any seasonal industry. In effect,
it was argued that the lumber industry was subsidized when laid-off
lumber workers received UIC and SAP payments, because such universal programs could be built into the industry's labour force planning
and served to keep laid-off workers available until an upturn began.
Similarly, medicare premiums in B.C. were much lower than the costs
to employers and employees of similar health insurance in the U.S.,
thus indirectly underwriting a company's labour costs.

These kinds of pressures — threatened countervails against B.C.'s
lumber products entering the U.S. on the basis of alleged unfair and
hidden subsidies — were seen as part of a relentless campaign to
increase the export of raw logs to the U.S. and to protect the U.S. domestic industry from Canadian competition. At first the FTA seemed good
for the B.C. lumber industry, since the U.S. was its biggest market and
the Canadian industry already enjoyed approximately 30 per cent of the
U.S. market due to the quality and price of its products. Under the FTA,
completely free access to the U.S. market could have been a bonanza for
B.C. But free access had not been obtained and the harassment of B.C.'s
lumber exports raised growing anxiety, not just about increasing B.C.'s
American market shares but also about the ability to retain existing
market shares, without giving up a great deal in terms of harmonizing
Canadian forestry and social policies with those in the U.S.

The time was a pivotal one for the B.C. industry. The decline in
old-growth forests of large trees available for cutting had led to a log
shortage for B.C.'s coastal mills, which could only process large trees.
Furthermore, an earlier loss of access to old-growth forests had already
caused the permanent closure of many similar U.S. mills. As well, B.C.
forestry companies made larger profits on the export of raw logs than

on processing. Thus, there emerged a growing confrontation between competing interests — environmentalists against loggers, the declining U.S. industry against the threatened Canadian industry, forestry companies eager for quick and easy returns against provincial governments seeking a policy for the long-term and stable exploitation of a resource now at risk, and workers desperate for jobs against the long-term public interest.

Obviously what was needed in forestry, just as in agriculture and energy, was a co-ordinated set of national and provincial policies to balance these competing claims, to sustain the industry for the long term, to ensure the re-tooling and modernization of the industry while at the same time husbanding the forests, and to plan and pace the transition. But neo-liberal governments had nothing to offer but the free market and free trade, and the final logic of their ideological commitment was clearly to let the market shape the future of forestry. The vacuum of coherent provincial and national leadership worsened the situation, leading to confrontation, controversy, and growing despair about the future.

The only issue that provokes as much anxiety in B.C. as the forests is water. B.C.'s copious and valuable supplies of fresh water, unlike raw logs, were not exempted from the FTA. Ever since the controversial 1961–62 Columbia River Treaty, widely seen as a total capitulation to the U.S. in exchange for short-term cash benefits from the sale of hydro-electric power, the people of B.C. have been particularly uneasy about American designs on the vast potential of the Rocky Mountain Trench.[124] In 1964, hard on the heels of the Columbia fiasco, the Frank M. Parsons Company of Los Angeles presented Canada with a proposal called the North American Water and Power Alliance (NAWPA), provoking near-complete knee-jerk opposition in Canada, and especially in B.C.[125] At the time, the idea was dismissed as colossally expensive, as well as socially, politically, economically, and environmentally insane. B.C. residents were particularly upset at a plan which proposed turning the entire Rocky Mountain Trench into a reservoir, wiping out rich agricultural valleys and settlements and flooding Prince George. But such were the growing hunger for Canada's water in the U.S., and the technical advances in the intervening 25 years, that the idea of massive water exports from Canada to the U.S. again became an issue for serious debate in the late 1980s and early 1990s.[126] Indeed, during the free trade negotiations there were repeated rumours that Simon Reisman, Canada's chief negotiator, intended to use the lure of Canada's abundant water as a trump card to clinch a deal. As it turned out, a continental energy agreement, a long-sought U.S. objective, proved to be sufficient enticement for the U.S. But it was clear that a continental water pact, giving the U.S. access to Canada's water, was only a matter of time, money, and political will.

One suspects that the reason water was not clearly on the table during the free trade negotiations was because the Canadian people were not then ready to accept the proposal that the resource commodity of the future, was, in many powerful minds, Canada's water. This was particularly true of B.C., a place that figures large in any continental water deal. Due to fears and publicly expressed worries, in November 1987 Ottawa announced a national water policy which prohibits massive diversions of water, particularly inter-basin transfers. But certain events of the last few years show that this may be just window dressing, since Canada appears to be on the threshold of positioning itself as a major exporter of water to the U.S. This has been partly in response to pressure from the U.S. and partly in response to pressure from those in Canada who see the wealth potential of water exports as irresistible.

Despite Ottawa's 1987 policy, the planning and lobbying have gone on. Grandco Ltd., a Canadian engineering consortium, with the public support of Simon Reisman, continued lobbying efforts in favour of its $100 billion Grand Canal diversion project to take water from James Bay to the Great Lakes and thence to the U.S. southwest. The U.S. Army Corps of Engineers continued to develop alternative plans to divert water from the Great Lakes to the U.S. midwest and southwest, including a $26 billion proposal to pump water out of Lake Superior and send it through a 1,000 kilometre aqueduct to the Missouri. And, of course, dreams about the Rocky Mountain Trench have not disappeared. Some supporters of such schemes are highly placed in Canada. The late Québec premier, Robert Bourassa, before his re-election, strongly favoured diverting James Bay water to the U.S., expressing great excitement at the enormous wealth to be generated by water exports. And although Ottawa has rejected, at least for now, diversion schemes, the comparatively tiny Garrison Diversion project at least sets a significant precedent.

Besides prohibiting large water-diversion projects, Ottawa's 1987 policy took a significant step toward a recognition of water as a saleable resource export commodity by permitting provinces to sell water by supertanker. B.C. had already moved in this direction in 1983 by approving supertanker exports from Ocean Falls, B.C. to southern California. Since that time B.C. has issued at least five export permits to four companies. One company even obtained a letter of agreement to ship 50 million gallons a day to Abu Dhabi in the Middle East. The supertanker export of water has yet to become a routine reality, but the companies are raising capital and positioning themselves to build the infrastructure necessary to get down to the serious water export business.

Meanwhile, the U.S. southwest is getting desperate. Water experts estimate that natural water sources, like the Ogallala Aquifer, located under the U.S. midwest and southwest, could dry up in the 2000s. Furthermore, Environment Canada continues to predict imminent serious water shortages in southern Ontario, Saskatchewan, Manitoba, and the B.C. interior. And the geopolitical fact remains that Canada, especially Canada's vast north, contains virtually all the North American continent's unexploited water.

The FTA has become a crucial factor in any decision Canada makes regarding water and its sale and export. Since water is not excluded from the FTA, under Article 409 water will have to be treated just like any other resource for export. By agreeing to sell water by tanker to Abu Dhabi and southern California, water has clearly become an export commodity. Should Canada move to major internal diversions to solve water shortages in Canada, say by allowing southern Ontario to purchase diverted water from James Bay, or the Prairies to purchase water from B.C., then water will have become, like oil or natural gas or hydro power, a resource for sale. It will be at this point that the FTA will make it impossible for Canada to deny exports of water to the U.S. Articles 105 and 502 of the FTA ensure "national treatment" to U.S. firms, as well as "treatment no less favourable than the most favourable treatment accorded." Once water has become a resource for sale, and has been sold as a commodity, there will be no way, under the FTA, to deny the U.S. access to our water.

Canada has often referred to itself, with some longing for diversification, as a "hewer of wood and drawer of water." In the next century the second half of that metaphor could become literal. And, indeed, in B.C., the first steps to adding the drawing of water to the hewing of wood have already been taken. Many in B.C. believe that neo-liberals would be only too eager to export water if they could get away with it, and the policies of both the Mulroney and Vander Zalm governments pointed down that road. Like so much else in the neo-liberal agenda, the main obstacle was popular resistance. Unfortunately, neo-liberal governments continued to see the resistance of their own people as something to be overcome, rather than something to be respected and acted upon.

THE FALL OF BRIAN MULRONEY

Mulroney's career as prime minister was ended, and his neo-liberal agenda stalled and significantly discredited, as a result of both economic and regional political forces. The brief economic recovery from 1988 to 1990 — when unemployment temporarily fell and the FTA allegedly held out the promise of instant prosperity — faltered and then collapsed. Although just barely sufficient to assist the prime minister's re-election, the recovery had really been a largely regional affair confined mainly to Ontario and less so to Québec. Clearly aspects of what will probably come to be recorded in history as the Second Great Depression could not be blamed completely on the Mulroney government though many did assign such blame — in February 1991, 57 per cent of Canadians expressed a lack of confidence in the federal government's ability to lead an economic recovery.[127]

The farm crisis on the Prairies was chronic, resulting from forces beyond Ottawa's control. The continuing low world prices for oil and natural gas and the collapse of the Atlantic fishery could not be blamed on Ottawa. The uncertain market for B.C.'s forestry products, and attacks on Canada's access to the U.S. softwood lumber market, were hardly Mulroney's fault. Yet critics did argue that Mulroney's neo-liberal economics aggravated a bad situation: he made too many FTA-related concessions to the U.S. on agriculture; resisted calls for a new national policy on industry and agriculture; granted too much to the foreign fish harvesters and failed to ensure aggressive enforcement of existing fish conservation regulations, resulting in years of over-fishing; allowed low world oil prices to lead to the over-exploitation of Canada's 24 karat reserves of easy, conventional oil and natural gas; failed to obtain free access to the U.S. market for B.C.'s lumber industry.

Some blame for the depression could be assigned to the effects of the FTA. Mulroney's promise of great prosperity if the FTA were passed came back to haunt him. The worst fears of the FTA's opponents appeared to be quickly realized, and free trade came to be seen by the public as the largest single cause of the depression, particularly in Ontario. In 1990 the conservative Conference Board of Canada made it official, announcing that Canada was in the second longest economic decline since the Great Depression.[128] In 1991, labour organizations estimated that about 200,000 jobs had been lost in Ontario over two years, primarily as a result of U.S. branch plants moving south under the FTA.[129] In July 1992 alone, 129,000 jobs disappeared from the Canadian economy.[130] A year later, it was announced that 43,000 jobs were lost just during July 1993 in the goods producing sector, and 1.6 million Canadians were unemployed, a rate of 11.6 per cent, the highest in a decade.[131] By 1991 the Geneva-based World Economic Forum had placed Canada in fifth place among the sixteen leading industrial nations. By 1993 Canada's ranking had fallen to eleventh place.[132] To add insult to injury, the Canadian economy was now bleeding to death as a result of a massive jump in cross-border shopping, which the FTA and lower U.S. prices now made considerably more attractive to Canadians. In 1989, there was a 20 per cent surge in shopping trips by Canadians to the U.S.[133] In 1992 experts estimated that in 1991 the Canadian economy lost $10.4 billion to cross-border shopping.[134]

Some pro-FTA experts insisted that most of these negative effects were due to normal restructuring and could not be blamed on the FTA. Others argued that this re-adjustment was temporary, if painful to many workers and industries, and after "restructuring" prosperity would return. (Canadians recalled that the prime minister had promised a program to assist workers and industries adjust to any negative impacts of the FTA, but had not delivered.) Anti-FTA experts claimed otherwise and continued to win the public relations and statistics war. Canadians, by and large, believed the FTA was to blame. In September 1990, Gallup reported that only 5 per cent of Canadians believed Canada had benefitted more from free trade than the U.S., while 71 per cent insisted the U.S. got the greater benefits, including 59 per cent of loyal Tories, and 69 per cent of Westerners.[135] By spring 1992, only 4 per cent of Canadians wanted to keep the FTA, 27 per cent favoured abrogation and 61 per cent favoured modifications to it.[136] A series of Gallup polls recorded the continuing and growing opposition to the NAFTA deal, culminating in an autumn 1992 poll which recorded that 64 per cent of Canadians believed the deal would hurt Canada most.[137] Despite this overwhelming opposition, including 54 per cent on the Prairies and 58 per cent in B.C., Mulroney rushed to have the NAFTA deal ratified by the House of Commons before he left office, invoking closure for the seventeenth time in his government's life and for the fifth time since his re-election, another record for the prime minister.[138] In one bold move, on the eve of his retirement, the prime minister had again reminded Canadians of his contempt both for their views as well as for Parliament.

THE COLLAPSE OF MULRONEY'S ALLIANCE

The unprecedented regional alliance Mulroney had fashioned between the West, most significantly in Alberta and B.C., and Québec, turned out to be a house of cards. In retrospect, given the political gulf usually separating the two regions, this was not surprising. Indeed, what was astonishing was Mulroney's ability to forge the alliance in the first place and maintain it long enough to win his second majority in

1988, a testimony to the man's political artfulness. What had made the alliance possible had been Mulroney's ability to give both regions what each wanted, or at least to appear to give both regions what each wanted. To the West, particularly its strong right-wing element, he gave the articulation and implementation of some of neo-liberalism's most cherished beliefs, long husbanded in what had been the right-wing backwaters in B.C. and Alberta: a free market in energy, a commitment to provincial rights, a weakened federal government, free trade, and many seats around the cabinet table in Ottawa. To Québec, particularly its nationalist element, he gave the Meech Lake Accord, including a unique "distinct society" clause for Québec in the constitution and a weakened Ottawa, free trade, and very large doses of patronage. The alliance was cemented for 1988 around provincial rights and free trade, though deep divisions over Meech had begun to emerge.

After the 1988 election, the Meech Lake Accord blew up in Mulroney's face. A key ingredient in the rejection of Meech in English Canada, particularly among the traditional Tory right-wing constituency in the West, was an increasing and inflexible unwillingness to grant Québec the "distinct society" clause in the preamble of the constitution. In an effort to salvage Meech from English Canadian opposition, Mulroney agreed to re-open the agreement — something he had steadfastly refused prior to the election — and to consider some modifications to quiet English Canadian anxieties and francophobia. To the surprise of most, the prime minister was sandbagged first by his old friend and new Québec lieutenant, Lucien Bouchard. Bouchard, a committed nationalist, had made it clear from the outset that the Meech Lake Accord was the absolute bare minimum he could accept. The "distinct society" clause, he argued, had already been diluted significantly by the premiers when the deal was first struck in 1987. In protest against this tampering with distinct society, Bouchard resigned from cabinet and then from the Tory party. He was quickly followed by seven other Québec nationalist MPs and the group founded the Bloc Québécois with Bouchard as leader— the first time in history that a Québec separatist party enjoyed representation in the House of Commons. Very soon the Bloc forged an alliance with the Parti

Québécois, and declared its commitment to furthering the cause of Québec sovereignty in the House of Commons. While the initial resignation by Bouchard may have been seen by many as an act of political self-immolation, in the context of the growing anger in Québec over English Canada's hostility and francophobia, Bouchard and the new Bloc proved enormously popular in Québec, scoring a decisive by-election victory in Laurier-Ste. Marie in August 1990. Bouchard had replaced Mulroney as Québec's favourite son in Ottawa.

From then on, the Bloc support in Québec went up dramatically, just as that of Mulroney and the Tories declined sharply. A Gallup poll just after the by-election victory gave the Bloc 21 per cent to the Tories' 29 per cent.[139] A year later, the Bloc led all parties in Québec, enjoying 42 per cent, while the Tories, at 16 per cent, languished in the basement with the NDP.[140] Not only had Mulroney lost the Québec nationalist anchor of his alliance, but his creation — Québec nationalists successful in federal politics, including his friend and advisor Bouchard — had turned on him. Mulroney's strength in Québec against Bouchard was tested during the 1992 referendum on the Charlottetown Agreement which went down to defeat, 57 per cent to 43 per cent.

The right-wing base of the Tory party in the West also turned on Mulroney, depriving him of the second pillar of his alliance. In the West, disillusionment with Mulroney certainly centred in part on the Meech Accord and the Charlottetown Agreement — because Mulroney tried to give Québec too much. But other factors played a significant role as well. The prominence of Westerners in the federal cabinet had not really changed very much. The Ottawa government, Liberal or Tory, remained the captive of Central Canada and pandered excessively to Québec. As one alienated Tory activist in Joe Clark's Yellowhead riding said, "I don't think Joe represents us to Ottawa. I think Joe represents Ottawa to us."[141] While Mulroney mouthed a good neo-liberal line — deficit reduction, cuts in social spending, privatization, the free market, and an end to big government — he just didn't go far enough fast enough with the right-wing agenda. As Tory support collapsed in the West — down to 18 per cent in B.C. and 17 per cent on the Prairies by August 1990 — that support didn't just dissipate into inactive despair, or go to the Liberals or the NDP, as might have been the case in the past. Rather, the disaffected Tory base found a new political home in Preston Manning's fledgling Reform party.[142]

THE RISE OF THE REFORM PARTY

In May 1987 the Reform party was founded in Vancouver by Manning with the backing of like-minded, influential conservatives and a clutch of wealthy entrepreneurs.[143] It was a carefully crafted effort to graft an extreme version of neo-liberal ideology onto western alienation, while weeding out the unrestrained right and those strongly committed to western separatism. While eliminating the separatist spectre, Manning initially retained the knee-jerk, anti-East regional grievances that characterized the western separatist movement of the early 1980s and attached to it the familiar right-wing lamentations of the formerly tiny, lonely and increasingly disillusioned group of true believers on the far right of the Tory party. By thus tying fundamental far-right ideas to the very real sense of western grievance, Manning began very quickly to succeed in winning a new legitimacy and credibility for what became the neo-liberal era's strongest rendition of the usual far-right bromides.

Attaching the new party's slogan of western alienation, "The West Wants In," to an urgent version of the neo-liberal agenda, proved effective in winning the party a western following. In the 1988 election, declaring itself exclusively a western regional party, the Reform party ran in 72 of the West's 86 seats, including full slates in B.C. and Alberta.[144] The platform focused on demands for a Triple-E Senate, deficit reductions and cuts in government spending, an end to bilingualism, opposition to Meech Lake, and support for free trade. The party won almost 276,000 votes, representing over 7 per cent of the total western vote. In Alberta, Reformers won 15 per cent of the vote, and came second in 9 seats. Manning himself ensured a lot of national media attention by challenging Joe Clark in Yellowhead, claiming that Clark did not represent the West on abortion, capital punishment, agriculture and energy,[145] cutting Clark's 30,000 vote margin in the 1984 election to 6,700. Electoral credibility was gained in March 1989 when Reformer Deborah Grey won a federal by-election in

the Alberta riding of Beaver River, which runs east of Edmonton to
the Saskatchewan border.[146] Then in October 1989 Reformer Stan
Waters won a smashing victory in a province-wide vote in Alberta's
Senate election,[147] called by Alberta premier Don Getty in defiance
of Ottawa.[148] Reform party membership, though concentrated in
Alberta, skyrocketed, going from 20,000 members in 1987 to a peak
of 137,000 in 1992 during the Charlottetown referendum.[149]

In 1991, the Reform party decided to go "national," organizing
in Ontario and Atlantic Canada, though not in Québec, in order to
present in Manning's words, "a program that would take in people
from other alienated Canadian regions that have the same problems
as the West."[150] The new slogan was, "Building the New Canada." By
1992, according to Gallup, the Reform party could boast the support
of 15 per cent of Canadians, 3 points ahead of the Tories, including 39
per cent in Alberta, 19 per cent in B.C. and 12 per cent in Ontario.[151]
The Reform party, in less than 5 years, had moved from a marginal,
right-wing, western protest party to a national neo-liberal party that 39
per cent of Canadians saw as a serious contender in the coming federal
election.[152]

In the initial phase, the folksy members of the Reform party were
best known for supporting a better deal for the West in Confederation
and a Triple-E Senate. They wanted to lock up the bothersome "French
fact" inside Québec and made it clear they didn't much like Third
World immigration, demanding it be reduced. They wanted a tough,
no-nonsense anti-abortion law. Further, they occupied the usual Tory
fiscal turf, though with much more shrillness, and were over-zealous
in their adherence to the principles of neo-liberalism.

They were also blunt and frequently brashly, even naively, honest in stating their views, to Manning's frequent annoyance. At one
very successful Edmonton rally in 1991 Manning gave his usual anti-
bilingualism and end multiculturalism code-word speech.[153] The
success, however, was lost in the media when one Reformer said,
"You're a fine white person. You know, we are letting in too many
people from the Third World, the low blacks, the low Hispanics.
They're going to take over the province." Matters weren't much helped

when another stood up and declaimed passionately, "Let them go. We don't need Québec." Even new MP Deborah Grey was a bit too frank when she said, "We're ultra-conservative, but we're not a wild, radical bunch."[154] Stories like the recruitment of four members of neo-Nazi groups in Ontario (they were kicked out),[155] or Manning's purge of the Manitoba Reform organization and the support he lent to a take-over by what some unhappy Reformers called "evangelical, Christian zealots,"[156] continued to feed the perception that the party was racist as well as far-right and full of religious fanatics. Perhaps even more damaging were the observations of people like *The Globe and Mail's* political columnist Jeffrey Simpson who attended the 1991 Saskatoon convention and commented on how unrepresentative the delegates seemed: " . . . no French-speaking Québeckers." Nor, with the exception of one woman from British Columbia, were there black, yellow or brown faces . . . a paucity of names of non-British origin."[157] This gave people like Sheila Copps, deputy leader of the federal Liberal party, the opening to call the party the "Regress party": "I know the Reform party says they're not bigots, they're not sexists, they're not elitists — they're really just populists. But I say, if it looks like a duck, walks like a duck, and quacks like a duck, then probably it is a duck and Preston Manning is a duck."[158]

This posed for Manning his biggest internal problem — to contain the extreme red-neck element of the party, to keep it under control and out of public view. If a perception of the party as red-neck became widespread, it would kill the Reform party, just as it had killed the western separatist movement in the early 1980s. What Manning did not need were loose cannons commenting to the media, or candidates like Vancouver broadcaster and columnist Doug Collins, a well-known right-winger who won a nomination in B.C. in 1988 and then refused to repudiate racism, forcing Manning to fire him as a candidate.[159] The language of the platform was moderated through the use of code words like opposition to "hyphenated Canadianism," the enhancement of "the national culture," immigration based on "economic and labour force needs," "genuine refugees," and "a strong and united Canada that includes a New Québec."[160] Contrary to

Manning's claims of populism and direct democracy, the party was tightly controlled from the top from the beginning in order to ensure that the local leaderships and nominated candidates were members of the respectable and restrained right. Manning hired political experts, like Frank Luntz, a former Republican party consultant and advisor to ex-president Reagan, and sought advice from a Hollywood television producer, to help him polish the party for public consumption. Under Manning's patient tutelage and autocratic control, the Reform party went to great lengths to disguise an extreme right-wing agenda in code words and nuances.

The most important impact of the Reform party on national politics after the 1988 election was the ratcheting of the general political debate significantly to the right. The outer limits of political debate lurched far to the right, and ideas and proposals that were previously beyond the political pale were now part of routine, daily political discourse. Given the 1988 results, Reform's two electoral triumphs, and the poll results, Manning could no longer be dismissed as a lonely voice in the right-wing political wilderness. More important, given that the growth in Reform strength had occurred almost entirely at the expense of the Tories, the Mulroney government began to steal pieces of the Reform platform in order to win back the support hijacked by the Reformers. In many ways, the Reform party began to set the agenda for the Tory government, and it was a more strident and breathless version of neo-liberalism.[161]

No sooner would Manning announce that Reform would end universal medicare, target pensions, and end business subsidies, than the Tory government would begin to discuss similar proposals.[162] Manning would announce a plan to cut the federal cabinet from 39 to 24 ministers and to amalgamate some departments and eliminate others, and a few months later Ottawa would actually do it.[163] Or Manning would announce a plan to cut unemployment benefits and then Ottawa would carry out the cuts.[164] Sometimes it was reversed — Ottawa would announce an intention to cut spending enough to eliminate the deficit in five years, whereupon Manning would outbid the government with proposed cuts to do it in three years.[165] The net effect, of course, was to push the government into a speedier and bloodier-minded implementation of the neo-liberal agenda. Never before in Canadian history had the leader of a regionally based, marginal party had such an immediate, almost day-to-day impact on a government's detailed actions.

The neo-liberal counter-revolution began in the West with B.C.'s Socred premier Bill Bennett in 1983. Ten years later, the Reform party and Preston Manning, with deep western roots, were hurrying its speedier implementation at the national level. Yet the strongest resistance to neo-liberalism also occurred in the West. The NDP denied Mulroney a western coronation in 1988 by taking 32 of 86 seats, including one in Alberta. And at the provincial level, the NDP in Saskatchewan and B.C., together with labour and a variety of popular organizations, sustained a spirited war on the ground to resist the agenda's implementation, finally sweeping the neo-liberal governments from office.

Strong policy leadership was needed to deal with the crises threatening the three pillars of the West's resource-based economy. The inability of the federal and provincial governments of the eighties to offer such leadership contributed to the popular rejection of the neo-liberal agenda in the West. Besides the extra-parliamentary resistance campaigns mounted by labour, social justice coalitions, and NGOs, the NDP, both in Ottawa and in provincial legislatures in the West, provided a significant focus of parliamentary opposition. NDP MPs and MLAs played a key role in mobilizing, focusing, and legitimating opposition, if only by criticizing the neo-liberal measures and articulating clear policy alternatives. As long as the NDP in the House of Commons and the Legislatures continued in this role, public opinion resisted neo-liberal arguments. Gallup polls reported repeatedly that the vast majority of Canadians wanted to sustain public spending on health, education, and social assistance; believed in spending public funds on a national day care program; insisted that hungry people should be fed; remained deeply committed to investing public dollars in regional development programs; opposed privatization while remaining staunch supporters of public ownership in the traditional key areas of the economy; and refused to be stampeded by the deficit/debt hysteria argument.

By the early 1990s, there was every reason to believe that the neo-liberal agenda had been stopped and that a process of damage repair and policy renewal would commence. The election of Bob Rae and the NDP in September 1990 in Ontario, the victories in October 1991 in Saskatchewan and B.C., the exit from the political stage of Getty and finally of Mulroney in 1993, all seemed to point to the beginning of a new era in Canadian politics. By their reckless and destructive actions, the business lobby and the neo-liberal governments had provoked a profound debate about the nature of Canadian society. After a decade, they appeared to have overwhelmingly lost that debate. For many this seemed like a mandate not only to regain lost ground, but to go even further in advancing a new and more progressive consensus by embarking on further innovation in social program development and economic intervention. This sense of hope, mixed with foreboding about the extent of the neo-liberal wreckage, was particularly strong in western Canada, especially in B.C. and Saskatchewan, where the NDP had survived and remained strong and continued to be seen both as the champions of workers, farmers and small business people against the corporate capitalist agenda, as well as of western Canada's struggle for a better deal in Confederation.

10

THE TRIUMPH OF THE RIGHT, 1993–2013: THE NATIONAL CONTEXT

The September 6, 1990, victory of the Ontario NDP, a comfortable majority government with only 38 per cent of the vote, caught the nation by surprise. The Ontario NDP's program, "An Agenda for People," advocated a reversal of the neo-liberal agenda, proposing accepting temporary public debt to fight the recession.[1] To neo-liberal charges of fiscal irresponsibility, Ontario NDP leader Bob Rae replied, "True fiscal irresponsibility is leaving people unemployed and idle, and others hungry and overtaxed, at a time when we are in a recession."[2] Upon election, Rae moved moderately in the NDP's traditional direction.[3]

In the government's first budget — openly targeted to fight the recession through stimulation rather than the deficit through spending cuts — a $9.7 billion deficit was projected simply to hold the line on traditional spending on health, education, and social assistance, thanks to federal downloading and rising unemployment.[4] The budget, hardly an experiment in radical social democracy, provoked a furor in business circles, leading to a mass street protest by Bay Street brokers. Thereafter the business lobby pounded the Rae government into submission. The Toronto Board of Trade's president described the government as "downright unfriendly" to business.[5] A banker accused the government of "putting the Ontario economy at risk."[6] A survey of Ontario's largest companies indicated many were commencing a capital strike by withholding investment to bludgeon the government.[7] General Motors warned the government: "Ontario needs to be seriously concerned about how the province is evaluated by business investors. Critical investment decisions will be made in the near future which will dictate the industrial base in Ontario for the year 2000 and beyond."[8] This was nothing short of economic blackmail, and it worked.

In its second budget, staggering as a result of the continuing recession and federal downloading, the Rae government capitulated, embracing neo-liberalism.[9] With a growing deficit of over $14 billion, Ontario began to cut spending and raise taxes. Rae then took an opposite tack: "The old conflicts, the old ritual battles between ... social justice and fairness and ... economic efficiency and productivity and competitiveness are battles we can no longer afford."[10] In 1993 cuts of $4 billion in spending, including a proposal to eliminate 11,000 jobs in the public sector, rivaled the hopes of even the most ardent neo-liberals. In order to carry out the spending cuts and job eliminations, the Rae government proposed a "social contract," re-opening existing collective agreements to achieve a public sector payroll cut of $2 billion. Public sector unions were given a choice: negotiate the cuts voluntarily or face compulsory cuts.[11] Although able to force most unions to submit, the Rae government paid a high political price. The NDP was riven by anger, and the labour movement turned on the government. NDP support collapsed from 60 per cent in January 1991 to 13 per cent after the 1993 imposition of the social contract.[12]

Unlike Rae, new NDP premiers in Saskatchewan and B.C. did not raise hopes. Both Roy Romanow and Mike Harcourt were on the right of the party, and expectations were low. In Saskatchewan, Roy Romanow made his neo-liberal position clear in March 1990. At a $125-a-plate business dinner, Romanow promised a balanced budget in his first term, the elimination of the deficit in 15 years, and a diminished role for the government in the economy.[13]

No one anticipated how far Romanow would go.[14] Over two budget cycles — 1992 and 1993 — the NDP government went much further in cuts to health and education programs than Devine had gone: three years of outright reductions in grants to universities, school boards, and hospitals; the effective end to the prescription drug and children's dental plans; user fees on selected health services; and a massive health care reform that effectively cloaked cuts in spending and in quality of care. The government even contemplated health care premiums ranging from $200 to $400 a year, depending on family income levels, provoking a caucus rebellion. Citing the debt, "we're on the verge of a financial crisis," said Romanow, declaring there were no "sacred cows ... [since] protecting them could mean we lose the whole herd." The message to the public was clear: Devine, Mulroney, and the other neoliberals were on the correct course after all. The province's debt and deficit made it impossible to do anything but cut social, health, and education spending. A year after winning 51 per cent of the vote, support for the Romanow government fell sharply.

In B.C., NDP premier Mike Harcourt initially took some decisive action on environmental and forestry policy while reassuring the business lobby. Speaking at a Wall Street meeting of investors in Canada, he announced, "We're determined to lower our deficit; you can't spend your way out of recession."[15] Harcourt had assured business he believed in "orderly good government" with a strong business orientation.[16] He did, however, continue to insist on a role for public ownership and declared his government's golden rule for business was clear: "Don't mess up the environment, pay your fair share of taxes, and treat your employees fairly..." These traces of moderate social democracy, including a commitment to reform the province's trade union laws, were too much for the business lobby.

Harcourt's first budgets included cuts in spending and announced the reduction of B.C.'s comparatively modest deficit and debt would take priority.[17] This wasn't enough. The business lobby accused the premier of being the captive front man for a gang of left-wing ideologues.[18] Labour law reform was denounced as an attack on business. The B.C. Chamber of Commerce declared a loss of confidence in a government "driven by ideology and not by good sense." The B.C. mining industry embarked on a capital strike, imposing a 50 per cent cut in exploration investment to force the government to abandon policies on environmental protection, tax rates, mineral rights, and land tenure regulations. The Harcourt government's efforts to appease the business lobby failed to win it over, while undermining public support for the NDP. A June 1993 Angus Reid poll reported Harcourt's approval fell to 23 per cent, lower than Vander Zalm's ever was, and 56 per cent of 1991 NDP voters disapproved of his performance.

The NDP's parliamentary leadership's right turn to neo-liberalism was completed in Ottawa in April 1993. Federal NDP leader Audrey McLaughlin fired Ontario MP Steven Langdon as finance critic for criticizing the Rae government's social charter. McLaughlin uttered words that shocked NDP supporters across Canada: "I don't think there's anyone in Canada, in any province, in any territory, or indeed federally, who doesn't believe that we have to be conservative in the sense of addressing the budget and the deficit."[19] This move to neo-liberalism by the three NDP premiers and the national NDP leader was a heavy blow for many NDP supporters. The NDP had provided a decade of resistance to the neo-liberal agenda in the House of Commons and in the B.C. and Saskatchewan legislatures, confronting the two most dedicated provincial neo-liberal governments in Canada. When the NDP's parliamentary leadership turned to neo-liberalism, support for the federal party fell steeply. From 1988 to June 1992, NDP support fluctuated between 20 and 40 per cent, according to Gallup. By November 1992, NDP support had fallen to 14 per cent. The downward slide reached 8 per cent in July 1993, the lowest for the party in 30 years.[20]

Confronted by a business lobby determined to keep a decade of gains and dedicated to bringing social democracy to heel, Canada's social democratic leaders lost their way, abandoned their popular base, and joined the neo-liberal consensus. Canada's social democratic leaders betrayed the trust and the expectations of those who put them in high office. Social democracy was dying in Canada, largely from wounds inflicted by its most successful leaders.

A shift of enormous significance took place in public opinion in the aftermath of the right turn of the NDP leadership. A decade of unsuccessful efforts to shift the public consciousness to share in a new neo-liberal political and economic consensus at the core of Canadian public policy finally bore fruit.[21] It appeared that what Mulroney, Vander Zalm, and Devine had failed to accomplish was quickly accomplished by the NDP premiers and the national NDP leader. It was a watershed in Canadian political history, and politics and political debates moved sharply right.

The three NDP premiers were not alone in their post-victory betrayal of the public trust by adopting the essentials of the neo-liberal agenda. They were quickly joined by Jean Chrétien when he became prime minister. When Brian Mulroney was driven from office, announcing his retirement on February 24, 1993, he was the most reviled prime minister in Canadian polling history. Canadians turned against Mulroney because of his policies and their effect on Canada. His loyal efforts to implement the corporate agenda were destructive. His attacks on social spending placed Canada's social, education, and health systems at serious risk and increasingly established a two-tiered system of access, one for the rich and another for the poor. Programs of privatization and deregulation crippled the national transportation system while loosening the legislated bonds of social responsibility on corporate behaviour in a variety of areas, from drugs to the environment to advertising. Tax relief for the rich and the corporate sector, combined with a regressive taxation attack on ordinary Canadians' wages and salaries, embittered middle-income Canada and set the stage for a mass, anti-government tax revolt orchestrated by the business lobby. The free trade initiatives, which had only marginal public support, were initially economically catastrophic for the Canadian economy and legions of wage earners, sending the country into a downward spiral of deindustrialization. Mulroney's clumsy constitutional initiatives deepened the chasm between English Canada and Québec and sped the emergence of the Bloc Québécois in Québec and the francophobic Reform party in the West. Mulroney deliberately weakened the federal power, encouraged the assertion of provincial rights, and left the federal government incapable of governing. The people were deprived of a central democratic state to defend them from unrestrained corporate power in an unregulated global market.

When Mulroney's immediate successor, Prime Minister Kim

Campbell, set the election date for October 25, 1993, it was a foregone conclusion that she was fated to be punished for Mulroney's sins.[22] Her dogged adherence to neo-liberalism, a variety of campaign gaffes, and her shallow knowledge of the issues made her an easy target for Liberal leader Jean Chrétien. She was shredded, with the Liberals leading by 28 points at the end of the campaign. The Liberals read the polls carefully and tailored their campaign to address Canadians' two central concerns. First, Canadians were deeply anxious and angry about Mulroney's neo-liberal agenda and its consequences. Second, with the rise of the Bloc in Québec and the Reform party in the West, Canadians were very uneasy about national unity. During the 1993 federal election the national unity issue was not as central as it was to become afterwards, when the Bloc won enough seats to form the Official Opposition, and especially in 1994, when Jacques Parizeau and the Parti Québécois swept to power in Québec promising an early referendum on sovereignty. The big issue in 1993 was the neo-liberal agenda.

The Liberals' platform, *Creating Opportunity: The Liberal Plan for Canada*, anointed the Red Book, carried messages of hope, of turning the corner, of reversing the neo-liberal agenda, of returning to a strong, caring, and interventionist central government.[23] The Red Book's persuasive package of promises was summed up:

> *For far too many Canadians, after nine years of Conservative government, [the Canadian dream] has turned into a nightmare. Our economy is in disarray… Over a million Canadian children live in poverty. Many of our national institutions have been shaken. Our cultural and social fabric has been weakened … [H]ope for tomorrow has turned into fear of the future … For Canadians, the next election is about one simple question: what kind of country do we want for ourselves and our children?*

Everywhere he went, Chrétien waved the Red Book, and repeated its promises, carefully crafted to be vague and general. Chrétien shrewdly wrote off the right, over which the Tories and the Reform party were squabbling, and went after the traditional Liberal centrist base and sidled left to woo NDP voters. For the duration of the campaign, Jean Chrétien sounded like a moderate social democrat, slightly to the left of Bob Rae and Roy Romanow, with no hint that after the election he would become an advocate of neo-liberalism.

The results were devastating for the NDP and the Tories, the former for having signed onto neo-liberalism, the latter for originating and implementing the agenda in the first place. The Tories won only two seats — one in Québec and one in New Brunswick — with 16 per cent. The NDP, though reduced to 7 per cent, won nine seats because what remained of its vote was concentrated in the West — one seat in Manitoba, five in Saskatchewan, two in B.C., one in the Yukon. In B.C. and Ontario, both with NDP provincial governments pursuing neo-liberal policies, the federal NDP's collapse was spectacular. In B.C. the NDP fell from 37 per cent and 19 seats in 1988 to 16 per cent and two seats in 1993. The NDP in Ontario was crushed, falling from 20 per cent and 10 seats in 1988 to 6 per cent and no seats in 1993.

The big news, shaping the next decade of politics in Canada, was the stunning success of the Bloc in Québec and the Reform party in the West. The Bloc took 49 per cent of the vote and 54 of 75 seats in Québec, becoming Her Majesty's Official Opposition. Coming from nowhere in 1988 (2 per cent and no seats), the Reform party won 52 seats with 19 per cent, including 51 of the West's 86 seats and even one in Ontario. The West voted for a party favouring a more ruthless pursuit of the neo-liberal agenda.

Chrétien won his majority government, with 177 of 295 seats, as a result of sweeping Ontario and Atlantic Canada: Ontario gave him 98 of 99 seats, and Atlantic Canada delivered 31 of 32 seats. To put him over the top, erstwhile NDP voters in the West went Liberal in large enough numbers to give Chrétien an unprecedented 27 seats. The 19 seats won in Québec were enough to give him his majority. He never looked back.

On the big issues Chrétien and his finance minister, Paul Martin, got quickly on side with the neo-liberal agenda and carried out a program of cuts in federal spending far in excess of Mulroney's. As fears about national unity increased — with the growing strength of the Reform/ Alliance party in the West and the near win by the sovereigntists in the 1995 referendum — Chrétien was able to win two more majority governments in 1997 and 2000 while continuing massive cuts in federal transfers to the provinces for health, post-secondary education, and social assistance, and a significant downsizing of federal programs and the federal civil service.

With Chrétien on side and able to win majority governments with ease thanks to the Reform/Alliance party in the West and the Bloc in Québec, the victories of the corporate agenda were unprecedented, and loyally delivered by Chrétien's pro-business finance minister, Paul Martin.[24] When Martin introduced his multi-year program of spending cuts in 1995 he bragged that by the next year federal spending would be the lowest, relative to gross domestic product, since 1951. The impact was dramatic as the social and economic wreckage spread across the nation. By the late 1990s, Ottawa had cut payments to provinces for health, post-secondary education, and social assistance by 60 per cent, pushing the provinces to the wall. Ottawa's direct transfers to individuals were cut by $35 billion, dramatically impacting those eligible for unemployment insurance — prior to the cuts 58 per cent of the unemployed were eligible for benefits, but after the cuts only 38 per cent qualified. In 1970 federal spending amounted to 19 per cent of gross domestic product. By 2004 this had fallen to 11.5 per cent.[25]

The federal government, and all provincial governments, were pushed further to the right by a stern ideological and political discipline from two sources: the organized business lobby and the Reform party as it struggled through a variety of transformations over the decade. From the election of Mulroney in 1984, Canada's organized business lobby had never been so powerful since its halcyon days of the late 19th century, when the Canadian Manufacturers' Association (CMA) wrote the tariff schedules desired to protect industry, and John A. Macdonald passed them through the House of Commons unchanged into law. Yet Macdonald's coziness with the CMA offended capitalists in other economic sectors, some of whom supported Liberal

policies of tariff reduction and free trade. Indeed, Canadian political history until the Royal Commission on the Economic Union and
Development Prospects for Canada in the early 1980s was full of conflict and contention between industrial, financial, resource, and retail/
wholesale factions of the capitalist class. Many of the conflicts within
the capitalist class involved the clash of regional interests and popular
mobilizations. In a sense, this lack of unity among the capitalist class
opened up political spaces for successful popular mobilizations and
even some significant popular victories. The last dramatic confrontation of this sort occurred with Joe Clark's 1979 budget. Resource-based
capitalists in the West, particularly the oil and natural gas interests,
supported Clark's budget, while elements of the capitalist class
involved in manufacturing and other resource sectors dependent on
a cheap energy policy, largely located in Central and Atlantic Canada,
opposed it and initially applauded Trudeau's re-election on promises
of energy price controls. However Trudeau's final years in office, characterized by the National Energy Program, which included heavy government intervention in the energy sector, and a further expansion of
the welfare state, served to unite Canadian capitalists in a move to the
global neo-liberal strategy, already underway in the UK under Margaret
Thatcher and the U.S. under Reagan.

Dominant Canadian capitalists, under the leadership of Thomas
d'Aquino, leader of the Business Council on National Issues (BCNI),
now the Canadian Council of Chief Executives (CCCE), began to speak
with one neo-liberal voice.[26] Supported by right-wing think tanks —
most notably the Conference Board of Canada and the Fraser and C.D.
Howe Institutes — and by multiplying free enterprise foundations (ten
by 2003 with assets of hundreds of millions of dollars), the organized
business lobby reached a loud, single-voice consensus. The policy declarations of these organizations received high profile media coverage,
giving the new capitalist consensus the aura of general public wisdom.
The frame of public debate shifted far right, and even moderate social
democratic voices were largely absent from the public discourse.

From 1984 onward Canada experienced a business dictatorship, as
each new party elected to power on an anti-business, anti-neo-liberal

platform was hammered into line. This contributed to a massive decline in public participation in elections. The public became disillusioned as they elected governments on one set of promises and discovered that, upon winning power, the neo-liberal agenda continued to be imposed, often with greater ferocity. For elected governments to take on the organized business lobby required political courage, deliberate polarization through popular mobilization, and acceptance of high-stakes political risks. The new crop of freshly minted and newly elected leaders, including social democrats, possessed none of these. The political victories of the organized business lobby were so complete d'Aquino expressed amazement at the extent of his success.

While the organized business lobby exercised harsh right-wing ideological discipline on governments throughout the decade, the Reform party and its offshoots imposed severe political discipline.[27] Preston Manning was a committed right-wing ideologue with a big idea — the construction of a principled right-wing electoral coalition to defeat the federal Liberals. In the 1988 federal election, Manning's Reform party had linked Western alienation to an extreme version of neo-liberalism and thereby began to win chunks of the electoral base of both the Tories and the NDP in the West. With no seats, and only 2 per cent of the national vote, all concentrated in the West (mainly Alberta), many viewed the Reform party as a temporary Western protest with no staying power. But Manning, backed by wealthy donors, doggedly continued to build the party and national events provided unprecedented political opportunities. The Québec crisis, provoked by the unravelling of the Meech Lake Accord in 1990 and the defeat of the referendum on the Charlottetown Agreement in 1992, served the Reform party well. As leader of the only political party opposing the unpopular Charlottetown Agreement, Manning's national status grew, especially in the West where support for Québec was low. Manning was thereby able to add anti-Québec posturing during a national catharsis to his already strong elixir of Western alienation and an unambiguous right-wing program.[28]

During the 1993 federal election the Reform party proposed stern fiscal measures to cut the deficit to zero in three years and to enact punitive social policy reform. Using shallow populist rhetoric and appeals to break with the "old line" parties, which now included the NDP, Reformers presented themselves as champions of the West in Confederation. Furthermore, in the wake of the Meech and Charlottetown fiascos, Manning appealed brazenly to the deep anti-Québec current in English-Canadian politics: attacks on bilingualism; contemptuous condemnation of Québec's sovereigntists; personal attacks on Chrétien's Québec roots, allegedly rendering him incapable of dealing firmly with Québec; and sneering denunciations of Québec as the "spoiled child" of Confederation. The Reform party's victory in the West was striking: 51 of 86 seats (and one in Ontario) with 19 per cent of the national vote, largely concentrated in the West and most particularly in Alberta. From then on the Reform party was on a roll, provoking fear among all incumbent political leaders, especially those in the West who were not sufficiently right-wing.

The Québec issue continued to dominate federal politics.[29] The sovereigntist Bloc Québécois won 54 of 75 Québec seats and became the Official Opposition in Ottawa. The Parti Québécois, led by militant sovereigntist Jacques Parizeau, won the 1994 Québec election and moved quickly to a referendum on sovereignty in 1995. After the near victory for sovereignty in 1995, Manning and the Reform party began to provoke Québec sovereigntists in order to sustain the anti-Québec anger in English Canada that had borne such promising fruit in the 1993 election.

After the 1995 sovereignty referendum Chrétien embarked on a risky but ultimately effective strategy to block both the sovereigntists in Québec and the Reform party's effort to break out of its Western corral. In addition to adopting the neo-liberal agenda Chrétien took a very hard line against Québec sovereignty, effectively checkmating charges he was soft on Québec. Appealing to Canadians on the basis of national unity, asking for their support to save Canada from the divisions fostered by Reformers and sovereigntists, Chrétien was able to win majorities in 1997 and 2000, effectively blocking the aspirations of both Reformers and sovereigntists. In doing so, he also created the political conditions that led to the fall of his two main antagonists — Reform's

Preston Manning and Québec sovereigntists' Lucien Bouchard both announced their exits from politics in 2001.

Convinced by the election results of 1993 and 1997 that as long as the right in Canada was split between Tories and Reformers Liberal electoral hegemony could not be overcome, Manning boldly dissolved the Reform party. He stepped down as leader and asked Canada's right to join him in a fresh new alliance of the right. The new party, the Canadian Reform Conservative Alliance, united Reformers and right-wing Tories. But in a stunning upset, Stockwell Day, former Provincial Treasurer of Alberta and a Christian fundamentalist embracing a literal interpretation of the Bible, defeated Manning for the leadership of the Alliance.

Eager to catch the new Alliance off balance, and sensing some ebbing of the momentum of the sovereignty movement in Québec, Chrétien called a snap election for November 2000 against the nearly unanimous advice of his advisors.[30] It turned out to be a shrewd move. Despite a disastrous campaign, Day still managed to improve on the 1997 result. The Alliance took 67 seats, up seven from 1997, and 25 per cent of the vote, up 6 per cent. Day even picked up two Ontario seats. But the Alliance was still firmly a Western phenomenon. Canadians in other regions refused to support the Alliance and voted even more strategically than in 1997. Ontario gave the Liberals 100 of 103 seats and Atlantic Canada gave them 19 of 32. Due to the stall in sovereignty momentum in Québec, the Liberals picked up 36 seats there, and even won a baker's dozen of Western seats. As a result, Chrétien emerged with an even stronger majority government: 171 of 301 seats.

It was clear that Canadian voters didn't trust Day's social conservatism, his literal Biblical beliefs, and his evasive manner. Facing internal party criticism, Stockwell Day began to unravel in one of the most bizarre spectacles in Canadian political history. Blaming not only the hated media but also internal sabotage for his electoral failure, Day began purging party staff and surrounding himself with personal loyalists, right-wing extremists, and Christian fundamentalists, feeding growing levels of paranoia that he would kill the party's credibility.

Dissent among Alliance MPs accordingly grew and the caucus fractured as public demands for Day's resignation became almost daily events. Stockwell Day's decline was recorded in the media and the polls. His public disintegration was embarrassing to watch, as his own Western base turned against him. Day was named newsmaker of 2001 as he fought his ouster bitterly, pushing his party to the precipice of extinction, before finally tendering his resignation and calling a leadership convention. Out of the wreckage, Preston Manning's dream of a new united right was reborn, thanks to Manning's protégé Stephen Harper. Harper won the Alliance leadership, campaigning on a commitment to bring the Alliance and the Tories together. Harper succeeded where all others had previously failed: the Alliance and the Progressive Conservative party were dissolved, despite resistance from red Tories and staunch Reformers, and the Conservative Party of Canada was born and officially registered in December 2003. Canada's right was finally united.[31]

Successfully uniting the right under the Tory banner was the first and most important step in Harper's march to power. The bitter lessons of Jean Chrétien's three Liberal majority governments in 1993, 1997, and 2000 helped. Chrétien won majorities with popular votes in the 40 per cent range. Harper patiently targeted the 40 per cent territory. The tables now turned in Harper's favour. The anti-Tory vote was split among the Liberals, the NDP, the Bloc in Québec, and the Green party Harper's task was more difficult than Chrétien's. The Liberal vote was spread across the country with key concentrations in Atlantic Canada, Québec, and Ontario, and that vote generously translated into seats. The West was not likely to go Liberal, but a smattering of seats in the region, especially in some B.C. areas, was important. The key to winning a majority was seat-rich Ontario.

Harper's problem was that a great deal of the Tory popular vote was concentrated in the West, especially Alberta, where the Tories won seats with massive majorities. While pushing up their popular vote, this did not translate into extra seats. In order to win, Harper not only had to break the Liberal stranglehold on Ontario, but also gain a significant share of seats in Atlantic Canada and, for good measure, pick up at least a few Québec seats. The first step was to replace the Liberals as the minority government.

Prime Minister Paul Martin inadvertently handed Harper a minority government on a silver platter. Martin, in an unprecedented act of disloyalty and divisiveness, and with a lot of help from the media, declared open war on Chrétien to drive him from office.[32] The battle deeply divided the party as Martin, still serving as minister of finance, openly built a party within the party, organizing across the country. Chrétien finally caved, retiring in December 2003. Chrétien handed Martin not only a party ripped to shreds by the internecine leadership battle provoked by Martin, but also the task of dealing with the fallout from the sponsorship scandal.[33]

There is no doubt Chrétien and the Liberal party were under a cloud over the fast-breaking scandal. Allegations of financial irregularities, kickbacks, and fraud were largely confirmed in the 2004 report of the Auditor General, which landed on Martin's desk. Upon release of the report there were deafening calls for a judicial inquiry, uniting the opposition parties and the media. Chrétien advised Martin it was a mistake to convene a public judicial inquiry at a cost of millions, creating a political circus to be exploited by enemies of the Liberal party. The scandal would eventually die a natural death as those guilty were found and prosecuted.

But Martin refused to listen and, in February 2004, promptly convened a judicial inquiry led by retired Justice John Gomery. Thus hoping to have put the issue to rest, Martin called a June 2004 election. The end of vote splitting on the right delivered 29.6 per cent of the popular vote and 99 Tory MPs, forcing a minority Liberal government. Liberal support slipped by 4 per cent to 36 per cent, suggesting the sponsorship scandal had begun to wound the Liberals. Most importantly, the new Tory party made a significant breakthrough in Ontario (24 of 106 seats). But the fact remained that the bedrock of the new Tory party remained in the West, which delivered handsomely (68 of 92 seats). It had taken 16 years for Manning's 1988 dream of creating a new, united conservative alliance to reach fruition. But the new Tory party, still led out of Alberta and still carrying a lot of Reform baggage, was not yet fully trusted in Ontario and Atlantic Canada. In Québec, the party went nowhere, winning less than 10 per cent of the vote.

The sponsorship scandal turned out to be the gift that kept on giving to Harper. Gomery released his Phase I report in November 2005, blaming Chrétien and his chief of staff for a failure to provide adequate oversight, while exonerating Martin, even though he was minister of finance at the time. If Martin believed Gomery's report would save him, he was wrong. The sponsorship scandal dominated the news. As Chrétien had warned, the story wouldn't die, largely due to the public hearings of day after day of damning testimony. The opposition parties rejected Martin's promise to call an election within one month of the release of Gomery's final report, uniting to pass a motion of non-confidence in the Liberal government, alleging corruption. The election was set for January 23, 2006.

The sponsorship scandal was the biggest issue in the campaign as Liberal support continued to slip. But in December Liberal support rallied, giving the Liberals a slight edge. The outcome could be a Tory or Liberal minority, depending on how the votes broke down on a seat by seat basis. The defeat of the Martin government was assured by RCMP Commissioner Giuliano Zaccardelli on December 23, 2005, in a letter faxed to NDP MP Judy Wasylycia-Leis announcing a criminal investigation into the office of Liberal finance minister Ralph Goodale, probing possible corruption in the handling of the government's November decision on income trust taxation policy changes.[34] Allegations were made that the highly secret details of the policy changes were leaked to insiders, allowing them to make a killing on the stock market. Wasylycia-Leis promptly shared the letter with the media, and the RCMP officially confirmed a criminal investigation was underway. Liberal support tracked irreversibly down until election day.

Harper became prime minister of a minority government, winning 124 seats (a gain of 25) with 36 percent of the popular vote (up 6 points). Meanwhile the Liberals lost 32 seats and dropped over 6 per cent in the popular vote. Sixty-five of the Tory seats were in the West, but Harper had made a big breakthrough in Ontario, winning 40 seats.

Prime Minister Harper was another step closer to majority power, thanks to RCMP Commissioner Zaccardelli's Christmas gift.

In his drive for majority power, Harper transformed electoral politics in Canada into a blood sport, following successful scripts devised by U.S. Republicans in electing Reagan and Bush, and winning control of the House and Senate. Manning and his chief strategist, Tom Flanagan, brought in Republican strategists to assist the Reform party, and this continued when Harper won the leadership of the Alliance. Upon uniting the right, Harper became relentless in applying the electoral tactics that had proven so successful south of the border.

The most important tactic was the never-ending election campaign. Rather than following the Canadian tradition of elections beginning in earnest when the writ was dropped, Harper's team campaigned continuously between elections, ratcheting it up dramatically during the official campaign. The Tories spent freely year round, while only officially reporting expenditures during the formal election campaign, thus circumventing the spirit if not the letter of the law imposing limits on election spending.

A never-ending election campaign required never-ending fundraising. The Tory fundraising machine was unique in Canadian political history, largely because it relied on a well-organized mass base of dedicated right-wingers and traditional conservatives. Targeted fundraising appealed to those with socially conservative values and beliefs, such as evangelical Christians, anti-choice activists, noose enthusiasts, and gun lovers. More restrained fundraising targeted those tired of high taxes, beleaguered middle- and upper-middle income earners, those worried about crime, those leery of expensive big government, and free market true believers. The Tories were always flush with funds, which they spent freely in their never-ending election campaign.

Harper's Tories made attack ads central to the never-ending campaign. When Manning's Reform party first introduced attack ads there were loud protests from the other parties and many media commentators who called them an American phenomenon that would never work in Canada, and might in fact hurt those who use such tactics more than those targeted by the ads. They were dead wrong. The purpose of attack ads is to discredit an opponent in the public mind by attacking his motives and character, stating baldly that he can't be trusted and distorts the truth. The psychological goal is to plant a negative impression of the target in the mind of the voter, and to do so before the target can establish a widely shared positive impression. The fact is attack ads work, often exceedingly well. Harper's team used attack ads masterfully, launching and sustaining relentless, give-no-quarter attacks on Martin's successors — first Stéphane Dion and then Michael Ignatieff. The first mass media exposure of Dion and Ignatieff to millions of Canadians was via Tory attack ads, placing both men on the defensive from the moment each secured the Liberal leadership.[35]

Another key feature of Tory campaigning was carefully crafted appeals to key demographic groups assessed to be potentially receptive to Tory messages. Such detailed micropolitics characterizes the approach of all parties, but the Tories were able to swamp the other parties. Flush with funds, the Tories hired experienced experts, acquired state of the art technology, and unleashed an army of paid staff and dedicated volunteers. The Tory team delivered well-targeted, nuanced messaging to various demographic groups, seeking the keys to their votes, gradually building toward 40 per cent majority territory.

The traditional Tory rural base in Ontario and Atlantic Canada was solid. Saskatchewan and Alberta were impenetrable bastions. Manitoba and B.C. still included unconquered enclaves of Liberal and NDP support in the cities, the suburbs, and the north. Québec remained beyond the reach of the Tories. Ontario was the key. To break into Ontario the Tories focused on the sprawling suburbs, which increasingly characterized Canada's new urban dwellers. Inner cities, traditional core middle class neighbourhoods, and old working class urban districts were largely dominated by the Liberals and the NDP. That domination had spread somewhat unevenly into the suburban areas and newly developed urban areas. But that support was identified as soft, and many of those seats were won by small margins. The Tories were determined to make the suburban middle class demographic their own, dreaming of a new political coalition between the West led by the rock solid Tory base in Alberta, traditional rural areas across

Canada, and the suburban sprawl around the major cities in Ontario and B.C. Such a new political coalition might make the Tories the new "natural governing party," Harper's ultimate ambition.

The suburban middle and upper-middle classes were united in expectations and levels of affluence with the remnants of the unionized and entitled working class. This broad middle income group was particularly susceptible to the Tory message after over 20 years of neo-liberal battering. Many entitlements of the traditional welfare state had been stripped through means tests. The reductions in federal funding for health and post-secondary education, and the resulting cuts imposed by the provinces, off-loaded increasing costs on family incomes. The cost of housing skyrocketed, putting off many people's dreams of owning a home, or, when those dreams were realized, making many "house poor" as mortgage payments became difficult to manage. Families scrambled to do their best to cover these growing demands on family incomes — incomes that were stagnating or falling in real dollars. The publicly funded infrastructure was crumbling around them. The tax burden was increasingly unfairly shared, with a heavier comparative burden imposed on the struggling and relatively affluent middle income group. Political disengagement increased as elections brought no positive change, no relief, and greater uncertainty about the future. Meanwhile, politicians, due to broken promises and scandals about the misuse of public funds, dropped below used car salesmen on measures of public trust.

The politics of resentment and selfishness replaced the old politics of the benign welfare state. The neo-liberal agenda had successfully reconstructed the political consciousness and expectations of growing numbers of Canadians. The socially and economically interventionist state had been killed by increasing public debt, deep cuts in social programs, and the new mantra that Canada could no longer sustain its historic commitment to the socially benevolent welfare state. Told that the government could no longer solve social and economic problems, and convinced by their daily lives that this was true, more and more people tuned out of politics. Governments were no longer seen as the tool of the people in a democracy to seize control of the national agenda and shape the character of the nation; that was to be left to the global market. Each was therefore alone in a war of each against all. Middle and upper-middle income groups were increasingly receptive to the Tory message of resentment — resentment of the poor, the welfare recipient, the dysfunctional family, the criminal, all consuming their hard-earned dollars paid in taxes. There was resentment against public servants with their fat salaries, job security, and sweet pension plans. There was resentment against those with an inflated sense of entitlement, and those who encouraged this: socialists, liberals, and fuzzy-thinking do-gooders.

The politics of selfishness is the reverse side of the coin of the politics of resentment. In tandem with the relentless anti-tax campaigns by the business lobby demanding tax cuts, the Tories appealed in micromessages to this soft middle income base with promises of small tax cuts here and there, while defending large tax cuts to the wealthy and the corporate sector as essential for economic growth in an increasingly competitive global market place. Many grasped these small straws in the rising tide of neo-liberalism, seeking at least some small personal advantage when they voted for Harper.

None of this would work if the Tories continued to be ripped apart in public by internal divisions, public attacks on the leader, and expressions of extreme views by backbench MPs. This lack of discipline, and the public fears provoked, plagued the Reform party, and reached a crescendo during Day's tenure as Alliance leader. It was clear that voters outside the West did not trust the new right. To prevent this, Harper imposed harsh, centralized control on every aspect of party activities in public. All speeches and public appearances by MPs, no matter how minor, and all press releases, had to be vetted and scripted by his office. During elections the same controls were imposed on candidates. Loose cannons were slapped quickly into line by threats of expulsion from the caucus, or firing as candidates.

Harper continued this approach even more aggressively as prime minister after 2006. Harper changed the traditional practices of Canadian parliamentary democracy. Harper and his staff in the PMO controlled all aspects of the party's performance in Parliament and in public. All cabinet ministers had to adhere to the new rules even more strictly — no public speeches, no press releases, no public appearances that had not been vetted and scripted in detail by the PMO. MPs were given a strategy and tactic book for parliamentary committees which included, during the period of opposition, how to disrupt committees and do damage control in the interests of the party. After winning minority power, it become even more important to undermine parliamentary committees and make them spectacles of dysfunctional failure in order to help persuade the public that Harper needed a majority in order to make Parliament work. Harper successfully imposed one-man rule on his party and then on his government. Harper's caucus submitted to this discipline willingly because it had worked, just as Harper had promised when he won the leadership of the Alliance and went on to unite the right.

Harper proved himself a masterful political strategist and a superb parliamentary tactician in his drive for majority power. Granted he faced a divided Liberal party, unable to find a leader who could successfully engage the Canadian public. Martin's successor, Stéphane Dion, played key roles in the governments of both Chrétien and Martin, coming to prominence in the battle against Québec sovereigntists and as a passionate advocate of saving the environment. Despite these strong credentials, few expected Dion to win the leadership. This seemed confirmed by his third place showing on the first ballot at the leadership convention. Bob Rae, former NDP premier of Ontario, and Michael Ignatieff, a political novice with the backing of most of the party establishment, were considered the favourites who would finally face off on the final ballot. But losing candidate Gerard Kennedy endorsed Dion, giving Dion a slight lead on the third ballot with Ignatieff second and Rae third. As he was dropped from the ballot, Rae endorsed no one. Dion won an unexpected victory.

Dion faced immediate attacks on three fronts. The Harper government launched a sustained series of attack ads which proved effective in undermining Dion. The media did not take Dion seriously, and he received considerable negative attention. Dion faced enemies within the Liberal party, as supporters of Ignatieff made it clear Dion had neither their confidence nor support. In the October 2008 election, Dion's "Green Shift" platform of imposing taxes on carbon emissions was savaged by both the Tories and the NDP. The Tories claimed it was an unfair tax grab aimed at the energy industry and the West, while the NDP insisted it would hit consumers hardest since the costs of the tax would be passed on by the industry.

The results took Harper another step closer to a majority (143 seats with just under 38 per cent). Dion's Liberals were crushed (77 seats and 26 per cent) in the party's worst showing since Turner's 1984 rout. The results seemed to confirm the wisdom of Harper's incremental strategy. The West delivered enthusiastically, while Harper approached the mid-point in Ontario with 51 seats. Atlantic Canada remained a problem, giving Harper only 10 of 32 seats, partly due to Newfoundland premier Danny Williams's ABC campaign (Anybody But a Conservative) over Harper's broken promise to exclude offshore oil revenues when calculating equalization payments. Québec continued to be elusive, giving Harper only 10 of 75 seats. But the fact is Québec no longer figured prominently in Harper's plan. Québec was not a key part of his effort to construct a coalition for a new "natural governing party."

Michael Ignatieff's fate at the hands of Harper was even more inglorious than Dion's. Ignatieff was hand-picked by key members of the Liberal establishment as the crown prince to replace Martin. An internationally recognized academic, scholar and writer, Ignatieff made his home in the UK for many years, dividing his time between teaching at top universities, writing fiction and non-fiction books, and successful, high-profile journalism. In 2000 he took a position at Harvard. In 2005 he accepted a post at the University of Toronto, the year after he was recruited to seek the Liberal leadership. (This long absence from Canada — most of his adult professional life — was used against him in a series of nasty, devastatingly effective Tory attack ads.) In preparation for the expected coronation, Ignatieff won a Toronto seat in the 2006 election. But the crown slipped from his grasp with Dion's upset victory. When Dion stepped down after the 2008 electoral disaster, Ignatieff assumed the leadership. Michael Ignatieff's political career will go down in history as one of the shortest of any major party leader in Canadian history. In May 2009 Ignatieff was declared Liberal leader in an uncontested leadership vote at a party convention. In the May 2, 2011, election he led the party to its worst defeat in history. Ignatieff lost his seat and resigned as leader the day after the election.

Harper's electoral coalition finally succeeded, giving him a comfortable majority of 166 of 308 seats with 39.6 per cent. The West delivered 72 of 92 seats. In Ontario the Tory coalition of rural and suburban voters garnered 73 of 106 seats. The Tories stumbled in Québec, winning only 5 of 75 seats. Atlantic Canada remained a disappointment, 14 of 32 seats. The Liberals were decimated, reduced to third party status, with 34 seats and 18.9 per cent of the vote. The NDP's surge shocked everyone, including themselves, winning the status of Official Opposition with 103 seats and 30.6 per cent of the vote due to an unprecedented breakthrough in Québec, 59 of 75 seats. The Green party's Elizabeth May won a seat.

The 2011 election was a watershed in Canadian politics for a variety of reasons. Preston Manning launched the Reform party in 1987 with the slogan "The West Wants In," attempting to capture the West's profound alienation in Confederation. Harper's reconstructed right-wing Tory party was the offspring of that movement. The West was now in — the prime minister, 72 of 166 MPs, and over half the cabinet were Westerners. The West had never before had such clout in Ottawa. For the first time in Canadian history the Liberal party was no longer one of the two dominant parties in the House of Commons. The NDP breakthrough in Québec defied all previous historical trends in Canadian federal elections. Not only did the NDP win the status of Official Opposition, but it did so thanks to Québec, which for 80 years repeatedly rejected the CCF/NDP. Ironically, the NDP, with its historical roots firmly planted in Western agrarian populism and working class protest, no longer spoke for the West, winning only 15 of the West's 92 seats. Lost in the bigger news of Harper's majority and the NDP's coup, was the election of the first Green MP, thanks to growing public anxieties about the environment and climate change.

The 2011 election signalled a deepening malaise in Canadian democracy. Only 61 per cent of the electorate voted, reflecting the continuing public disengagement from electoral politics that began after the 1988 free trade election and the rapid imposition thereafter of the neo-liberal agenda. Harper's majority government was based on winning just under 40 per cent of those who voted. This kind of democratic deficit is built into our "first past the post" parliamentary system where the power to rule is based on seats won rather than actual popular support. As a result governments can impose the will of the governing party and its leader despite overwhelming popular opposition. This contributes to increased disengagement, as governments with low public support impose unpopular policies despite a dubious democratic mandate.

Many warned Harper would begin to implement his far-right "secret agenda" upon winning power. Harper's agenda was certainly right-wing by contemporary Canadian standards, even harshly so. But the principles of neo-liberalism had already been adopted by all parties as the new economic policy consensus. Granted, Harper's version was marked by steely, unfeeling determination. But Harper never made a secret of his views during his days as a Reform MP (1993–97), as leader of the right-wing National Citizens' Coalition (1997–2001), as leader of the Canadian Alliance (2002), and then of the new Tory party (2004), or as leader of the Opposition in the House of Commons (2002–06). Harper's agenda was an open book, and he never pretended he would deviate from the policies and principles he long advocated.

Throughout his political life Harper was dedicated to uniting the Canadian right into a political force capable of winning power. But he did not seek power for its own sake. From the beginning his mission was to reshape Canada from its foundations upwards. He was deeply devoted to the principles at the core of his ideological mission. Harper saved the Reform/Alliance party from becoming firmly locked up as a cranky regional phenomenon. Though personally committed to social conservatism, Harper publicly fought Reform/Alliance members who would use government powers to impose religious or personal values, arguing the state should not legislate on matters of conscience. For Harper this was tactically essential if the right ever hoped to win power

in order to implement the more important, nation-changing policies. In pursing this goal, Harper first broke with his mentor, Preston
Manning, and then openly defied and defeated Stockwell Day. Upon
ascension to leadership he effectively muzzled far-right members of his
parliamentary caucus.

Harper's critical assessment of the Canada constructed by successive
Liberal governments was brutal — "Canada is a Northern European
welfare state in the worst sense of the term, and proud of it."[36]
He lamented the socialist tendencies of Liberal governments, especially Trudeau's. Harper advocated stronger but smaller government,
intervening far less in the economy and the daily lives of citizens.
Governments listened too much to experts and intellectuals, seeing
itself as a social work agency rather than the possessor and wielder
of the discipline of the state to impose law and order, to manage the
economy, to seek global trade opportunities, and to militarily defend
Canada's privileged place in the world. The welfare state had gone
too far in disrupting the operation of market forces, weakening the
competitive health of the economy. Protection from the full force
of the discipline of the market — whether through overly generous
unemployment insurance payments or the pooling principles of the
Canadian Wheat Board — had gone on for so long under the Liberals
that the Canadian economy was at risk. Harper was a true believer in
the unflinching application of neo-liberal principles and to the use
of state violence in furthering Canada's geopolitical and economic
interests.

Harper criticized the strong, centralized state which characterized
the Canadian federation, foisted on Canadians by weakening provincial powers. He proposed the withdrawal of the federal government
from areas of provincial constitutional jurisdiction. Harper foresaw a
federal government strong and active in areas of federal jurisdiction,
while refraining from using fiscal discipline to impose federal programs that trampled on provincial constitutional rights.

Harper argued the federal government had gone too far in regulating
expanding areas of business that touched the lives of everyone — consumer products, drugs, food, and environmental impact reviews. The

red tape and delays were a drag on the robust evolution of business ventures. The government was out of control, and it was time to curtail its growth, to reduce its size, and to trim its activities, which imposed an impenetrable underbrush of regulations touching the work of all businesses and the lives of all citizens. This would be achieved by cuts in budgets, thus limiting the capacity of government agencies to continue their former levels of activity, and cuts in public service positions, reducing the number of bureaucrats with a shrinking mandate as downsizing went forward.

Harper lamented Canada's failure to take a more aggressive stance in foreign affairs, arguing the Canadian military had been cut to disgraceful and dangerous levels. Canada had failed to pay its fair share, in blood and treasure, in defending its economic interests in the world. Yet Canada benefited from the efforts of the U.S. and other NATO powers to defend the interests of the advanced capitalist countries. While in Opposition he denounced the Chrétien government for failing to join U.S. president Bush's "Coalition of the Willing" to invade and occupy Iraq and enthusiastically supported Canada's intervention in Afghanistan. It was clear that a Harper government sees itself as an active junior partner in future imperialist military adventures to retain economic and geopolitical domination in the world. Harper championed a revival of the true conservative traditions of old-fashioned patriotism, love of the monarchy, an ideologically sanitized conservative version of Canadian history, and uncritical support for a government at war and Canadian troops in combat. Harper argued that Canada should join far more zealously in the U.S.-led "War on Terror," and accept that the nation had to develop a higher level of war-readiness, in both military expenditures and popular support, to participate in what could be a global war without a foreseeable end.[37]

All this, and more, was known before Harper ascended to high office to begin his work. It was the most public "secret agenda" on record. Upon winning his majority Harper began the reconstruction of Canada. He again rummaged around in the American political tool box, adopting the routine use of the "omnibus bill," a common budgeting process in the United States. (An omnibus bill includes any number of legislative enactments that a government can defend as related.) In the U.S. the practice is routine for annual budget bills — all departments' budgets are rolled into one bill to which "earmarks" on sundry spending measures are added. These earmarks constitute patronage spending targeted to particular congressional districts or whole states demanded by members of the House of Representatives or the Senate for supporting the bill. They can range from building a daycare or a community centre in a congressional district to the location of major defence spending in a state. Earmarks commonly make up billions of dollars in each year's budget, and have little or nothing to do with the administration of federal spending and everything to do with buying votes in the House and Senate in order to get the budget approved in a timely manner.

Omnibus bills in the British parliamentary tradition are rare, typically meeting determined resistance from the Official Opposition and a public outcry against such an attack on democracy. In 1968 Trudeau introduced an omnibus crime bill with 120 clauses involving a long-overdue reform of the Criminal Code. In response to protests from the Opposition, the bill was divided. In 1982 the Trudeau government presented an omnibus energy bill, resulting in the Opposition withdrawing from the House of Commons and refusing to vote. Following weeks of a stalled House, the government relented, dividing the bill. In 1994 Reform MP Stephen Harper denounced the Chrétien government for tabling a budget bill that was too diverse, thus hampering the ability of MPs to vote their consciences on matters of principle. The bill was 21 pages long. And in 2005 Opposition leader Harper threatened to defeat Martin's minority government over the insertion of a single change in employment insurance in the budget bill.

In an act of breathtaking hypocrisy, during his first year with majority power Harper introduced two massive omnibus budget bills, Bill C-38, tabled in March 2012, and Bill C-45, tabled in October 2012. Prior to this he tested the waters with an omnibus crime bill, Bill C-10, tabled in October 2011. *The Safe Streets and Communities Act* included 38 provisions previously defeated by the House of Commons during Harper's minority years, rolling into one bill his entire "tough on crime/law and order" agenda: longer sentences, jailing categories of young offenders, curbs on judicial discretion in sentencing, strengthened victims' rights, increases in ministerial discretion, mandatory minimum sentences, tougher prison regimes, and on and on. The bill was rammed through the House using closure repeatedly to limit debate, finally passing the House 45 days after tabling. In 45 days Harper achieved what he had failed to achieve during five years of minority rule.

Arguably Harper's crime bill, though unwieldy and diverse, remained somewhat in the tradition of omnibus bills — it dealt with crime, extremely loosely and broadly conceived, just as Trudeau's 1982 bill had dealt with energy. But the sheer speed and effectiveness of the omnibus strategy, given a tame majority in the House of Commons, was irresistible. But Harper's omnibus budget bills, Bills C-38 and C-45, dealt with virtually anything on Harper's broad reconstruction agenda he wished to throw in. The Orwellian titles of the bills were sweeping: Bill C-38, *The Jobs, Growth and Long-term Prosperity Act* contained 753 clauses in 385 pages; Bill C-45, *The Jobs and Growth Act*, 516 clauses in 357 pages.[38] Despite strong opposition the bills were rammed through using closure (C-38 passed on June 13, 2012; C-45 on December 5, 2012). The business lobby, especially the oil and gas industry, expressed delight with the measures.

The two bills proceeded to dismantle the welfare state and the interventionist government dedicated to protecting the public interest. The measures included: cuts of over 19,000 federal civil servants; large budget cuts in major government departments, agencies, and crowns; the gutting of Statistics Canada; large multi-year cuts to the CBC; the privatization of some Via Rail routes; wholesale cuts in major regulatory agencies for food, drug, and consumer products; hamstringing the Federal Grain Commission; and the final death of the Canadian Wheat Board.[39]

Harper's attack on the federal welfare state included extending the age for eligibility for old age security from 65 to 67. This carried great symbolic significance, since the 1927 *Old Age Pensions Act* was the first brick in the construction of the welfare state. While the 1927 measure signaled the beginning of the welfare state, the 1935 *Employment and Social Insurance Act* became its foundation.[40] The 1935 act, ruled unconstitutional by the Supreme Court, led to a constitutional amendment that made unemployment insurance a federal responsibility. As a result, the *Unemployment Insurance Act* was finally adopted in 1940. Though initially narrow in application (only about 4 in 10 in the labour force were covered) and niggardly in benefits, over the years Canada's unemployment insurance program was expanded dramatically. Unemployment insurance became a version of a guaranteed annual income for individuals active in the labour market, a support system for seasonal workers and seasonal industries — hence a measure to reduce regional economic disparities — and a mechanism for delivering a variety of social support programs. The 1971 amendments extended coverage to over 9 in 10 wage and salary earners in the labour force; minimum weeks of work required for eligibility was reduced to eight; benefits were increased to 75 per cent of the wage lost; the disqualification period was cut in half; and benefits were provided for job loss due to illness, maternity leave, and retirement until age 70. Benefits could be enjoyed for up to 51 weeks.

The attack on Canada's unemployment insurance program began in 1976 and intensified under successive neo-liberal Conservative and Liberal governments during the 1980s and 1990s. By 1996, when the program was renamed "employment insurance" (EI), wage replacement rates had fallen from 75 to 55 per cent, benefit periods and insurable earnings reduced, penalties increased, clawback provisions of 100 per cent were targeted to repeat users in certain circumstances, and eligibility rules tightened regarding job searching and work willingness. Harper's additional changes, in effect from January 6, 2013, placed a ceiling of $501 per week on coverage and dramatically reduced benefit eligibility periods. The net effect of the changes meant less than half of officially unemployed Canadians were eligible for benefits. Support for seasonal workers effectively ended since claimants must be willing to accept a pay cut of up to 30 per cent in a new job and be willing to travel 100 km to a job designated "suitable" by EI bureaucrats. A generous bonus system was introduced for EI enforcers to track down and cut off those ineligible for benefits under the increasingly complex and cumbersome rules deliberately designed to reduce the number of benefit recipients. Harper signaled there was more to come, including a possible devolution of employment insurance to the provinces.

Harper's interest in devolution to the provinces extended beyond employment insurance. The Harper government decided the Canada Health and Social Transfer (CHST), a $40.4 billion transfer of funds to the provinces in 2012–13, will face limited growth until 2016–17, with serious cuts thereafter.[41] The program is up for renegotiation in 2024 and Harper made it clear that these areas of provincial constitutional responsibility should ideally devolve back to the provinces. The Equalization Program, designed to offset regional economic disparity, is constitutionally protected under 32(6) of the *Constitution Act, 1982*, and will therefore survive in some form in spite of Harper's ideological doubts about the program. (In 2012–13 it delivered $15.4 billion to the poorer provinces). Harper will devote himself to the task of curtailing the amount of federal funds Ottawa is constitutionally required to devote to the program in future years, setting the stage for constitutional challenges from poorer provinces facing reductions.

Harper's devotion to severely diminish government regulation of the economy focused most importantly on federal environmental regulatory laws, programs, and agencies. Having already cut as many environmental programs as the opposition allowed while a minority prime minister, all inhibitions were eliminated with a majority government. A key theme throughout the two omnibus bills was a systematic assault on the federal environmental regulatory regime. The cuts focussed most importantly on paving the way for a more rapid expansion of Canada's petro-economy by giving the energy sector virtual free reign on developments with scant environmental oversight. The sheer number and complexity of the changes swamped the opposition, the media, and the public. Most importantly the new laws gave the federal cabinet the final authority to determine the scope and details of the environmental assessments of any development proposal. This was defended as necessary in order to drive the energy sector forward faster.

Many current federal environmental powers will devolve to the provinces and the territories, which, in the past, have been notoriously willing to engage in shallow, *pro forma* environmental assessments, and fast track approval procedures, in order to get desperately desired economic activity moving forward quickly.[42] Public interventions in environmental assessments were sharply curtailed and controlled. The number of environmental experts employed by the federal government was cut dramatically, and those remaining were effectively muzzled. The number of waterways under federal protection was reduced catastrophically.

The single most important objective of gutting the environmental assessment process, and giving cabinet the final authority to approve projects, was to push the oil and gas industry forward more rapidly. The expansion of Alberta's tar sands developments will accelerate. Perhaps more urgently important, several key pipeline proposals designed to speedily expand Canada's pipeline network and capacity to the West coast, the Gulf States in the U.S., and the east coast of Canada and the U.S. were mired in public opposition and extensive environmental assessments. The Harper government insisted these developments were vital to developing new, more lucrative markets, particularly by tanker to Asia. Delays in pipeline construction, the government alleged, will cost Canada $1.3 trillion in economic output by 2035, as well as a loss of $281 billion in tax revenues.[43] Harper instantly gained the reputation as leading a government of the oil industry, for the oil industry, and by the oil industry.

A number of measures in the bills reaffirmed Canada's more aggressive, hard-edged position on the world stage.[44] Foreign policy, particularly foreign aid programs, will be conducted on the business-first model. Accordingly, the forty-year-old Canadian International Development Agency was terminated, and its programs transferred to a new department on foreign affairs and trade. Canada will take positions to defend its economic and geopolitical interests. Canada will no longer be a friend of the United Nations — indeed it will join the U.S. and Israel in resisting UN activities that appear to give aid and comfort to the perceived enemies of the privileged nations. Foreign aid will be explicitly tied directly to foreign trade and investment, and Canada's aid programs will be designed to create, enhance, and complement Canada's economic interests and activities in recipient countries. In line with Harper's insistence that the economy and economic growth must be the centerpiece of the entire program of his government, Canada's role in foreign affairs will focus primarily on negotiating and signing as many free trade agreements as possible in order to expand existing, and gain new, markets for Canada's exports, especially energy exports. From the beginning Harper tied his political star to managing the economy and maximizing economic growth, and he was determined to focus all Canada's efforts on the world stage on that task.

Harper's Canada, as laid out in the two omnibus bills, was a very different Canada from that Canadians embraced for years: a land ruled by a shrinking and mean-spirited government, rushing to imprison people, curtailing regulatory protection of the public interest, bloody-mindedly callous about the environmental consequences of unregulated economic growth, eager to strut arrogantly on the world stage rattling its rather small sabre. The new reality was survival of the fittest and minimal help and comfort for those who fall by the wayside. The market was king, the arbiter of all things, but each was alone in the market and the guiding light became *caveat emptor*. It was a Canada Harper described openly and bluntly for many years before winning power.

11

THE TRIUMPH OF THE RIGHT, 1993–2013: PROVINCIAL CONSOLIDATION

From 1993 the West supported the reconstruction of the right. By the end of the decade the new right-wing Tory party, bereft of red Tories, enjoyed political hegemony in the West's political culture. Western protest, having created social democracy and militant trade unionism in the past, turned solidly right. By 2000 the West was the anchor in Harper's electoral coalition which finally gave him a majority in 2011 — the West, rural Canada, and suburban Ontario. Neo-liberal ideological hegemony in the West was consolidated among all political parties in the four western provinces.

SASKATCHEWAN

CCF/NDP premiers of Saskatchewan largely earned places in history for progressive contributions to Canada. T.C. Douglas (1944–61) pioneered the welfare state, public ownership of key economic sectors, and medicare. His successor, Woodrow Lloyd (1961–64), battled the medical profession and the united right during the 1962 Doctors' Strike punctuated by the vicious "Keep Our Doctors" campaign, successfully implementing medicare when many, even some in his own party, counseled surrender. If one person earned the title of Father of Medicare, it was Woodrow Lloyd. Lloyd also earned a place in history as the only provincial party leader to support the left-wing Waffle Manifesto at the 1969 NDP national convention in Winnipeg.

For that, he was ousted from the leadership by a caucus cabal led by Roy Romanow. Premier Allan Blakeney (1971–82) won significant concessions for the West in Trudeau's patriated constitution — an effective western constitutional veto, more complete provincial powers over natural resources, and the constitutionalization of the right of poor provinces to equalization payments. Blakeney implemented an aggressive strategy of public ownership of resources during the 1970s: nationalization of half of the potash industry, creation of a large crown in oil, and significant public partnerships in uranium development. In marked contrast, one rummages through the record of Roy Romanow (1991–2001) in a fruitless search for such contributions. Romanow is remembered for his betrayal of social democratic principles, loyal service to the business lobby, and coziness with Liberal prime minister Jean Chrétien.[1]

On October 21, 1991, Romanow won a convincing popular mandate, easily enough to end the neo-liberal agenda in the province, roll back Grant Devine's cuts, improve labour laws, and re-acquire public assets sold at fire sale prices. The Tory party was in a state of collapse. After 1993 the Tory party was totally discredited as trials began in the Tory caucus fraud scandal involving the fraudulent misappropriation of nearly $1 million from MLA communication allowances between 1986 and 1991. By the end of the trials, 16 had been convicted or pleaded guilty, including 14 former Tory MLAs, 11 of whom were of cabinet rank, most prominent among them former deputy premier Eric Berntson.[2] Romanow had two full terms to carry out an aggressive social democratic agenda with the right in disarray.

Upon victory, Finance Minister Janice MacKinnon made the rounds to speak privately to academics known as NDP sympathizers.[3] Her message was disturbing. Dealing with the deficit and debt required huge cuts in spending and large increases in taxes on wages and salaries. The government faced the strongest opposition from NDP members and supporters. She sought to persuade intellectuals to support the government. Romanow saw his own party, its supporters and the labour movement as his primary adversaries. Such quiet visits were buttressed by a relentless propaganda campaign and dramatic speeches by the premier up and down the province, designed to whip up public hysteria about the deficit and debt. There followed a three-year cycle of cuts in social, education, and health spending, involving hundreds of millions of dollars and hundreds of public sector jobs, as well as an increased tax burden on wages and salaries. Relief at Romanow's defeat of Devine died, replaced by anger and apathy.

Romanow's last full term as premier (1995–99) witnessed the end of Romanow's political magic. Those who voted for him, most importantly NDP activists and supporters, experienced an even deeper sense of betrayal. Shortly after re-election in 1995 Romanow announced his election promises of an end to cuts and hard times could not be met due to the nasty feds in Ottawa. Writing the shabbiest chapter in NDP political history, Romanow feigned surprise at the looming cuts in federal transfer payments for health, post-secondary education, and social assistance. Not only did Romanow know of the coming cuts, he was well aware of their magnitude and the manner in which they would be staged in long before he called the 1995 election. Federal finance minister Paul Martin had been remarkably candid, and officials in Ottawa and Regina had already crunched numbers indicating that the cuts would hit Saskatchewan with an estimated $108 million cut in 1996 followed by between $200 and $300 million in each subsequent year. But that did not deter Romanow from claiming all promises from 1995 were swept from the table because of the sudden federal cuts.

While the further alienation of Romanow's own base jeopardized his political future, the effective restructuring of right-wing political parties ended Romanow's cakewalk in politics. In August 1997 the national executive of the Reform party agreed to target Saskatchewan for a move into provincial politics, filling the vacuum on the right created by the collapse of Tory credibility. The Reform party was confident, having won eight of Saskatchewan's 14 seats with 36 per cent of the vote in 1997. In response, the Saskatchewan right moved quickly to establish the Saskatchewan Party to forestall Reform's intrusion. Tory leader Bill Boyd announced the four Tory MLAs would dissolve the Tories and join the new party. Four right-wing Liberal MLAs defected. On August 9, 1997, the Saskatchewan Party was founded, stealing the mantle of

Official Opposition from the Liberals. Reform party members rushed to join the new party easily overwhelming the Tories and right-wing Liberals. Inevitably, former Reform MP Elwin Hermanson won an easy victory as leader. In the coming 1999 election Romanow faced a formidable and fresh right-wing foe, capable of uniting much of the free enterprise, anti-NDP vote. This shift in mood on the right — from a defeatist conviction Romanow was unbeatable to a sense victory was within reach — was manifested in increased cockiness in the legislature, and on the hustings as the Saskatchewan Party mobilized popular support.

Romanow strategists were convinced that the NDP could easily win a June 1999 election. The Saskatchewan Party was not yet ready. The still lively Liberal party would pull enough right of centre votes to help the NDP. The public was mistrustful of the right-wing agenda of the Saskatchewan Party and uneasy about Elwin Hermanson as premier. Though unhappy, the NDP's supporters on the left, the centre left, and in the labour movement had nowhere else to go and could be pulled out to work to stop Hermanson. Polls during 1998 and early 1999 suggested the NDP could win a majority in June. The whole plan was derailed by the nurses' strike in April 1999, bringing into sharp relief two strategic miscalculations of the Romanow government.

First, the Romanow government assumed it could do anything with the health care system — cut, slash, underfund, restructure — and get away with it by constant reference to Tommy Douglas and the NDP's devotion to medicare. Who would dare question the founders of medicare and the inheritors of the mantle from Douglas? This worked well at first. Most people saw Romanow and the NDP as trustees of medicare. But by 1999, especially after the 1995 election, it was no longer true for growing numbers of the electorate. Increasingly Romanow and the NDP were seen as just another government lying and spinning to cover painful cuts to health care.

Second, the Romanow government assumed that labour was a permanent political captive. Labour had no alternative but to support the NDP over the Saskatchewan and Liberal parties. This was and remains largely true. But Romanow became so cavalier with labour that he assumed labour's demands could be forever ignored, and as a result, labour won very little from the Romanow government. You can deny your popular political base only so long before there's growing anger. Labour had been denied repeatedly by the Romanow government, and the fiasco of the nurses' strike deepened their sense of betrayal.

In April 1999, 8,400 nurses went on strike.[4] Within hours Romanow rammed a back-to-work law through the legislature. Defying the law, the nurses embarked on a 10-day illegal strike. Relations between the NDP government and labour deteriorated to the lowest point since 1982, as the government embarked on a negative propaganda campaign against the nurses while labour likened Romanow's unseemly rush to a back-to-work law as in the worst tradition of right-wing, anti-labour governments. The nurses were particularly incensed by Romanow's constant refrain that he had no choice because patients were at risk. Saskatchewan Union of Nurses (SUN) leaders denounced this as a "bold-faced lie," since detailed provisions had been made to ensure emergency staffing. As the strike went on, public opinion shifted dramatically in the nurses' favour, the government caved, and a settlement was quickly achieved. But the political damage was done. The planned June election was postponed to September. It marked the end of Romanow's career.

Romanow was confident as the 1999 campaign started. In an August interview with *The Globe and Mail*, the journalist assumed Romanow was walking to an easy victory. Asked to characterize his secret to success, a confident Romanow said, "Call it Third Way or Tony Blair–style socialism…"[5] Faced with growing anger in rural areas afflicted by the chronic farm crisis, now almost two decades old, Romanow played Pontius Pilate as he washed his hands of the farm crisis, pointed the finger at Ottawa, and declared he would not put the province's treasury at risk as Devine had done in the 1980s. During the campaign, Romanow avoided large meetings in rural areas, opting for small meetings of carefully selected rural supporters. His decision to call the election in the middle of harvest further estranged the farm vote. (Tommy Douglas had always advocated June elections, after seeding and when hope was high, while avoiding harvest elections). Farmers, and those who depend upon them, already angry, became furious.

If Devine used his infamous "rural strategy" to win in 1986, Romanow embarked on an urban strategy, counting on a lock on his captive vote in urban Saskatchewan and hoping to win just enough rural votes to top up NDP support to win a majority. It failed. Romanow retained a tenuous hold on power despite winning 3,600 fewer votes than the Saskatchewan Party which successfully united the right-wing, anti-NDP vote and swept rural Saskatchewan. Voter turnout remained low at 65 per cent. Reflecting an epidemic of abstentions, turnout was lowest in the urban seats. Reflecting the aroused anger of rural voters, turnout was highest in rural seats.

Chastened, Romanow cobbled together a coalition with two of the three Liberals (including the Liberal leader), both of whom were put in the cabinet, and announced his retirement from politics upon selection of a new leader at an early 2001 convention. The Romanow era ended. He led the party from a major victory in 1991, when over 83 per cent of the electorate voted, to near defeat in 1999, when just over 65 per cent turned out. Upon election in 1991, Romanow pushed the party hard to the right, abandoned its founding principles, and throttled social democracy. As a newly minted neo-liberal, Romanow cut health care and education heavily, while cozying up to the business lobby. He repeatedly beat up on the NDP's traditional constituencies — labour, the activist left, environmentalists — refusing them major concessions, while paying devoted attention to business. The left, labour activists, and environmentalists left the party in large numbers, or drifted into inaction.

A common view among Romanow's critics on the left was he refused to reverse the neo-liberal agenda, to repair the damage done by Devine and steer the government in a moderate social democratic direction. The evidence leads to an even harsher conclusion. Romanow intensified the neo-liberal agenda begun by Devine and demanded by the business lobby. Romanow completed the privatizations of public assets. From 1991 to 1994 he completed the privatization of the Potash Corporation of Saskatchewan (PCS). In 1989, when the PCS was privatized, the province received 35 million shares and immediately sold off 13 million. Thus when Romanow came to power he had the necessary tools to reverse the privatization. Romanow removed the concessions Devine had been politically compelled to make during the 1989 privatization battle, including the restrictions that no person or group, except the government of Saskatchewan, could hold more than 5 per cent of shares and that non-residents of Canada could not own more than 45 per cent of the shares, thus ensuring effective control of the corporation remained in Canada. The loss between 1989 and 1996, both in underselling assets and lost dividends, amounted conservatively to half a billion dollars. Over the lifetime of the potash industry the losses will be a hemorrhage of foregone public revenues.

In 1997 Romanow sold the province's 50 per cent interest in Saskfor, a forestry partnership with MacMillan, losing average annual dividends of $6 million. In 1998 he sold the province's shares in the Crown Life insurance company for $150 million and the Lloydminster Upgrader (destined to become a huge cash cow) for $308 million. Between 1991 and 1996 Romanow reduced the province's stake in Cameco, a partnership with the private uranium industry, from 30 to 10 per cent. Clearly, Devine began the privatization of public assets, but Romanow finished the job.[6]

Defenders of privatization argue the most important source of public resource revenues come from royalties and taxes, while the dividends paid from ownership hardly compensate for the public capital frozen in the asset and the risks associated with equity investment. This was contradicted by the evidence. For example, between 1976 and 1988 PCS paid provincial taxes and royalties of over $372 million and dividends of over $228 million, and the province still owned its investment. That total came close to the one-time payment the province received for privatization. The crown oil company, SaskOil, was consistently a very good money maker for the province. Despite the claims royalties delivered the real benefits without risk, Devine had cut royalties for all resources dramatically. For example, the Blakeney government took 50 per cent of the total sales of oil as royalties and taxes. Devine cut this to 27 per cent. But Romanow went further, cutting it to 17 per cent. In 1979–80 the Blakeney government obtained about 21 per cent of total revenues from resource rents. Certainly Devine changed that dramatically, but by 1994–95, given Romanow's refusal to reverse Devine's reductions, Saskatchewan obtained just over 8 per cent of revenues from resource rents. A return to a resource rent policy approximating Blakeney's, and a re-acquisition of cash-producing public assets, would have more than offset Devine's deficit and debt from the 1980s (which was largely created by tax and royalty cuts), and easily sheltered the province from the federal cuts of the 1990s. Romanow not only retained Devine's cuts in resource rents, but actually increased them in 1998.[7]

On the matter of labour law there was more continuity than discontinuity between Devine and Romanow. Romanow legislated striking power workers back to work in 1998 and striking nurses in 1999.[8] He refused to amend trade union laws to tilt the relations of power a bit from capital to labour in order to facilitate organizing the unorganized. He rejected anti-scab laws. Romanow refused to include workers in large agro-industrial enterprises in rural areas, like hog barns and feedlots, under the labour code. He routinely rejected individuals recommended by labour as preferred labour representatives on boards and commissions. Symbolic of the relationship were the amendments to labour standards to help part-time workers by granting more senior part-timers the right to take additional hours of work as they became available in their places of employment. These were passed but never proclaimed, sitting forlornly on public display.

Overall, as political economist John Warnock concluded in 2003, in each and every policy area — privatization, deregulation, agriculture and rural development, taxation, labour, social programs, the environment — "the Romanow government decided to continue the restructuring of capitalism as demanded by the business community," while jettisoning the "promised . . . return to the social democratic orientation of the Blakeney government."[9]

Romanow's departure led to a process of renewal and a slight shift to the left. Many disgruntled members returned to the fold to support Lorne Calvert for premier in 2001, widely seen as a moderate social democrat in the Blakeney tradition. Calvert distanced himself from the Romanow legacy — a little more went into health care and education, the Crowns were somewhat re-centred in government policy, there was more social democratic talk.[10] When Calvert called an election in 2003, the pundits predicted defeat.[11] Calvert turned slightly left, very publicly called home the disillusioned among the party's faithful, defended public ownership, and made health and education top priorities. Calvert won 45 per cent of the popular vote compared to the Saskatchewan Party's 39 per cent. But this translated into a narrow victory in seats, 30 to 28. His promise of a new left-leaning direction worked beyond expectations — voter turnout jumped to 71 per cent as the total NDP vote increased dramatically.

Yet by 2005 Calvert had not yet broken with the Romanow legacy. Indeed, Calvert caved on the most important issues defining his government. When he moved to proclaim the available hours law, the business lobby and the Saskatchewan Party launched an hysterical attack. Calvert surrendered, promising not to proclaim the law and to wipe it off the statute books. The message to Calvert was clear: even a modest pro-labour measure will be met by the implacable opposition of the business lobby, the Saskatchewan Party, and the media. Calvert continued to lower royalty rates on resources, especially oil and potash. Indeed, the share of oil sales going to revenues fell to 17 per cent under Romanow, and after Calvert's additional concessions it fell to 14 per cent.

Defenders of Calvert noted with a narrow one-seat majority in the legislature, and a group of Romanow-era pro-business cabinet ministers led by Industry Minister Eric Cline, Calvert remained a captive of the Romanow legacy. Perhaps that was true, but the fact remained that under Romanow the NDP government was neo-liberal in words and actions. Under Calvert the NDP government was neither fish nor fowl, one day staggering in a moderate social democratic direction and the next day, facing attacks by the business lobby and the media, staggering in a neo-liberal direction.

Calvert's failure to break with neo-liberalism and to reassert a social democratic approach heralded the final hegemonic consolidation of neo-liberalism in provincial politics. All parties, with the exception of the tiny New Green Alliance, embraced neo-liberal principles and policies with only minor variations. This approach characterized Calvert's record up to the 2007 election. In fact, his retreat on the available hours law was but the first step in a complete capitulation to neo-liberalism. Calvert agreed to the demands of the oil and gas industry in a deal negotiated in secret. Royalty and tax rates on new production were cut dramatically, the capital surcharge was cut, and a complex new regime of industry-friendly volume incentives was announced. He declared his government open to the possibility of uranium refining in the province in response to an orchestrated campaign of pressure by the nuclear industry. This was a mistake, since uranium refining had a history of deep opposition among the public. His budgets were clearly pro-business: extensive concessions to the oil and gas industry and the implementation of the totality of the Vicq Committee's pro-business tax cut proposals were centerpieces.[12] In response, the Saskatchewan Party accused Calvert of stealing their program, offering the public "Sask Party Light" rather than the real deal. Though Calvert softened this capitulation to the business lobby by increasing funding for social, health care, and education programs, the NDP political base expressed concern about the rightward shift in economic policy.

Calvert was responding to political reality. Defeat in the next election appeared a foregone conclusion. Support for the Saskatchewan Party under new leader Brad Wall grew dramatically.[13] Wall skillfully positioned himself as a centrist in marked contrast to the previous leader, Elwin Hermanson. He laundered the party program of harsh right-wing measures and weeded out extreme right-wingers as candidates. He promised not to privatize the Crowns. He promised to hold out a helping hand to the poor. He embraced medicare with enthusiasm. He even allowed that unions were okay, as long as members didn't listen to union bosses. Wall was determined to focus the coming campaign on vague themes: it's time for a change, and the NDP had been too long in power with nothing new to offer. Wall did not want a campaign polarized around the big issues, nor, it appears, did Calvert. Calvert adopted virtually the entire Saskatchewan Party economic agenda, hoping to deflate Wall on the hustings. This was a miscalculation.

Brad Wall's Saskatchewan Party won two back-to-back landslide victories, 38 of 58 seats with 51 per cent in 2007, and 49 of 58 seats with 64 per cent in 2011. In 2011 the NDP was reduced to 9 seats and 32 per cent. Wall's goal became to make history by winning a third term in 2016 and replacing the NDP as the natural governing party. In 1944 a fundamental political realignment occurred in Saskatchewan when the CCF swept to power, uniting middle-level farmers, the urban working class, and teachers.[14] Saskatchewan was on the cusp of embracing the Saskatchewan Party as the new natural governing party. The unprecedented victory of Wall in the 2011 election, with 64 per cent, the highest popular vote victory in the province's history, arguably marks a second fundamental realignment in Saskatchewan's political history. Wall swept city, town, and country, decimating the NDP.

The previous victories of anti-CCF/NDP, pro-business election coalitions — Ross Thatcher's Liberals in 1964 and 1967; Grant Devine's Tories in 1982 and 1986 — proved ephemeral, ending in large victories for the NDP after two terms (Blakeney in 1971 and Romanow in 1991). While in opposition the NDP remained committed to a moderate social democratic vision and ran on social democratic platforms to regain power. But the process of political realignment was already well underway. The class transformation of Saskatchewan agriculture — the emergence of growing numbers of conscious capitalist farmers and the decline of the middle-level farmer leading to rapid rural to urban population shifts — saw the CCF/NDP's rural base wither in its capacity to win seats.[15] More and more, the NDP relied on a solid urban base rooted in what was mistakenly viewed as impregnable working class support.[16] The Saskatchewan Party enjoyed hegemony in rural Saskatchewan beginning with the 1999 election. In 2011 Wall's Saskatchewan Party routinely won rural seats with pluralities of 60 to 70 per cent.

In urban Saskatchewan the Saskatchewan Party's assault on the NDP's 27-seat urban base won no seats in 1999, 3 in 2003, 10 in 2007, and 20 in 2011. While political realignment in rural areas was clear and apparently permanent, the 27 urban seats remained contested terrain. At the partisan electoral level, the 2016 election will test the extent to which realignment has occurred in urban Saskatchewan. Should Wall win an unprecedented third majority government with a continuing solid foundation in urban Saskatchewan, it can be reasonably concluded that the 2011 election involved a critical, structural realignment of politics in the province. Wall's soft neo-liberalism, combined with his wisdom in taking care not to provoke an urban/rural polarization like that engineered by Grant Devine, might well succeed in sustaining a substantial urban base.

At the ideological level the political realignment in Saskatchewan arguably occurred with Romanow's 1991 victory. After winning a large majority based on promises to reverse the neo-liberal agenda, Romanow embraced neo-liberalism and continued its aggressive implementation. From then on, both major parties supported neo-liberalism and the social democratic option disappeared from electoral politics. Calvert's brief flirtation with social democracy polarized the province in the 2003 election, giving the NDP an unexpected victory. But Calvert abandoned social democracy and continued the imposition of neo-liberalism.

After Calvert's defeat in 2007, the NDP narrowly rejected the centre-left vision of Ryan Meili in leadership contests in 2009 and 2011, selecting Romanow's deputy premier Dwain Lingenfelter in 2009 and Cam Broten in 2011, both of whom adhered to the NDP's commitment to neo-liberalism. Under its current leader, Cam Broten, the NDP will take a cautious, traditional electoral approach, criticizing the Wall government on the margins while waiting for the government to stumble or the economy to weaken. Neo-liberalism will therefore remain hegemonic in Saskatchewan politics. Nevertheless, given the solid base of residual social democratic support among NDP party members, should Wall win a third term the NDP may go through a major internal battle between the two wings of the party — the neo-liberal wing versus those with a residue of social democratic principles which enjoy significant sway among many in the rank-and-file.

Clearly Wall's victories confirm that Saskatchewan was a solid foundation in the neo-liberal fold in Canada, successfully combining economic neo-liberalism and muted social conservatism. Upon election in 2007 Wall did not have a big job to do since the essential features of neo-liberalism had already been implemented by Devine, Romanow, and Calvert.[17] There was not much left to do, particularly since Wall had solemnly promised not to privatize the province's big Crowns.

Wall contented himself with fiscal conservatism (balancing the budget, paying down the debt), a series of small downsizing measures against the Crowns, and a slightly bigger push in increasing privatization of selected aspects of health care. During 2012–13 Saskatchewan enjoyed a potash revenue windfall, due to high world prices and demand. In late 2013 and early 2014 the potash situation darkened as increased competition, and collapse of managed marketing, witnessed a sharp fall in prices and serious declines in provincial revenues. A potash crisis could end Wall's honeymoon with the electorate.

In the area of social policy Wall improved the situation of some of the most needy by increasing welfare benefits to the disabled and to poor seniors, and taking thousands of low income earners off the provincial income tax rolls. The biggest defining moment in his first term was the violation of pure free market ideology by opposing the hostile takeover of the Potash Corporation of Saskatchewan by Australian-based BHP Billiton, and successfully lobbying the Harper government to deny the takeover. Such actions did not sit well with some members of his own party and elements of the business lobby. He was increasingly quietly criticized for his NDP-like spending habits and his lack of sufficient enthusiasm for neo-liberal economic principles. These elements of the Saskatchewan Party, which include the old far right from the Reform party, deeply committed right-wing Tories, and right of centre Liberals, will join the business lobby to pressure Wall to implement more tax cuts, especially for business, and to lead a bigger push to privatizations in health care and of larger pieces of the Crowns.

On one key feature of neo-liberalism, however, Wall was zealous, and this earned him strong support from the business lobby and anti-labour rural voters. Upon election in 2007 Wall declared war on the trade union movement. Saskatchewan now has the most anti-union labour laws in Canada.[18] The CCF pioneered progressive, pro-union labour laws in 1944. Wall is now a Canadian pioneer of the right on labour law. Angered by the ad campaign against his government by the province's trade unions, Wall announced upon his electoral victory in 2011 his intention to seek legislative means to prevent unions from using members' dues for political purposes. The war between organized labour and the Wall government will continue.

One thing was clear in Saskatchewan in 2013: neo-liberalism was triumphant while social democracy in its Canadian cradle was dead. When it came to the important social and economic questions it mattered little which party governed.

BRITISH COLUMBIA

The CCF/NDP became the "natural governing party" in Saskatchewan by 2013, holding power for 47 of the 81 years since the founding of the CCF in 1932. In British Columbia the CCF/NDP became the "natural opposition party," retaining the position of Official Opposition from 1932 to 2013, with only brief episodes in power covering 13 of the 81 years (1972–75; 1991–2001). The business lobby in B.C. ran the province, creating and discarding anti-CCF/NDP electoral coalitions as circumstances warranted. When the CCF/NDP won power, the business lobby, with the help of the media, was unrestrained in its campaigns to discredit the government, including nasty character assassinations of NDP premiers. As a result, NDP governments in B.C. were under constant siege, governing in an atmosphere of crisis manufactured by the business lobby and the media. What is striking about the CCF/NDP record in B.C. is not their years as the opposition, but the fact they won power in three elections in the last 81 years, given the powerful forces determined to keep the "socialists" chained to the opposition benches.

Mike Harcourt's victory in 1991 was decisive in seats, but tenuous in popular vote. Together with NDP premiers Rae of Ontario and Romanow of Saskatchewan, Harcourt embraced the turn to neo-liberalism, thereby immediately losing substantial support among his supporters. His decision to support the Charlottetown Agreement, which grew increasingly unpopular across the West, and particularly in B.C., further undermined his political stature. Meanwhile the business lobby and the media continued a relentless attack, accusing Harcourt of having a secret left-wing agenda and of incompetence in managing the economy.

The final blow to Harcourt was the "Bingogate" scandal.[19] Though completely innocent of any wrongdoing, Harcourt was smeared by his political opponents and the media in a feeding frenzy that drove him from office. Dave Stupich, an NDP MLA for many years, a federal MP for one term, and minister of finance and agriculture in the old Barrett government, was involved in an elaborate fraud involving siphoning off funds from charitable bingos, mostly for personal gain though some funds were also channeled into the NDP. Over the years it was alleged that close to $1.5 million was misdirected. The scandal broke in 1992 when individual complaints led to Stupich's charitable organization, the Nanaimo Commonwealth Holding Society, pleading guilty in 1994 to misappropriating funds and faced fines and restitution orders. In response to media pressure, Premier Harcourt ordered an independent forensic audit. That report was leaked and alleged that the scheme involved stealing from charities for political purposes. The media and the opposition were hysterical in their demands for mass resignations and firings of NDP staff and ministers, as well as the laying of charges against sundry people all the way back to former premier Dave Barrett. In response, Harcourt announced his resignation in November 1995.

After investigation by a special prosecutor and the convening of a judicial inquiry, charges were finally laid against Dave Stupich, his spouse, his daughter, and a former party secretary. It turned out that the whole scheme was largely for personal gain, though some funds did find their way into the NDP. Harcourt knew nothing of "Bingogate," but the scandal, and the atmosphere created by the media and his political foes, ended his career. It was widely assumed the NDP faced certain defeat in 1996.

Few expected Harcourt's successor, Glen Clark, to win in 1996. Clark was on the left of the party and signaled a return to social democratic policies. An effective speaker, a formidable organizer, and deeply rooted in the labour movement, Clark's victory was unexpected, especially by the media and the business lobby, who were mesmerized by the overconfident prediction of an NDP defeat in the wake of "Bingogate." The political right, with the support of the business lobby, abandoned the thoroughly discredited Socreds as the favoured anti-NDP coalition, and orchestrated the ouster of left-leaning Liberal leader Gordon Wilson and his replacement by Gordon Campbell. Gordon Campbell was supposed to become premier. But Clark took 39 seats with just over 39 per cent of the vote, while the Liberals, though outpolling him, took 33 seats. The Reform party of B.C. played the role of spoiler for the Liberals, pulling 9 per cent and two seats, while the left-leaning Progressive Democratic Alliance (led by ousted Liberal leader Gordon Wilson) played a similar role for the NDP, pulling 6 per cent and winning one seat. (Wilson won and joined Clark's cabinet.)

The next few years were among the most tumultuous in B.C. political history.[20] Clark plunged ahead with his social democratic agenda, while making some concessions to the business lobby with tax cuts, especially targeted at small business. Faced with tough economic times, due to a slump in the forestry sector and the fishery, the Clark government began to run up deficits — almost $100 million in 1998 — and refused to cut programs. Indeed, Clark promised to spend a billion dollars more on infrastructure, especially health care and education, despite an almost $31 billion debt. In 1999, the Clark government went even further, announcing another $2.2 billion in new spending. Finance Minister Joy MacPhail declared, "Unlike other provinces, we intend to grow our way out, not cut our way out." The increased spending led to an $890 million deficit and saw the public debt grow to almost $35 billion. Further, Clark proved himself willing to think big and take political risks by launching an expensive, ultimately ill-fated, fast ferry program both to reduce crossing times to Vancouver Island, and to revitalize B.C.'s languishing shipbuilding industry.

From the business lobby's point of view, Glen Clark was a dangerous man. From working class roots in East Vancouver, he was tough and courageous, he thought big, and he refused to back down in a fight. That made him potentially dangerously popular in the bare-knuckled brawl of B.C. politics. It was clear that Clark intended to stay on course and go to the people on his record in 2000. In the meantime, he was battling the business lobby and refusing to submit. He successfully faced down aluminum giant Alcan and got a better deal for the province in Kitamat. He ended 25 years of fighting with the

U.S. over changes to the Columbia River Treaty, winning concessions that benefited B.C. with a $5.6 billion power deal. He refused to grovel before the all-powerful forestry industry and developed a public plan that he claimed was better for the industry's sustainability and won wide support among forestry workers. He took a hard, anti-U.S. line on the salmon dispute with the Alaskan fishery and he dragged his feet on renewing the lease on the Nanoose Bay weapons testing range off B.C.'s coast unless more help came from Ottawa for the province's fishery, the Americans signed an acceptable deal on managing the harvest of salmon, and a ban on testing weapons designed for a nuclear capability were imposed. He pushed through the Nisga'a treaty against virulent right-wing and racist opposition, thereby potentially breaking the logjam blocking the settlement of scores of outstanding aboriginal land claims in the province. He was feisty in the legislature and an easy match for Gordon Campbell, who was looking less and less like a viable premier. And most worrisome to the business lobby, there were signs in 1999 that the economy was improving, particularly the forestry sector upon whose fate governments in B.C. routinely rose and fell.

The NDP's traditional political opponents — the business lobby, Campbell's Liberals, and the media — combined hysteria and brutal determination to discredit the Clark government. The attack campaign became desperate. Clark's economic approach was characterized as "totally irresponsible," "another mad spending spree." The province was "headed for economic disaster." The dark economic mood purveyed couldn't have been greater had the province entered another Great Depression. Besides verbal hyperbole, Clark's foes took action. Using the province's recall law, whereby a petition signed by 40 per cent of voters on the list of the previous election could vacate a seat, the business lobby launched a campaign to recall the entire NDP caucus. Spearheaded by the Canadian Taxpayers Federation and the Concerned Citizens for BC, both well-funded front groups of the business lobby, the effort to recall the entire caucus was finally dismissed by a judge as "an effort to overthrow the government." Help B.C., a provincial front group funded by the right-wing National Citizens Coalition, launched unsuccessful legal challenges accusing the NDP government of having lied about the deficit, thereby defrauding voters and hence violating B.C.'s *Elections Act*. This costly campaign was a propaganda dream for Clark's opponents and a nightmare for the increasingly beleaguered government, particularly given the consistently prominent coverage provided by the media of the antics of what were essentially a bunch of right-wing crackpots. The message from the business lobby was the same as that sent during the Barrett regime of 1972–75 and the Harcourt regime of 1991–96 — the NDP will simply not be allowed to govern B.C., a province owned by big business and run only by those anointed by big business.

Then one of the sleaziest character assassinations of a sitting premier in Canadian history began. As a dirty political trick it ranks right up there with the Brinks Affair in the 1970 Québec election.[21] On March 2, 1999, the RCMP, without warning, raided Clark's home in working-class East Vancouver.[22] The media were tipped off and the whole thing was captured on TV and broadcast endlessly over the coming weeks. The information used to justify the search warrant was kept secret until August 1999, although at the time a judge commented that "an awful lot of hearsay evidence" was used. Clark was accused of breach of trust and receiving a benefit. It was alleged that a friend and neighbour, Dimitrios Pilarinos, did some renovations for Clark and in exchange Clark attempted to help him get a casino license in Burnaby. The whole story did not come out until Clark's 136-day trial in 2002 in which he was completely exonerated. The judge noted he showed "poor judgment" in his relations with Pilarinos, but this was not "behaviour requiring criminal sanctions."

The roles of the Liberal party, including Gordon Campbell and an RCMP officer known to be connected to the Liberal party, were not fully detailed until the trial. The initial source of the hearsay evidence used against Clark came from a staff member in Gordon Campbell's constituency office. Pilarinos was bragging he had the premier in his pocket and would get a contested gambling license. The initial police investigation concluded there was no foundation to the hearsay allegations and claims. But then RCMP Staff Sergeant Peter Montague, who was twice asked to run for the Liberals, was appointed as one of two officers in charge of a re-investigation. Montague's superior described him as a "very, very good friend" of a prominent Liberal. During the course of the re-investigation many of the hearsay witnesses changed their stories.

As a result of the re-investigation the search warrant was obtained. A local news station was tipped off about the exact day and time of the raid, giving them ample time to set up and be ready to roll as soon as the raid occurred. One senior RCMP crime investigator, speaking to *The Globe and Mail* on condition his name not be published, noted that the raid smacked more of politics than a police investigation: "This is not the way you conduct a case … someone is after the Premier, what they've done is convict him without a trial." It was bizarre, the home of the premier of the province was raided as if he were the local kingpin in drug trafficking. The media and Clark's political opponents savaged Clark for weeks and months, but he denied wrongdoing, proclaimed his innocence, and fought to retain his position. Then, as the party dropped in the polls, his own party turned on him as two cabinet ministers resigned and prominent NDPers called openly for his resignation. Only the labour movement stood by Clark in those dark days. The final blow was delivered by Clark's Attorney General Ujjal Dosanjh when he convened a press conference to announce Clark was under criminal investigation. On August 21, Clark resigned as premier.

What could have been done? Once the slime was thrown on Clark by the police raid, it stuck. Perhaps, though, his own party could have circled the wagons and defended him, since the evidence of a possible Liberal plot and possible abuse of police power by one of the RCMP officers in charge had leaked early on. Perhaps the Attorney General could have shut down the criminal investigation of Clark and called in an outside investigator to look into the allegation of a Liberal/RCMP conspiracy. In retrospect, given the trial evidence, there are clear grounds for such an investigation and perhaps a suit by Clark against the Attorney General and the police for malicious prosecution (though Clark may have been compelled to waive such remedies before the province agreed to pay his estimated $1 million legal bill). The fact remains that the most politically effective anti-business NDP leader, who had won an unexpected victory in 1996 and who just might have managed another such coup in 2000 or 2001, was ruined and driven from elected office by a savage, groundless smear. And his own Attorney General, his own cabinet, and, indeed, his own party allowed it to happen.

Premier Ujjal Dosanjh led the NDP to its worst defeat in history in May 2001. Gordon Campbell's Liberals took 77 of 79 seats with 58 per cent of the vote. The NDP was crushed, winning 2 seats with 22 per cent. Declaring a determination to end Clark's "class-warfare agenda," Campbell in fact reversed it. The ferocity of his attacks on public sector workers, the labour movement and the underclass was without precedent.[23] Over three years, Campbell re-imposed a virulent neo-liberal program. By the time he was finished, Campbell had the credentials as the premier of the most right-wing, cut and slash government in Canada. Critics accused Campbell of cutting B.C. into a deep recession, and by 2005 both the deficit and the public debt were higher than their peaks under Clark.

Campbell elevated tensions between aboriginals and non-aboriginals.[24] The "special treatment" accorded aboriginals has long been a bugbear of the right in Canada. The issue is particularly contentious in B.C. where over $500 million has been spent in largely unsuccessful efforts to resolve 50 outstanding land claims covering almost the entire province. When the Clark government and Ottawa successfully concluded an agreement with the Nisaga'a in 1998, the right wing in the province exploded in protest. The treaty was attacked in the House of Commons by the Reform party and in the B.C. legislature by Gordon Campbell, using what critics alleged were racist code words. Campbell tried to block the treaty with a hopeless court challenge, given previous Supreme Court decisions. Even Bill Vander Zalm rose from his political grave to carry a picket sign against the treaty. Upon election Campbell got his revenge.

In 2002 he held a referendum to seek public input on principles to guide his government in such negotiations. Aboriginal leaders denounced the move as "racist" and "divisive." A scant 36 per cent bothered to vote on the eight principles, but gave the government 85 to 95 per cent majorities on all principles. These principles were long advocated by Preston Manning and many others on the right:

no expropriation of private property, respect for all existing leases, access for all to all Crown lands, all parks protected, imposition of the province's environmental laws, aboriginal government must be like municipalities with only delegated powers from the province and Ottawa; an end to all tax exemptions. The whole thing was an exercise in negative propaganda, since it had no legal effect given the Canadian constitution and many Supreme Court precedents. But it appeased bigots and cranks on the right, while angering the aboriginal community. It also imposed impossible constraints on the ability to negotiate in good faith. The whole sorry episode set back negotiations a decade. The aboriginal community in turn got revenge by rejecting Campbell's proposal for a settlement to extinguish the Haida's claims to the Queen Charlotte Islands. The uncertainty in B.C. due to the outstanding claims continued, worsened by the lack of trust in the provincial government among the aboriginal community.

High on Campbell's agenda was to tame B.C.'s labour movement, the most militant in Canada outside Québec.[25] The business lobby insisted labour had made too many gains during the Harcourt/Clark years, gains that had to be stripped away. After cutting public sector workers by one-third, those who remained had to be paid less, have fewer benefits, and fewer rights guaranteed in labour law. The door to the privatization of the public sector, especially the huge health care sector, had to be cracked open. An aggressive pro-business, anti-labour government would dampen the demands and expectations among all workers in both the private and the public sectors. The last major neo-liberal assault under Bill Bennett back in May 1983 provoked the creation of Operation Solidarity, a coalition of labour and social activist groups, which mounted huge protest demonstrations and drove toward a October 31, 1983, general strike. Last-minute negotiations led to major concessions by Bennett and the strike was averted.

Despite this history, and fully expecting major confrontations, Campbell commenced a multipronged attack on labour from his first day in office. In a wave of anti-labour legislative changes, Campbell rescinded the moderately pro-labour changes made by Harcourt and Clark, taking labour rights back 20 years to the dark days of Socred governments. The business lobby was delighted, applauding the "dramatic improvement" in the business and investment climate.

Labour fought back. Legal, wildcat, and illegal strikes became commonplace. Laws ordering transit workers, nurses, and health-sciences professionals back to work, and imposing contracts by law, passed quickly with little debate (the Opposition had only two MLAs). When 10 months of negotiations failed to achieve a settlement with teachers, Campbell imposed a settlement, leading to a series of protests and walkouts by teachers. Growing labour unrest led inevitably to a major confrontation in spring 2004 when the government took on the 40,000 member Hospital Employees' Union (HEU). In order to achieve reduction targets in spending and public sector job numbers, the HEU's contract had to be shredded and the back of the union broken. During negotiations the government, through the association of public sector employers in health, demanded massive concessions — a 16 per cent pay cut, reduced sick leave, disability benefit reductions, fewer vacation days, reduced benefits for part-timers, an end to pay equity implementation, as well as dozens of pages of wording changes to reduce the union's power and its members' protections. The most provocative demand was the unfettered right of employers to lay off public health workers and contract out the work to the private sector. The employers began a massive layoff and contracting out campaign involving over 2,000 workers while negotiations were going on, provoking a strike on April 25.

Three days later the government passed a back-to-work law, imposing a legislated settlement containing the major concessions. The key concessions were a 15 per cent wage cut retroactive to January 1, 2004, which workers would have to repay, an increase in the work week, and no limit on an employer's right to lay off public workers and contract out the work to the private sector. The HEU defied the law and appealed to the BC Federation of Labour (BCFL) for support. Spontaneous wildcat strike activity began to occur all across the province and, on April 30, hundreds of workers, mostly in the public sector, walked off the job to join HEU picket lines. The BCFL called a general strike for May 3, 2004. A last-minute deal on May 2 between

the BCFL, HEU, and the government ended the HEU strike and cancelled the general strike: wage cuts were not retroactive, annual caps on
the layoffs and contracting out were imposed, severance pay was provided for those laid off, no penalties were imposed for strike activity.
The government claimed victory, as did the HEU and the BCFL. But in
the end Campbell's larger restraint program and curtailment of labour
rights remained in place. Many among the rank and file expressed bitterness, and a few wildcat walkouts occurred but petered out quickly.
Campbell had faced down labour and, unlike Bennett in October
1983, he did it with fewer concessions and without a huge drop in his
personal popularity. After 1983 Bennett was unelectable. After May
2004 Campbell still appeared confident of a second term.

The business lobby was content with Campbell, though expressing some concern about his approach to aboriginal land claims. As
for the cuts in public sector jobs, the huge reductions in government
spending, the large tax cuts, and the attack on labour, the business
lobby had nothing but good things to say. Indeed, Campbell was just
carrying out the plans laid down at two sessions of the B.C. Business
Summit in 1998 and 1999, convened to attack the Clark government
and to mobilize opposition to the regime.[26] Both sessions declared
confidently that tax cuts, government spending cuts and pro-business
changes in labour laws would turn the economy around, leading to
prosperity. Though that did not appear to be happening in 2004–05,
the business community and the wealthy were doing very well.

Polls indicated the electorate was largely on side. Campbell's brush
with two scandals in 2003 revealed a charmed life.[27] He was charged
with drunk driving and speeding during a vacation in Hawaii, and he
was not fully honest about it back home until the truth caught up with
him. The legislature offices of two Liberal ministerial aides were raided
by the RCMP in connection with an investigation into an organized
crime drug case involving smuggling and money laundering. Such
events might have brought down an NDP premier, but the media did
not begin a witch hunt, and prominent members of the business lobby
remained silent. It appears two standards exist in B.C. when a premier
is touched by scandal: if it's an NDP premier, hang him high; if it's a

pro-business premier, slap his wrist.

The 2005 election was crucial for both parties. Gordon Campbell's Liberals faced a popular test of the depth of support for, or opposition to, the painful cuts imposed since 2001. Furthermore, Campbell's image had been tarnished by scandal, and this was a measure of how much damage was done. The NDP, under new leader Carole James, desperate to exorcize the Clark ghost, shifted rightward, abandoning old ideologies, reducing trade union influence, attempting a broader appeal, and warmly embracing business. Campbell was convinced there was widespread support for his neo-liberal crusade, dismissing the disorder of many strikes and public demonstrations as an obstreperous minority of special interests out of tune with the silent majority. The results were unexpectedly bad for the Liberals — a loss of 31 seats and 12 per cent of the popular vote. The NDP had nowhere to go but up after the 2001 debacle, but did much better than expected, gaining 31 seats. Though the Liberals were returned with a majority — 46 seats to the NDP's 33 — the popular votes of the two parties were close (Liberals, 45 per cent; NDP, 42).

In response, Campbell and the Liberals were recast as neo-liberals with a human face and helping hand. During its second term the Liberal government made many rhetorical commitments to more social spending, an improved housing policy, and greater devotion to protecting the environment, even delivering on a successful carbon tax against the oil industry's wishes. The government reopened treaty negotiations with B.C.'s First Nations and engaged in more reasonable negotiations with public sector unions. Much of this was show, leading to no significant reversal of the destructive changes imposed during the first term, but a friendly media ensured that a positive public spin prevailed for the reborn Campbell government. The reality was that the neo-liberal revolution was not over, it had merely passed successfully through its open class warfare phase during which much pain was administered to impose the agenda. With the basic agenda in place, all government actions, in health care, education, social policy, and economic planning occurred in the firm context of market-driven neo-liberal ideology.

Meanwhile the NDP under James decided that if a rightward shift had brought dramatic improvement in 2005, then the road to victory in 2009 was to continue the march to the right. The James NDP declared itself business-friendly and anti-tax, even opposing the carbon tax, the one decent environmental accomplishment of the Campbell government. There were no promises of a reversal of the neo-liberal revolution, nor a return to even the most modest social democratic orientation in economic and social policy.

The media proclaimed that the NDP and Liberals were colliding in the centre of the political spectrum. In reality, they both occupied the right/centre-right, with the NDP claiming to be more prepared than the Liberals to govern with compassion for the needy and afflicted. The 2009 election was a "non-election," with the results echoing those of 2005. Both parties gained from an electoral redistribution that increased the total number of seats. The Liberal majority improved by 3 seats to 49; the NDP gained 2 seats, winning 35. The popular vote shares remained substantially unchanged. It was truly a Tweedle-Dee/Tweedle-Dum election. The electorate seemed to share that view as voter turnout fell to 51 per cent, down seven points from 2005.

Though both leaders could claim some success, surprisingly the 2009 election quickly led to their ouster. Having lost two consecutive elections, James neglected to consult her caucus regarding her continued leadership. Dissent within her caucus over her arrogant leadership style grew. Jenny Kwan, a popular, left-leaning Vancouver MLA led a public rebellion demanding an immediate leadership convention. Her position enjoyed strong support in the caucus. The bill of indictment against James was lengthy: suppression of debate, all power in the leader's office and her cabal, key decisions taken and presented to the media before MLAs learned of them, no clear direction, no vision of the future, secret backroom deals, hiding from controversial and important public issues. Kwan issued her public attack on December 1, 2010. James resigned on December 6.

The departure of Campbell was a bit messier. Two months after re-election Campbell announced the government's intention to proceed to impose a Harmonized Sales Tax (HST) — rolling into one tax Ottawa's 5 per cent GST and B.C.'s 7 per cent sales tax. This had the effect of dramatically increased taxation since previous sales tax exemptions would disappear. A firestorm of opposition erupted, encompassing the media, the broad public, most popular organizations, and even members of Campbell's own party (including caucus and cabinet members). Only the business lobby embraced the proposal, since the additional tax revenue from this increasingly regressive consumption tax would leave more room for further business tax cuts. The premier was caught in a lie when he insisted that the HST plan was not on the government's list of intentions prior to the election. Later it was discovered that the government had a full HST plan in place before the election. Former Socred premier Vander Zalm rose again from his political grave to lead the anti-HST fight, even coyly threatening a possible return to politics. A petition for a referendum on the issue under B.C. law was successful, and in the summer of 2011 the referendum defeated the HST (55 to 45 per cent). This result was binding on the government — the HST was dead.[28]

The HST mess wounded Campbell mortally, as his popularity and credibility fell like a stone, bottoming out at 9 per cent in 2010. His political career was over. Perhaps the final nail was revelations that the premier appeared to have lied to the public and the legislature during the never-ending scandal that broke over the privatization of BC Rail in 2004.[29] His initial lies about his 2003 drunk driving and speeding charges in Hawaii were revisited. Public trust in Campbell was gone. On November 3, 2010, Campbell announced his intention to resign; on March 14, 2011, he finally did so. Campbell's fall from grace was broken by a velvet cushion provided by Prime Minister Harper — Campbell was appointed High Commissioner to the United Kingdom. Meanwhile, Carole James continues to toil away as a backbench NDP MLA representing a Victoria seat.

When Christy Clark won the Liberal leadership and became Premier of B.C. on March 14, 2011, it was widely assumed she would lead the party to defeat in 2013.[30] A former Liberal MLA, deputy premier and cabinet minister, Clark quit politics in 2005 for an unsuccessful run at Vancouver mayor and to work in the media. She returned to the legislature in a May by-election in Campbell's vacated seat. Her government suffered negative fallout from the HST debacle and the taint of the BC Rail scandal. Clark herself faced internal opposition, losing prominent cabinet ministers. There were internal calls for her resignation as her government fell far behind the NDP in the polls.

New NDP leader Adrian Dix, former chief of staff for Glen Clark, vowed he would heal the wounds in the party resulting from the fall of James and his own hard fought third ballot victory as leader.[31] As the May 2013 election approached, Dix and the NDP were confident of victory, consistently outpolling the Liberals, often dramatically. Dix embarked on a cautious campaign, couched in generalities, promising specifics after election. He refused to take clear stands on key issues, including the debates raging over pipeline construction to the B.C. coast. Dix appeared to be trying to sneak into power, focusing on reassuring the public and the business community they had nothing to fear from an NDP government. His most fatal mistake was to take the high road of a positive campaign, free of aggressive attacks on Clark and the Liberal record, thus failing to meet the Liberal attack head on. As Stephen Harper has proven repeatedly, attack ads work and the only remedy to them is to strike back aggressively. The Liberals campaigned hard on jobs, economic stewardship, strong demands that B.C. be protected from environmental calamity with the construction of oil pipelines, and a demand for a fair share of the oil wealth for B.C. The Liberals spent heavily on media advertising, including scary attack ads demonizing Dix and the NDP. The Liberal media blitz, relentless campaigning by Clark, and positive media coverage worked. Christy Clark won an unexpected majority government victory: 49 seats with 44 per cent, compared to the NDP's 34 seats and 40 per cent. Large numbers of voters were clearly not engaged, as turnout limped up from 51 per cent in 2009 to 52 per cent in 2013.

Almost immediately the knives were out in the NDP, as the usual debate emerged. The consensus seemed to be to apply the old formula — a further shift to the right was necessary to overcome the public's fear of the NDP. Ever since the NDP abandoned clear social democracy for neo-liberalism under Harcourt — but for the brief Clark interlude

— the doctrine had been that in order to win the NDP had to abandon the remnants of its old ideology and its organic links to the working class through the trade union movement, clearly embrace market-oriented economic policy, and strive to bury its allegedly radical past. It was the same argument used to persuade the party in past years to abandon socialism for moderate social democracy in order to achieve victory. It didn't work then, and it had yet to prove its viability in the neo-liberal era. A strong group on the left of the party insisted the road to victory was to clearly embrace social democratic policies, polarizing the province around the need for a decisive break with neo-liberalism. On September 18, 2013, Dix announced his resignation as leader.

During the 2013 provincial election, B.C.'s governing and opposition parties embraced neo-liberalism as the hegemonic political ideology within which all political contestation must occur. Yet neo-liberalism failed to solve the continuing problems of the forestry industry and of the crises afflicting the salmon fishery, both economic pillars of the B.C. economy.[32] The population's resistance to this new reality can be gauged by the growing disengagement from electoral politics — half the electorate now routinely declines to vote. At the federal level, B.C.'s adherence to neo-liberalism was solid, contributing to Harper's majority victory in 2011 — 21 of 36 B.C. seats and 46 per cent of the vote.

ALBERTA

The neo-liberal revolution was never in doubt in Alberta, the heart and soul of conservative and free market ideology in Canada.[33] The oil and natural gas industry dominated the province's economy and politics, and governments and premiers rose and fell according to the industry's agenda. When Premier Don Getty fumbled badly in 1989 and was finally pushed from office and replaced by Ralph Klein, the province was in serious difficulty from the perspective of the business lobby. The combined opposition vote in 1989 reached 45 per cent and the NDP became the Official Opposition. The oil and natural gas industry was in recession, not booming again until 1998, and Klein's Tories won two difficult victories. In June 1993, the Tories took 51 of 83 seats with 44 per cent of the vote, and in March 1997 63 of 83 seats with 51 per cent. The NDP was put back in its place — no seats in 1993, 2 seats in 1997. The Liberal threat was real in 1993, 40 per cent and 32 seats, but abated by 1997 to 33 per cent and 18 seats. During those years Klein faced serious choices. The elections were hard fought, but Klein found his stride. One key focus was relentless Ottawa bashing, a favoured tactic of all successful Alberta premiers since Aberhart. But Klein developed Ottawa bashing into an art form: Ottawa was plotting to take Alberta's wealth; the federal Liberals had no sympathy for Alberta, indeed were downright hostile to Albertan interests; the Chrétien government was a constant threat. And Klein took it that extra step, coyly encouraging separatist sentiment and often appearing to walk part way down that road.

In 1993 the freshly minted Klein government faced a $22.7 billion debt and a $3.2 billion annual deficit, a politically unacceptable situation in the province that spawned Manning's Reform party. Over his first two terms, Klein acted ruthlessly, cutting transfers to cities and towns by 78 per cent, cutting all departments by between 12 and 30 per cent, closing hospitals, increasing class sizes, slashing the size of the public service and rolling back the wages of those who survived the cuts. Welfare rates were cut by 20 per cent and thousands of employable recipients were struck from the rolls. The lowest minimum wage in Canada was imposed. Liquor stores and motor vehicle registration offices were privatized. Electricity was deregulated on the grounds it would provide savings both to the public purse and consumers. Health care premiums were raised and raised again.

These measures provoked both public protest and labour resistance, as teachers, hospital workers, and retail clerks went on strike or engaged in illegal walkouts. By 1997, Alberta, with the lowest unionization rate in Canada at 22 per cent, had over triple the national average of days lost to industrial conflict. But Klein always prevailed because Alberta had the strongest job market in Canada, paying the highest wages in the West, even after the cuts. By 2002 Alberta replaced B.C. as the destination of choice for Canadians looking for opportunity. Thus the labour confrontations were episodic, never developing into a generalized movement against the Klein agenda. Even as the economy turned around, Klein dragged his feet on increasing social spending to the point where even Alberta government reports admitted serious social deficits in high rates of teenage pregnancy, neglect of the elderly, serious literacy problems, excessive rates of industrial accidents, problems of water quality, severely neglected environmental problems and an increasingly desperate underclass of the chronically poor.

The burdens of debt and deficit reduction were not imposed on the business sector. Indeed, the explicit, three-pronged economic strategy of the Klein government was proudly proclaimed as the "Alberta Advantage": maintaining a pro-business climate, keeping taxes the lowest in Canada, and a very non-interventionist government. As a result, even during tough times business not only prospered, but the government took steps to ensure that prosperity. In Alberta, a "hands off" government meant no interference in the free market unless approved by business. But the government was very "hands on" in furthering the business agenda. By 1998 Alberta boasted the lowest taxes and resource rents in Canada. In the 1970s and 1980s, Lougheed took about $5 a barrel of oil as government revenue. By 1997 this was down to just over $2 and Klein promised further cuts. When electricity was deregulated it turned out to amount to a $4 to $5 billion transfer of public wealth to private companies each year for five years — as well as increased prices to consumers. Getty's dreams of a huge forestry industry faltered when Millar Western and Alberta-Pacific, the two big firms created to build mega pulp plants and lumber mills to harvest Alberta's timber with virtually no regulation, couldn't make good on government loans. Millar Western was forgiven a $245 million loan for a payment of $28 million, while Alberta-Pacific, with a debt of $450 million in loans and outstanding interest, was forgiven for a one-time payment of $260 million. The government made clear that the "Alberta Advantage" applied only to business, not to school kids, public sector workers, or those on welfare. Due to its vital economy and low unemployment rate, in 2001 Alberta had the lowest poverty rates in the West, but it also had welfare benefit rates far below other western provinces.

After the 1997 election Alberta's economy began to improve dramatically, thanks to hefty increases in the price of oil and natural gas and the insatiable demands of the U.S. market. Every $1 US increase in the price of a barrel of oil brought $153 million more into government coffers. Every 10 per cent increase in the price of natural gas netted an additional $142 million. As prices increased, each year the government announced an embarrassment of riches and increased budgetary surpluses. Though there was a slight dip in 1998 when oil fell to $20(US), from then on prices marched upwards, reaching $32(US) in 2000, $38(US) in 2003, and into the $40 to $50(US) range in 2004–05, even occasionally going over $50(US). Wells drilled doubled and then tripled as exploration proceeded at a frenzied pace. Alberta enjoyed an unexpected windfall of $10 billion in 2001 alone, and anticipated budget surpluses from $2 to $6 billion every year from 2000 onward.

In 2005 Klein declared Alberta the only debt-free province in Canada (Ontario groaned under a $112 billion debt load and B.C. faced $35 billion). Experts began predicting $100(US) oil. New technology reduced the cost of extracting oil from the tar sands to $14 a barrel, making it handsomely profitable. This resulted in plans for an additional $34.5 billion investment in the tar sands over 10 years by five major consortia. Though the sweet crude of the Western Basin was being pumped out at an alarming rate, Alberta's tar sands contained an estimated 177 billion barrels of recoverable oil. The possibility of a never-ending boom seemed real. But boom talk in Alberta is nervous talk. Albertans have been through many booms — the 1970s boom was supposed to be never-ending but it busted in the 1980s and never fully recovered until the mid to late 1990s. And though each $1(US) price rise in oil and each 10 per cent price rise in natural gas brought in about an extra $300 million, each fall of $1(US) or 10 per cent brought losses of the same order. And as oil and gas prices spiked up and down with world markets, each year remained an uncertain gamble. Consequently, boom times in Alberta are always tempered by lingering fears of the bust that can come as suddenly as the boom.

Ralph Klein had delivered, reaching the peak of his popularity. The March 12, 2001, election was therefore more of a coronation than an election contest, as Klein's Tories took 62 per cent of the popular vote and 74 of 83 seats. During his victory speech Klein uttered those famous words — a sort of oxymoron of trailer park humility and pomposity that only Klein could pull off — "Welcome to Ralph's world." Those are the words remembered rather than the rest of his befuddled speech. Nevertheless there were serious problems that wouldn't go away, making the government vulnerable and contributing to Klein's decline.

The discovery of bovine spongiform encephalopathy (BSE), or "mad cow disease," in one Alberta cow in May 2003 led to the closure of the U.S. and world markets to Canadian beef and cattle, creating a meltdown in the Canadian industry. Klein did not handle the situation particularly well. His most damaging comment was, given what had happened, perhaps the cattleman in question should have "shot, shoveled, and shut up," and this might inevitably become a future approach. The comment ricocheted around the world, undermining confidence in Canada's regulatory trustworthiness. Farmers and cattle producers were not reassured by Klein's handling of the problem. The deregulation of electricity also created continuing problems for Klein, suggesting the decision was not well thought out. After it became clear that electrical deregulation was going to be very costly to both residential consumers and businesses, Klein imposed regulation on the deregulation process to the amusement of many. His handling of electricity deregulation became an embarrassing joke.

Mishandling the BSE crisis and electricity deregulation created problems, but ready cash for cattle bailouts and energy rebates easily limited any serious political damage. Growing concern about environmental problems in Alberta was another matter. Albertans have an ambivalent attitude to the environment. They are proud of the grandeur and diversity of the province's natural gifts and are sensitive to environmental degradation. Yet the vigorous exploitation of natural resources is the foundation of the province's wealth and prosperity. The automatic choice of economic development over the environment created a looming catastrophe. Klein's cavalier approach to environmental problems resonated less and less among growing numbers of Albertans.

Though environmental concerns due to the oil and gas industry were greatest, Albertans increasingly complained about forest stripping for pulp and lumber mills, huge open pit coal mines, and the incredibly rapid deterioration of Alberta's lakes, rivers, and streams due to industrial pollutants. Some environmental scientists described the rapid degradation of Alberta's environment a "powder keg" which must inevitably explode. But Klein's response to such claims was to pooh-pooh them, dismissing such people as alarmists. Anyone who dared to rain on Alberta's prosperity parade was written off as a crank. But that approach was less and less effective as the degradation became more widespread and palpable to growing numbers of Albertans.

Klein's handling of the health issue made him both the *bête noir* of supporters of medicare and an increasingly ridiculous figure due his constant equivocations. For Stephen Harper, Klein became an unwitting ally of Martin's Liberals during the 2004 federal election when Klein's eleventh hour promise to reveal Alberta's plan for health care reform was seized upon by Martin as proof of Harper's "secret agenda" to privatize medicare. Klein made no secret of his determination to develop a "Third Way" in health care delivery in Alberta involving a mix of public and private delivery systems, constantly berating Ottawa and the *Canada Health Act* which forbids private delivery, promising "stormy times" in the battle for health care reform.

Klein wanted Alberta to become the first province to take the next comprehensive step — a two-tiered health system: one publicly funded and accessible to all, the other topped up by private funding and accessible to those with the means to pay extra to obtain speedier and better quality services. Health experts contended it would lead to an increasingly underfunded, low grade public system for lower income Canadians, while attracting the more competent physicians and other health professionals to the more luxurious private tier. The Canadian public, including Albertans, while willing to concede some privatization on the margins (hip, knee, cataracts, MRIs) due to the growing incapacity of the public system to provide timely care, was strongly opposed to any move to a fully developed two-tiered system.

There is no doubt that national resentment of Alberta grew during Klein's premiership, and not just over the medicare battle. Klein's bombast about Alberta's prosperity and his dog-in-the-manger approach to hoarding Alberta's wealth and defending it against all claims, did not go down well with other Canadians. As other provinces struggled with debts, deficits, and cuts, Klein rubbed salt into already raw wounds as he bragged about Alberta's repeated windfalls and its debt-free wonderland. In a speech to an Edmonton business audience in August 2001 Prime Minister Chrétien called on Alberta to share the wealth in order to help solve Canada's social problems, saying, "We have to make sure that every person in every part of Canada benefits from the potential and the wealth that belongs to the people of Canada [who have] the right to have their share." Klein and the Alberta business lobby lamented once again Ottawa was about to loot Alberta's wealth just as they had with the National Energy Program (NEP).

As oil and gas increase in cost, creating a bonanza for Alberta and economic hardship for the energy-consuming provinces, there will be increased public pressure from Canadians outside Alberta, or outside the energy-producing West and the coastal provinces, for a national policy on energy. Attitudes like Klein's, and the earlier "let the eastern bastards freeze in the dark" slogan expressed during the battle over the NEP in the 1980s, will outrage Canadians. In the 1980s Trudeau backed off due to his constitutional aspirations and considerable public sympathy for the West's argument that resource booms were temporary and the West had a right to use such booms to increase economic diversification. There will be little such sympathy during the next, much more serious and inevitably global, energy crunch, as Canada's hunger for reliable and reasonably priced energy from the tar sands and offshore becomes desperate and trumps any absolutist notion of provincial rights. The Klein years of "in your face" nose thumbing at Ottawa and the rest of Canada will be remembered as the people of Canada impose their democratic will on Alberta.

After 2001 Klein began to disintegrate, and his own caucus and the public were less forgiving. The media began to take a more critical and investigatory approach to the Klein regime. A key event marking the beginning of this decline occurred in December 2001, just nine months after his electoral triumph. Klein, drunk, staggering, slurring, and abusive, made a midnight visit to an Edmonton homeless shelter, getting into a loud argument with two homeless men, telling them to get jobs and allegedly contemptuously tossing $70 on the floor as a handout. Though Klein publicly apologized and admitted a drinking problem, his reputation never fully recovered. Such a spectacle on the part of a premier was not easily erased from public memory.

When he was hit with a cream pie in August 2003, Klein reacted angrily, with neither humour nor grace, and the prosecutor of the student perpetrator sought a maximum penalty. In 2004, mumbling he'd had "enough of this crap," Klein stalked angrily away from a media scrum on the BSE crisis, an event he, as a seasoned TV journalist, usually effectively dominated. Klein insisted Chilean dictator Pinochet did what he did because socialism forced him to take extreme measures. He promised to open up the books on cabinet expenditures and air flight logs, and then refused to follow through. He promised receipts of a trip he made to India, and then refused to cough up. When his caucus forced him to back off on the public release of his health care reform plan, his behaviour was so churlish that one of his MLAs commented "something's not quite right."

Klein increasingly became a national spectacle, and a provincial embarrassment, on the issues of same-sex marriage and anti-smoking health policy. His battle against same-sex marriage became hilariously Quixotic as he promised to use provincial constitutional powers that did not exist to retain the traditional, religious definition of marriage while denying any right to same-sex marriage. Klein took a strong stand against bans against smoking in public spaces, despite all the advice of health experts on the dangers of second hand smoke and contrary to growing public support for smoking bans. Such events, when combined with his mishandling of files on electricity deregulation, health care reform, relations with Ottawa, and the BSE crisis, led *Edmonton Journal* columnist Graham Thomson to note in 2004 Ralph Klein had become a "train wreck that won't stop," as one car piled up on the other. Klein was demonstrably falling apart as an effective premier in full public view.

In retrospect Klein's unraveling and his inexplicable behaviour may have reflected early onset symptoms of the progressive dementia which resulted in his death in 2011.[34] But no one knew that at the time and variously attributed his behaviour to alcohol and to the arrogance of power too easily won. Klein further annoyed many by calling an unnecessary election for November 2004, though to general relief he announced it was his last. Facing a chorus of criticism, an increasingly unfriendly and critical media, and deepening public disaffection, Klein was absent during much of the campaign which many dubbed a "non-election." Klein paid an embarrassing price at the polls, losing 22 seats and witnessing a decline in popular vote to 47 per cent, a fall of 15 per cent from the previous election. More significantly, public disenchant-ment with the Klein regime was reflected in voter turnout falling to 45 per cent. It was a victory for the "None of the Above" party.

Klein attempted to cling to power, ignoring the wide consensus among the public, the media, the business elite, and his own party that it was time for him to go.[35] Though promising to step down, he remained endlessly vague about the date. Klein's foot-dragging forced the hand of the party. In March 2006, convention delegates gave Klein a humiliating 55 per cent approval rating. In the past Klein had easily won 90 per cent. In April Klein announced his resignation, remaining in office until his successor, Ed Stelmach, was sworn in. In January 2007 Klein resigned his seat.

Despite the mess he created in his last years as premier, Klein had delivered in spades to the Canadian neo-liberal movement. Alberta remained the bedrock foundation of the right in Canada. Provincially the right was without effective opposition, and in federal elections Alberta voters loyally delivered huge victories in votes and seats to Harper's Tories. As one Alberta wag put it, "the Tories could win in Alberta with Ronald McDonald as leader." That may be an exaggera-tion, but it is perhaps enough simply to note that Ralph Klein won four majority governments with relative ease.

The problems of the Alberta Tories persisted in the years following Klein's departure. From the outset Klein's successor, Ed Stelmach, was under siege: attacked by elements of his own party and the growing far right which coalesced around the Wildrose Party.[36] The media con-sidered him a lightweight second stringer. Upon entering provincial politics in 1993 Stelmach became a Klein loyalist, serving in various cabinet posts. He was neither charismatic nor comfortable in the public eye. He was burdened with the reputation of a mediocre lieutenant of Klein, gaining the nickname "Steady Eddie." During the leadership race few expected him to win against two prominent front runners. His low-key, grassroots campaign paid off when he secured an upset second ballot victory.

Stelmach earned a place in history as the shortest-serving premier of the Lougheed Tory dynasty. Sworn in as premier on December 14, 2006, Stelmach was a bad luck premier. He faced storms of controversy over the tar sands and had the ill-fortune to be in office when the 2008 world-wide economic collapse began. Stelmach pushed tar sands development with little concern for the environment, dismissing critics as wrong and ideologically motivated. He spent billions on carbon capture technology, much to the industry's delight, despite the advice of experts it was money wasted on technology unproven to lower green house gas emissions. He was a stalwart climate change denier. When 1,600 ducks died in a Syncrude tailings pond, his government first covered it up and then lied, claiming only 500 had died. The issue — and the images of the ducks covered in muck — received world attention, feeding the growing campaigns in the U.S. and the European Union against the "dirty oil" from Alberta's tar sands. In an effort to combat the increasingly successful negative propaganda campaign against tar sands development, Stelmach re-branded the province with a new slogan, "Freedom To Create, Spirit To Achieve," dropping Klein's successful "The Alberta Advantage." The new brand was ridiculed widely, becoming a major embarrassment, particularly when it was revealed that some of the photos showing children running happily in pristine environments were locales outside the province. It seemed everything Stelmach touched turned into a political liability.

The early years of Stelmach's term enjoyed boom times, the previously successful trump card against naysayers. During his first year as premier, 2007, the government enjoyed a surplus of almost $9 billion — the best ever. In 2008 the surplus was about $5 billion, and the government projected surpluses of between $1 and $2 billion over the next few years. It was not to be. The December 2008 economic collapse resulted in falling oil prices.[37] By April 2009 the Stelmach government was projecting a deficit of just under $5 billion — the first deficit in over ten years, and the worst on record. Stelmach admitted deficits would probably continue over the next three to four years. In response, the government began cutting spending and proposed going into debt to stimulate the economy with infrastructure renewal projects. Talk of going into debt was widely seen as a betrayal of the major accomplishment of the Klein regime, and galvanized criticism within the party and among the growing disaffected right outside the party. The oil industry was assisted with cuts in royalty rates, a controversial move as the economic downturn resulted in cancelled projects, decreased drilling, and job cuts as the industry prepared to weather the world economic storm.

Stelmach's sole election victory as party leader, 2008, at first appeared to be a triumph. But it turned out to be a hollow victory, as his troubles started and the 2008 economic downturn began to take its toll. Though winning 53 per cent of the popular vote and 72 of 83 seats, voter turnout collapsed to 41 per cent, the lowest in history, indicating an epidemic of public disengagement. In the wake of his government's repeated missteps, and the economic crisis, by 2009 the government's popularity fell and the right-wing Wildrose Party was rising rapidly, particularly after the young, right-wing, and charismatic media personality, Danielle Smith, a former paid lobbyist for the Canadian Federation of Independent Business, became leader in 2009.[38] An upset by-election victory in Calgary, with the Tories running third, gave the new party its first seat in the legislature. Defections by three Tory MLAs contributed to the upsurge and the growing credibility of the party. Old Reformers and hard Tories began to flock to the new party.

By 2010 the Wildrose Party was besting the Tories in some public opinion polls, and there was more and more talk that once again Albertans were about to switch *en masse* to a new governing party. In 2010 the party claimed its 1,400 members had grown to 15,000 in less than a year, and then skyrocketed to 25,000 in 2011. It became a foregone public conclusion that Stelmach, despite his triumph in 2008, was on a downward spiral to inevitable defeat in 2012. Stelmach, under siege from inside and outside his party, the object of a media consensus that he was among the walking political dead, and threatened by a major caucus rebellion, announced his intention to resign in late January 2011. After his replacement was selected, Stelmach resigned on October 7, 2011. The unanswered question was could his successor save the party from defeat at the hands of the Wildrose Party?

In October 2011, contrary to most expectations, Alison Redford won a third ballot victory as leader.[39] Redford was a newcomer to provincial politics, elected in 2008 and serving Stelmach as Attorney General and Minister of Justice. Redford, an adviser to Joe Clark in the 1980s, was considered a red Tory, unlikely to succeed in rural Alberta. She proposed Alberta break with the past and embrace a positive engagement in national debates, a suspect position among the old Reform base. Alberta, she argued, as the leading economic powerhouse in Canada, must embrace a place of primacy in national debates. She surprised many by proposing increased spending on social programs, health care, and education. In March 2012 Redford called an election.

Repeated polls recorded substantial leads for the Wildrose Party.[40] The Wildrose attack on Redford was a relentless, right-wing rant: a return to "firewall Alberta" with a new provincial constitution including referendum and recall, entrenched property rights, and unfettered gun ownership; an aggressive attack on Ottawa's equalization program; more private health care and a move to a two tier system; cuts in spending and lower taxes — all the usual bromides of the right. Redford stood her ground, advocating a positive role for Alberta in national politics, more spending on education and health programs and a moderate, responsible tax policy. Redford argued forcefully that Alberta must embrace the future of Alberta's economy, emphasizing the need to win the pipeline debate to reach new markets. She recognized that tar sands oil was under international siege as "dirty oil," and that climate change denials and refusals to get serious about the environment were not helping Alberta win allies. Redford was proposing a significant shift in the political culture of the old Klein Tories. The polls indicated Redford was on track to defeat.

A media blitz and strong messages of support from the oil and gas industry gave Redford a boost, but it was not enough to stop the Wildrose surge. The game changer was Peter Lougheed's intervention in the campaign's final week. Urging Tories attracted to Wildrose to reconsider their decision, he endorsed Redford as representing the hope for the future of Alberta. "I want them to think about it and I want them to listen carefully to what Alison Redford is saying, to reflect on what I've been saying, to look forward to Alberta in the future."[41] This was the first time Lougheed had publicly endorsed a Tory premier during an election campaign.

On April 23, 2012, Redford won, defying all the polls and media reports giving Wildrose an upset victory right up to the moment ballots were cast. Redford's Tories won 61 of 83 seats with 44 per cent of the vote — a fall in seats of 11 and popular vote of 9 per cent. Smith's Wildrose took 17 seats with 34 per cent, becoming the Official Opposition. The Liberals dropped 17 per cent, suggesting many Liberal supporters voted strategically, shifting support to the Tories at the last moment to stop Wildrose. Voter turnout surged 16 per cent to 57 per cent. Wildrose support was locked up in rural southern Alberta. The Tories swept the cities and rural areas north of Wildrose's rural fortress.

Redford's insecure victory was based on an eleventh hour intervention by Lougheed and last-minute strategic voting by Liberal supporters. The government immediately faced a series of crises. In 2011 wildfires and flooding near oil production facilities cut production by over 30,000 barrels a day until the fires were controlled and the water receded.[42] Headlined as a major natural calamity, it was eclipsed by the June 2013 flood.[43] Five days of heavy rain (160 to 300 mm) and heavy spring runoff from the Rockies quickly inundated areas near the Elbow, Bow, and Highwood rivers: downtown Calgary and many suburbs were flooded, bringing city life to a halt; the town of High River, 40 kilometres south of Calgary, was wiped out; four people died. It was an unprecedented disaster with major economic consequences: half the province's oil and gas export capacity was shut down until waters receded. An estimated $5 billion was needed to rebuild the devastated infrastructure, and uncounted millions in revenues were foregone due to production cuts. Redford handled the crisis well, and political blame can hardly be laid for a natural disaster. But coming on top of the ongoing crises afflicting the province's oil and gas industry, it had potentially negative political fallout. The financial burden of the disaster came at a time when the province's revenue stream was in serious trouble. The extreme weather — unprecedented torrential rains over three days combined with an unusually heavy snow runoff — awakened the greenhouse gas and climate change debate at a sensitive time for the tar sands. The glory days of the Klein boom years were over, and the future did not look bright.

The promise of an endless bonanza from tar sands oil was fading.[44] Previous projections indicated tar sands oil production would double or triple by 2030, assuming it could be delivered to markets. But oil production in Alberta had already exceeded existing pipeline capacity, hence much of the oil was locked in. New pipelines were therefore vital, since moving such quantities of oil, especially heavy crude, by rail and truck was expensive and controversial. (Pipelines were out of the public's sight and mind, at least until a serious breach occurred; endless trains on tracks through populated areas and highways clogged with huge tanker trucks full of oil upset the public, and accidents were more visible and potentially dangerous.) Public resistance to new pipelines was growing, and although it was widely expected that the proposed pipelines would eventually be approved, the need was urgent and political opposition had slowed the approval process to a snail's pace.

In addition Alberta faced lower oil prices resulting in growing government deficits. Though the world price continued to hover between between $90 and $100 a barrel, Alberta heavy oil faced growing price discounts in the U.S. market. Tar sands oil always faced a discount since it is more costly to upgrade and refine. But such discounts in the past had been relatively small, given strong demand in the U.S. In 2013 Alberta heavy crude faced discounts per barrel of $40 in January and $15 in July — the discount moved up and down depending on supply and demand. In order to be commercially attractive tar sands oil needed prices ranging from $80 to $100 per barrel, and future developments, given rising costs of construction and labour, will need guaranteed prices in excess of $100. Hence tar sands expansion began to slow, some projects were delayed, others cancelled. Huge projected future developments seemed increasingly unlikely, as $9 billion in new investment awaited approval of the Keystone Pipeline.

The price discount was importantly driven by competition from expanded oil production in the U.S. The Alberta dream of a limitlessly prosperous future had been premised on the U.S. market remaining insatiable for all the oil Alberta could deliver, including the heavy crude from the tar sands. That was no longer true. New horizontal drilling technology led to opening long shut-in wells in all the traditional oil producing states in the U.S., bringing a flood of new lighter crude onto the market. Further, new hydraulic fracturing ("fracking") technology made the recovery of oil and natural gas from shale deposits commercially viable. The new Bakken field, including areas in the Dakotas, Saskatchewan, and Manitoba, with the largest concentration in South Dakota, provided an unexpected gush of new oil and natural gas on the market. These new developments were so successful that in 2012 experts were predicting not only future energy independence for the U.S., but the U.S. will become a net exporter of oil and natural gas. The U.S. was projected to surpass Russia as the world's biggest oil and natural gas producer in 2013, devastating news for the future of Alberta's tar sands.

As this new oil and natural gas came on stream Alberta's heavy crude faced stiff competition, resulting in heavy price discounts. The solution was to find new markets — in Asia and Central and Atlantic Canada. This required a greatly expanded pipeline network throughout the continent and to Canada's West coast for export to Asia. This solution faced strong political resistance.[45] In the meantime, the prices Alberta received for oil and natural gas remained depressed. Natural gas, once a great source of revenue, saw prices fall to historic lows. The new discoveries and production created a glut, with huge surpluses in storage across North America. To get Alberta's natural gas on the U.S. market in 2013 required a 50 cent per gigajoule discount — a 10 cent drop represents a $23 million loss in Alberta's revenue. Alberta had 3,400 trillion cubic feet of natural gas with no place to go. In 2006–07

Alberta received $6 billion in annual natural gas revenues. By 2013 this was down to $965 million. Alberta slipped from the leading continental supplier of natural gas to serving Canada's western region. Alberta perhaps received some solace to learn it was not the only major world oil producer suffering as a result of increased production in the U.S. Some OPEC exporters face serious difficulty if the volatility in world oil prices continues. The marginal cost of shale oil production in North America was $65 per barrel. Some OPEC states need $100 per barrel or face serious budget deficits. Some need prices ranging from $120 to $145, most notably Venezuela and Iran. Experts predicted that 2014 will be a tipping point, with prices falling from 10 to 20 per cent.[46]

Given these economic circumstances the Redford government was in serious difficulty.[47] The March 2013 budget was bad news. Redford warned Albertans of tough times ahead due to the fall in oil and gas prices, creating a $6 billion revenue shortfall. The province faced its sixth consecutive deficit, and the 2012 deficit came in at $4 billion, $3 billion higher than forecast. The 2013 deficit was projected at $6 billion, reflecting the $6 billion gap between revenues and expenditures. Redford announced the cancellation of the spending promises made in 2012 and warned Albertans the province would have to cut spending, increase some taxes, delay programs, and borrow $12.7 billion for infrastructure projects. Attacked from the left for reneging on spending promises and from the right for leading the province into a morass of deficit and debt, support for Redford's Tories fell sharply.

By February 2014 Redford's government was in serious trouble. Leaked private polls put the Wildrose Party 10 points ahead of the Tories as Wildrose support moved out of its southern rural enclave, growing across the province. By March 2014 Redford's approval rating fell to under 20 per cent. Redford faced a caucus rebellion, allegedly over her lavish travel expenses and abrasive leadership style, but much more related to her loss of connection with, and support from, the Tory popular base. Redford had little support in the caucus when she unexpectedly won the leadership, and what little support she had withered rapidly with the prospect of certain defeat in 2016. Uneasy about the growing fragmentation of the Redford government, leading elements of the oil and gas industry expressed private concerns about the government's credibility during difficult negotiations about the industry's future. The Tory machine always promptly ousted leaders who couldn't deliver . . . Getty, Klein in his final sad term, and Stelmach. On March 19, 2014, Redford resigned. Redford's brand of a softer neo-liberalism, and her efforts to pull Alberta out of its isolation to play a more reasonable and central role in national debates, was sandbagged by the economic crunch, replacing Stelmach as the shortest-serving premier of the Lougheed dynasty.

MANITOBA

Tory premier Gary Filmon appeared to lead a charmed political life.[48] As neo-liberal governments toppled in the early 1990s, Filmon managed to retain power. Learning from the errors of former Tory premier Sterling Lyon, an early pioneer of the neo-liberal agenda, who imposed a harsh program of restraint and cuts from 1977 to 1981, Filmon moved cautiously. Lyon was defeated after one term by Howard Pawley and the NDP. Pawley was in turn defeated by Filmon in 1988 after implementing some neo-liberal measures — large tax increases that hit ordinary wage and salary earners hard while largely sheltering business, a large jump in automobile insurance rates, underfunding of health and education, and supporting the unpopular Meech Lake Accord.

Pawley's successor as NDP leader, Gary Doer, described Filmon as a "masterful strategist" with a solid sense of what works in Manitoba's moderate political culture. Winning only minority government status in 1988 (Tories, 25 seats; Liberals, 20; NDP, 12), Filmon pursued a hybrid agenda, posing as both a self-styled "social progressive" and "fiscal conservative." As patronage poured into Manitoba from the Mulroney Tories in Ottawa, Filmon's stature grew. Filmon carefully tread through the minefield of the Québec issue, providing only lacklustre support for the Meech Lake Accord and the Charlottetown Agreement. While declaring health care, education, and social programs safe from heavy cuts, Filmon pursued balanced budgets and tax cuts as a neo-liberal. In September 1990 Filmon won a majority government (Tories, 30 seats; NDP, 20; Liberals, 7). Continuing his careful neo-liberal approach, after 1990 Filmon did not sound all that different from the new NDP premiers in Saskatchewan and B.C. Though pursuing a somewhat tougher neo-liberal agenda, Filmon held back from the excesses of Mike Harris in Ontario, or the earlier excesses of neo-liberal premiers in B.C. and Saskatchewan. As a result, Filmon was rewarded with another majority government in April 1995, though the increasing shift of the Liberal vote to the NDP from 1988 to 1995 created growing anxiety among Tory strategists.

After the 1995 victory the Filmon government faltered and then began to disintegrate. Filmon forgot that Manitobans were leery of either extreme — extreme neo-liberalism or extreme social democracy — and preferred modest, sensible governments which acted as the prudent trustee of health, education, and social programs and Manitoba's small but important public sector. The Manitoba electorate viewed health and education as more important than tax cuts, and Filmon began to deliver tax cuts at the expense of such programs. He became increasingly niggardly, particularly in health expenditures, cancelling some significant renewals of the health infrastructure contrary to public opinion. Suddenly Gary Doer's attacks on Filmon's neo-liberal agenda resonated more with voters.

In 1997 Filmon, in a very unpopular decision, privatized the publicly owned Manitoba Telecom System (MTS), declaring this a necessary fiscal measure and placing the proceeds in a Fiscal Stabilization Fund to be used to ensure future balanced budgets. The NDP criticized the privatization vehemently, claiming that making telephone communication and internet service a for-profit activity, rather than a public service, would lead to declines in service. The NDP also noted that the price paid for MTS was too low. Very soon the evidence was clear that declines in service began, particularly in the north and sparsely populated rural areas, which were expensive to service and netted no profit. And as the Fiscal Stabilization Fund began to drain to balance annual budgets, the wisdom of achieving a one-time financial benefit at the expense of selling off a valuable public asset seemed questionable. Such events began to erode Filmon's support. But what finally destroyed Filmon and his government was the Tory vote-splitting scheme during the 1995 election. In retrospect the whole vote-splitting scheme was a ridiculous failure, but it ruined Filmon's reputation and led to his defeat in September 1999.

In the 1988 election Liberal leader Sharon Carstairs parlayed her strong opposition to the Meech Lake Accord into 20 seats, becoming leader of the Official Opposition. She continued to battle Meech and became virtually a one issue leader, then fumbled the ball badly by her support of Meech in its final hours. After the collapse of Meech in June 1990, Carstairs claimed she was manipulated and browbeaten by Filmon into supporting the Accord. Her reputation never recovered and support for the Liberal party in the September 1990 election crashed. The Liberals were reduced to seven seats as much of their vote shifted to the NDP. From then on Tory strategists were frantic about a continuing shift of Liberal voters to the NDP as the 1995 election loomed.

In response, Taras Sokolyk, Filmon's chief of staff, devised a vote-splitting plot to defeat the NDP in three safe northern seats by draining votes away from the NDP to three independent aboriginal candidates running under the Independent Native Voice banner. The nomination of the three independent candidates was arranged with the help of Tory party officials, and Tory party funds were diverted to their campaigns. Further, individual donations were solicited by Tory officials from prominent and well-heeled Tory supporters. Two of the three independent candidates ultimately admitted involvement in the scheme. One candidate, Daryl Sutherland, claimed he was given cash and a car. This was all in clear violation of the *Manitoba Elections Act*. The story broke in the media just days before the election, but was vig-orously denied by Tory campaign officials. After the election the Chief Electoral Officer investigated the allegations and cleared the Tories, though the government refused to make the report public. But the allegations wouldn't go away, as the NDP alleged a cover-up. Filmon dismissed the allegations as "sleaze-mongering" and denied any Tory money was ever diverted to the three candidates. Filmon denied any knowledge of the scheme until the summer of 1998 when it leaked to the media that he in fact knew about it when Sutherland made his public admission in June 1998, because Sokolyk told Filmon about it at that time. Filmon convened a judicial inquiry and Sokolyk resigned.

Manitoba Chief Justice Alfred Monnin's inquiry revealed most of the details of the scheme, reporting in 1999. The Tories indeed engineered the vote-splitting campaign of the three independent candidates and provided party funds for their campaigns. The scheme was largely hatched by Sokolyk. Other officials of the Tory campaign were involved in the scheme, including the party's campaign accountant. The secretary of the Treasury Board was involved in a cover up of the paper trail tracking the money involved. False invoices were issued and the books were cooked. A couple of friends of the premier, wealthy and prominent Winnipeg businessmen, admitted writing personal cheques, at the request of Tory campaign officials, to support the vote-splitting candidates. Millionaire businessman, Robert Kozminski, a fraternity pal of the premier, even appeared proud of what he had done, testifying "I would do anything to take votes away from the NDP."

By the end of the inquiry Monnin could find no evidence of Filmon's direct knowledge or personal involvement, but the chief justice was also uncertain that he had been able to get to the bottom of the scheme. As he said in his report, "In all my years on the bench, I have never encountered as many liars in one proceeding as I did during this inquiry." But the whole scheme in its intent, despite its ridiculous and amateur character (the three candidates pulled only 2 per cent of the vote and the NDP held all three seats), led the chief justice to conclude that it was nevertheless an "unconscionable debasement of the citizen's right to vote." The justice regretted that no civil or criminal charges could be laid since the statute of limitations had passed.

Though Filmon had not been fingered directly, with five of his friends and top advisors implicated he had no choice, as premier, but to take responsibility for what had happened and apologize to the public. But the damage was done. Filmon's years of stonewalling and denial, the apparently ineffectual and tainted probe by the chief electoral officer, and the involvement of his inner circle all made it difficult for the public to accept his claims of innocence. Filmon continued to minimize what had happened as merely "poor judgment" and an excess of zeal. The NDP charged that the premier repeatedly lied to the public and to the legislature. In September 1999 the NDP's Gary Doer defeated Filmon (NDP, 32 seats; Tories, 24; Liberals, 1), ending his 11-year career as premier. There was no doubt that the vote-splitting scandal had handed the premiership to Doer as the Liberal vote collapsed largely in the NDP's favour.

Premier Doer styled himself as a social democrat in the Blair and Romanow "Third Way" tradition, committed to "fiscal prudence with a human face." Doer carefully walked the neo-liberal line already pioneered by Romanow in Saskatchewan — "balanced priorities," first, health and education, followed by modest tax cuts and balanced budgets. Indeed Doer's style and approach to governance was very much in the Filmon tradition, though he embarked on more modest cuts in program spending, a carefully blended mixture of tax cuts here and tax increases there, and a moderate reform of the income tax system in a more progressive direction. Doer presided over a slowly shrinking government, as attrition and small cuts were allowed to reduce the civil service, and the overall rate of government spending declined. Even in the face of growing social deficits in poverty and declines in education and health quality, Doer persisted with neo-liberal measures. The Doer government was, therefore, neither fully social democratic nor fully neo-liberal, as he zigged and zagged opportunistically from one side of the spectrum to the other. It was a successful political formula.

During his first term, Doer diligently appeased the business lobby by giving business pretty much everything asked of the government. There was, however, one exception. He remained attentive to labour's demands, sometimes even courting sharp conflict with the business lobby. This was understandable, given Doer's background and road to success. Doer's roots were in the trade union movement, which provided his career ladder to the top. Beginning his public life as a corrections officer, he rose quickly in the ranks. A dedicated trade unionist, he served as president of civil service union from 1979 to 1986, when he became an NDP MLA. Prior to entering politics with strong union support, Doer was one of the most prominent trade union leaders in the province. Strong union backing helped him win the NDP leadership in 1988. As a rookie MLA he was not a front runner, but won a narrow third ballot victory. When Doer became leader, the NDP appeared dead, running a distant third in the polls. Some even predicted the party's demise during the new reality of neo-liberalism. Doer proved his leadership and organizational abilities by quickly rebuilding the party and preparing the ground for the 1999 victory.

The Doer formula for success became clear as his years in power accumulated: give the business lobby most of what it asked for; give trade unions enough of what they demanded to keep them content; pursue balanced budgets religiously (every budget during the Doer reign was balanced); slowly reduce the size of government through a "death of a thousand cuts" strategy; cut taxes overall, especially business taxes, but disguise this agenda with targeted modest tax increases in order to sustain revenues; and, most importantly, embark on no controversial reforms of any significance.

Doer won his second mandate in June 2003 with an increased majority (NDP, 35 seats; Tories, 20; Liberals, 2), and his third in 2007 (NDP, 36 seats; Tories, 19; Liberals 2). But political interest waned as voter turnout collapsed from 68 per cent in 1999 to 54 per cent in 2003, staying there in 2007 and 2011. Manitoba's politics had never been as dramatic as those in the other three western provinces, at least not since the days of the Winnipeg General Strike in 1919 and the United Farmers of Manitoba government in the 1920s. By 2003 Manitoba's provincial politics had become positively boring, as Doer strove to avoid confrontation and controversy, diligently applying his formula for success. On August 27, 2009, Doer announced he would not seek re-election, and on August 28 Harper named him ambassador-select to the United States. Harper's stamp of approval reveals a great deal about Doer. Harper considered him a reliable, pragmatic, and, most importantly, politically effective neo-liberal. Some cynics suggested that with the unbeatable Doer gone, Harper hoped to clear the way for a Tory win in Manitoba in order to make the entire west unmistakably blue. If this indeed was part of Harper's plan, it failed. Greg Selinger, Doer's minister of finance, easily won the leadership, becoming premier. Selinger continued Doer's style of governance until calling an election in October 2011, reproducing the results of Doer's last election (NDP, 36 seats; Tories, 19; Liberals, 2). It appeared Doer's dynasty might have considerable staying power.

Manitobans initially resisted the West's strong support for the new right in federal politics, only sending three Reform MPs out of 14 to Ottawa in 1997, and only four Alliance MPs in 2000. However in 2004 Manitobans embraced the West's rightward drift, still with something less than enthusiasm, by sending seven Harper Tory MPs to Ottawa with 39 per cent of the vote. Harper's patient incremental construction of a majority government continued to pay off in Manitoba: 2006, 8 Tories and 43 per cent; 2008, 9 Tories and 49 per cent; 2011, 11 Tories and 54 per cent. Moderate, cautious Manitoba finally embraced Harper's neo-liberalism. Perhaps Doer's patronage plum was an expression of gratitude by an indebted Harper for Doer's role in gradually snuffing out the flickering flame of moderate social democracy.

The election of anti-neo-liberal parties in the early 1990s in Ontario, Saskatchewan, B.C., and Ottawa reflected the public's opposition to the neo-liberal business agenda. The failure of those parties to deliver on their promises and, indeed, their zealous continuation of that agenda deeply disillusioned the public, undercutting faith in our democratic system. More importantly, the continued implementation of the agenda accelerated the economic trends and problems noted in the previous chapters.[49] As governments in the West and in Ottawa withdrew from the economy and cut programs sheltering people, the free market became the arbiter of economic and social policy. As Ottawa bowed to provincial rights, premiers, yielding more and more power to the provinces, funds from Ottawa for health, post-secondary education and social programs were often diverted to whatever use the province wished. Ottawa would announce programs in health, education and child care, sign agreements with the provinces, but had no power or will to enforce national standards or even to monitor the actual use of the funds. As Ottawa yielded ground on energy policy to the provinces — Alberta, Saskatchewan, Newfoundland, and Nova Scotia — the possibility of a national energy strategy disappeared from the radar. Less activist and interventionist governments set the nation adrift, allowing the inexorable pull of the continental market to draw Canada deeper and deeper into integration with the U.S.

The free trade agreements, primarily NAFTA, continued the structural re-shaping of the Canadian economy. By the turn of the century, Canada's net loss of jobs as a result of free trade approached 300,000 and the east/west national economy had virtually disappeared. Over half of Canadian manufactured goods went to U.S. markets. And free trade was only truly free for the U.S., as the U.S. repeatedly denied Canadian softwood lumber free access to their markets — and as Canada won one challenge, another one was immediately issued. Indeed, the U.S. repeatedly bowed to powerful domestic interest groups threatened by Canadian competition, whether it was the U.S. softwood lumber industry, or the U.S. cattle and beef industry keeping the border closed beyond reason over a single case of BSE. The U.S. took this a step further with the Byrd amendment which distributed proceeds from trade dispute duties to U.S. interests — thus the duties Canadian exporters of softwood lumber paid were distributed among their U.S. competitors (in effect from 2000 to 2005). The worst fears regarding NAFTA's Chapter 11 were realized as Canada faced repeated challenges and penalties for government laws and policies on the grounds that they did not accord U.S. investors "national treatment." As a result Canada's sovereignty was undermined repeatedly.

Free of government constraints, more and more industries decamped from Canada to low wage areas in the southern U.S. and offshore. The final accounting of two decades of neo-liberalism and free trade was clear: Canada no longer had a viable national, east-west economy. Deeper integration into the U.S. had occurred. There was a net loss of good, secure jobs for Canadians, and real wages stagnated while corporate profits soared. The pre-existing economic dependencies of the various regions were exaggerated as their regional economies responded to U.S. market needs. Thus energy grew in importance in the West, and Ontario became virtually a one-industry economy as a key player in the continental automobile industry. The new Canadian economy was less vital and diverse, increasingly shaped by the pull of U.S. market forces.

Integration with the U.S. was most advanced in the West due to the energy sector. Between 1991 and 2001 there was a 90 per cent increase in the export of crude oil to the U.S. as Canada became the U.S. market's biggest single supplier. By 2002 Canada supplied 15 per cent of American natural gas consumption. The U.S. declared that Alberta's tar sands were a "U.S. pillar" for future "energy and economic security." By the turn of the century Canada produced more energy for the U.S. than it did for its own national needs. In 2001 President George W. Bush called for more pipeline infrastructure for the delivery of Canadian oil and natural gas, including a mega-pipeline to bring natural gas from the Arctic. It was initially estimated that Canada would drill over 200,000 new oil and natural gas wells in the West by 2011 to meet U.S. energy hunger. That turned out to be an underestimate. Though oil and natural gas were most important, the U.S. also became increasingly dependent on Canadian hydro-electric power from B.C. and Québec. The pressure to speed up the construction of infrastructure for access to Canadian energy, pipelines, and power grids, increased powerfully after 911, as the State Department insisted that the U.S. must cut dependency on "unstable oil sources" and rely more on Canada. In the post-911 political environment U.S. ambassador Paul Cellucci's call for a continental plan for energy integration between Canada and the U.S. created hardly a stir. Between 2002 and 2004 Canada's national economic growth pattern shifted significantly westward largely due to the energy boom.

The economic benefits for the West from energy were somewhat off-set by the continuing disaster in agriculture. By the end of the second decade of neo-liberalism, agriculture in the West was a basket case. The loss of markets and low prices due to the wheat wars were worsened by bad weather and poor crops. Trade disputes hurt agriculture as attacks continued on Canada's managed marketing system in dairy and egg products, which was declared illegal by the World Trade Organization in 2002. The United States and the European Union (EU), continued to defy free trade rules with huge subsidies for grain farmers, which had already been catastrophic for Canadian farmers as market after market was lost to the U.S. and the EU. In response, Canadian farmers began to diversify into crops like peas, lentils, and chickpeas, and the

U.S. responded by extending its subsidies for American farmers to the new crops in order to go after these new Canadian opportunities. The U.S. slapped duties on Canadian wheat (in great demand for pasta-making in the U.S.), on the grounds that Canada's Canadian Wheat Board and Crow Rate subsidies to the railways were unfair trade practices. Canadian farmers found free trade a bitter experience as they faced repeated border battles for access to the U.S. market for their hogs, cattle, and wheat. Realized net farm income fell dramatically and the number of farmers driven off the land had only been greater during the Great Depression. Prairie agriculture never recovered from the first decade of neo-liberal policies and the full implementation of free trade worsened the situation.

As for Canada's water, the U.S. made it abundantly clear they wanted access, sooner rather than later. In 2001 U.S. president Bush announced the U.S. wanted a deal with Canada to build water pipelines from Canada to the dry southwest U.S., proposing a continental water pact. Both Newfoundland and B.C. earlier indicated a desire to export water to the U.S., and Ottawa continued to equivocate, declaring opposition for domestic political consumption while doing nothing tangible to legally secure Canada's water. It was clear that the U.S. had a comprehensive strategy for the integration of Canada with the U.S. that included natural gas, oil, electricity, and water. The debate continues about whether NAFTA makes water exports inevitable. Some experts insist that water is protected by NAFTA. Others say water is not mentioned in the text and therefore not exempt. They argue that water exports will kick in inevitably under one of two scenarios. First, if there were ever a serious water crisis in the U.S. (an inevitable situation in the southwest), NAFTA provisions will compel granting the U.S. access to Canada's water. Second, if Canada ever begins to sell water, then NAFTA will compel similar access to the U.S. All experts agree that under NAFTA, once the water tap is turned on, it can never be shut off, nor can new taps be prohibited. By the early 2000s it was clear that under the present regime of the neo-liberal business agenda, and the free trade agreements, the export of Canada's water had become inevitable.

Two events accelerated the neo-liberal reconstruction of Canada and the West: the 2008 economic crisis and the elections that brought Harper to power, and finally to a majority government. As the economic crisis hit the U.S., Canada's manufacturing sector was hit hard as U.S. markets collapsed, especially for Ontario's autos and auto parts industry. Meanwhile, the West was able to weather the economic slump due to strong world demand for its resources, especially oil and potash. The U.S., while declining as an export destination for Canada's manufactured goods, remained a strong market for the energy sector. The importance of the energy sector, firmly rooted in Alberta, became more and more central to Canada's national economy. Indeed, with the push from the Harper government to make energy Canada's central industry, Canada became essentially a petro-economy. By 2012 the energy sector accounted for one-quarter of the value of Canada's S&P/TSX index, attracting over $55 billion in investment in that year. In 2011, oil and gas made up 11 per cent of Canada's gross domestic product, and crude oil accounted for 20 per cent of the value of all Canada's exports (a doubling since 2000). By 2013, 74 per cent of all Canada's exports went to the U.S. — a doubling since the pre–free trade era. Oil and natural gas accounted for 24 per cent of all exports, while autos and auto parts fell to 13 per cent. Autos and auto parts were projected to fall a further 25 per cent by 2020. The energy sector, primarily crude oil from the West, replaced autos and auto parts as the main economic driver of the national economy. Power shifted dramatically westward, both politically and economically.

The developing crisis in Canada's energy sector due to the new technologies for recovering oil from old shut-in wells, and for mining oil and natural gas from shale deposits, has not shifted Canada's dependence on energy as the central economic driver. As the U.S. market imposed hefty price discounts on Canadian oil and natural gas, due to dramatic increases in U.S. production, the scramble for new markets in Asia and Atlantic and Central Canada pushed the pipeline construction agenda, and witnessed a dangerous shift to moving oil and gas by rail and tanker truck. The message from the Harper government became the national economy needs new pipelines if Canada hopes to flourish in the future. This will result in even deeper continental integration, and set the stage for staggeringly costly environmental disasters.

Harper's majority victory allowed him finally to eliminate the remaining traditional benefits won by the West as repayment for the price it shouldered in early nation building: a final end to the Crow Rate benefit, the dismantling of the Canadian Wheat Board (CWB), repeal of Canada's elaborate environmental regulatory regime, sharp curtailment of the regulation of food and food products going to market, and systematic destruction of the network of supports for the family farm built up over generations. The proposed trade agreement with the European Union, if finalized, will see an end to the remnants of orderly marketing, since the dismantling of protection for Canada's egg, poultry, and dairy industries will be required to achieve a final agreement. Western farmers became naked as they faced the world market. In 2013 Prairie farmers harvested bumper crops in grains, but grain prices, which had been very good in the spring, began to drop like a stone as harvest approached. With the CWB gone, those farmers in need of ready cash to pay down debt and prepare for the next season were forced to sell at depressed prices, while larger farmers were able to store their harvest until prices improved. This was exactly the scenario Prairie farmers fought against when they established cooperative pools and finally won the CWB. Further, free of close oversight by the CWB and Ottawa, Canada's railways failed to deliver the 2013 crop quickly to the market, preferring moving more lucrative goods, especially oil by tanker car. This sort of rail blockade of grain had earlier pushed farmers to successfully gain oversight of the railways, ensuring the timely shipment of grain. Such routine oversight no longer occurred in the neo-liberal era. The final result can only be the acceleration of the corporate transformation of agriculture and the final end of the family farm as we have known it.

The West was created as a market and a resource-producing region as a key element of Canada's founding economic strategy. The West resisted the role of "hewer of wood and drawer of water" in the national economy and fought repeatedly for a better deal. Concessions were won, but never the structural changes necessary to satisfy the West's aspirations for a balanced, secure, and diversified economy delivering fairness and justice. Activist and interventionist governments in the Western provinces attempted to overcome the West's resource dependency and pioneered the welfare state and modest public ownership strategies. While gaining some relief, security and prosperity, the West was never able to break out of its economic destiny as laid down in the National Policy. But from settlement to the Great Depression, the West learned that unregulated capitalism and free markets did not deliver the security, prosperity, and economic justice demanded by those who did the work, took the risks and produced the wealth.

New generations forgot those lessons and the struggles that led to the popular gains made after the Great Depression and World War II. New generations of Westerners were swept away by the apparently novel free market magic proclaimed by the business lobby and its political parties in the 1980s. After three decades, that political process has inevitably kept the West in its place as resource hinterland, not for the national economy, but now for a continental economy dominated by the U.S.

Canada as a national project largely ceased to exist, and few in the West mourned its end given the long years of unsuccessful battles for new terms of national integration. Led now by the business lobby and neo-liberal political parties, the West turned south to realize a new dream of prosperity through economic integration with the U.S. But this turn south was not the result of a political debate and a democratic political decision. Rather it was the result of surrendering to the inexorable logic of free market capitalism liberated from government regulation and constraint.

Western Canadians have returned to the past as they survey the wreckage of much of the welfare state, and the end of governments committed to interventions to defend the common good.

12

FRACTURED FEDERATION

Although this book focuses on the West, it is really about Canada. Can Canada survive as a federal state in the absence of a strong central government with national policies to balance the needs of all regions in a manner that heals wounds and binds Confederation together? Can a nation composed of fractious regions — of which the West is only one — long endure in the absence of strong political and economic ties sustaining a viable federation in which benefits outweigh costs? In the 1970s the nation was fractured by fault lines between the West and Central Canada, and between Québec and English Canada. Those confrontations were unsatisfactorily resolved for the West by constitutional reforms granting the West an amending formula including a regional veto, a clearer affirmation of provincial control of natural resources, and a guarantee of the principle of equalization payments to the poorer provinces. But these concessions to the West were granted only by further isolating Québec to simmer in dreams of sovereignty, setting the stage for the constitutional crises around Meech and Charlottetown in the 1980s and early 1990s.

During the first neo-liberal decade, 1982–93, Canada's business lobby and political elites moved to what was billed as a final solution to the regionalism afflicting Canadian politics since 1867. An overbearing central government would be stripped of many of its effective powers, while provincial powers would be greatly enhanced. Never again could Ottawa impose a national policy on a dissenting province, as in the case of the National Energy Program. Liberated by a free market and access to the American market through the FTA, and ultimately to the whole continental market through NAFTA, Canada's regions, each with unique economies, could finally realize prosperity by entering continental and world markets without federal constraints. With this courageous "leap of faith," the chronic problem of regional disparity, at the root of so much political confrontation, would dissipate in a wave of prosperity and growth. The heavy hand of government intervention in the economy would be lifted, and the entrepreneurial spirit would be freed of onerous regulation and taxation in order to usher in a millennium of economic innovation and the generation of new wealth. Thus stripped of many powers, and having surrendered the political will to generate sufficient public revenues, governments would have to reconsider spending levels for social, health, and education programs and increasingly withdraw from public entrepreneurship. The Québec conundrum would be finally resolved, not by giving Québec special status in the federation, something English Canada has always refused, but by essentially giving all provinces what Québec has been demanding since the Quiet Revolution.

In order to bring off this shift in the nature of Canada, Brian Mulroney fashioned an unprecedented political alliance among the corporate elite, the nationalist elite of Québec, and the regional elite of Western Canada, on the sole basis of an unremitting hatred for the central government in Ottawa and a determination to disarm that government. The Western regional elite — the dependents and servants of international resource companies, the oil and gas industry, small and large regional capitalists, rich farmers, and the business lobby in general — wanted rid of federal constraints on their ability to exploit the region's natural wealth without regard to the environment, the future or the public interest. The West entered this alliance uneasily. There was great discomfort in Alberta about making common cause with Québécois nationalism, a foe long opposed. That uneasiness was increased as the Reform party nipped at the heels of the traditional Western Tory bloc. Furthermore, a great many in the

West — especially labour and the family farmer — were reluctant to give up gains made from, and the security provided by, a strong central government able and willing to establish national support programs in agriculture, regional development, unemployment insurance, education, health, and social assistance. It was not surprising that the alliance collapsed during Mulroney's second term. Nor was it surprising that the collapse had constitutional and economic roots.

Constitutionally, the support for the alliance in the West collapsed for two reasons. First, the continuing francophobia among many Westerners just could not bear to grant Québec status as a distinct society, however meaningless. Second, and more significantly, a great many Westerners proved finally unwilling to countenance a dramatic weakening of federal powers, believing the West needed federal policies and supports due to the region's unstable resource economy. Economically, the alliance collapsed because a decade of neo-liberalism and free trade did not produce the promised results. The recession of the early 1980s became a full-scale, decade-long second Great Depression in the West. Oil and natural gas prices stayed low, and many Westerners saw their conventional oil and gas squandered at indefensibly low prices, accelerated by a lack of regulation and the establishment of a free continental energy market. The world wheat wars provoked the worst crisis in agriculture since the 1930s. Neo-liberal parsimony in social spending was offset by profligacy in public spending on private economic development through grants, loans, loan guarantees, and reduced taxation for private enterprise. Yet despite growing deficits and debts, the promised economic diversification was not realized.

Canada was not well served by Mulroney's alliance, hailed as an example of the new era of the politics of unity rooted in neo-liberalism and free trade. The collapse of the alliance left Québec more embittered by the unwillingness of English Canada to make even minimal concessions. For the first time, separatist sentiment was represented in the House of Commons and the unthinkable had happened. The leading federal party in Québec was separatist and Québec seemed on a trajectory to sovereignty. In the West, the move to neo-liberalism left the fragile regional economy vulnerable, and the main economic pillars of the West — agriculture, energy, and forestry — at risk. The cuts in government spending for the social security system and regional development could not have occurred at a worse time. The West's new self-appointed political champion, the Reform party, was determined to carry through the neo-liberal counter-revolution, regardless of consequences. Meanwhile, the traditional champion of the West, the NDP, joined the neo-liberal crusade. As the wreckage was surveyed, Canadians had never been worse off, or so it seemed. The wheat economy was in tatters. The fishery, the economic pillar of Atlantic Canada, was shut down and pronounced dead, only fitfully re-emerging from decades of crisis. Ontario was ravaged by depression, as de-industrialization acceler-ated after the FTA, pushing the province into the worst downturn since the 1930s. The regional cleavages between English Canada and Québec , between Central Canada and the West, between Atlantic Canada and the rest of the nation, now turning its back on helping the poorer regions, were never so deep. In truth, Canada was at risk.

Federal and provincial neo-liberal governments were defeated in the early 1990s with the election of Jean Chrétien's Liberals in Ottawa and NDP governments in Ontario, Saskatchewan, and B.C., all promising a reversal of the neo-liberal business agenda. Popular relief was quickly replaced by bitterness as the former critics of neo-liberalism became its quickly converted champions, imposing the agenda even more harshly. During the second decade of neo-liberalism, 1993–2005, the public increasingly lost faith in our democratic institutions. Regardless of which party was elected, Canada lived under a business dictatorship. All parties — Liberal, Tory, and NDP — when in power, imposed the neo-liberal business agenda.

Public faith in political parties and governments as tools of the democratic popular will fell dramatically. Public participation in the electoral process declined steeply. Politicians became objects of pub-lic contempt, viewed as the most untrustworthy category of citizen in poll after poll. The Reform party, which metamorphosed into the Alliance and then the new pristine right-wing Tory party, won political hegemony across the West. The West turned right as never before, seeking some revenge on liberals and social democrats who spoke one way in a cynical effort to win votes and then governed in the opposite way. There was no national vision offered except vague talk of distinctive Canadian values mixed with anti-Québec rhetoric. The wreckage caused by neo-liberal social policies, and free trade and free markets, spread as the West was further integrated into the U.S. market. Never had the Canadian national project been so deeply rejected by Westerners, now under the political leadership of the extreme right and the business lobby. In truth, however, the Canadian national project ceased to exist, as regions battled for two main things: free access to the U.S. market and more "no strings" cash from Ottawa.

A third decade of neo-liberalism began with Harper's ascension to power, first as a minority government in 2006, setting the stage for his majority victory in 2011. He fashioned a new electoral coalition firmly anchored by solid support in the West, and in rural Canada from coast to coast. To this he was able to add enough of the suburban middle class and the entitled, better paid working class in Ontario to win. This "middle income" or "middle class" stratum had grown increasingly unhappy about declines in public spending on education, health, and social programs; limits on their eligibility for such supports; and a growing tax load. Harper pandered to a politics of selfish resentment to win them over. Upon victory, Harper began the zealous implementation of a full neo-liberal reality in the new Canada. Nation building, public obligation to support the weak and vulnerable, and the politics of compassion were dead.

A strong current of opinion in analyses of Canadian historiography views the rebellions of the West as the result of unfortunate sectionalism. Blinded by purely local interests and grievances, such movements indicate an unwillingness to embrace the great task of nation building. If only Westerners were able to see beyond immediate grievances to behold the great national vision that lies behind the Canadian project, their lamentations would subside as they accepted some discomfort as the patriotic price of building a great nation against impossible odds. The West's resistance to national policies, and its continuing fractiousness, have prevented the final realization of a united, vital, and strong Canada. Though perhaps understandable, the West's complaints, the argument goes, have been largely ultimately destructive.

This sort of condescending Central Canadian attitude to the West — remarkably parallel to the one inflicted on Québécois nationalists by English Canada — contributed to the West's deepening sectionalism, helped to create the Western separatist spasm of the 1970s, and set the stage for the emergence of the Reform party in the 1980s and early 1990s. In many ways, the early Reform party was the ultimate expression of sectionalism, spawned in the West, nurtured by oil money and the extreme right of the business lobby, seeking to unite backward, redneck elements across all English Canada in an effort to dismantle the sometimes carefully crafted, sometimes jerry-built, consensus that had managed to sustain the federation since Confederation.

In retrospect, this was understandable, if only because history has largely vindicated the West's grievances while at the same time indicting Central Canada and successive governments in Ottawa for failing to act. The genocide committed against the Métis and several First Nations now stands exposed as one of the monumental crimes of the 19th century. Canadians today recognize the injustices done, but have failed to stop the injustices and pay historical debts. The complaints of the early farmers in the West were repeatedly vindicated by government investigation, and the list of concessions to Western grain growers are a testament to the nation's recognition of the justice of these complaints. The great agrarian crusade of the 1910s and 1920s, when a new vision of Canada was offered, again forced significant concessions. The brave agitations of the Western working class, together with the efforts of workers all across the Dominion, have been vindicated by the fact that most of what they asked has been implemented. The agitations of the 1930s, led by the Social Credit party and the CCF, articulating a critique of capitalism and a new vision of Confederation more responsive to the needs of the common people, though failing to win the nation, modified the polity and the economy markedly, resulting in the establishment of the welfare state consensus, the prime target of the neo-liberal counter-revolution from 1980 to 2013. In the 1970s the clash between the West and Central Canada during the energy and constitutional wars led to minor constitutional concessions on the amending formula, an enhancement of the provinces' control of natural resources, and guarantees of equalization payments to poorer provinces. The record of concessions, more than anything else, supports the West's complaints. But the West was not just seeking concessions, though those made were gladly accepted. The West was challenging the very nature of the political and economic structure of Confederation.

On no fewer than five occasions the West called on Canada for basic progressive changes in national direction. In 1869–70, Riel and the white settlers of the Red River asked that the West not be unceremoniously incorporated into Canada as a colonial possession. The West ought to enter Confederation on the same terms as any other province, they argued. Further, the new nation ought not to be created by overriding the Métis and Western First Nations. Rather these peoples should be embraced and helped to join the westward expansion. The Dominion did not listen and created the postage stamp province, retaining the remainder of the vast Western territory as a colonial possession.

Riel called from the West a second time in 1885. Again he asked for recognition of the land claims of his people, a fairer deal for the First Nations, as well as responsible government. Again he pleaded for help for his people to participate in the expansion. Again he asked for provincial status. He was again not heard and was sent to the gallows for his efforts. Provincial status for the rest of the West was denied until 1905. Control of natural resources was denied to the Prairie provinces until 1930. The Dominion justified this on the grounds that local legislatures might impede settlement and expansion. And when the provinces of Alberta and Saskatchewan were finally established, Western opinion was ignored as two provinces rather than one, with regimes loyal to the ruling Ottawa Liberals, were established.

In the 1910s and 1920s the agrarians from the West, in union with organized farmers across English Canada, called for a less corrupt, more responsive political system and an economy freed from the control of the "Special Interests." Though they had a great impact, they were defeated. Two different voices emerged on the Prairies during the Great Depression — Social Credit and the CCF. Both asked for political and economic changes to humanize the political and economic face of Confederation and of capitalism. Again, though they had a great impact, they were defeated in their efforts to win national support.

None of these movements was primarily a manifestation of regional grievance. Riel's movements were articulations of a national grievance by a people about to be crushed by westward expansion. The organized farmers, Social Credit, and CCF agitations were primarily expressions of grievances from the perspective of "the middle sort" of farmer and their labour allies. Each of the latter three movements proposed alternative systems of economic organization, and new terms for Confederation, more attuned to the popular aspirations of the common people. And each of the three presented itself to the whole Dominion in an effort to win support for the changes proposed.

In fact, the regionalization of the movements was imposed upon them by the structure of Confederation and of the national economy, which so clearly divided the economic interests of Canada's regions. Failing to win national mandates, the movements, in the case of the victorious Social Credit in Alberta and the CCF in Saskatchewan, retreated to provincial strategies as they struggled for political survival and economic improvement.

As the movements fought to win and hold office, increasingly they articulated their positions in regional terms. Thus the lowest common denominator in Saskatchewan and Alberta that united farmer, worker, and small business was a very real Western regional perspective: the bad treatment of the West in Confederation, the economic injustices perpetuated by Central Canadian interests, the need to diversify a vulnerable resource economy to even out the "boom-bust" cycle, to fight Ottawa for more concessions, and to give sound Western-oriented government. As the movements became increasingly confined in the West, this retreat to provincial strategies and regional perspectives became characteristic of all competing political parties in the region. The movements lost their vision of a new Canada.

The resource confrontation of the 1970s confirmed regional politics remained in command in the West. In the absence of structural changes to alter the West's place in the national economy and its political weakness in Confederation, the West was forced to battle to defend its interests as a subordinate region. After the collapse of oil prices in the early 1980s followed by the collapse in world prices for much of what the West produced, ushering in a decade of depression, many Westerners, desperate for economic diversification, once again toyed with the mystical promise of unfettered capitalism, while seeking revenge on the structures of federalism that frustrate their aspirations. Many Westerners, therefore, with the eager help of the business lobby and the Tory party, had come full circle, yearning for a return to the very economic system earlier movements had sought to transform. Perhaps this was understandable. Despite all the agitations and concessions, despite all the booms and busts, the Western economy remained vulnerable and fragile, rooted in the export of natural resources to uncertain world markets and increasingly integrated into the U.S. market.

At the root of the West's continuing unhappiness in Confederation, an unhappiness that often intensifies during boom times due to resentment at missed opportunities, and turns into deep anger during busts, is fed by a sense of chronic insecurity and vulnerability. Good times are rarely enjoyed as Westerners wait for the inevitable bust. This structural economic inequality, built into the very fabric of the national economy, combines with the inevitable insecurity that haunts resource-based economies to sustain an ongoing sense of injustice in the West. Western disaffection, and its continuing expression in increasingly regional politics, is the defensive reaction of the people of the West who have fought repeatedly for structural changes, only to be defeated each time. And each defeat has made an all-class regional sense of grievance the inevitable focus of electoral politics. The defeats, and growing Western sectionalism, culminated in the West's disastrous flirtation with neo-liberalism from the 1980s on. Like separatism in Québec , the West's sectionalism, now expressed in its most extreme form in national politics by a commitment to hard,

right-wing conservatism, represents the politics of a disintegrating
Canada, of a defeated national dream, a dream that frequently seemed
to mock the West with the privileges and powers of the Ontario-based
capitalist class as it imposed its will on Confederation, indifferent to
the consequences for the West.

At the end of three decades of neo-liberalism characterized by massive cuts in program spending, and the end of interventionist governments inspired by programs of province and nation building, there
was no longer even a pretence of a national project uniting the regions
in the pursuit of the Canadian dream. At the end of that era, federal-
provincial meetings, rather than concentrating on debates about
constitutions and national policies, focused on the "fiscal imbalance"
among the provinces, and between the provinces and Ottawa. Canada
became a debate about bookkeeping and accounting.

The idea of the "fiscal imbalance" had roots in the Rowell-Sirois
Commission which reported in 1940 that the provinces had enormously expensive constitutional responsibilities — health, education, and social welfare — but lacked the taxing powers to pay for
the explosion in public expectations for programs in those areas. As a
result, from 1940 onward Ottawa responded both by granting more
taxation room to the provinces, and by establishing federal-provincial
cost sharing for such programs. By 2000 the concept of "fiscal imbalance," purveyed by aggressive provinces seeking more federal powers
and federal funds, had come to mean a crude comparison between
the amounts provinces paid into Ottawa as a result of federal taxes,
and the amounts flowing into the provinces from Ottawa in cash and
programs. If more was sucked out of a province than was paid into
the province by Ottawa, then there was a "fiscal imbalance." Such an
approach to federalism was a final step in fragmentation and disintegration as increasingly powerful provinces pummelled the federal government, weakened by self-inflicted wounds and political cowardice,
into handing over program cash with no strings, with no imposition
of national standards, with no federal powers to ensure the funds were
spent on the programs designated by the federal government.

Even the "fiscal imbalance" pretence of a national vision ended with

Harper's ascension to majority power. With single-minded determination he quickly began a wholesale dismantling of the nation building programs put in place over the last hundred years. Already deeply cut and partially dismantled during the Mulroney and Chrétien years, welfare state and regulatory systems faced further deep cuts or outright cancellation. Harper announced an end to federal/provincial first ministers meetings, refusing to meet premiers except one-on-one in private. He reaffirmed his commitment to withdraw federal involvement in areas of provincial jurisdiction, signalling that future federal funding for shared cost programs would face further cuts. He warned that Ottawa would curtail the amount of funds put into the equalization formula. He began dismantling the elaborate structures of federal regulation and oversight designed to ensure national standards and to protect public safety. Harper's vision was simple and clear: the free market will rule, with little oversight and regulation by governments. The future of Canada will not be determined by the democratic will of the people, but by the market and the rich and powerful who control it. Each province, each region was on its own, free to shape its fate in the global marketplace. The Canadian national project, directed by interventionist democratic governments, was over.

WHAT CAN BE DONE?

Before we can contemplate solutions to the problem of the West in Confederation, we must accept we are not dealing with a regional but a national problem. Focusing simply on the grievances of this or that region, and proposing half-measures and concessions to placate the West, to defuse resentment in Atlantic Canada, or to undercut separatism in Québec, leaves the basic national problem unresolved. We are not dealing with the continuing irrationality of Québécois nationalism, or the quaint complaints of Atlantic Canada, or the folksy alienation of the West. We are dealing with a nation that has no national politics. Western provinces, Québec, and Newfoundland and Labrador are no more guilty of regional self-seeking than Ontario. Due to its size and wealth, Ontario has often been successful in wrapping its own brand of sectionalism in the Canadian flag. But Ontario has nevertheless proven just as adept at playing the regional game as the West. Indeed, in 2005 Ontario joined the "fiscal imbalance" bandwagon, insisting that Ottawa owed Ontario $23 billion.

Regionalism dominates politics in every province and is used to mobilize the united opinion of people with quite diverse interests — business people, farmers, workers, the poor — in the ongoing battle of the regions. Class struggles are eclipsed by regional struggles. The Québécois worker, farmer, and entrepreneur are united to defend the nation from the abuses of English Canada. The Atlantic fisher, farmer, worker, and entrepreneur, encouraged by the new potential of off-shore wealth, are united to enlarge the region's share of the pie. In the West, the farmer, worker, and entrepreneur, with the eager support of the energy lobby, unite to battle the rest of Canada for control of the West's increasingly valuable resources. And in Ontario, the traditional big capitalist, rooted in Canada's large financial, commercial, and industrial enterprises, seeks support from the threatened farmer, work-er, and small entrepreneur to defend Ontario's traditional privileges.

The regional structure of the Canadian economy, and the polit-ical design of Confederation, make such brokerage politics inevitable. Indeed, Canada's regions merely replay, again and again, the kind of bargaining engaged in by the elites of the various colonies when Confederation was first negotiated. Confederation began as a busi-ness deal among the elites of the colonies. And Canada remains a business deal among the elites of the various regions, bargaining and squabbling over sharing the wealth. There are therefore no viable national politics in Canada, nor perhaps have there ever been. The successful politician — federal and provincial — is the one who can set one region against the other in a bid for electoral power. There is no party of Confederation, there are only parties representing sectional interests, defending traditional ruling class privileges, and imposing the policy will of the business lobby. After three decades of weakened non-interventionist governments, free markets and free trade, there is a new twist to the problem. In the past Canada's regions squabbled over their places in the national economy and concessions could be granted and accommodations made. As the national economy disappears and is replaced by a continental and global economy, the regions increasingly see the federation as a costly encumbrance as they seek prosperity and economic expansion. Having been instructed for three decades to seek market advantages as the first priority in economic, political, and social life, it is not surprising that many in the West, and even more so in Québec, increasingly argue for freedom from the shackles of Canada.

Our present crisis has its roots in the energy and constitutional wars of the 1970s when Canadian politics became even more deeply poisoned by regionalism. Lougheed bashed the "feds" and won overwhelming mandates while ignoring the fact his provincial economy was the private preserve of the multinational oil companies, for whom he frequently spoke while posing as the West's champion. Premier Bill Davis of Ontario won confidence by bashing the West, making it clear that he would not let the "blue-eyed sheiks" of Alberta take Ontario for a ride. Peckford of Newfoundland made his name by standing up to Ottawa. Blakeney in Saskatchewan initially did well by bashing the "feds," but upon his first accommodation his electorate punished him, as the Tories accused him of betraying the West. Trudeau, defeated by the regions in 1979, won in 1980 by slamming the West, mobilizing Central and Atlantic Canada behind him. Meanwhile resource companies, the oil and gas lobby, and eager entrepreneurs in the West funded separatist organizations in order to battle federal interference in energy. In Ottawa, the federal Liberal government responded in kind. Assured of Québec and a divided Atlantic Canada, the Liberals wrote off the West while making efforts to win Ontario, the province deciding who would govern.

The Liberals posed as the party of Confederation merely because they won elections. The recipients of most of the support of big business and industry, simply because they alone seemed able to provide stable government, the Liberals were able to win because their near-total hegemony in Québec allowed them to focus on appeals to Ontario. Atlantic Canada, deeply dependent on federal handouts, typically judiciously divided its loyalties between the two major parties. The federal Tories at the time, deprived of hope in Québec because of historical sins, degenerated into a party that brought together a whole series of contradictory regional grievances on the basis of a grab bag of anti-Québec sentiment, regional resource capitalist anger, and conservative hysteria about big government. The party's sad efforts to unite the demands of the Alberta Tory regime for higher energy prices with those of the Ontario Tory regime for lower energy prices tore the 1979 Clark government to shreds in a few short months. Each major federal party was locked into representing regional interests in national politics. The NDP, as well, had become increasingly split along regional lines. Desperate for a national breakthrough, the federal party tried to downplay its strong Western roots in a bid for electoral support in Ontario. Meanwhile, the Western wing, which elected most NDP MPs, strove to retain its position as the reform voice of the West in Confederation. There was therefore, no national voice in Canada's federal politics — just the continuing clamour of regional interests striving to win their way in each of the three main parties.

This gridlock set the stage for Mulroney's counter-revolution of the 1980s. Successfully fashioning an unprecedented and unexpected alliance between the two most bitterly anti-Ottawa regions — Québec and the West — Mulroney won back-to-back victories in 1984 and 1988. With the eager support of the newly aggressive business lobby, determined to shed itself of any commitment to Canada's national project, Mulroney ushered in not only three decades of an abandonment of nation building, but also of frontal assaults on the essence of the evolved Confederation consensus. As Mulroney's reckless adventure spun out of control and collapsed, regional divisions widened to yawning chasms, as the Bloc Québécois in Québec and the Reform party in the West rose to prominence. When the NDP parliamentary leadership stumbled and failed to deliver, the social democratic option in Canadian politics, so vital in forcing the construction of the welfare state/interventionist government consensus, appeared on the verge of extinction. The final chapter was the failure of the Liberal party under Chrétien to reverse the neo-liberal agenda. The Liberals chose instead to accelerate it, as they lost Québec to the separatists and faced a growing threat from the right in the West. Harper rode the collapse of the traditional party system to power. Uniting the right in a new hard Tory party, he cobbled together a new electoral alliance between the West, rural Canada, and suburban Ontario to win a majority. In a sort of revenge, Harper wrote off Québec , just as Chrétien had written off the West, in his drive to power.

Whatever the final outcome of the volatile morass of Canadian politics in the aftermath of three decades of neo-liberalism, one fact is clear. In this next era of Canadian political history a viable mechanism for balancing Canada's regional strains and stresses will have to be developed. Further, during that journey of discovery, a new shared vision of Canada for the century urgently needs articulation, a vision including concrete national policies.

During the 1992 Charlottetown referendum, Canadians clearly rejected a reformed Senate as a viable mechanism for the resolution of Canada's regional problem. Canadians also rejected the excessive devolution of federal powers to the provinces. Whether the federation will be saved or lost will be determined by the House of Commons, just as it should be in a democratic society. Yet the House of Commons, under our current "first past the post" electoral system, has proven unable to provide fair and balanced representation to Canada's regions. As a result, parties receiving a minority of votes can win huge parliamentary majorities based on opportunistic regional alliances, and then proceed to impose unpopular policies on resistant regions. Thus, in 1980 Trudeau could write off the West, win a majority government, and proceed to force the National Energy Program on the West. In 1988 Mulroney could lose in English Canada, yet proceed to impose the FTA, as well as a series of deeply unpopular neo-liberal policies, with a comfortable parliamentary majority. Chrétien, with far less than 50 per cent of the vote, could win three majority governments in 1993, 1997, and 2000, effectively writing off both the West and Québec by racking up a huge majority of seats in Ontario, while the right was split between the Tories and the various incarnations of the Reform party. Harper was able to win his 2011 majority, though 60 per cent of the electorate opposed him, by writing off Québec and cobbling together his unprecedented coalition between the West, rural Canada, and the suburbs of Ontario.

The House of Commons must become a more representative and responsive institution if Canada hopes to reconcile the regions and regain the confidence of Canadians in a very undemocratic political system. Similarly, political parties must be rescued from the necessity of thinking primarily in terms of regional horse-trading and allowed to begin to think about the future of the federation as a whole. The most obvious way to ensure our federal political parties begin to think federally and to create a truly national politics would be to abolish the present "first past the post" system of election in favour of proportional representation in the House of Commons based on a sharing of each province's federal seats according to the parties' actual popular support. There would thus be MPs from all provinces committed to all parties. The advantages of the system are obvious: the true popular support for each party in the regions and in the nation would be faithfully reflected in the House of Commons. Each of the parties would therefore be forced to confront the particular problems of each region and develop policies that attempted to seek a balance between conflicting perspectives.

Yet many argue that the main disadvantage of such a system is that Canada would never be able to elect a majority government, except as a result of an exceptional popular sweep by a party. Thus Canada would be plagued with political instability. But a case can equally made that this vice is really a virtue. In Canada's history, minority governments have had a consistently more responsive record than majority governments. Minority governments are forced to concede, to compromise, and to innovate. Majority governments, smug and secure in their mandates, need not remain responsive to the needs and aspirations of the people. And perhaps it is more democratic to ensure that no government shall have a clear majority unless it has earned a majority popular mandate. Clearly proportional representation would go a great distance in reconciling Canada's divided regions, and deepening our imperfect democracy.

There is very little support for thorough-going proportional representation among any of the established parties or the existing provincial regimes. This should not be surprising since the system would lead to uncertainty and the prospect of never having a comfortable majority. Our governments and politicians would have to work harder at governing better. Perhaps the time is now ripe, after enduring three decades of neo-liberalism — contrary to the popular will expressed both in elections and in poll after poll — for Canadians to insist that it is exactly what is needed: a truly representative House of Commons in which party majorities would be rare, therefore requiring our political parties and MPs to roll up their sleeves to achieve workable compromises on an ongoing basis.

A Trudeau minority government would never have been able to impose the NEP without addressing many of the West's central grievances. A Mulroney minority government would not have been able to impose the FTA and then NAFTA, and many other central features of the neo-liberal agenda. A Chrétien minority government would never have gotten away with running against neo-liberalism and then implementing it more harshly. A Harper minority government would never have been able to ram two omnibus budget bills through the House of Commons to complete the dismantling of the old Canada and the construction of the new neo-liberal Canada.

None of these reforms will work, however, in the absence of a new national policy with deep popular support in each region. In the absence of that, no political tinkering will change the regional impasse we confront and have confronted since Confederation.

A NEW NATIONAL POLICY

After three disastrous decades of no national policy but that of weak governments, free markets and free trade, Canada desperately needs a new national policy to articulate the aspirations of the regions in a new political and economic structure, while reflecting the desire of the people for a society based on economic and social justice. A vision of what Canada could be is urgently needed; a vision to overcome the regional loyalties to which we have all been so well trained by our local political and economic elites; to allow us to break out of regional constraints in order to unite Canadians of all regions in a quest for a Canada able to flourish into the future.

The first step is to open each region to the complaints and grievances of all other regions, to reciprocally recognize the basic justice
of the complaints of the regions. As a first principle, Canadians must
declare a willingness to take the risks necessary to be generous to
redress regional grievances as a matter of national policy. Québec
must be granted the unqualified right to self-determination, as well as
the unquestioned right of special status, as the political expression of
the Québécois nation, in any new regime of Confederation. The West
must be finally freed from the quasi-colonial status that has haunted
it since 1869, not just rhetorically, but with significant reparations in
recognition of the costs the region has repeatedly borne in building
Canada. First Nations must be granted forms of autonomy and self-
government, and at the same time fair and generous settlements of
all outstanding land claims must be made. Atlantic Canada needs to
be assured economic development will be fostered and supported by
national policies. All Canadians must be assured that the nation is
dedicated not just to a basic national minimum level of well-being,
but to programs that will lead to a genuine equality of condition for
all. Such commitments will begin to remove the regional poison from
our politics, allowing us to focus on the great general issues of social
and economic justice, rather than on regional bartering and trade-offs.

But a new national policy would be worthless without a new economic
strategy for national development. Three decades of neo-liberalism have
again made that clear to all but free market ideologues. The FTA and
NAFTA must be either abrogated, or profoundly modified and replaced
by a series of sectoral agreements with the U.S., and bilateral and multi-
lateral agreements with other countries, as part of a new economic strategy. Canada, of all nations, due to the regional nature of its economy,
needs serious economic planning and active government intervention at
federal and provincial levels in order to achieve regional justice and balance. Such a strategy need not negatively affect Central Canadian industry. The tariff system was largely gone even before the FTA, and Central
Canadian industry is struggling to find its new place in world markets. A
new industrial strategy, building on existing strengths, is clearly essential
if Central Canada is to resist further de-industrialization and if Canada is

to retain its place as a major industrial nation. But surely a new industrial strategy can also focus on the beginnings of meaningful industrialization in the resource regions. And given the high levels of education among the Canadian population, a strategy that involved massive investments in education to further develop our human capital could set the stage for Canada to play a significant role in the new technological and information economy.

In these neo-liberal times this sounds like dreaming in technicolour. Public political disengagement has gone so far that almost half of eligible voters don't bother to vote. There is a spreading political contagion encouraging the conviction that our democratic political system is a sham, that our participation will have little impact. This is the final victory of neo-liberalism — successfully persuading the people that democracy cannot deliver significant change, and governments are unable to shape history, and, hence, the popular will is powerless to remake our political and economic system. History provides an antidote for this contagion.

Canada's modern capitalist political economy can be usefully divided into two epochs. During the first nation building epoch, from Confederation to the 1980s, the dominant elements of Canada's capitalist class implemented a strategy of industrial modernization based on linkages imposed by the federal state, integrating Canada's diverse regional economies into a coherent national economy to compete on the world stage. The second neo-liberal epoch began in the 1980s, with the 1988 free trade election as the pivotal event, when the dominant elements of Canada's now mature capitalist class abandoned a national economic strategy in favour of seeking their futures in the emerging neo-liberal global economy. Both epochs were characterized by intensive class struggles, and neither outcome was inevitable.

During the nation building epoch the class struggles of farmers and workers successfully won a re-definition of the nation building policies which originally sought capital's unfettered extraction of wealth from the enterprise and labour of farmers and the labour of workers. Farmers and workers fought back relentlessly. These class confrontations continued and matured, resulting in class organization into political parties, as the class consciousness among farmers and workers transformed them into active classes-for-themselves. Many concessions were won heralding the establishment of the Canadian version of the welfare state and the interventionist democratic government protecting the public interest. These concessions became precedents in the functioning of Canada's political economy. The principle of using government powers to regulate the operation of the national plan in the interests of farmers, workers, and the general population was grudgingly added to the overriding imperative to use the power of the state to further the interests of the dominant capitalist class. Political contestation in Canada thereafter focussed on the use of state power to regulate society and the economy to accommodate diverse and conflicting interests. The regulation of "free enterprise" on behalf of capital was compelled to yield some small space to modest regulation in response to the interests of the lesser classes and the hinterland regions. The welfare state was not yielded up easily and voluntarily by the capitalist class. All the concessions granted were won under political threat.

The importance of the victory of the CCF in Saskatchewan should not be underestimated. Aggressively using provincial powers, the CCF positively transformed the lives of citizens in Saskatchewan in ways never before believed possible. The Saskatchewan model of moderate democratic socialism, which proved that "pie in the sky" could be had after all, inspired the subordinate classes across Canada. Threatened by this popularity, the established capitalist parties adopted central features of the CCF's welfare state program, and even began to move to public ownership in "natural monopolies" like utilities and transportation. Without the CCF victory in Saskatchewan, there is no doubt the Canadian welfare state would never have gone as far as it did in responding to the needs of the people. At the height of the welfare state in the 1970s the richest 10 per cent of market income earners earned 21 times the income earned by the bottom 10 per cent. In terms of family income, the richest 10 per cent of families took 23 per cent of all earnings, while the poorest 20 per cent took only 4.5 per cent.[1] In terms of total wealth (all assets minus all liabilities) the top 10 per cent possessed 43 per cent of all wealth, while the bottom 20 per cent possessed six one hundredths of 1 per cent. Still Canada could brag about having one of the most egalitarian societies in the world, especially when the "social wage" provided by social program spending was taken into account.[2]

The neo-liberal epoch was also characterized by intensive class struggles. While the class struggles of the nation building epoch were initiated from below by farmers and workers, the class struggles of the neo-liberal epoch were initiated from above by the dominant capitalist class. These class struggles were counter-revolutionary, seeking to take back the gains made by the subordinate classes by dampening market wages and salaries; dismantling the welfare state; reducing the share of the total wealth produced in Canada going to the state for redistribution through education, health, and social programs; withdrawing governments from interventions in and oversight over the economy; and dramatically reducing the tax burden on the wealthy and the corporate sector. While the subordinate classes became ascendant and aggressive in the nation building era, in the neo-liberal era they were unprepared for the onslaught. They were taken by surprise, naively believing that the welfare state consensus, and the class peace it had engendered, was fixed and inviolable. In confrontation after confrontation — fights over inflation, free trade, reductions in social spending — the subordinate classes were defeated as the neo-liberal agenda was rolled out over three decades. Even when they appeared to win a major battle, such as the free trade election in 1988 when a majority of Canadians voted for parties opposed to free trade, or the successful elections of anti-neo-liberal governments in the early 1990s, they were betrayed as all parties, even the cherished social democratic NDP, embraced and implemented neo-liberalism. As a result the class struggles of the subordinate classes, and their organizations, became defeatist and defensive, scrambling to save what they could of their former victories from the neo-liberal attack. Today the popular classes are disarmed, without effective organizational tools to go on the offensive. The neo-liberal triumph is reflected dramatically in more recent income and wealth shares. By the 2000s the richest 10 per cent of market income earners took 314 times the income earned by the poorest 10 per cent. In terms of family income, the richest 10 per cent earned 30 per cent, while the poorest 20 per cent had been pounded down to less than 3 per cent. In terms of total wealth, the top 10 per cent possessed 45 per cent of all wealth while the bottom 20 per cent possessed seven one thousandth of 1 per cent. This growing income and wealth inequity was intensified by large cuts in the "social wage." Canada now had bragging rights to one of the most inequitable distributions of income and wealth in the advanced world.

The Canadian architects of neo-liberalism could congratulate themselves that Canada now spends a lower proportion of its gross domestic product on welfare state programs than it did in the 1950s, and the wealthy of Canada are now back to their 1923 shares of wealth possessed and incomes earned. As one walks the streets of any major Canadian city, except for the clothing fashions and the automobiles, the social landscape of today is more reminiscent of the 19th century than of Canada in the 1970s: extremes of wealth and poverty; exclusive neighbourhoods, sometimes gated and patrolled for the rich; slums full of a desperate and hopeless underclass; streets teeming with beggars and the homeless (until they are rounded up and moved on by the police). Substitute top hats and frock coats for the silk suits, and horses and carriages for the limos, and dress the homeless and beggars in rags rather than donated clothing, and it is a page right out of a Dickens novel. The neo-liberals can brag they have turned Canada once again into a social obscenity.

The 2008–09 economic crisis remains with us, and experts, including billionaires among the world's super rich, warn that further worsening crises are inevitable given the advanced economies have become unstable houses of cards built on the ephemeral foundation of world finance capitalism. Nobel Prize economists warn the accelerating gap between rich and poor is the most pressing problem facing late capitalism, predicting growing social and political instability into the future.[3] As these crises occur Canada's popular classes will discover the basic truth that they are victims of a complex class war in which they suffered repeated defeats from the 1980s on. As that awakening occurs, along with the conviction that this world we have fashioned is a human construction, visions of a new Canada will again emerge premised on democratic and social justice principles relevant to the new millennium. Once again the people will embrace the fundamental truth that a new political and economic world can be fashioned serving the needs of the people, rather than the needs of the market and capital, and those who control them. Canada is a wealthy country, endowed with fabulous wealth and an educated, skilled and productive labour force. The New Jerusalem on earth envisioned by the early Christian socialists can be built. The "pie in the sky" ordinary people were told would never be theirs could, in fact, be grasped. But first, Canada's current political and economic élites will have to be swept aside.

Sir Wilfrid Laurier was wrong. The 20th century was not Canada's. Canadians needed it to work through the messy legacy of 1867. The 21st century could be Canada's, but first we must build a Canada that serves the people, and that the regions can embrace.

NOTES

CHAPTER 1: INTRODUCTION: THE WEST IN CANADA

1   Statistics Canada. *Gross Domestic Product: Canada and the Provinces*, Millions of Current Dollars, 1981–2010. CANSIM Series; Statistics Canada. *Gross Domestic Product, Expenditures Based, by Province and Territory*. 19 November 2012. CANSIM Series. http://www.statcan. gc.ca/tables-tableaux/sum-som/101/cst0/econ15-eng.htm. Retrieved 10 October 2013.

2   Statistics Canada. *Net Farm Income, 2007–2011*. CANSIM Series. http://www.statcan. gc.ca/tables-tableaux/sum-som/101/cst01/agric01a-eng.htm. Retrieved 10 October 2013.

3   Statistics Canada. *Personal Disposable Income per Capita (in current $): Canada and the Provinces, 1981–2010*. CANSIM Series; Statistics Canada. *Median Total Income, by Family Type, by Province and Territory*. CANSIM Series, table 111-0009, 2 October 2013. http://www.statcan.gc.ca/tables-tableaux/sum-som/101/cst01/famil108a-eng.htm. Retrieved 10 October 2013.

4   Statistics Canada. *Canadian International Merchandise Trade, July 2012*, 11 September 2012. http://www.statcan.gc.ca/daily-quotidien/1120911/dq/20911a-eng. htm. Retrieved 10 October 2013; Statistics Canada. *International Merchandise Trade, Annual Review 2011*, Catalogue no. 65-208-X; Statistics Canada. *Canada's Mineral Production, Preliminary Estimates, 2012*. Catalogue no. 26-202X; Statistics Canada. *Energy Statistics Handbook, Fourth Quarter 2010*. Catalogue no. 51-601-X.

5   Jonathan Bendiner, "Release of 2012 Provincial, GDP Confirms Momentum Advantage in the West," *TD Economics*, 3 May 2013. http://www.td.ecom/economics. Retrieved 10 May 2013.

6   Canada, Department of Finance. "Equalization Program," 19 December 2011. http:///www.fin.gc.ca/fedprov/eqp-eng.esp. Retrieved 11 October 2013; TD Financial Group, "Ontario Poises to Collect Equalization in 2011–12," 29 April 2008. http://www.td.com/economics/special/db0408_equal.jsp. Retrieved 14 July 2009.

7   Statistics Canada. *Manufacturing Sales by Province and Territory*, 17 September 2012. CANSIM Series. http://www.statcan.gc.ca/tables-tableaux/sum-som/101/manuf28-eng htim. Retrieved 10 October 2013.

CHAPTER 2: "THE LAST BEST WEST"

1   *London Times*, 13 April, 1865, quoted in P. B. Waite, *The Life and Times of Confederation, 1864-1867* (Toronto: University of Toronto, 1962), p. 323.

2   Waite, ibid., p. 329. A phrase used by George Brown during the 1865 Confederation debates

3   The phrase appears in a letter from Macdonald to Captain Strachan, 9 February, 1854, see J. K. Johnson and Carole B. Stelmarl, (eds.). *The Letters of Sir John A. Macdonald, 1836-1857* (Ottawa: Public Archives, 1968), p. 202.

4   Stanley B. Ryerson, *Unequal Union: Confederation and the Roots of Conflict in the Canadas, 1815-1873* (Toronto: Progress Books, 1968), pp. 276-77.

5   From an 1865 speech by Macdonald in the Assembly of Canada, reproduced in P. B. Waite (ed.), *The Confederation Debates in the Province of Canada* (Toronto: McClelland & Stewart, 1963), p. 39.

6   G. P. Browne (ed.), *Documents on the Confederation of British North America* (Toronto: McClelland & Stewart, 1969), p. 95.

7   Ibid., p. 133.

8   Ibid., p. 98.

9   Ibid., p. 51.

10   D. G. Creighton, "Economic Nationalism and Confederation," in R. Cook (ed.), *Confederation* (Toronto: University of Toronto, 1967), p. 4.

11   M. C. Urquhart and K. A. H. Buckley (eds.), *Historical Statistics of Canada* (Toronto: Macmillan, 1965), p. 14.

12   Quoted in J. W. Dafoe, *Clifford Sifton in Relation to His Times* (Toronto: Macmillan, 1931), pp. 273-74.

13   These figures are from G. F. G. Stanley, *The Birth of Western Canada: A History of the Riel Rebellions* (Toronto: University of Toronto, 1936), p. 13.

14   New York *World*, 29 May, 1867, quoted in Waite, *The Life and Times*, p. 305.

15   Parliamentary Debates (1870), quoted in Lewis G. Thomas, *The Prairie West to 1905: A Canadian Sourcebook* (Toronto: Oxford, 1975), p. 80.

16   C. A. Dawson, and Eva R. Younge, *Pioneering in the Prairie Provinces* (Toronto: Macmillan, 1940), pp. 11-12.

17   Norman MacDonald, *Canada: Immigration and Colonization, 1841–1903* (Toronto: Macmillan, 1966), p. 187.

18   W. A. Mackintosh, *The Economic Background to Dominion-Provincial Relations* (Toronto: McClelland & Stewart, 1964), pp. 30-32.

19   Details on the CPR contract are provided in H. A. Innis, *A History of the Canadian Pacific Railway* (Toronto: University of Toronto, 1921), pp. 98-99.

20   R. E. Caves and R. H. Holton, "An Outline of the Economic History of British Columbia, 1881- 1951, " J. Friesen and H. K. Ralston (eds.), *Historical Essays on British Columbia* (Toronto: McClelland & Stewart, 1976), pp. 152-66.

21   Dr. John Sebastian Helmcken, quoted in Martin Robin, *The Rush for Spoils: The Company Province, 1871–1933* (Toronto: McClelland & Stewart, 1972), p. 46.

22   Urquhart and Buckley, ibid., p. 14.

23   *Report of the Royal Commission on Dominion- Provincial Relations, Book I* (Ottawa: King's Printer, 1940), p. 61. Hereafter cited as *Rowell-Sirois Report, I.*

24   Ibid., p. 57.

25   All figures used on growth on the Prairies are from the *Rowell-Sirois Report, I.*

26   Ibid., p. 74.

27   Quoted in ibid., p. 73.

28   Quoted in V. C. Fowke, *The National Policy and the Wheat Economy* (Toronto: University of Toronto, 1957), p. 66.

29   Urquhart and Buckley, ibid., p. 14.

30   Robert A. J. McDonald, "Victoria, Vancouver, and the Economic Development of British Columbia, 1886-1914, " W. Peter Ward and Robert A. J. McDonald, *British Columbia: Historical Readings* (Vancouver: Douglas and McIntyre, 1981), pp. 369-95.

31 A. Ross McCormack, *Reformers, Rebels and Revolutionaries: The Western Canadian Radical Movement, 1899–1919* (Toronto: University of Toronto, 1977), p. 4.

32 The figures on homestead failures are from Fowke, ibid., p. 285.

CHAPTER 3: AGITATION AND REBELLION

1   A.S. Morton, *History of Prairie Settlement* (Toronto: Macmillan, 1938), pp. 93-95.

2   Lewis G. Thomas, *The Prairie West to 1905: A Canadian Sourcebook* (Toronto: Oxford, 1975), pp. 96-97.

3   E. H. Oliver, "Saskatchewan and Alberta: General History, " in A. Shortt and A. G. Doughty, *Canada and Its Provinces, Volume XIX, Prairie Provinces-I* (Toronto: Glasgow, Brook and Co., 1914), p. 168.

4   D. A. MacGibbon, *The Canadian Grain Trade* (Toronto: Macmillan, 1932), pp. 23-28.

5   M. C. Urquhart and K. A. H. Buckley, (eds.). *Historical Statistics of Canada* (Toronto: Macmillan, 1965), pp. 14, 351-52.

6   The following figures on wheat prices are from ibid., pp. 41-44, and W. A. Mackintosh, *Economic Problems of the Prairie Provinces* (Toronto: Macmillan, 1935), pp. 283-84.

7   Quoted in Oliver, ibid., p. 168.

8   Quoted by M. Chester, "Political History of Manitoba, " in Shortt and Doughty, ibid., p. 112.

9   Morton, ibid., p. 95.

10 Quoted in G. F. G. Stanley, *The Birth of Western Canada: A History of the Riel Rebellions* (Toronto: University of Toronto, 1936), p. 319. See also the highly sympathetic and moving account of Riel's stuggles in Joseph Howard, *Strange Empire: Louis Riel and the Metis People* (Toronto: Lorimer, 1974).

11 George Woodcock, *Gabriel Dumont* (Edmonton: Hurtig, 1975).

12 Quoted in Stanley, ibid., p. 395.

13 H. A. Innis, *History of the Canadian Pacific Railway* (Toronto: University of Toronto, 1921), p. 128.

CHAPTER 4: "THE MAN BEHIND THE PLOW"

1   Details on the early grain marketing infrastructure are from Harald Patton, *Grain Growers Cooperation in Western Canada* (Cambridge, Mass.: Harvard, 1928).

2   Details on early agrarian grievances are from Hopkins Moorhouse, *Deep Furrows* (Toronto: McLeod, 1918).

3   "Story of the Early Days — Hon. W. R. Motherwell, Regina," selections from the transcript of an interview by Hopkins Moorehouse in 1916, in *Saskatchewan History, VIII: 3*, Autumn, 1955, pp. 108-9.

4   Quoted in Brian McCutcheon, "The Patrons of Industry in Manitoba, 1890-1899," in Donald Swanson (ed.), *Historical Essays on the Prairie Provinces* (Toronto: McClelland & Stewart, 1970), p. 115.

5   Paul Sharp, *The Agrarian Revolt in Western Canada* (Minneapolis: University of Minnesota, 1948), p. 33.

6   The activities of the Manitoba Patrons are outlined in L. A. Wood, *A History of Farmers'Movements in Canada* (Toronto: Ryerson, 1924), pp. 123ff and in W. L. Morton, *Manitoba: A History* (Toronto: University of Toronto, 1967), p. 258.

7   Quoted in Edward and Annie Porritt, *Sixty Years of Protection in Canada, 1846–1912* (Winnipeg: Grain Growers' Guide, 1913), p. 407.

8   Ibid., p. 440.

9   Ibid., p. 435.

10 Census of Canada, 1911, Vol. IV, *Agriculture*, p. x.

11 Quoted in W. L. Morton, *The Progressive Party in Canada* (Toronto: University of Toronto, 1957), p. 298.

12 All information on the 1911 election is from Paul Stevens, *The 1911 General Election* (Toronto: Copp-Clark, 1970).

13 Porritt, ibid., p. 4.

14 Ibid., p. 15.

15 Census of Canada, 1911, Vol. 1, *Area and Population*, p. 530.

16 M. C. Urquhart and K. A. H. Buckley (eds.), *Historical Statistics of Canada* (Toronto: Macmillan, 1965), pp. 59, 351.

17 V. C. Fowke, *The National Policy and the Wheat Economy* (Toronto: University of Toronto, 1957), p. 72.

18 Quoted in Morton, *Progressive Party*, p. 300.

19 The following quotes are all from Moorhouse, ibid., pp. 244-47, 281-86.

20 Minutes, 19th Annual Convention, Saskatchewan Grain Growers' Association, 1920, Saskatchewan Archives at Regina.

21 First Grain Growers' Sunday of the S. G. G. A., 27 May, 1917, Saskatchewan Archives at Regina.

22 Moorhouse, ibid., pp 289-90.

23 Ibid., p. 292.

24 All economic data are from the *Rowell-Sirois Report, I.*

25 Quoted in Morton, *Progressive Party*, p. 43.

26 Ibid., pp. 302-6.

27 Howard Scarrow, *Canada Votes: A Handbook of Federal and Provincial Election Data* (New Orleans: Hauser Press, 1962), pp. 34-35.

28 See Patton, ibid., pp. 389-90.

29 Morton, *Progressive Party*, pp. 211-12.

30 See Patton, ibid., pp. 230ff and D. A. MacGibbon, *The Canadian Grain Trade* (Toronto: Macmillan, 1932), pp. 343-44.

CHAPTER 5: SOCIALISM AND SYNDICALISM

1   The characterizations here of early situations faced by Western workers, as well as subsequent struggles, are based on the following: David J. Bercuson, *Fools and Wise Men: The Rise and Fall of the One Big Union* (Toronto: McGraw-Hill, 1978); A. Ross McCormack, *Reformers, Rebels and Revolutionaries: The Western Canadian Radical Movement, 1899–1919* (Toronto: University of Toronto, 1977); Paul Phillips, *No Power Greater: A Century of Labour in B.C.* (Vancouver: B.C. Federation of Labour, 1967); Warren Carragata, *Alberta Labour: A Heritage Untold* (Toronto: Lorimer, 1979); S. M. Jamieson, *Times of Trouble: Labour Unrest and Industrial Conflict in Canada, 1900–1966* (Ottawa: Privy Council, 1968); Martin Robin, *Radical Politics and Canadian Labour, 1880–1930* (Kingston: Queen's University, 1968); Charles Lipton, *The Trade Union Movement In Canada, 1827–1959* (Montreal: Canadian Social Publications, 1967); Dorothy G. Steeves, *The Compassionate Rebel: Ernest E. Winch and His Times* (Vancouver: Boag Foundation, 1960). Three articles in W. Peter Ward and Robert A. J. McDonald, *British Columbia: Historical Readings* (Vancouver: Douglas and McIntyre, 1981) were also useful: D. J. Bercuson, "Labour Radicalism and the Western Industrial Frontier, 1897–1919" (pp. 45Iff); A. Ross McCormack, "The Industrial Workers of the World in Western Canada, 1905–1914" (pp. 474ff); and Stuart Jamieson, "Regional Factors in Industrial Conflict: The Case of British Columbia" (pp. 500ff).

2   McCormack, *Reformers, Rebels, and Revolutionaries*, pp. 8-9 and Bercuson, *Fools and Wise Men*, pp. 2-4-.

3   This description of the 1906 streetcar strike is based on: D. J. Bercuson, *Confrontation at Winnipeg: Labour, Industrial Relations and the General Strike* (Montreal: McGill-Queen's, 1974), pp. 11-15 and Jamieson, *Times of Trouble*, pp. 84-85.

4   Quoted in McCormack, Reformers, Rebels and Revolutionaries, p. 6.

5   Quoted in R. C. Brown and R. Cook, *Canada: 1896–1921: A Nation Transformed* (Toronto: McClelland & Stewart, 1974), p. 116.

6   This description of the strike is based on Jamieson, *Times of Trouble*, p. 123-26; Jack Scott, *Plunder-bund and Proletariat* (Vancouver: New Star, 1975), pp. 82-84; and Phillips, ibid., pp. 55-61.

7   Quoted in Scott, ibid., p. 84.

8   R. E. Caves, and R. H. Holton, "An Outline of the Economic History of British Columbia, 1881–1951," in J. Friesen and H. K. Ralston (eds.), *Historical Essays on British Columbia* (Toronto: McClelland & Stewart, 1976), p. 152.

9   *Census Reports*, 1931.

10   W. T. Easterbrook and H. G. J. Aitken, *Canadian Economic History* (Toronto: Macmillan, 1967), p. 564.

11   An estimate based on 1911 and 1921 census figures and G. V. Haythorne, *Labour in Canadian Agriculture* (Boston: Harvard, 1965), p. 9. For the 1911 and 1921 census figures see M. C. Urquhart and K. A. H. Buckley (eds.), *Historical Statistics of Canada* (Toronto: Macmillan, 1965), pp. 351, 354, 355, 364. The 49,000 farm wage labour figure is a 1911 figure.

12   Quoted in L. A. Wood, *A History of Farmers' Movements in Canada* (Toronto: Ryerson, 1924), p. 104.

13   Quoted in W. A. Mcintosh, "The United Farmers of Alberta, 1909–1920, " M. A. thesis, University of Calgary, 1971, p. 32.

14   Quoted in Jamieson, *Times of Trouble*, p. 111.

15 Quoted in Steeves, ibid., p. 273.

16 Brown and Cook, ibid., p. 273.

17 J. H. Thompson, *The Harvests of War: The Prairie West, 1914–1918* (Toronto: McClelland & Stewart, 1978), pp. 160-61.

18 Information on events leading up to, during and after the Winnipeg General Strike was provided by the following: D. C. Masters, *The Winnipeg General Strike* (Toronto: University of Toronto, 1950); Norman Penner (ed.), *Winnipeg, 1919* (Toronto: Lorimer, 1973). Previously cited sources were also used.

19 Easterbrook and Aitken, ibid., p. 569.

20 J. W. Scallon, President, Address to the 1920 Convention, United Farmers of Manitoba, *UFM Year Book*, 1920, Manitoba Archives.

21 J. W. Scallon, President, Address to the 1921 Convention, United Farmers of Manitoba, *UFM Year Book*, 1921, Manitoba Archives.

22 *Farmers' Platform Handbook*, special issue of *Grain Growers' Guide*, 2 July, 1919, Manitoba Archives.

CHAPTER 6: DEVASTATION AND PROTEST

1   *Rowell-Sirois Report, I*, p. 144.

2   Ibid., p. 150.

3   Ibid., p. 146.

4   Ibid., p. 149.

5   Alberta, *The Case for Alberta: Alberta's Problems and Dominion-Provincial Relations* (Edmonton: King's Printer, 1938), Part 1, p. 94.

6   *Report of the Saskatchewan Reconstruction Council* (Regina: King's Printer, 1944), pp. 51 and 57.

7   *Rowell-Sirois Report, I*, p. 168.

8   Martin Robin, *The Rush for Spoils: The Company Province, 1871–1933* (Toronto: McClelland & Stewart, 1972), p. 235.

9   E. J. Hanson, "A Financial History of Alberta, 1905–1950," Ph.D. thesis, Clark University, n. d.

10 "Year by Year, the Load Grows Heavier, " CCF party pamphlet, 1938 election, Saskatchewan Archives at Regina.

11 W. L. Morton, *Manitoba: A History* (Toronto: University of Toronto, 1957), p. 429.

12 *Rowell-Sirois Report, I*, p. 172.

13 W. Allen and C. C. Hope, *The Farm Outlook for Saskatchewan* (Saskatoon: University of Saskatchewan, 1936), also cited by S. M. Lipset, *Agrarian Socialism: The Co-operative Commonwealth Federation in Saskatchewan* (Berkeley: University of California, 1971), p. 119.

14 *A Submission by the Government of Saskatchewan to the Royal Commission on Dominion-Provincial Relations* (Canada, 1937) (Regina: King's Printer, 1937), p. 148.

15 Ibid., p. 187.

16 Alma Lawton, "Urban Relief in Saskatchewan During the Years of the Depression,

1930-37, " M. A. thesis, University of Saskatchewan, 1969, pp. 46ff.

17 *Rowell-Sirois Report, I,* p. 164.

18 All per capita income declines are from ibid., p. 150.

19 *Case for Alberta,* part 1, p. 6.

20 Dorothy Steeves, *The Compassionate Rebel: Ernest E. Winch and His Times* (Vancouver: Boag Foundation, 1960), p. 87.

21 L. M. Grayson, and Michael Bliss (eds.), *The Wretched of Canada: Letters to R. B. Bennett, 1930–1935* (Toronto: University of Toronto, 1971), p. 75.

22 Ibid., p. 160.

23 Quoted in S. M. Jamieson, *Times of Trouble: Labour Unrest and Industrial Conflict in Canada, 1900–1966* (Ottawa: Privy Council, 1968), p. 217.

24 The political events in Saskatchewan and Alberta leading up to and following the CCF and Social Credit victories are detailed in J.F. Conway, "To Seek a Goodly Heritage: The Prairie Populist Resistance to the National Policy in Canada, " Ph. D. thesis, Simon Fraser University, 1979.

25 *Journals,* Alberta Legislature, 1932, Vol. XXIX, pp. 6-10.

26 Calgary *Albertan,* 21 January, 1932.

27 Calgary *Albertan,* 23 January, 1932.

28 Dean E. McHenry, *The Third Force in Canada: The Co-operative Commonwealth Federation, 1932–1948* (Berkeley: University of California, 1950), ch. 1 and 11. See also Walter D. Young, *Anatomy of a Party: The National CCF, 1932-62* (Toronto: University of Toronto, 1969), ch. 1 to 3.

29 All quotations from the Manual are from Wm. Aberhart, B. A. *Social Credit Manual: Social Credit as Applied to the Province of Alberta; Puzzling Questions and Their Answers,* 1935, Saskatchewan Archives at Saskatoon.

30 Aberhart promised all "bona-fide" citizens of Alberta a "basic monthly dividend." For those 21 years and older, it was to be $25; children up to 16 years old, $5; those 17 and 18, $10; those 19, $15; those 20, $20. Many detractors of Aberhart argue that this promise of monthly dividends won Aberhart the election. It doubtless helped but was not decisive. In 1940, after admitting he could not deliver the dividends, Aberhart was still returned as premier with a solid majority. See John Irving, *The Social Credit Movement in Alberta* (Toronto: University of Toronto, 1959) for an account of the Social Credit movement's drive to power.

31 All election results are from Howard Scarrow, *Canada Votes: A Handbook of Federal and Provincial Election Data* (New Orleans: Hauser, 1962).

32 *Financial Post,* 31 August, 1935.

33 *Financial Post,* 19 September, 1936.

34 *Montreal Gazette,* 12 May, 1938, quoted in J. R. Mallory, *Social Credit and the Federal Power in Canada* (Toronto: University of Toronto, 1954), p. 106.

35 "Bankers' Toadies, " Social Credit pamphlet collection, Glenbow Museum, Calgary. The text was also reproduced in its entirety in the *Financial Post,* 9 October, 1937.

36 *Journals,* Alberta Legislature, 1940, Vol. XLI, pp. 6-13.

37 Edmonton *Bulletin,* 22 February, 1940.

38 Quoted in J. J. Schultz, "A Second Term: 1940," *Alberta Historical Review*, X(1), 1962.

39 Quoted in Schultz, ibid, *Financial Post*, 30 March, 1940.

40 Constitution and By-laws, Farmers' Union of Canada, 1925, Saskatchewan Archives at Regina.

41 D. S. Spafford, "The Origins of the Farmers' Union of Canada, " *Saskatchewan History*, 28(3), 1965 and "The Left-Wing, 1921–1931," in N. Ward and D. S. Spafford (eds.), *Politics in Saskatchewan* (Toronto: Longmans, 1968).

42 Quoted in David E. Smith, *Prairie Liberalism: The Liberal Party in Saskatchewan, 1905–1971* (Toronto: University of Toronto, 1975), p. 99.

43 L. D. Courville, "The Saskatchewan Progressives," M. A. thesis, University of Regina, 1971.

44 W. Calderwood, "The Rise and Fall of the Ku Klux Klan in Saskatchewan, " M. A. thesis, University of Regina, 1968, and P. Kyba, "Ballots and Burning Crosses — the election of 1929," in Ward and Spafford, ibid.

45 The record of the 1929 Co-operative Government is described in P. A. Russell, "The Co-operative Government in Saskatchewan, 1929–1934: Response to the Depression," M. A. thesis, University of Saskatchewan, 1970.

46 United Farmers of Canada, Saskatchewan Section, The U. E. C. Economic Policy and Convention Resolutions, 1932, Saskatchewan Archives at Regina.

47 Quoted in G. J. Hoffman, "The Saskatchewan Provincial Election of 1934," M. A. thesis, University of Regina, 1973, p. 58.

48 Quoted in G. J. Hoffman, "The Saskatchewan Farmer-Labour Party, 1932-34," *Saskatchewan History*, XXVIII(2), 1975.

49 Hoffman, "1934 Election," p. 278.

50 Minutes, First Annual CCF Convention, Saskatchewan, 1936, Saskatchewan Archives at Saskatoon.

51 Program and Manifesto of the Co-operative Commonwealth Federation, Saskatchewan Section, 1934, Saskatchewan Archives at Saskatoon.

52 Liberal party pamphlet collection, 1938 election, Saskatchewan Archives at Regina.

53 G. H., Williams, *Social Democracy in Canada* (Regina: McInnis Brothers, n.d. (1938?), p. 32, Saskatchewan Archives at Regina.

54 "Is Social Credit Coming or Going?" CCF pamphlet collection, 1938 election, Saskatchewan Archives at Regina.

55 "CCF Debt Adjustment and Land Policy," CCF pamphlet collection, 1938 election, Saskatchewan Archives at Regina.

56 S. Silverstein, "The Rise, Ascendancy and Decline of the Co-operative Commonwealth Federation Party of Saskatchewan, Canada," Ph. D. thesis, Washington University, 1969.

57 Quoted in F. Steininger, "George H. Williams: Agrarian Socialist," M. A. thesis, University of Regina, 1976, p. 328.

58 See Martin Robin, *The Rush for Spoils: The Company Province, 1871–1933* (Toronto: McClelland & Stewart, 1972), ch. IX, "Business Government, 1929–1933," pp. 232ff, and Martin Robin, *Pillars of Profit: The Company Province, 1934–1972* (Toronto: McClelland & Stewart, 1973), ch. 1, "Socialized Capitalism: 1934–1937, " pp. 9ff.

CHAPTER 7: CONCESSION AND COMPROMISE

1   M. C. Urquhart and K. A. H. Buckley (eds.), *Historical Statistics of Canada* (Toronto: Macmillan, 1965), pp. 625-26.

2   Regina *Leader-Post*, 31 October, 1938. My thanks to Professor M. Knuttila for drawing this poll to my attention.

3   United Farmers of Canada (Saskatchewan Section), *Applications for Reductions in the Tariff*, Regina, 1927, Saskatchewan Archives at Regina.

4   Alberta, *The Case for Alberta* (Edmonton: King's Printer, 1938), Part 1, pp. 8-10.

5   All election results are from Howard Scarrow, *Canada Votes: A Handbook of Federal and Provincial Election Data* (New Orleans: Hauser, 1962).

6   Walter D. Young, *Anatomy of a Party: The National CCF; 1932–1961* (Toronto: University of Toronto, 1969), p. 110.

7   Roger Bothwell, et al., *Canada Since 1945: Power, Politics and Provincialism* (Toronto: University of Toronto, 198 1), especially ch. 10, "Making a Better Country," pp. 99ff.

8   Social Credit Board, Alberta, *Annual Report*, 1942 (Edmonton: King's Printer, 1943), p. 18. C. B. Macpherson, *Democracy in Alberta* (Toronto: University of Toronto, 1962) provides a good account of ideological developments in the Social Credit movement.

9   Speech from the Throne, *Journals*, Alberta Legislature, 1944, Vol. XLV, pp. 6-10.

10   Social Credit election advertisement, *Edmonton Journal*, 5 August, 1944.

11   From a speech by a Social Credit candidate, *Edmonton Journal*, 29 July, 1944.

12   From a speech by Premier Manning, *Edmonton Journal*, 22 July, 1944.

13   From a speech by a CCF candidate, *Edmonton Journal*, 27 July, 1944.

14   *Financial Post*, 19 August, 1944.

15   *Edmonton Journal*, 9 August, 1944.

16   *Financial Post*, 12 November, 1936.

17   Ibid.

18   Alf Hooke, *30 + 5: 1 know, I was there* (Edmonton: Co-op Press, 1971), p. 215.

19   *Edmonton Journal*, 15 August, 1935.

20   *Edmonton Journal*, 9 August, 1935.

21   "CCF Program for Saskatchewan," CCF pamphlet collection, 1944 election, Saskatchewan Archives at Regina.

22   Ibid.

23   CCF pamphlet collection, 1944 election, Saskatchewan Archives at Regina.

24   S. Silverstein, "The Rise, Ascendancy and Decline of the Co-operative Commonwealth Federation Party of Saskatchewan, Canada," Ph. D. thesis, Washington University, 1968.

25   T. C. Douglas, Premier, "Address in Reply to the Speech from the Throne," February 18 and 19, 1946, *Journals*, Saskatchewan Legislature, 1946, Vol XLV.

26   *Financial Post*, 3 July, 1948.

27 V. C. Fowke, *The National Policy and the Wheat Economy* (Toronto: University of Toronto, 1957), p. 93.

CHAPTER 8: OF RESOURCES AND CONSTITUTIONS

1   Details of the deal are from Philip Mathias, *Forced Growth* (Toronto: Lorimer, 1971), ch. 6, pp. 124ff.

2   Details of the deal are from Mathias, ibid., ch. 4, pp. 81ff.

3   Martin Robin, *The Rush for Spoils: The Company Province, 1871–1933* (Toronto: McClelland & Stewart, 1972) and *Pillars of Profit: The Company Province, 1934–1972* (Toronto: McClelland & Stewart, 1973).

4   Information on per capita incomes and provincial unemployment rates is from Canada, Department of Finance, *Economic Review*, 1982.

5   Canada, *Canadian Agriculture in the Seventies: Report of the Federal Task Force on Agriculture* (Ottawa: Queen's Printer, 1969).

6   *Parliamentary Guide*, 1969 and 1979.

7   Details on Western resource developments and controversies are from John Richards and Larry Pratt, *Prairie Capitalism: Power and Influence in the New West* (Toronto: McClelland & Stewart, 1979).

8   A. Blakeney, Text of a speech to the *Financial Post*'s Conference, "Resource Development in Saskatchewan, " August 29, 1979, Saskatoon.

9   P. Lougheed, Text of speech to Radio and Television Directors' Association, Edmonton, 20 June, 1981.

10 A. Blakeney, *Financial Post* Conference speech, August 29, 1979.

11 Data on the 1979 federal election are from *Report of the Chief Electoral Officer*, Ottawa, 1979.

12 An interesting account of Clark's period in power is contained in Warner Troyer, *200 Days: Joe Clark in Power* (Toronto: Personal Library, 1980). A better account, which provides a good description of how Clark was caught in the squeeze over energy policy, is provided in Jeffery Simpson, *Discipline of Power* (Toronto: Personal Library, 1980).

13 *The Globe and Mail*, 11 September, 1980.

14 *Financial Post*, 16 August, 1980.

15 *The Globe and Mail*, 21 May, 1981.

16 *The Globe and Mail*, 5 February, 1981.

17 All GDP figures are rough calculations based on data from *The Globe and Mail*, *Report on Business*, "Outlook, 1981 " series published during January, 1981.

18 All per capita income figures are from Canada, Department of Finance, *Economic Review*, 1982, pp. 140-41.

19 *Report of the Chief Electoral Officer*, Ottawa, 1980.

20 Canada, Department of Energy, Mines and Resources. *The National Energy Program*, Ottawa, 1980.

21 Regina *Leader-Post*, 8 June, 1981.

22 Regina *Leader-Post*, 6 May, 1981.

23 Details on the constitutional struggle are available in David Milne, *The New Canadian Constitution* (Toronto: Lorimer, 1982).

24 A. Blakeney, Text of speech delivered to law students at Queen's University, 10 April, 1980.

25 *The Globe and Mail*, 8 November, 1980.

26 *The Globe and Mail*, 11 November, 1980.

27 Regina *Leader-Post*, 1 November, 1980.

28 *Financial Post*, 1 November, 1980.

29 Regina *Leader-Post*, 3 November, 1980.

30 The study was done by the Sample Survey and Data Bank Unit, University of Regina, 1980.

31 *The Globe and Mail*, 17 November, 1980.

32 Regina *Leader-Post*, 2 January, 1981.

33 *The Globe and Mail*, 14 February, 1981.

34 *Financial Post*, 28 March, 1981.

35 Regina *Leader-Post*, 8 April, 1981.

36 Regina *Leader-Post*, 25 April, 1981.

37 Regina *Leader-Post*, 6 May, 1981.

38 Regina *Leader-Post*, 17 January, 1981.

39 *The Globe and Mail*, 21 May, 1981.

40 Regina *Leader-Post*, 20 January, 1981.

41 Regina *Leader-Post*, 8 May, 1981.

42 *The Globe and Mail*, 2 June, 1981.

43 *The Globe and Mail*, 16 March, 1981.

44 *Financial Post*, 21 August, 1982.

45 *The Globe and Mail*, *Report on Business*, 4 March, 1982 and *Financial Post*, 19 March, 1983.

46 *The Globe and Mail*, *Report on Business*, 6 November, 1982; 5 February, 1983; and 12 April, 1983.

47 Regina *Leader-Post*, 6 January, 1983.

48 Regina *Leader-Post*, 19 May, 1983.

49 Regina *Leader-Post*, 2 February, 1983.

50 *The Globe and Mail*, *Report on Business*, 17 August, 1982.

51 *The Globe and Mail*, 16 March, 198 1; 23 January, 1982; *Financial Post*, 18 April, 198 1; Regina *Leader-Post*, 1 May, 1982.

52 *The Globe and Mail*, *Report on Business*, 16 March, 1981: Regina *Leader-Post*, 1 May, 1982.

53 Regina *Leader-Post*, 3 September, 1982; 31 March, 1983.

54   Regina *Leader-Post*, 3 May, 1983.

55   *The Globe and Mail, Report on Business,* 17 September, 1983.

56   *Report of the Chief Electoral Officer,* Saskatchewan, 1982.

57   *Financial Post,* 24 July, 1982.

58   *Report of the Chief Electoral Officer,* Alberta, 1982.

59   *The Globe and Mail,* 24 January, 1981 and Regina *Leader-Post,* 27 January, 1981.

60   *The Globe and Mail,* 14 April, 1982.

61   John Gallagher, *To Kill the Crow* (Moose Jaw: Challenge Publishers, 1983).

CHAPTER 9: THE RISE AND FALL OF THE NEO-LIBERAL PARTIES, 1982–1993

1   *The Globe and Mail,* 6 September, 1984; 18 March, 1986; and Regina *Leader-Post,* 5 September, 1984.

2   John Sawatsky, *Mulroney: The Politics of Ambition* (Toronto: Macfarlane Walker and Ross, 1991); N. Auf der Maur, R. Chodos, and R„ Murphy, *Brian Mulroney: The Boy from Baie-Comeau* (Halifax: Goodread Biographies, 1985).

3   *The Globe and Mail,* 6 September, 1985.

4   Canada, Department of Finance, *A New Direction for Canada: An Agenda for Economic Renewal.* Ottawa, 8 November, 1984.

5   *Financial Post,* 5 September, 1988.

6   *The Globe and Mail,* 19 November, 1988.

7   John Calvert, *Government Limited: The Corporate Takeover of the Public Sector in Canada* (Ottawa: Centre for Policy Alternatives, 1984); Duncan Cameron (ed.), *The Free Trade Papers* (Toronto: Lorimer, 1986); Stephen Clarkson, *Canada and the Reagan Challenge* (Toronto: Lorimer, 1985); Daniel Drache and Duncan Cameron (eds.), *The Other Macdonald Report* (Toronto: Lorimer, 1985); Cy Gonick, *The Great Economic Debate* (Toronto: Lorimer, 1987); Herschel Hardin, *The Privatization Putsch* (Halifax: Institute for Research on Public Policy, 1989); J. Krieger, Reagan, *Thatcher and the Politics of Decline* (New York: Oxford, 1986); James Laxer, *False God: How the Globalization Myth Impoverished Canada* (Toronto: Lester, 1993); James Laxer, *Leap of Faith: Free Trade and the Future of Canada* (Edmonton: Hurtig, 1986); Warren Magnusson and others, *The New Reality: The Politics of Restraint in British Columbia* (Vancouver: New Star, 1984); M. Patricia Marchak, *The Integrated Circus: The New Right and the Restructuring of Global Markets* (Montreal: McGill-Queen's, 1991); Lawrence Martin, *Pledge of Allegiance: The Surrender of Canada in the Mulroney Years* (Toronto: McClelland & Stewart, 1993); Stephen McBride and John Shields, *Dismantling a Nation: The Canadian Agenda* (Halifax: Fernwood, 1993); Linda McQuaig, *Behind Closed Doors* (Toronto: Penguin, 1987); Linda McQuaig, *The Wealthy Banker's Wife: The Assault on Equality in Canada* (Toronto: Penguin, 1993); John W. Warnock, *Free Trade and the New Right Agenda* (Vancouver: New Star, 1988); Mel Watkins, *Madness and Ruin: Politics and the Economy in the Neoconservative Age* (Toronto: Between the Lines, 1992); Allan Tupper and G. Bruce Doern, (eds.), *Privatization, Public Policy and Public Corporations in Canada* (Halifax: Institute for Research on Public Policy, 1989); James J. Rice and Michael J. Prince, "Life of Brian: A social policy legacy," *Perception,* June 1993, pp. 6-8, 30-33.

8 Bryan D. Palmer, *Solidarity: The Rise and Fall of an Opposition in British Columbia* (Vancouver: New Star, 1987).

9 Unless otherwise noted, material on Saskatchewan is taken from Lesley Biggs and Mark Stobbe (eds.), *Devine Rule in Saskatchewan* (Saskatoon: Fifth House, 1991); James M. Pitsula and Ken Rasmussen, *Privatizing a Province* (Vancouver: New Star, 1990); and J. F. Conway, "The Saskatchewan Electoral Boundaries Case, 1990-91, " Canadian Political Science Association, Learned Societies, June, 1993. Unless otherwise noted, material on responses in the West to the Meech Lake Accord and the Charlottetown Agreement is taken from J. F. Conway, *Debts to Pay* (Toronto: Lorimer, 1992).

10 Regina *Leader-Post*, 27 April, 1988.

11 *The Globe and Mail*, 20 March, 1986.

12 *The Globe and Mail*, 11, 16, 28, 30 April and 1, 3 May, 1986; *Financial Post*, 1 March, 1986, 19 April, 1986, and 17 May, 1986.

13 *The Globe and Mail*, 19 to 30 April, 1988; Regina *Leader-Post*, 26 and 27 April, 1988; *Financial Post*, 2 May, 1988.

14 *Report of the Chief Electoral Officer*, Ottawa, 1988.

15 *The Globe and Mail*, 3 November, 1988.

16 *The Globe and Mail*, 31 August, 12 October, 17 November, 1988.

17 *The Globe and Mail*, *Report on Business*, 7 October, 1988.

18 Regina *Leader-Post*, 19 October, 1988.

19 *The Globe and Mail*, 3 November, 1988.

20 Regina *Leader-Post*, 7 July, 1989.

21 *The Globe and Mail*, 3 October, 1988.

22 Regina *Leader-Post*, 15 July, 1989.

23 *The Globe and Mail*, 19 November, 1988.

24 *The Globe and Mail*, 13 August, 1988.

25 *The Globe and Mail*, 26 October, 1988.

26 F. Leslie Seidle (ed.), *Interest Groups and Elections in Canada, Vol. 2*, Research Studies, Royal Commission on Electoral Reform and Party Financing. (Toronto: Dundurn Press, 1991), pp. 20-29.

27 *The Globe and Mail*, 12, 22, and 28 September, 1988; *Financial Post*, 12 September, 1988.

28 *The Globe and Mail*, 19 November, 1988.

29 *The Globe and Mail*, 24 November, 1988.

30 Regina *Leader-Post*, 22 April, 1988.

31 *The Globe and Mail*, *Report on Business*, 21 July, 1988.

32 *The Globe and Mail*, *Report on Business*, 6 August, 1988.

33 *The Globe and Mail*, *Report on Business*, 28 July, 1988.

34 *The Globe and Mail*, *Report on Business*, 17 October, 1990.

35 Regina *Leader-Post*, 9 October, 1990.

36 Regina *Leader-Post*, March to June, 1987.

37 Regina *Leader-Post*, 27 April and 15 June, 1988; April and May, 1989; 3 November, 1989; 23 and 26; May, 1990; 28 September and 17 October, 1990; 4 May, 1991. *The Globe and Mail, Report on Business*, 20 July, 1989 and 28 September, 1990.

38 *The Globe and Mail*, 4 October, 1989.

39 *The Globe and Mail, Report on Business*, 21 July, 1988.

40 *The Globe and Mail*, 28 February, 6 and 12 March, 1992.

41 *The Globe and Mail, Report on Business*, 13 September, 1983, 21 July, 1989, 12 March, 1990, 8 November, 1990, 22 May, 1992, 8 March, 1993; *Report on Business Magazine*, November, 1989, May 1991, and August 1993; *The Globe and Mail*, 21 April, 1988, 12 and 15 March, 1990, 9 February, 6 and 12 March, 2 November, 1992; Regina *Leader-Post*, May-June 1989, 8 February and 26 December, 1990, 14 July, 1993; *Financial Post*, 21 January, 1984.

42 *The Globe and Mail*, 19 October, 1990.

43 Canada, Department of Finance, *Economic Reference Tables*, August, 1992, p. 58.

44 Ibid., p. 3 1.

45 Saskatchewan Agriculture, *Agricultural Statistics 1991*, November, 1992, pp. 3, 13.

46 *The Globe and Mail*, 14 April, 1992.

47 *The Globe and Mail*, 14 November, 1992; *The Globe and Mail, Report on Business*, 14 October, 1992; *The Globe and Mail, Report on Business*, 8 March, 1993.

48 *The Globe and Mail, Report on Business*, 19 January, 1988 and 9 September, 1988; Regina Leader-Post, 5 May, 1988.

49 *The Globe and Mail, Report on Business*, 24 and 27 February, 1989.

50 The study was suppressed by the government but obtained under the *Access to Information Act*. The story was broken by Francis Russell in the Winnipeg *Free Press* on 13 March, 1991 and 9 October, 1991. A laundered version of the article was published in June, 1991: H. Mimoto and P. Cross, "The Growth of the Federal Debt, " *Canadian Economic Observer*, Statistics Canada, Catalogue No. 11-010, June 1991, pp. 3.1-3.18. A copy of the original unlaundered study is in the possession of the author.

51 *Sask Trends Monitor*, April 1990 and September 1991.

52 *The Globe and Mail*, 31 March, 1 and 10 April, 1989; 24 to 30 November, 1990.

53 *The Globe and Mail*, 5 August, 1991.

54 *The Globe and Mail* 19 July, 1989.

55 *The Globe and Mail*, 19 October, 1989, 31 March, 1991; *The Globe and Mail Report on Business*, 31 March, 1991.

56 *The Globe and Mail*, 14 November, 1989.

57 *The Globe and Mail*, 24 to 30 November, 1989.

58 Pitsula and Rasmussen, op. cit., pp. 262 ff.

59 Regina *Leader-Post*, 31 May, 1989; 22 and 30 June, 1989

60 *The Globe and Mail* 1 October, 1989; 19 October, 1990.

61 Regina *Leader-Post*, 17 February, 1990; 26 September, 1990.

62 *The Globe and Mail*, 16 February, 1991.

63 Pitsula and Rasmussen, op. cit., pp. 249ff; M. Rasmussen and H. Leeson, "Parliamentary Democracy in Saskatchewan, 1982-89, " in Biggs and Stobbe, op. cit., pp. 49ff.

64 Conway, "Electoral Boundaries Case," op. cit.

65 *The Globe and Mail*, 18 and 22 June, 1991; Regina *Leader-Post*, 30 May, 1991; 19 and 20 June, 1991.

66 *The Globe and Mail*, July and August, 1988; September, 1989; 11 December, 1990; 8 January, 1991; 18 February, 1991.

67 *The Globe and Mail*, 10 September, 1988.

68 Graham Leslie, *Breach of Promise: Socred Ethics Under Vander Zalm* (Madeira Park, B.C.: Harbour, 1991); cited in *The Globe and Mail*, 30 March, 1991.

69 *The Globe and Mail*, 15 February, 1991.

70 *The Globe and Mail*, 11 December, 1990.

71 *The Globe and Mail*, 19 April, 1988; 22 July, 1988; 15 and 18 June, 1989; *Financial Post*, 11 July, 1988.

72 *The Globe and Mail*, 21, 23, 26 and 30 September, 1989; 5 and 14 October, 1989; 1 November, 1989; 11, 13, and 28 December, 1989; 16 and 18 January, 1990; 20 September, 1990; 19 December, 1990; 8 January, 1991; 9 and 18 February, 1991; 21, 22, 30 March, 1991; 2 and 3 April, 1991; 20 May, 1992; 26 June, 1992; 12 September, 1992. See also, David J. Mitchell, *Succession: The Political Re-shaping of British Columbia* (Vancouver: Douglas and McIntyre, 1991).

73 *The Globe and Mail*, 28 January, 1989; 18, 19, 21, 22 April, 1989; 2 and 13 May, 1989; 28 July, 1989; *The Globe and Mail, Report on Business*, 29 March, 1989; 17 April, 1989, 10 June, 1989; 29 October, 1990.

74 *The Globe and Mail*, 22 March, 1989.

75 *The Globe and Mail*, 30 June, 1992.

76 *The Globe and Mail*, 16 June, 1993.

77 *The Globe and Mail*, 8 April, 1991.

78 *The Globe and Mail*, 2 June, 1991.

79 *The Globe and Mail*, 4 June, 1993.

80 *The Globe and Mail*, 12 September, 1990.

81 *The Globe and Mail*, 4 December, 1992.

82 *The Globe and Mail*, 8 January, 1991, 28 November, 199 1; Regina *Leader-Post*, 19 and 20 October, 1988, 16 March, 1989.

83 *The Globe and Mail*, 10 June, 1988.

84 *The Globe and Mail*, 22 September, 1989.

85 *The Globe and Mail*, 18 June, 1988, 25 October, 1989, 11 December, 1989; *The Globe and Mail, Report on Business*, 13 December, 1989.

86 British Columbia, *Report on the Chief Electoral Officer, 1991 Election*.

87 Regina *Leader-Post*, 3 May, 1989.

88 Regina *Leader-Post*, 20 July, 1990.

89 Regina *Leader-Post*, 5 May, 1991.

90 Regina *Leader-Post*, 4 and 5 May, 1988.

91 Saskatchewan, *Report on the Chief Electoral Officer, 1991 Election*.

92 Regina *Leader-Post*, 19 December, 1990; 13 February, 1992; 8 April, 1992.

93 *The Globe and Mail, Report on Business*, 25 February, 1992.

94 *The Globe and Mail*, 25 February, 1993.

95 *The Globe and Mail, Report on Business*, 24 June, 1992.

96 *The Globe and Mail, Report on Business*, 29 April, 1989; 3 June, 1989; 9 August, 1993.

97 *The Globe and Mail, Report on Business*, "Report on Canada, " 22 to 25 January, 1991; 26 April, 1991; 30 May, 1991.

98 Regina *Leader-Post*, 28 and 31 May, 1988; 24 September, 1990; 17 and 30 October, 1990; 28 April, 1993; *The Globe and Mail*, 27 June, 1989; 29 November, 1990; 24 February, 1992; 1 February, 1993; *The Globe and Mail, Report on Business*, 18 October, 1990; 26 November, 1990.

99 J. F. Conway, "The Distribution of Benefits of the 1986 Saskatchewan Farm Production Loan Program: A Preliminary Research Note and a Case for Targetting," Learned Societies, Laval University, Canadian Association for Rural Studies, June, 1989; Peter Finkle and W. H. Furton, "Net Farm Income Insurance: A New Direction for Farm Policy," mimeo, 1988; I. L. McCreary and W. H. Furtan, "Income Distribution and Agricultural Policies," mimeo, 1988.

100 *The Globe and Mail, Report on Business*, 15 March, 1990; 16 and 26 November, 1990; 15 January, 199 1; *The Globe and Mail*, 29 November, 1990; Regina *Leader-Post*, 4 October, 1990; 30 March, 1991; 5 April, 1991.

101 Regina *Leader-Post*, 4 October, 1990.

102 *The Globe and Mail*, 25 January, 1989.

103 *The Globe and Mail*, 20 July, 1993.

104 Regina *Leader-Post*, 16 March, 1993; 28 April, 1993.

105 *The Globe and Mail*, 21 September, 1988.

106 *The Globe and Mail, Report on Business*, 15 May, 1986.

107 *Financial Post*, 12 September, 1988.

108 *The Globe and Mail, Report on Business*, 22 December, 1989.

109 *The Globe and Mail, Report on Business*, 22 December, 1989; 15 January, 1990; 16 March, 1990.

110 *The Globe and Mail, Report on Business*, 3 July, 1990.

111 *The Globe and Mail, Report on Business*, 14 March, 1991.

112 *The Globe and Mail, Report on Business*, 12 and 26 March, 1992; 12 December, 1992.

113 *The Globe and Mail, Report on Business*, 19 May, 1988, 17 March, 10 April and 22

July, 1989, 16 and 27 March, 1990, 29 January, 1992.

114 *The Globe and Mail, Report on Business,* 16 March, 1989.

115 *The Globe and Mail, Report on Business,* 20 March, 1989.

116 *The Globe and Mail, Report on Business,* 25 July, 1989.

117 *The Globe and Mail, Report on Business,* 5 December, 1990.

118 *Financial Post,* 1 March, 1986; Regina Leader-Post, 26 March, 1990.

119 *The Globe and Mail, Report on Business,* 3, 12, 23, 24 October, 1990; 12 and 27 December, 1990; 28 March, 1991; *The Globe and Mail,* 24 November, 1990; 25 December, 1990.

120 *The Globe and Mail,* 18 July, 1991.

121 *The Globe and Mail, Report on Business,* 5 July, 1988.

122 *The Globe and Mail, Report on Business,* 22 April, 1988; 5 June, 1989; 5 December, 1990; 28 March, 1991; Regina *Leader-Post,* 11 and 14 July, 1989.

123 *The Globe and Mail, Report on Business,* 24 and 27 February, 1989; 22 to 25 January, 1991.

124 James G. Ripley, "The Columbia River Scandal," *Engineering and Contract Record,* April, 1964.

125 James Laxer, *The Politics of the Continental Resources Deal* (Toronto: New Press, 1970).

126 J. F. Conway, "Trade pact could force Canada to export water to U.S.," Regina *Leader-Post,* 27 June, 1988.

127 *Gallup Report,* 14 March 1991.

128 *The Globe and Mail, Report on Business,* 11 October 1990.

129 *The Globe and Mail, Report on Business,* 2 July 1991.

130 *The Globe and Mail,* 8 August 1992.

131 *The Globe and Mail, Report on Business,* 7 August 1993.

132 *The Globe and Mail, Report on Business,* 22 June 1993.

133 Regina *Leader-Post,* 23 June 1989; *The Globe and Mail, Report on Business,* 26 October 1991.

134 *The Globe and Mail, Report on Business,* 24 June 1992.

135 *Gallup Report,* 1 October 1990,

136 *Gallup Report,* 11 May 1992.

137 *Gallup Report,* 28 September 1992.

138 *The Globe and Mail,* 13 August 1992; *The Globe and Mail, Report on Business,* 24 June 1993; *The Globe and Mail,* 28 May 1993; Regina *Leader-Post,* 31 May 1993; *Gallup Report,* 15 April 1993.

139 *Gallup Report,* 23 August 1990.

140 *Gallup Report,* 21 November 1991.

141 Regina *Leader-Post,* 28 October 1988.

142 Murray Dobbin. *Preston Manning and the Reform Party* (Toronto: Lorimer, 1991).

143 Dobbin, *Preston Manning*, Ch. 4 & 5; Elections Canada, Registered Party Fiscal Period Return on behalf of the Reform Party of Canada, 1989–1992.

144 *Toronto Star*, 30 October 1988; Dobbin, Preston Manning, pp. 80ff.

145 *The Globe and Mail*, 28 May 1988.

146 *The Globe and Mail*, 15 and 18 March 1989.

147 *The Globe and Mail*, 25 October 1989.

148 *The Globe and Mail*, 11 July and 23 October 1992; 23 March 1993.

149 Regina *Leader-Post*, 26 November 1988.

150 *The Globe and Mail*, 6 and 29 April 1991; The Reformer, May 1991.

151 *Gallup Report*, 23 June and 13 July 1992.

152 *The Globe and Mail*, 30 March 1991.

153 *The Globe and Mail*, 15 March 1989.

154 Regina *Leader-Post*, 10 April 1992.

155 *The Globe and Mail*, 28 December 1992.

156 *The Globe and Mail*, 11 April 1991.

157 Regina *Leader-Post*, 16 March 1991.

158 Dobbin, *Preston Manning*, pp. 121-22.

159 *The Globe and Mail*, 23 October 1992.

160 Reform Party of Canada, *Principles and Policies, 1990*; *Reform Party of Canada*, "Who are the Reformers?" party pamphlet, 1993; *The Globe and Mail*, 11 April 1991.

161 Sydney Sharpe and Don Braid. *Storming Babylon: Preston Manning and the Rise of the Reform Party.* (Toronto: Key Porter, 1991); *The Globe and Mail*, 26 February 1992.

162 *The Globe and Mail*, 12, 15, and 16 June 1992.

163 *The Globe and Mail*, 10 November 1992 and 23 April 1992.

164 *The Globe and Mail*, 30 March 1993.

165 *The Globe and Mail*, 23 April 1993.

CHAPTER 10: THE TRIUMPH OF THE RIGHT, 1993–2013

1   Ontario NDP, "An Agenda for People," 1990, pamphlet in possession of the author.

2   *The Globe and Mail*, 20 August 1990.

3   *The Globe and Mail*, 30 November 1990.

4   *The Globe and Mail, Report on Business*, 18 and 27 June, 1991; 30 July 1991.

5   *The Globe and Mail, Report on Business*, 18 June 1991.

6   *The Globe and Mail, Report on Business*, 27 June 1991.

7   *The Globe and Mail, Report on Business*, 28 August 1991.

8   *The Globe and Mail, Report on Business*, 15 January 1992.

9   *The Globe and Mail*, 6 April 1992; 22 January 1993.

10 *The Globe and Mail, Report on Business,* 20 March 1993.

11 *The Globe and Mail,* 5 May, 21 June, 8 July, 24 August 1993.

12 *Gallup Report,* 27 March 1991; 30 April 1991; 18 December 1992; 24 July 1993.

13 Regina *Leader-Post,* 14 March 1990.

14 Regina *Leader-Post,* 27 January, 5 February, 19 February, 13 April, 8 May and 9 November 1992; 2 January, 26 February, 17–22 March, and 17 June 1993. *The Globe and Mail,* 15 February, 11 and 13 April, 8 and 9 May, and 9 November 1992; 15 and 19 March, 5 May, 1993.

15 *The Globe and Mail, Report on Business,* 24 January 1992.

16 *The Globe and Mail,* 19 October 1991; 8 January 1992.

17 *The Globe and Mail,* 6 November 1991; 9 November 1992.

18 *The Globe and Mail,* 2 April and 6 November 1992; 23 January, 12 March and 6 April 1993. *The Globe and Mail, Report on Business,* 19 October 1991; 3 June 1993.

19 Regina *Leader-Post,* 30 April and 1 May 1993. *The Globe and Mail,* 30 April, 7 May, 8 and 9 July 1993.

20 *Gallup Report,* 21 December 1989, 20 June 1991, 24 June 1993, 15 July 1993.

21 *Gallup Report,* 3 October 1991, 7 May 1992, 11 May 1992, 24 April 1993, 29 April 1993, 3 May 1993, 17 May 1993, 30 August 1993, 9 September 1993. *The Globe and Mail,* 10 May 1993.

22 Details on the elections of 1993, 1997, and 2000 are taken from: J. F. Conway, *Debts to Pay: A Fresh Approach to the Québec Question,* second edition (Toronto: Lorimer, 1997) and J. F. Conway, *Debts to Pay: The Future of Federalism in Québec,* third edition (Toronto: Lorimer, 2004).

23 Liberal Party of Canada, *Creating Opportunity: The Liberal Plan for Canada,* 1993, copy in possession of the author.

24 The following characterization of the details and impacts of Martin's cuts is taken from the following sources: Ellen Russell, "What Should We Do with the Federal Budget Surplus?" *Alternative Federal Budget 2005,* Technical paper #1 (Ottawa: Canadian Centre for Policy Alternatives, 2005); Canadian Centre for Policy Alternatives, *Alternative Federal Budget 2005: It's Time* (Ottawa: Canadian Centre for Policy Alternatives, 2005); Anne Curry-Stevens, *When Markets Fail: Exploring the Widening Gap between Rich and Poor in Canada* (Toronto: CSJ Foundation for Research and Education, 2001); Steve Kersteller, *Rags to Riches: Wealth Inequality in Canada* (Ottawa: Canadian Centre for Policy Alternatives, 2003); Joanne Naiman, *How Societies Work: Class, Power and Change in a Canadian Context* (Toronto: Thomson-Nelson, 2004); Todd Scarth, ed., *Hell and High Water: An Assessment of Paul Martin's Record and Implications for the Future* (Ottawa: Canadian Centre for Policy Alternatives, 2004).

25 Andrew Jackson, "Paul Martin's Economic Record: Living Standards of Working Families and Prospects for Future Prosperity," *Alternative Federal Budget 2004,* Technical Paper #2 (Ottawa: Canadian Centre for Policy Alternatives, 10 December 2003); and *The Globe and Mail,* 17 and 19 January, 2003.

26 Jamie Brownlee, *Ruling Canada: Corporate Cohesion and Democracy* (Halifax: Fernwood, 2005).

27 For the following material on the transformation of the Reform party to the Alliance party to the Conservative party, the fall of Preston Manning, and the rise

and fall of Stockwell Day see: Murray Dobbin, *Preston Manning and the Reform Party* (Toronto: Lorimer, 1991); Trevor Harrison, *Of Passionate Intensity: Right-wing Populism and the Reform Party of Canada* (Toronto: University of Toronto, 1995); Trevor W. Harrison, *Requiem for a Lightweight: Stockwell Day and Image Politics* (Montreal: Black Rose, 2002); Claire Hoy, *Stockwell Day: His Life and Politics* (Toronto: Stoddart, 2000); Preston Manning, *Think Big: My Life in Politics* (Toronto: McClelland & Stewart, 2003); J. F. Conway. *Debts to Pay: The Future of Federalism in Québec*, third edition (Toronto: Lorimer, 2004, especially from Chapter 7, pp. 138 ff.); J. F. Conway, "Reflections on Canada in the Year 1997–98," in Leen d'Haenens (ed), *Canadianness: Visions of Canada's Politics, Culture and Economics* (Ottawa: University of Ottawa, 1998, pp. 7–28); J. F. Conway, "Reflections on Canada in the Year 1994," *Journal of Canadian Studies*, 29:3 Fall 1994; J. F. Conway, "The 'Folksy Fascism' of the Reform Party," *Literary Review of Canada*, June 1996, pp. 8–11; J. F. Conway, "The Alliance's First Mistake," *Prairie Dog*, 27 July 2000, p. 4; J. F. Conway, "Parson Manning and the Politics of Hate," *Briarpatch*, July/August 1997, pp. 18–19; J. F. Conway, "The Reform Party: Taking a Few Pages from an Old Western Book ," *The Globe and Mail*, 21 March 1991; J. F. Conway, "Once again Day Relying on Fundamentalist Backing," Regina *Leader-Post*, 19 February 2002; J. F. Conway, "View from the Left: Vive Stockwell Day," Kitchener-Waterloo *Record*, 29 August 2001; J. F. Conway, "Day Far From Being Popular with Voters," Montreal *Gazette*, 7 August 2000; J. F. Conway, "Reform's Message Still the Same," Regina *Leader-Post*, 19 June 1996. A news record of some of the more important events in the evolution of the right are found in the following issues of *The Globe and Mail*: 11 March 1998; 12 September 1998; 19 to 22 February 1999; 3 June 2000; 23 October 2001; 14 December 2001; 9 and 10 July 2001; 3, 13 and 26 December 2001; 4, 10, 16, 17 and 22 August 2001; 9 and 11 September 2001; 4, 5, 17 and 20 July 2001.

28 Reform Party of Canada, *Twenty Realities of Secession*. Reform party pamphlet, 1995, copy in possession of the author; Tom Flanagan, *Waiting for the Wave: The Reform Party and Preston Manning* (Toronto: Stoddart, 1995).

29 John F. Conway, *Debts to Pay: The Future of Federalism in Québec*, third edition (Toronto: Lorimer, 2004, chapters 8 to 13).

30 All election results are taken from the Elections Canada website. There were two key elections in Harper's drive to majority power. In the 2006 election, Harper first won minority power, ending the long reign of the Liberal party, and in 2008 he held on to minority power while increasing his popular vote and seats won (124 to 143 seats; 36 to 38 per cent). See Jon H. Pammett and Christopher Dornan (eds), *The Canadian Federal Election of 2006* (Toronto: Dundurn, 2006) and by the same authors, *The Canadian Federal Election of 2008* (Toronto: Dundurn, 2009).

31 For details on Harper's rise to power, his approach to winning and holding power, and his aggressive right-wing agenda see: Lloyd Mackay, *The Pilgrimage of Stephen Harper* (Toronto: ECW Press, 2005); William Johnson, *Stephen Harper and the Future of Canada*, second edition (Toronto: McClelland & Stewart, 2006); Chantal Hébert, *French Kiss: Harper's Blind Date with Québec* (Toronto: Vintage, 2007); Paul Wells, *Right Side Up: The Fall of Paul Martin and the Rise of Stephen Harper's New Conservatives* (Toronto: McClelland & Stewart, 2007); Howard Cody, "Minority Government in Canada: The Stephen Harper Experience," *American Review of Canadian Studies*, 38:1, 2008, pp. 27–42; Gerry Nicholls, *Loyal to the Core: Stephen Harper, Me and the NCC* (Toronto: Freedom Press, 2009); Bob Plamandon, *Blue Thunder: The Truth about Conservatives from Macdonald to Harper* (Toronto: Key Porter, 2009); Bob Plamandon, *Full Circle: Death and Resurrection in Canadian Conservative Politics*, second edition (Toronto: Key Porter, 2009); Tom Flanagan, *Harper's Team: Behind the Scenes*, second edition (Montreal/Kingston: McGill-Queen's, 2009); Michael Behiels, "Stephen Harper's Rise

to Power: Will the 'New' Conservative Party Become Canada's 'Natural Governing Party' of the Twenty-first Century?" *American Review of Canadian Studies*, 40:1, 2011, pp. 118–145; Lawrence Martin, *Harperland: The Politics of Control* (Toronto: Penguin, 2011); Christian Nadeau, *Rogue in Power: Why Stephen Harper is Re-making Canada By Stealth* (Toronto: Lorimer, 2011);Yves Engler, *The Ugly Canadian: Stephen Harper's Foreign Policy* (Halifax: Fernwood, 2012); Ian Mackay, *Warrior Nation: Rebranding Canada in the Age of Anxiety* (Toronto: Between the Lines, 2012).

32 Details on Martin's relentless efforts to oust Jean Chrétien and replace him as prime minister are provided in the following: Robert Chodos *et al.*, *Paul Martin: A Political Biography* (Toronto: Lorimer, 1998); Susan Delacourt, *Juggernaut: Paul Martin's Campaign for Chrétien's Crown* (Toronto: McClelland & Stewart, 2003); Lawrence Martin, *Iron Man: The Defiant Reign of Jean Chrétien* (Toronto: Viking, 2003); John Gray, *Paul Martin: The Power of Ambition* (Toronto: Key Porter, 2007); Jean Chrétien, *My Years as Prime Minister* (Toronto: Knopf Canada, 2008); Paul Martin, *Hell or High Water: My Life In and Out of Politics* (Toronto: McClelland & Stewart, 2009). A running op-ed commentary was provided by this author: "The PM vs. PM Jr.," *Briarpatch*, May 2000, pp. 12–13; "Chrétien fights back and will likely win," Winnipeg *Free Press*, 2 June 2002; "Chrétien vs. Martin: Who is to blame?" Winnipeg *Free Press*, 8 August 2002.

33 A good review of the unfolding of events in the breaking scandal is provided in "The Sponsorship Scandal," *CBC News in Depth* (April 2004 and June 2005, online at http://www/cbc.ca/news/background); John Gomery, *Who Is Responsible: Phase 1 Report* (Ottawa: Public Works, 2005); John Gomery, *Restoring Accountability: Phase 2 Report* (Ottawa: Public Works, 2006); Francois Perrault, *Inside Gomery* (Toronto: Douglas & McIntyre, 2006); Kristen Kozolanka, "The Sponsorship Scandal as Communication: The Rise of Politicized and Strategic Communication in the Federal Government," *Canadian Journal of Communications*, 31:2, 2006 (online: http:www.cjc-online). Both Martin and Chrétien deal with the scandal from very different perspectives in their memoirs (see footnote 36). A running op-ed commentary on the scandal and its political impacts was provided by this author: "Bloodied Crown: New PM Martin is a Modern Macbeth," *Prairie Dog*, 11 December 2003, p. 7; "Martin's Gut Check: does the new PM have the mettle to weather the Québec sponsorship scandal?" *Prairie Dog*, 4 March 2004, p. 7; "Minority Rule: Canada's shifting political landscape and Martin's record," *Prairie Dog*, 13 May 2004, p. 6; "Martin's Gamble," Winnipeg *Free Press*, 23 May 2004; "The Way It Was: a long, last look at the 2004 federal election," *Prairie Dog*, 8 July 2004, p. 4; "Deep Impact: only Québec understands the real scandal of sponsorship," *Prairie Dog*, 17 February 2005, p. 10; "Unruly Alliance: same strategy, different goals for Liberal-hating opposition leaders," *Prairie Dog*, 28 April 2005, p. 8: "Martin's Revenge," *Prairie Dog*, 24 November 2005, p. 8; "The Martin Reign: Act I, Scene 2," *Prairie Dog*, 8 December 2005, p. 8; "The Secret of Stephen Harper's Success," *Prairie Dog*, 19 January 2006, p. 9; "Chrétien's Vindication," *Prairie Dog*, 9 April 2009, p. 8, 10.

34 The letter became an instant top story, creating a feeding frenzy in the media (see *The Globe and Mail* during the days following the release of the letter by NDP MP Judy Wasylycia-Leis on 28 December 2005). On 29 September 2006 and 6 October 2006, *The Globe and Mail* editorials called for Zaccardelli's resignation stating in October, "He has lost his credibility, and is a stain on any government that lets him stay on the job." Though the primary reason for demands for his resignation, and his resulting decision to resign, had more to do with the conflicting testimony the Commissioner provided to the O'Connor inquiry, and at a House of Commons committee investigation into the Mahar Arar scandal (Arar was illegally detained by the RCMP

knowingly using false information, and deported to Syria where he was imprisoned and tortured), the Commissioner's unprecedented intrusion into the campaign for the 2006 election had sullied his reputation and credibility. An investigation of Zaccardelli's political intervention by the RCMP's Public Complaints Commissioner concluded that Zaccardelli had not violated any policy since there was no policy to violate. However, the report revealed that Zaccardelli instructed his staff to include Liberal finance minister Ralph Goodale's name in the news release announcing the criminal investigation. He also told his staff how to word the release (*National Post*, 31 March 2008). Despite the destruction of his public reputation, Zaccardelli landed on his feet after his resignation on 15 December 2006, gaining a leadership position with Interpol in Lyon, France working with African police forces developing strategies to fight international criminal organizations. One suspects he would not have obtained such a prominent position with Interpol without the warm support of the Canadian government, now led by a very grateful Harper. The following op-ed articles by the author deal with the Zaccardelli affair: "The Secrets of Harper's Success," *Prairie Dog*, 19 January 2009, p. 9; "Giuliano Zaccardelli's Security Blanket," *Prairie Dog*, 12 October 2006, p. 10.

35 For additional details on the rise and fall of Stéphane Dion and Michael Ignatieff see: Linda Diebel, *Stéphane Dion: Against the Current* (Toronto: Viking, 2007); *Ottawa Citizen*, 27 September 2008; Ian Basen, "The Framing of Stéphane Dion," *Canadian Journal of Communication* (34:2, 2009, 297–305); Derrick O'Keefe, *Michael Ignatieff: The Lesser Evil?* (London: Verso, 2011); Peter Newman, *When Gods Changed: The Death of Liberal Canada* (Toronto: Random House, 2011).

36 "Text of 1997 speech by Stephen Harper to US right-wing think tank" http://www.sistersagesmusing.ca/2011/12/24, retrieved 8 February 2012. The speech has been widely posted on many websites. It was originally posted on CTV.ca, 14 December 2005. The speech was made to the U.S. Council on National Policy, widely seen as a front group of the right-wing of the Republican Party. Throughout the speech Harper's sneering contempt for Canada's managed economy, elaborate welfare state, and commitment to government intervention to protect a shared definition of "the public interest," constructed by successive Progressive Conservative and Liberal federal governments, was evident. Harper dismissed efforts to take the speech seriously, since he insisted the speech was just a big joke. But his actions in power uncannily echo the content of that early speech.

37 Ian Mackay, *Warrior Nation: Rebranding Canada in the Age of Anxiety* (Toronto: Between the Lines, 2012); Yves Engler, *The Ugly Canadian: Stephen Harper's Foreign Policy* (Halifax: Fernwood, 2012).

38 Details are provided in the Budget Speech delivered on 29 March 2012 by Finance Minister Jim Flaherty, "Economic Action Plan, 2012." Hon. Jim Flaherty. *Budget 2012: Jobs, Growth and Long Term Prosperity.* (Ottawa: Government of Canada, Department of Finance, March 2012). Seven pages of details and analysis on "Harper's Modest Revolution," as it was characterized, are provided in *The Globe and Mail*, 30 March 2012. The text of the bills can be viewed at Parliament of Canada online, "Bill C-38, An Act to implement certain provisions of the budget tabled in Parliament on March 29, 2012 and other measures," First reading, April 26, 2012; and "Bill C-45, A second Act to implement certain provisions of the budget tabled in Parliament on March 29, 2012 and other measures," First reading, October 18, 1012 http://www.par.gc.ca./HousePublications/.

39 Further details from the budget bills are from *The Globe and Mail*, 11, 17 and 30 April 2012; 7, 10 and 11 May 2012.

40 Jay Makarenko, "Employment Insurance in Canada: History, Structure and Issues," Mapleleafweb, September 2009. http://www.mapleleafweb.com/features/employment-insurance-canada-history-structure-and-issues. Retrieved 7 March 2013.

41 Canada, Department of Finance, "History of Health and Social Transfers." http://www.fin.gc.ca/fedprov/his-eng.asp. Retrieved 7 March 2013; "Federal Support to Provinces and Territories." http://www.fin.gc.ca/fedprov/mtp-eng.asp. Retrieved 8 March 2013; "Federal Transfers to Provinces and Territories." http://www.fin.gc.ca/access/fedprov-eng/asp. Retrieved 7 March 2013.

42 Harper is also moving quickly to devolve federal powers over the northern territories to local control in order to speed up resource development projects. The Northwest Territories is to be granted "province-like" powers over its natural resources, ending the current complex federal regulatory regime for northern developments. The government of the NWT is eager to accelerate resource development and dreams of becoming "a potential energy super power" in the future. Final inking of the deal awaits approval by five of the seven regional aboriginal governments. *The Globe and Mail*, 12 March 2013. The oil industry quickly picked up the signal and announced a new energy play in the NWT thanks to the anticipated simplification of the approval process. *The Globe and Mail, Report on Business*, 13 March 2013.

43 "Pipeline delays 'devastating' to Canadian economy, says report," *The Canadian Press*, posted 7 February 2013 on CBC Business News, http://www.cbc.ca/news/business/story/2013/02/07business-pipeline-report.html.

44 *The Globe and Mail*, 28 December 2011; 2 October 2012; 4, 5 and 7 December 2012; 23 January 2013; 23 March 2013.

CHAPTER 11: THE TRIUMPH OF THE RIGHT, 1993–2013

1 For the following discussion of the Romanow regime see op-ed commentaries by the author from 1991 to 2000: "NDP Giveaways to the Oil Industry as Generous as Tories," Saskatoon *Star Phoenix*, 18 November 1991; "Will Romanow Tame the Business Lobby?" Moncton *Times Transcript*, 30 November 1991; "Cuts Ripe with Messages," Kitchener-Waterloo *Record*, 14 April 1992; "Advice for Premier Romanow," *Briarpatch*, May 1992, pp. 10–11; "Social Policy: The Way Forward for the NDP," *Briarpatch*, December 1991/January 1992; "A Faith Abandoned: Weak Leaders and Big Business are the Death of Social Democracy," Kitchener-Waterloo *Record*, 2 April 1993; "New Democrats: Political Suicide ," Regina *Leader-Post*, 20 October 1993; "Manufacturing a Pro-uranium Convention: Strike Three Against Romanow," *NeWest Review*, February/March 1993, pp. 8–9; "Romanow Betrays the Douglas Legacy," *Prairie Dog*, August 1994, p. 6; "NDP Defeat Certain: Romanow's Remarkable Feat," *Canadian Dimension*, October/November 1994, pp. 22–24; "By-election Lessons for the NDP," Regina *Leader-Post*, 26 February 1994; "Romanow Rolls the Electoral Dice," *Prairie Dog*, June 1995, p. 4; "Saskatchewan: Non-election of a non-government," *Canadian Dimension*, October/November 1995, p. 22; "The Death of the Saskatchewan Myth," London *Free Press*, 18 February 1995; "Romanow Government has Failed to Collect Taxes in a Fair Manner," Regina *Leader-Post*, 13 March 1996; "Saskatchewan Way Meets a Fork in the Road," Kitchener-Waterloo *Record*, 12 February 1996; "The Saskatchewan NDP Government in 1996," *Prairie Dog*, January 1996, p. 5; "The Saskatchewan Right Plays Musical Chairs," *Prairie Dog*, September 1997, p.9,18; "Mangled Right Warrants Romanow a Durable Future ," Edmonton *Journal*, 7 September 1997; "Romanow's Alamo?" *Prairie Dog*, May 1999, p. 6; "Trouble in Romanow Land," *Briarpatch*, September 1999, pp.13–14; "NDP Erred by Postponing Election," Regina *Leader-*

Post, 10 August 1999; "Echoes of 1986 Election," Regina *Leader-Post,* 30 September 1999; "Romanow's Decision Made for Him," Regina *Leader-Post,* 5 October 2000. See the following more summative and scholarly works: J. F. Conway, "From 'Agrarian Socialism' to 'Natural' Governing Party: CCF/NDP in Saskatchewan, 1932–2002," in Murray Knutilla and Bob Stirling (eds.), *The Prairie Agrarian Movement Revisited.* (Regina: Canadian Plains Research Centre Press, 2007, pp. 209–244); J. F. Conway, "Labour and the CCF/NDP in Saskatchewan," *Prairie Forum,* 31:2, Fall 2006, pp. 389–426; Erin Weir, *Saskatchewan at a Crossroads: Fiscal Policy and Social Democratic Politics.* (Ottawa: Canadian Centre for Policy Alternatives, March 2004); John W. Warnock, *The Structural Adjustment of Capitalism in Saskatchewan* (Ottawa: Canadian Centre for Policy Alternatives, 2003); Saskatchewan Institute for Social and Economic Alternatives, *The Privatization of the Potash Corporation of Saskatchewan: A Case Study* (Regina, June 1996); L. A. Brown *et al., Saskatchewan Politics from Left to Right '44 to '99.* (Regina: Hinterland Publications, 1999.

2   J. F. Conway, "The Devine Regime in Saskatchewan, 1982–1991: The Tory Caucus Fraud Scandal and Other Abuses of Power," in Dorothy E. Chunn, Susan C. Boyd, and Robert Menzies (eds.), *(Ab)Using Power: The Canadian Experience.* (Halifax: Fernwood, 2001, pp. 95–109); Gerry Jones, *SaskScandal: The Death of Political Idealism in Saskatchewan.* (Saskatoon: Fifth House, 2000).

3   The author was favoured with just such a visit from the minister of finance.

4   For the 1999 nurses' strike see the following: *The Globe and Mail,* 9, 12, and 13 April 1999; Regina *Leader-Post,* 9 to 20 April 1999, 3 July 1999.

5   *The Globe and Mail,* 31 August 1999.

6   Saskatchewan Institute for Social and Economic Alternatives, *The Privatization of the Potash Corporation of Saskatchewan: A Case Study* (Regina, June 1996); Regina *Leader-Post,* 15 May 1999, 15 February 2002.

7   Regina *Leader-Post,* 6, 10 and 11 February 1998.

8   *The Globe and Mail,* 24 October 1998; Regina *Leader-Post,* 20 October 1998; *The Globe and Mail,* 9, 12 and 13 April 1999; Regina *Leader-Post,* 9 to 20 April 1999, 3 July 1999.

9   John W. Warnock, *The Structural Adjustment of Capitalism in Saskatchewan* (Ottawa: Canadian Centre for Policy Alternatives, 2003, pp. 9 and 10).

10   A running review of the Calvert government is provided in op-ed commentaries by the author from 2001 to 2007: "The NDP knows what it must do to win," Regina *Leader-Post,* 25 January 2001; "Calvert caves to the oil industry," Winnipeg *Free Press,* 24 November 2002; "Slippery Business: Calvert caves to the oil industry," *Briarpatch,* April 2003, pp. 18–19; "The Vote in Saskatchewan," Kitchener-Waterloo *Record,* 29 October 2003; "Shrubgate: Saskatchewan NDP Government Panics," *Briarpatch,* September 2003, pp. 17–18; "Can Calvert Win?" *Prairie Dog,* 16 October 2003, p. 11; "NDP's Left Turn Pays Off," Winnipeg *Free Press,* 23 November 2003; "Earth to Calvert, Come In," *Prairie Dog,* 18 March 2004, p. 8; "Lorne's Revenge," *Prairie Dog,* 20 December 2004, p. 8; "Lies and Labour Laws," *Prairie Dog,* 3 February 2005, p. 7; "Pimpernell vs Pink Panther," *Prairie Dog,* 27 October 2005, p. 8; "The Vision Thing: Advice to Premier Calvert," *Prairie Dog,* 10 November 2005, p. 10; "Calvert's Gambit," *Prairie Dog,* 13 April 2006, p. 8; "Is Calvert Toast?" *Prairie Dog,* 20 July 2006, p. 7; "Divide and Conquer: Calvert's Road to Power," *Prairie Dog,* 3 August 2006, p. 8; "Calvert Goes for the Throat," *Prairie Dog,* 9 November 2006, p. 9; "Suicide Pact: NDP-Labour power plays help the Saskatchewan Party," *Prairie Dog,* 1 March 2007, p. 8; "Off the Cartoon Cliff: Sigma Poll Creams Wile E. Calvert, roadrunner style,"

Prairie Dog, 10 May 2007, p. 7; "Dare to Dream: slumping NDP needs return to pro-people roots," *Prairie Dog*, 7 June 2007, pp. 10–11; "Democracy's Slow Death: Voters tune out, turn off, even in Saskatchewan," 25 October 2007, pp. 46. See also summative and scholarly works on the Calvert government: David McGrane, "Which Third Way? A Comparison of the Romanow and Calvert NDP Governments from 1991 to 2007," in Howard Leeson (ed.), *Saskatchewan Politics: Crowding the Centre* (Regina: Canadian Plains Research Centre Press, 2008, pp. 143–64); David McGrane, "The 2007 Provincial Election in Saskatchewan," *Canadian Political Science Review*, 2:1, March/April 2008, pp. 64–71; Howard Leeson, "The 2007 Election: Watershed or Way Station?" in Howard Leeson (ed.), *Saskatchewan Politics: Crowding the Centre* (Regina: Canadian Plains Research Centre Press, 2008, pp. 119–140).

11 Elections Saskatchewan, *Statement of Votes: Twenty-fifth Provincial General Election, November 5, 2003* (Regina: Office of the Chief Electoral Officer, 2004); *Statement of Votes: Twenty-sixth Provincial General Election, November 7, 2007* (Regina: Office of the Chief Electoral Officer, 2008); *Statement of Votes: Twenty-seventh Provincial General Election, November 7, 2011* (Regina: Office of the Chief Electoral Officer, 2012).

12 Business Tax Review Committee. *Final Report of the Business Tax Review Committee* (Regina: Government of Saskatchewan, November 2005) (The Vicq Report). For a critical assessment see Erin Weir, "Money for Nothing: The Vicq Committee's Corporate Tax Cuts," *Saskatchewan Notes*, 4:6, December 2005 (Saskatchewan Section of the Canadian Centre for Policy Alternatives).

13 Key events in the rise of Brad Wall from a relative unknown to premier of Saskatchewan are provided in op-ed commentaries by the author: "Wall's World: Just Who is Brad Wall, Anyway?" *Prairie Dog*, 1 April 2004, p. 6; "Brad Wall: Ideas Man?" *Prairie Dog*, 2 March 2006, p. 8; "Stephen Harper's Pet Poodle," *Prairie Dog*, 8 June 2006, p. 8; "Brad's Fiddle-Diddle: fraud-forgiving Premier-wannabe has a funny definition of 'honest man'," *Prairie Dog*, 14 September 2006, p.8; "Welcome to Wall's World: The Saskatchewan Party Won: Let the Ruckus Begin," *Prairie Dog*, 20 November 2007, p. 8; "Prelude to a Rampage: barely in office, Wall pulls out right-wing play book," *Prairie Dog*, 6 December 2007, p. 11; " Wall's World: Prairie ruckus about to begin," *The Record*, 23 November 2007. See summative and scholarly assessments of the rise of Wall: Howard Leeson (ed.), *Saskatchewan Politics: Crowding the Centre* (Regina: Canadian Plains Research Centre Press, 2008).

14 Use of the term "political realignment" is based loosely on the work of Key, Burnham, and Mayhew. It refers to a dramatic and relatively permanent change in political behaviour. During such critical elections new coalitions of voters emerge that stabilize into future elections. The 1944 election of the CCF was such a political realignment — the CCF became the virtually hegemonic "natural governing party" of Saskatchewan. Wall's 2011 victory has features that may prove to represent a relatively permanent realignment. The CCF/NDP was gradually pushed out of rural Saskatchewan, but with Wall it has become a shutout. Wall's great gains in urban Saskatchewan, where he cobbled together an electoral coalition cutting across class lines, appears to have broken the back of the NDP's urban hegemony. It is too early to conclude definitively that the urban shifts constitute a political realignment with some stability. We will know more after the 2016 election. See the following: V. O. Key, "A Theory of Critical Elections," *Journal of Politics*, 17:1, 1955, pp. 3–18; Walter Dean Burnham, *Critical Elections and the Mainsprings of American Politics* (New York: Norton, 1970); and David Mayhew, *Electoral Realignment* (New Haven: Yale, 2004).

15 The consolidation of farms into fewer and much larger units accelerated dramatically starting in the late 1970s and, combined with general rural depopulation,

contributed to the political de-radicalization of rural Saskatchewan. By the 1980s, "the conservatives were able to play to an increasingly receptive rural audience in Saskatchewan, not because neo-liberalism *per se* was attractive, but because of the decline of social democratic populism" [Howard Leeson, "The Rich Soil of Saskatchewan Politics," in Howard Leeson (ed.), *Saskatchewan Politics: Into the Twenty-first Century* (Regina: Canadian Plains Research Centre, 2001, p. 7)]. While Devine's decisive victory in 1982 depended on an urban breakthrough accomplished by playing to pocket-book issues, his winning of a crucial second term depended on the Conservative's rural strategy in the context of the electoral implications of increasing urbanization for the respective weight of urban and rural seats. The Conservatives were able to position themselves as the party of a rural Saskatchewan in crisis, channelling anxiety among an ageing population about the closure of rail lines, grain elevators, rural hospitals, and the more general viability of rural communities, into a right-wing populism that combined regional grievances with hot-button social and cultural wedge issues [Kevin Whislow, "Rethinking the Polarization Thesis: the Formation and Growth of the Saskatchewan Party," in Howard Leeson (ed.), *Saskatchewan Politics: Into the Twenty-first Century* (Regina: Canadian Plains Research Centre Press, 2001, pp. 186 *ff.*)] Between 1981 and 2006, the proportion of farms with gross receipts under $50,000 was almost cut in half. Since 1991, the only category of farm to experience any relative growth was that with more than $100,000 in gross receipts. Since 2001, that honour has belonged exclusively to farms with upwards of $250,000 in receipts, and since 2006, to those with more than $500,000 in receipts. According to the preliminary results of the *2011 Census of Agriculture*, the number of farms with less than $500,000 in receipts has decreased by 21.6 per cent since 2006, while the number with more than $500,000 in receipts rose 44.9 per cent in the same period. Those with very large farms account for just 12.9 per cent of farms, but they generated 60 per cent of all farm receipts in Saskatchewan in 2010. See Statistics Canada, *Census of Agriculture, 2011* (based on provincial highlights available at: http://www.statcan.gc.ca/pub/95-640-x/2012002-eng.htm.)

16 In the last 30 years NDP urban working class support shifted from relatively impregnable to more contested political terrain. The NDP's role as "the natural governing party" brought it into repeated conflicts with the unions in the rapidly growing pink and white collar sectors of employment, especially those in the Crown corporations, the health care sector, and government employees. These conflicts eroded the sense of deep political identification with the CCF/NDP among these new, non-traditional elements of the working class. Among the trade union movement the balance of power shifted from the big traditional unions in the private sector to service unions in the public sector. As the sectoral composition of the employed labour force shifted away from the traditional working class occupations to the new service occupations, much of the urban working class became fertile ground for the growth of the right. Further, the relative growth of the private sector throughout the Devine and Romanow/Calvert years through privatization, subsidies, and taxation/regulatory relief, boosted by the resource and real estate booms of the 2000s, has, alongside the more general trend toward a service-based occupational structure, added complexity to the urban social forces available for electoral appeals and coalition building. The share of the labour force employed in education, health care, and social assistance experienced strong growth in the late 1980s and again in the 1990s — providing a key pillar of support for the NDP's recapture and retention of power. Between 1976 and 2012 this sector's share of the labour force grew by 43 per cent. But even more dramatic has been the growth, from a lower initial level, of the share of employment found in finance, insurance, and real estate, and in professional, technical, and business services. These categories of primarily urban and private sector workers and middle level professionals

grew twice as fast, nearly doubling as a share of the labour force between 1976 and 2012. Together with overwhelming support from an aggressive business lobby, it seems reasonable to conclude that the growth in size and influence of this more solidly neo-liberal urban grouping, along with employees and workers in the favoured resource extraction and construction industries, has been an important factor in the Saskatchewan Party's steady and growing urban breakthrough in recent elections, growing from 0 of 27 urban seats in 1999, to 3 in 2003, 10 in 2007, and 20 in 2011. The party's success has more generally been based on its ability to associate in the public consciousness the province's boom in resource industries and real estate with its brand of deregulatory pro-business boosterism in economic policy, despite the reality that global economic forces and domestic flows of credit into residential real estate have been the primary economic drivers. (The labour force figures are calculated from "Sectoral Composition of the Employed Labour Force, Saskatchewan, 1976–2012," CANSIM, Table 2820008.)

17   A running op-ed commentary by the author on the record of the Wall government is provided in: "The Push-over Premier: Brad Wall's federal suck-upping doesn't help Saskatchewan," *Prairie Dog*, 31 January 2007, p. 8; "Too Close for Comfort: Sask Party gets closer to Tories, Yankees…and NDP?" *Prairie Dog*, 27 March 2008, p. 6; "Dark Remarks: video reveals plenty about right-wing agenda," *Prairie Dog*, 10 April 2008, p. 9; "Strategy for unions: to get up off their knees," Winnipeg *Free Press*, 30 August 2008; "Beware Brad Bearing Gifts," *Prairie Dog*, 6 November 2008, p. 8; "Democracy is Broken," *Prairie Dog*, 21 May 2009, pp. 8, 10; "Top to Bottom Ugly: politics are a mess in our city, province, and country," *Prairie Dog*, 19 November 2009; "Political Ponzi: potash plunge wrecks Wall's wild promises," *Prairie Dog*, 17 December 2009, p. 9; "Three and Beyond: Brad Wall's Eye on the Bigger Prize," *Prairie Dog*, 30 December 2010, p. 9; "Lingenfelter's Fall: a chance for Saskatchewan NDP to re-tool," Edmonton *Journal*, 17 November 2011; "A Huge Fragile Victory," Winnipeg *Free Press*, 19 November 2011; "The Future of Wall," *Prairie Dog*, 27 June 2013. For summative and scholarly analyses see: John F. Conway, "Election 2011: the Looming Debacle," *The Bullet*, Socialist Project, E-Bulletin No. 503, 31 October 2011; John F. Conway, "Whither Brad Wall? Conservative Dilemmas," *The Bullet*, Socialist Project, E-Bulletin No. 850, 10 July 2013; Howard Leeson (ed.), *Saskatchewan Politics into the Twenty-first Century* (Regina: Canadian Plains Research Centre Press, 2001); Howard Leeson (ed.), *Saskatchewan Politics: Crowding the Centre* (Regina: Canadian Plains Research Centre Press, 2008); David McGrane (ed.), *New Directions in Saskatchewan Public Policy* (Regina: Canadian Plains Research Centre Press, 2011).

18   For details on Wall's attack on the trade union movement see: John F. Conway, "History Lesson: Battered labour movement needs to agitate like its 1944," *Prairie Dog*, 28 August 2008, pp. 11, 12; John F. Conway, "Wall Declares War on the Working Class," *The Bullet*, Socialist Project, E-Bulletin No. 239, 13 July 2009; Andrew Stevens, "Saskatchewan: A Beachhead of Labour Law Reform?" *The Bullet*, Socialist Project, E-Bulletin No. 812, 29 April 2013; Charles Smith, "The New 'Normal' in Saskatchewan: Neo-liberalism and the Challenge to Workers' Rights," in David McGrane (ed.), *New Directions in Saskatchewan Public Policy* (Regina: Canadian Plains Research Centre Press, 2011, pp. 121–152).

19   For details on "Bingogate," see the following: *The Globe and Mail*, 6 May 1998, 23 June 1998, 26 June 1999, 8 August 1999, and 4 September 1999. All B.C. election results noted can be found in: Elections British Columbia, *The Electoral History of British Columbia, 1971–1986* (Victoria: Queen's Printer, 1988); Elections British Columbia, *The Electoral History of British Columbia Supplement, 1987–2001* (Victoria: Queen's Printer, 2001); Elections British Columbia, *Statement of Votes, 37th Provincial General*

Election May 16, 2001 (Victoria: Queen's Printer, 2001); Elections British Columbia, *Statement of Votes, 38th Provincial General Elections, May 17, 2005* (Victoria: Queen's Printer, 2005); Elections British Columbia, *Statement of Votes, 39th Provincial General Election, May 12, 2009* (Victoria: Queen's Printer, 2010); Elections British Columbia, *Interim Statement of Votes, 40th Provincial General Election, May 14, 2013* (Victoria: Queen's Printer, 2013).

20 For what follows on the Clark government, see the following: *The Globe and Mail*, 6 August 1997, 1 October 1997, 5 November 1997, 2 December 1997; 3 and 4 February 1998, 3 March 1998, 16 September 1998, 3 and 4 January 1999,18 February 1999, 31 March 1999; *The Globe and Mail, Report on Business*, 14 May 1999; Regina *Leader-Post*, 30 March 1998.

21 Early in the morning on Sunday, April 27, 1970, two days before the first Québec election contested by René Lévesque and the separatist Parti Québécois, nine Brinks armored trucks pulled up to the front door of the Royal Trust building on Dorchester Boulevard. This was unusual, since Brinks never made pickups at that building on a Sunday, and usually the trucks used the garage entrance to the interior for security reasons. The media were already there waiting. The trucks, in full public view, were loaded with boxes of what were claimed to be "securities" and they drove to the Ontario border. Their route took them conveniently past waiting television cameras which recorded this "flight of capital." The item was then repeatedly broadcast for the next two days to buttress the screaming headlines in the newspapers about the disaster that would befall Québec if the separatists won power. Later it was learned that the boxes were empty and that the event had been elaborately staged by Royal Trust and the Brinks Company, with the obvious collusion of the media. Lévesque denounced this as an act of "economic terrorism." Up until the obvious conspiracy to destroy Clark, it was arguably the dirtiest trick in Canadian politics.

22 Details on the destruction of Clark can be found in: *The Globe and Mail*, 3 to 6 and 28 March 1999; 13, 14, 17 April 1999; 14, 29 May 1999; 20 and 23 July 1999; 21, 23, 25 August 1999; 13 and 10 September 1999; 19 and 21 February 2000; 6 September 2001; 14, 17, 19, and 23 January 2002; 27 and 29 June 2002; 29 to 31 August 2002. Further analyses of B.C. politics from the fall of Harcourt to 2013 are contained in: Michael Howlett, Dennis Pilon, and Tracy Summerville (eds.), *British Columbia Politics and Government* (Toronto: Edmond Montgomery Publications, 2009); William K. Carroll and R. S. Ratner, "The NDP Regime in British Columbia, 1991–2001: A Post-Mortem," *Canadian Review of Sociology and Anthropology*, 42:2, 2005, pp. 167–196; Daniel Gawthrop, *Highwire Act: Power, Pragmatism and the Harcourt Legacy* (Vancouver: New Star, 1996).

23 Income taxes were cut 25 per cent, providing the greatest benefits to corporations and the wealthy. On "Black Thursday," January 17, 2002, cuts of 11,550 public servants over three years were announced, with the aim of reducing B.C.'s 35,000 strong civil service ultimately to under 23,000. This was the largest cut in a civil service in history. Welfare rates were cut and limits were imposed restricting recipients without children to two years of benefits out of any five. Those with children exceeding the two year limit faced substantial benefit cuts. The aim was to reduce the welfare budget by one-third and to reduce B.C.'s welfare recipients from 250,000 to under two-thirds that number. By 2005 the number of homeless living on the streets of Vancouver had doubled, and food banks couldn't keep up with need. Medicare premiums were raised by 50 per cent. Pieces of B.C. Hydro were put up for sale. BC Rail was privatized. Hospitals, scores of government offices, and services in every area were shut down across the province. *The Globe and Mail, Report on Business*, 5 October 2001 and 26 November 2002; *The Globe and Mail*, 31 July, 21 August, 28 September, 21 November

2001; 18 to 21 January, 11 and 23 February, 3 and 24 April, 4 July 2002; 19 to 22 January, 30 December 2003; 1 to 6 January, 2 and 9 July 2004. Regina *Leader-Post,* 16 August and 10 December, 2001; 31 December 2003; 9 July 2004.

24 For what follows on the land claims issue see: *The Globe and Mail,* 11 November 1997; 25 February, 20 October, 3, 9, 10, 12 and 14 November 1998; 24 November 1999; 4 July 2002; 4 September 2003.

25 The Campbell government declared education an essential service thereby subject to fast-track back to work orders, thus angering the province's 45,000 teachers. He reduced benefits for injured workers, cut coverage for stress, ended permanent disability benefits at 65, changed minimum pay for call backs from four to two hours, took away the right to negotiate class size in the provincial teachers' contract, gave employers the tools they needed to fight union organizing drives, established "business viability" as a legal criterion to be considered when granting collective bargaining rights in a workplace successfully organized, declared the 40 hour work week could be averaged over two to four weeks before mandatory overtime kicked in. The list went on and on in a blizzard of changes in legislation and regulations. *The Globe and Mail.* 23 July, 9 and 15 August 2001; 28 January and 14 May 2002; 27 April to 10 May 2004; Regina *Leader-Post,* 8 May and 23 April 2004.

26 For details on the two Business Summits and generous business donations to the Liberals see: *The Globe and Mail, Report on Business,* 30 June 1999; *The Globe and Mail,* 18 June and 9 November 1998, 1 and 2 April and 30 June 1999; Regina *Leader-Post,* 27 April 2004 and 30 April 2005.

27 For basic information on the two scandals see: *The Globe and Mail* 22 January and 30 December 2003; 1 and 6 January 2004; Regina *Leader-Post,* 31 December 2003; John F. Conway, "The Haunting of Gordon Campbell," *Prairie Dog,* 12 May 2005, p. 11.

28 Elections British Columbia, *Report of the Chief Electoral Officer on the 2011 HST (Harmonized Sales Tax) Referendum, June 13-August 26, 2011* (Victoria: Queen's Printer, 2011). For further details on the HST battle see: *The Globe and Mail,* 12 June, 23 July, and 2 September 2010; *The Globe and Mail, Report on Business,* 1 July 2010; *The Globe and Mail,* 23, 27, 29 August and 1 September 2011

29 For details on the damage done to Campbell by the ongoing sandal see: *The Globe and Mail,* 14, 19, 21 April 2010; 29 March 2012.

30 See the following for details of the 2013 election: *Vancouver Sun,* 10 April and 15 May, 2013; *The Globe and Mail,* 3 and 15 May, 2013; Toronto *Star,* 15 May 2013; *The Huffington Post BC,* "BC Election 2013 Polls Wrong, Pollsters Lambasted," http://www. huffintonpost.ca/2013/05/15/bc-election-2013-pollsters-wrong_n_3276813.html, retrieved 26 August 2013; CBC News, British Columbia, "How did Christy Clark pull off a B.C. election stunner?", 16 May 2013, http://www.cbc.ca/news/canada/british-columbia/story/2013/05/05/f-bc-election-analysis.html, retrieved 26 August 2013; Nancy Macdonald, "10 reasons Christy Clark could actually win the B.C. election," *Maclean's,* 9 May 2013, http://www2.macleans.ca/2013/05/09/10, retrieved 30 August 2013; Gary Mason, "Anatomy of a comeback: how Christy Clark beat the odds," *The Globe and Mail,* 22 June 2013, pp. 1, 6–7.

31 For details on the problems associated with the Dix leadership, the NDP 2013 campaign, and post election fallout see: *The Province,* 13 March 2012; Vancouver *Sun,* 10 April 2013; *The Globe and Mail,* 2 and 22 February 2011, 17 April 2011; Dick Meissner, *The Canadian Press,* "B.C. NDP looks to rebuild party, drop Dix," http:// www.globalnews.ca/news/740406.html, retrieved 26 August 2013. For details on Dix's

resignation see: *The Globe and Mail,* 19 September 2013. For more on Clark's troubles and the role of the pipeline controversy in the election see: *The Globe and Mail,* 28 February and 1 December 2011; 8 February and 4 March 2012; *The Globe and Mail, Report on Business,* 7 and 8 February 2012; *The Globe and Mail,* 17 May 2013.

32 See the following for details on the continuing volatility of the forestry industry: *The Globe and Mail, Report on Business,* 10, 18, 19, 24 May 2010; 15 December 2011; 15 February and 18 May 2012. See the following for details on the recurring crises in the B.C. salmon fishery: *The Globe and Mail,* 25 and 26 August 2010; 11 May 2011.

33 For the following material on Alberta see: *The Globe and Mail,* 11 March, 11 May and 29 September, 1997; 9 and 15 January,10 and 13 February, 21 March, 18 September, 5 October, 1998; 23 February, 1 March, 25 and 29 June, 16 July 1999; 3 and18 February, 4 March 2000;11 July, 24 August, 22 November, 7, 17, 18 and 20 December 2001; John F. Conway, "Alberta, B.C., and Companies resist sharing oil and gas wealth," *The CCPA Monitor,* May 2001, p. 22; *The Globe and Mail,* 18 October 2002; 21 January, 31 March, 28 August and 9 September 2003; 2 January,11, 12, 14, 19, 24 April, 3, 5 and 7 July 2004. *The Globe and Mail, Report on Business,* 5 May, 19 September and 10 November 1998; 6 July and 11 November 1999; 30 June, 26 July, 26 September, 10 October, 10 November, 5 and 19 December 2001; 2 April and 17 October 2002; 4 January, 6 February, 13 and 24 March, 23 April and 29 August 2003; 10 July 2004. Regina *Leader-Post,* 1 March 1999; 18 April, 18 June, 19 October and 15 December 2001; 22 February and 11 December 2002; 28 February, 29 and 31 March 2003; 6 and 14 May, 24 and 30 June, 1, 5 and 7 July 2004; 3 May 2005. *Maclean's,* 16 February 2004, p. 26; 6 September 2004, p. 24-5; 6 December 2004, p. 35; 24 January 2004, p. 28. *Report on Business Magazine,* March 2001, pp. 40–46, 112-13. National Council of Welfare, *Welfare Incomes 2002,* Ottawa, Spring 2003. National Council of Welfare, *Poverty Profile 2001,* Ottawa, Autumn 2004. See the following for analyses of Alberta's shift to neo-liberalism: Trevor Harrison (ed.), *The Return of the Trojan Horse: Alberta and the New World (Dis)Order* (Montreal: Black Rose, 2005). All election results noted are taken from reports of Alberta's Chief Electoral Officer for the elections of 2004, 2008 and 2012. Upon his death, a remembrance of Weibo Ludwig, who had bombed oil facilities, was published in *The Globe and Mail,* 16 April 2012. Ludwig had become a folk hero to some, symbolizing the eco-terrorist movement to sabotage the oil and gas industry.

34 Edmonton *Journal,* 8 April 2011; *Vancouver Sun,* 8 April 2011; *The Globe and Mail,* 9 April 2011; *National Post,* 20 March 2013. Klein was diagnosed with frontotemporal dementia, an untreatable progressive mental deterioration that gradually erases the personality and leads inevitably to death.

35 John F. Conway, "Ralph's Reign," *Planet S,* 18 August 2005, p. 9; John F. Conway, "Bye, bye Ralph? Klein says this is his last hurrah, but some fear he'll run again," *The CCPA Monitor,* October 2005, p. 7; "Just go home, Ralph," *Prairie Dog,* 8 June 2006, p. 8.

36 The following material on the troubles of Stelmach leading up to and following the 2008 election is based on: Calgary *Herald,* 29 May 2008; *The Globe and Mail,* 22 January 2010; Edmonton *Journal,* 7 March 2010; *The Globe and Mail,* 29 January and 23 July 2011; Regina *Leader-Post,*31 January 2011; *The Globe and Mail, Report on Business,* 24 November 2011. See also, John F. Conway, "Alberta Election 2008: It was a stunning victory for 'None of the Above,'" *The CCPA Monitor,* April 2008, pp. 18–19; Ryan Katz-Rose, "Whatever It Takes: Protecting the Tar Sands, Protecting Capitalism," *The Bullet,* E-Bulletin No. 408, 26 November 2010.

37 For the fallout from the 15 September 2008 economic collapse and the impacts

on Alberta's oil and gas industry see: Kevin Carmichael, "Five Years Later," *Report on Business* magazine, September 2013, pp. 27–34; *The Globe and Mail, Report on Business*, 18, 28 and 29 May, 2010; 11 August 2011.

38 For the rise of the Wildrose Party see: *Vancouver Sun*, 9 October 2009; *National Post*, 4 January 2010; *The Globe and Mail*, 29 April, 26 June and 13 August 2010; *The Globe and Mail*, 24 January 2012; *Vancouver Sun*, 8 April 2012; *Toronto Star*, 12 May 2012.

39 For the following on Redford's leadership victory, her attempt at a shift in style and policy, and run up to the 2012 election see: *The Globe and Mail*, 5 March; 16, 17 19 and 29 September; 1 and 3 October; 5, 17 and 19 November; 28 December 2011; and 8 February, 28 and 29 March 2012.

40 For more details on the 2012 election and its results see: *The Globe and Mail*, 30 and 31 March; 3, 4, 6, 7, 11, 14, 15, 17, 22, 24, 25, 26 and 27 April 2012. Paul Kellogg, "Alberta Election — Party of Big Oil Defeats Party of Big Oil," *The Bullet*, E-Bulletin No. 628, 4 May 2012.

41 Quoted in Bill Graveland, "Alberta Election 2012: Wildrose Leader Danielle Smith Calls Peter Lougheed Endorsement for Conservatives 'Tragic,'" *The Canadian Press*, 15 April 2012, posted on *Huffpost Alberta*, http://www.huffingtonpost.ca/2012/04/15/alberta-endorsement-wildrose-tories_n-14 , retrieved 18 September 2013. For more details on Lougheed's comments see *The Globe and Mail*, 16 April 2012.

42 See the following for a report on the impacts of the 2011 wildfires and floods: *The Globe and Mail, Report on Business*, 17 May 2011.

43 See the following for details on the 2013 flood: *The Globe and Mail*, 21. 22, 24, and 25 June 2013; 21 August 2013; 24 September 2013.

44 Details on the various crises afflicting the oil and natural gas industry in Alberta can be found in the following: *The Globe and Mail, Report on Business*, 2010: 13, 29 April; 14, 18 and 29 May; 11 August/2011: 8 February; 22 September; 20 October and 4 November/2012: 4, 5, 17, 19, and 24 January; 8, 9, and 10 February; 13, 14, 16, and 27 March/2013: 6 June; 4 July; 20 August and 12 September.

45 For details on the ongoing debate about pipeline and rail methods of moving oil and gas see: *The Globe and Mail, Report on Business*, 2010: 13, 29 April; 14, 18, 29 May 13 July/2011: 8 February; 2 March; 2 and 26 August; 22 September; 20 October; 4, 11 November; 24 December/2012: 4, 5, 17, 19, 24 January; 8, 9, 10 February; 13, 14, 16, 27 March; 22 May; 31 August; 17 September; 12 October; 14 December/2013: 12 January; 28 May; 6 June; 4 July; 9, 10, 14, 15, 19, 20 August; 12 September; *The Globe and Mail*, 29 July 2013. The tragic derailment of an oil train in Lac-Mégantic in July focused public attention fully on the merits and dangers of moving oil by rail: *The Globe and Mail*, 8, 9, 10, 13, 14, 15 July and 14 August 2013; *The Globe and Mail, Report on Business*, 10 August 2013. See the following for discussions of the Lac-Mégantic disaster: Leo Panitch, "Why are Canada's Trains Vulnerable? Good Old Capitalist Cost-Cutting," *The Bullet*, E-Bulletin No. 852, 15 July 2013; The Ecological Network, "Lac-Mégantic: A Social and Ecological Tragedy," *The Bullet*, E-Bulletin No. 856, 19 July 2013; Harry Glasbeck, "The Presumed Innocence of Capitalism and Lac-Mégantic," *The Bullet*, E-Bulletin No. 858, 5 August 2013.

46 *The Globe and Mail, Report on Business*, 21 September 2013.

47 For details on the collapse in support for Redford and the Tories see: *National Post*, 7 March and 17 June 2013; *The Globe and Mail*, 4 March 2013. For details on Redford's fall from grace and resignation see: *The Globe and Mail*, 5 and 7 January. 1 and 27

February, 17, 19 and 20 March 2014; Regina *Leader-Post,* 19 March 2014.

48 For the following material on Manitoba see: *The Globe and Mail,* 1 November 1996; 11 February, 23 and 29 June, 1 July and 26 November 1998; 4 and 14 January, 10 February, 26 and 30 March, 3, 6, and 8 April, 17 November 1999; 8 January and 20 April 2004; 7 and 27 September; 3, 4 and 5 October, 2011; Regina *Leader-Post,* 12 March 1997; 13 August and 17 September 1999: Winnipeg *Free Press,* 1 November 1996; 27 August, 28 September 2009; 4 and 5 October. 2011. Ian Hudson, "Prelude to a Budget," C-Manitoba, April 2004. Errol Black and Jim Silver, "The Way Forward for Labour," CCPA-Manitoba, 2 May 2004. Barry Ferguson and Robert Wardbaugh (eds.), *Manitoba Premiers of the 19th and 20th Centuries* (Regina: University of Regina, CPRC Press, 2010, see pp. 307–419 for essays on Lyon, Pawley, Filmon and Doer). Paul Thomas and Curtis Brown (eds.), *Manitoba Politics and Government: Issues, Institutions, Traditions* (Winnipeg: University of Manitoba Press, 2010); Todd Scarth, *Business Lobby Cries Wolf over Manitoba's Labour Law Changes* [Winnipeg: Canadian Centre for Policy Alternatives (Manitoba), August 2010]. All election results are taken from reports of Manitoba's Chief Electoral Officer.

49 For the following material on economic impacts see: *The Globe and Mail,* 6 and 19 November 1999; 1 June 2000; 18 and 19 July, 13 August, 20 November 2001; 20 April, 3 May, 15 and 17 October, 9 December 2002; 5 October 2013; Regina *Leader-Post,* 5 October 2013; *The Globe and Mail, Report on Business,* 19 August 1997; 20 May 1999; 1 March 2000; 18 and 21 July, 31 October, 6 November 2001; 8 May, 25 June and 26 November 2002; 18 January, 14 and 27 March, 3 April, 8 and 9 September 2003; 6 and 23 January, 13 April, 8 July 2004; 29 September, 6, 8, and 11 October, 2012; 2 and 3 October 2013; Bruce Campbell and David Macdonald, *Big Business and the Canada-US Free Trade Agreement Fifteen Years Later* (Canadian Centre for Policy Alternatives, Ottawa, 22 December 2003); Darrin Qualman and Fred Tait, *The Farm Crisis, Bigger Farms and the Myths of "Competition" and "Efficiency"* (Canadian Centre for Policy Alternatives, Ottawa, 2004); Terris Turner and Diane Gidson, *Back to Hewers of Wood and Drawers of Water: Energy, Trade and the Demise of Petrochemicals in Alberta* (Edmonton: Parkland Institute, 2005); David Campanella and Shannon Stunden-Bower, *Taking the Reins: The Case for Slowing Alberta's Bitumen Production* (Edmonton: Parkland Institute, 2013); Larissa Sommerfield, *Stress Points: An Overview of Water and Economic Growth in Western Canada* (Calgary: Canada West Foundation, 2012); Roger Gibbins and Robert Roach, *Taking Stock of the Federation* (Calgary: Canada West Foundation, 2012); Michael Holden and Robbie Rolfe, *State of the West: Energy: 2012* (Calgary: Canada West Foundation, 2012); Elspeth Hazell, Kar-Gai Gee and Andrew Sharpe, *The Human Development Index in Canada: Estimates for the Canadian Provinces and Territories, 2000–2011* (Ottawa: Centre for the Study of Living Standards, 2012).

CHAPTER 12: FRACTURED FEDERATION

1 The income and wealth figures are compiled from the following sources: Armine Yalnizyan, *The Rise of Canada's Richest 1%* (Ottawa: Canadian Centre for Policy Alternatives, December 2010); Hugh McKenzie, *Canada's CEO Elite: The 0.01%* (Ottawa: Canadian Centre for Policy Alternatives, January 2012); Jordan Brennan, *A Shrinking Universe: how concentrated corporate power is shaping income inequality in Canada* (Ottawa: Canadian Centre for Policy Alternatives, November 2012).

2 The *Oxford Dictionary* defines the social wage simply as "the amenities provided within a society from public funds." Typically the term is used to include all social, educational, and health benefits funded by governments using revenues generated by taxation. The more progressive a tax system, the greater the contribution of the

social wage in reducing inequality, i.e., it becomes a significant program of income redistribution. As the social wage was cut, Canadians found themselves forced to divert more and more of their incomes to cover the gaps formerly funded publicly.

3   For evidence and argument on how increasing inequality is a major source of political instability and growing social crises see: Lars Osberg, *Instability Implications of Increasing Inequality: What can be learned from North America* (Ottawa: Canadian Centre for Policy Alternatives, May 2012); Richard Wilkinson and Kate Pickett, *The Spirit Level: Why Equality is Better for Everyone* (Toronto: Penguin, 2010); Linda McQuaig and Neil Brooks, *The Trouble with Billionaires* (Toronto: Penguin, 2011).

INDEX